Edexcel
Government and
Politics for A2
Ideologies Second Edition

Jenni Moore

Edexcel
Government and
Politics for A2
Ideologies Second Edition

Neil McNaughton

HODDER
EDUCATION
AN HACHETTE UK COMPANY

Orders: please contact Bookpoint Ltd, 130 Milton Park, Abingdon, Oxon OX14 4SB.
Telephone: (44) 01235 827720. Fax: (44) 01235 400454. Lines are open from 9.00 - 5.00,
Monday to Saturday, with a 24 hour message answering service. You can also order
through our website www.hoddereducation.co.uk

If you have any comments to make about this, or any of our other titles, please send
them to educationenquiries@hodder.co.uk

British Library Cataloguing in Publication Data
A catalogue record for this title is available from the British Library

ISBN: 978 0 340 98737 7

First Edition Published 2005
This Edition Published 2009

Impression number   10 9 8 7 6 5 4 3 2 1
Year   2013 2012 2011 2010 2009

Copyright © 2005, 2009 Neil McNaughton

Hachette UK's policy is to use papers that are natural, renewable and recyclable
products and made from wood grown in sustainable forests. The logging and
manufacturing processes are expected to conform to the environmental regulations of
the country of origin.

Cover photo © Sweetym/iStockphoto.com
Typeset by Dorchester Typesetting Group
Printed and bound in Italy for Hodder Education, an Hachette UK Company,
338 Euston Road, London NW1 3BH

Contents

Introduction   viii

Chapter 1   Liberalism   1

Chapter 2   Conservatism   35

Chapter 3   Socialism   70

Chapter 4   Anarchism   132

Chapter 5   Nationalism   159

Chapter 6   Feminism   192

Chapter 7   Ecologism   219

Chapter 8   Multiculturalism   241

Chapter 9   Conclusion: Critically assessing ideologies   260

Chapter 10   Answering examination questions   267

Bibliography   273

Index   275

Acknowledgements

The authors and publishers are grateful to the following for permission to reproduce illustrative material:

Picture on page 6 © Bettmann/Corbis; The Bridgeman Art Library Nationality for the picture on page 13; picture on page 25 © Hulton-Deutsch Collection/Corbis; Stock Montage/Getty Images for the picture on page 42; Illustrated London News for the picture on page 48; picture on page 50 © Julian Calder/Corbis; picture on page 70 © The Gallery Collection/Corbis; pictures on pages 83 and 84 © Bettmann/Corbis; Sutton-Hibbert/Rex Features for the picture on page 97; picture on page 136 © Bettmann/Corbis; picture on page 139 © Hulton-Deutsch Collection/CORBIS; Mary Evans Picture Library for the picture on page 152; Francois Gerard/The Bridgeman Art Library/Getty Images for the picture on page 160; picture on page 166 © Vasily Fedosenko/Reuters/Corbis; Illustrated London News for the picture on page 172; picture on page 182 © Bettmann/Corbis; The Granger Collection, NYC/TopFoto for the picture on page 193; The Bridgeman Art Library for the picture on page 208; picture on page 210 © Sophie Bassouls/Sygma/Corbis; AP Photo/Erlend Aas/Scanpix Norway for the picture on page 226; David Lomax/Rex Features for the picture on page 233; Dominique Faget/AFP/Getty Images for the picture on page 239; picture on page 244 © Chip East/X01370/Reuters/Corbis.

Every effort has been made to trace and acknowledge ownership of copyright. The publishers will be glad to make suitable arrangements with any copyright holders whom it has not been possible to contact.

Introduction

The new edition of this A2 textbook reviews all the major ideologies covered in the exam board specifications from 2008 onwards. The first eight chapters each deal with an important ideology, describing both its development and its core values. This is designed to develop your understanding of the subject; it is important that you are aware of the historical context of each ideology, how it has changed over time and its enduring values and beliefs. Whenever new concepts and terms are introduced, concise explanations of these are given in the Key Term boxes highlighted within the text.

Brief biographies of important authorities on each ideology are included. These place topics in context and provide useful examples that can be deployed when answering examination questions. Quotations from leading figures add colour to your exam answers and give insights into how such people expressed themselves. However, the list of thinkers is not exhaustive and you should also undertake some additional, more specialised reading. To help you do this, a small number of recommended texts is included at the end of each chapter. These are core writings from which additional examples and knowledge can be gleaned.

Towards the end of each chapter there is a section on the key issues relating to the ideology concerned. This will assist you with answering commonly asked questions by identifying the most important controversies surrounding them. These sections include some comparative material, since an understanding of ideologies can always be improved by making comparisons and contrasts. For example, considering how different ideologies view the concept of equality can assist our comprehension of them.

These chapters finish by listing a number of typical examination questions. They are divided into short questions, which should be answered in 15 minutes, and long questions, which should take 45 minutes to answer. These questions can be answered by referring to the relevant chapter and to the key issues section within that particular chapter. The examples and quotations you should include can be found in the text too.

The final chapter is a guide to answering typical examination questions on political ideologies. As well as offering general principles, it gives exemplars with detailed suggestions as to the content and structure of particular answers.

The bibliography that follows is divided into three parts. The first contains suggested extension reading to help you take your study of ideology further. The second gives useful websites. Finally, a list of classic works is included. It may interest you to go back to the primary texts, both to deepen your knowledge and to see how the great political thinkers throughout history have explained their theories. The comprehensive index that concludes this book is useful for quick references and highlights where the Key Terms feature in each chapter.

Tackling ideologies

The terms that make up most of the chapter headings in this textbook will be familiar to you. We all have ideas about what a liberal or a conservative is like. There are many images of anarchism or Marxism that we could conjure up – revolutionaries, sinister assassins or colourful demonstrators at international meetings. In the case of feminists and environmentalists, too, we may harbour stereotypes that can have little basis in fact.

Such images are often misleading. All ideologies have complex roots and include sophisticated ideas. In addition, they each have important variations and developments within them. It is therefore vital to guard against your prejudices and keep an open mind. You may find some of the ideas in these ideologies objectionable; in some cases, they may even be repugnant. It is important, however, to try to get inside the minds of an ideology's adherents. Remember that all these ideas have, at some time or other, been extremely popular. You must therefore ask what was, or is, their appeal.

Extreme forms of nationalism such as fascism, for example, illustrate the need for objectivity. The evils of genocide, concentration camps, war and conquest, which were the manifestations of this philosophy in the twentieth century, can prevent an effective examination of the ideology. Millions of Germans and Italians supported extreme nationalism or fascism freely and enthusiastically. How did this come about? What was the appeal of fascism? It is important to understand that there were features of the fascist ideology that had nothing to do with the Final Solution or with Hitler's attempt to dominate Europe. For example, did the fascist critique of democracy have any validity? Is there a place in certain historical circumstances for the kind of dynamic leadership that fascism offers? Is there anything we can learn about how societies can be bound together in order to carry out some acceptable form of collective enterprise?

Anarchism, too, presents problems. To most observers, it is an impractical philosophy based on an over-optimistic view of humankind and an unworkable set of propositions. However, anarchism provides a comprehensive critique of modern society. By examining the anarchist position, we can develop a deeper understanding of the workings of some societies. For example, what is the true nature and function of the state? How can private property be justified? What would humankind do if awarded complete, uninhibited freedom?

There are four questions that can be asked of each ideology:

1 What does it say about the fundamental nature of humankind?

2 How does it go about analysing society? For example, is its analysis based on social class, the nature of government, some view about a natural order or the historical development of the society in question?

3 Does it have any fundamental values that determine its thinking?

4 Does it base its ideas upon scientific analysis or simply upon basic principles?

You should also consider the main variations within each ideology. Some ideologies, such as liberalism, socialism and conservatism, have tended to change over time. Others have internal divisions that are based upon differences in underlying principles. For example, some anarchists have an individualistic view of human nature, while others believe that humankind is essentially social. This has led to two distinctive forms of the same ideology. Similarly, some feminists believe that the status of women will be improved only if there is a revolutionary change in the nature of male-dominated society. Others argue that the problem can be solved by reforming society in a more moderate fashion. One of our ideologies – multiculturalism – may indeed not be an ideology at all, so broad is its basis. Nevertheless it does conform loosely to our definition of ideology and so should be included.

Like the other ideologies it does include a number of key variations.

Note that these ideologies are not necessarily separate, discrete entities. There is a good deal of overlap and there are shared ideals between them. There are many examples of this, most strikingly that of neo-liberalism. This movement, which has dominated conservatism since the 1980s, is inspired by a brand of liberalism that was at its height in the mid-nineteenth century. Similarly, the ultimate goal of many anarchists is to create a communist form of society, which is reminiscent of the final stage of historical development foreseen by Marx. Multiculturalism is an aspiration that virtually all liberals support.

This blurring of distinctions can be a source of confusion when considering political parties. Don't assume, for example, that the ideas of liberalism are only to be found in Liberal parties. The UK Conservative Party has from time to time been relatively progressive in its outlook, notably under David Cameron since 2005. Indeed, liberal philosophy has influenced all mainstream political parties in the developed world.

Finally, be cautious when using terms such as socialism and social democracy. These have been used by parties from time to time to describe themselves, but it is their own interpretation of the term that they are using. You need to take a more detached view. This is especially true when reading American commentaries. The policies of President Barack Obama, for example, were often characterised by his Republican opponents as 'socialist' because he proposed some redistribution of wealth, while in a British context he is seen as no more than a progressive liberal.

The historical development of ideology

The term 'ideology' is believed to have been developed by the French philosopher Antoine de Tracy (1754–1836). He used it to mean the 'science of ideas'. This concept arose out of the Enlightenment period and the reconstruction of French society necessitated by the 1789 revolution.

The Enlightenment brought about new ways of understanding the world that were free from religious prejudices and the corruption of truth by absolute monarchies and aristocratic governments. For de Tracy, it was possible to study society, religion, politics and philosophy in an objective, scientific manner, and so comprehend society better. This was seen as a crucial development, since it was hoped that a rational form of society could result from a rational study of ideas. Thus, ideology did not begin life as a set of beliefs, but as a claim to understanding the world scientifically.

The new concept did not last long before it came under criticism. Far from being objective, it was argued, ideology was a utopian ideal – a vision of society not as it *was*, but as the advocates of ideological thinking *wished it to be*. A more vehement attack was provided by Karl Marx in the middle of the nineteenth century. He argued that ideology was merely a reflection of the ideas of the ruling class in any age, a corruption of truth designed to maintain the dominant position of that ruling class. For example, liberalism was the dominant ideology of capitalism. Its advocacy of individual liberty, free markets and the absence of government regulation all served the interests of the capitalist structure, its exploitative nature, and the bourgeois class that controlled it. Describing ideology as the ruling ideas of the age, Marx pointed out its links with the ruling class:

The ideas of the ruling class are in every epoch the ruling ideas, i.e. the class which is the ruling material force of society, is at the same time its ruling intellectual force.

From *The German Ideology*, 1846

However, Marx's critique of ideology was undermined by the success of his own philosophy. In a sense, the fact that Marxism itself became an ideology disproved his assertion that ideology must only be the possession of the ruling class.

Moreover, the dominant liberal ideology of capitalism came to be challenged by a range of ideologies, including socialism, anarchism and conservative forms of nationalism. This gave rise to a new perspective on the concept. The Marxists themselves amended Marx's own analysis by declaring that an ideology was, in fact, simply a view of the world adopted by any particular social class. While liberalism was a middle-class ideology, socialism was the ideology of the rising working class and conservatism was the ideology of the aristocracy and landed gentry. In the twentieth century, fascism became known as the ideology of the 'petite bourgeoisie' – members of the lower middle classes who earned their living independently. Ideologies had therefore become partial analyses of the world, proposing new social arrangements that would serve the interests of a particular class, and not merely the ruling class, as Marx had suggested.

Another definition of ideology is that it is a system of belief that is designed to maintain the status quo – a defensive view of the world, which sees all alternatives as false and dangerous. Conservatism appears to fit well into this category, as does the modern world consensus that encompasses liberal democracy, individualism and free-market capitalism. This consensual, ideological view of the world is under threat from both environmentalism and religious fundamentalism, and in response asserts that its values are eternal and uncontestable. Ideology in this sense is a return to the Marxist perspective, in as much as the opponents of the dominant *Weltanschauung* (world-view) of the USA and its allies see it as a distorted vision of the world that is designed to maintain the dominant position of the 'rich club' of nations.

The nature of ideology

These competing definitions of ideology, although interesting, will not help to clarify the

Key Term

Weltanschauung
This German word translates literally as 'view of the world'. It refers to the way in which various belief systems or ideologies see the world. When there is a dominant *Weltanschauung*, all other ideologies are considered to be flawed. For example, present-day liberal capitalism sees the world as a huge market in which free enterprise should be allowed to operate and in which all individuals should be free to progress through their own efforts. It competes with an alternative belief that the less economically developed countries of the world are exploited by rich nations.

issues raised in this textbook. A more neutral and universal idea of the concept is needed in order to compare the various ideologies. Below is a description of ideology that can be applied to all the ideas that this book explores:

- Ideology incorporates a collection of principles, values and doctrines that are interlocking, i.e. form a coherent whole.

- It includes a theory of society, with some explanation of the true nature of how people live in society and how society has developed.

- Ideologies that challenge the existing order offer a critique of existing society. Those that oppose change offer critiques of those movements that propose change.

- Ideologies develop a vision of how they believe future society should be. This may be a specific blueprint, or it could be a partial idea that includes generalised aims based on certain fixed principles.

This description of ideology may not be exhaustive and there may be others that are equally valid. It is possible, for example, to describe a belief system based on a single principle as an ideology. Thus libertarianism, which proposes absolute freedom, can be so described. There is also a looser definition, which may be better termed a 'philosophy'. A philosophy is a generalised way of looking at the world and its problems. It is therefore less rigorous than an ideology, ideologies being more specific in their aims. Conservatism is often seen as a philosophy, not an ideology. For many, conservatism is a state of mind and a way of thinking about the world, rather than a formula for social transformation. However, for the purposes of this book ideology is defined according to the criteria given above.

Multiculturalism presents problems with our definition of ideology. To some extent it is not an ideology at all. Certainly its main supporters – mostly liberals – do not see it as an ideology. Rather, they see it as a description of how a modern society should be arranged in order to accommodate the many different cultures that now have to coexist within Western states. Opponents of multiculturalism, perhaps ironically, often do see it as an ideology. Some see it as an ideological attempt to assimilate different cultures and therefore eventually eliminate them. Others see it as a concerted attempt to impose equality upon all ideologies, rejecting criticism of their values and asserting instead that all values are equal. Whether multiculturalism is indeed an ideology is of less concern than the fact that it stands at the centre of some of the most important political conflicts of the modern age.

At this stage, it is worth considering the distinction between utopianism and scientism. Utopianism refers to ideological thought that is based on a set of desirable outcomes, and not on any scientific or objective principles. Anarchism is often seen as utopian. Critics of such movements call them unrealistic, but their supporters argue that they are examples of purposeful idealism – the pursuit of desirable goals that will create a better society. Scientism, on the other hand, is based upon empirical, objective studies of history and society. Such movements either see the perfect society as an inevitable outcome of historical processes – e.g. Marxism – or they claim to have discovered truths about the nature of humankind and wish to construct a society that will allow the natural state of human nature and potential to develop.

Once you have read the descriptions of the main political movements and theories of the past 250 years or so, as they appear on the pages that follow, you can make up your own mind whether each ideology is utopian or scientific.

Chapter 1

Liberalism

Liberalism is a wide-ranging political movement that has its origins in the Enlightenment. Its central value is that individuals have a fundamental right to personal freedom. However, liberals accept that liberty entails responsibility. At its minimum, this responsibility implies that the actions of an individual should not harm others or curtail the individual's own freedom. Liberals support the existence of the state and its laws to enforce this kind of responsibility. The liberal state must be formed by popular consent and must be accountable to the people. This is to ensure that it does not curtail freedom without justification. The liberal state should be limited in its scope and only act in such a way as to advance freedom and opportunity. Liberals demonstrate strong attachments to equal rights for all groups, tolerance, diversity and equality of opportunity. More recently, they have also embraced the idea of social justice, accepting that people are naturally unequal but insisting that all should have equality of opportunity, and that wealth should not be achieved at the expense of the poorer members of society. In modern politics, liberalism can be compatible with both conservative and social democratic movements.

Introduction

It could be argued that liberalism has been the dominant ideology in Western society since the early part of the twentieth century. This is not to say that it has prevailed everywhere. It has been challenged and, on occasions, defeated by communists, socialists, fascists and conservatives. Nevertheless, it has always returned as the central element of political cultures in the West. Liberal parties, as such, may not have won elections or formed governments with any great regularity, but all mainstream parties in modern democracies have liberal values as part of their core identity. Conservative and social democratic parties, which tend to win most democratic elections, have come to accept many key liberal beliefs. It could be said, indeed, that liberalism has seeped into the social and political culture of all economically developed countries.

During the nineteenth century, liberalism did not enjoy such pre-eminence. Conservatives placed themselves in direct opposition to liberal values, seeing them as a threat to the preservation of order. Later, socialists associated liberalism with capitalism and so challenged it on the most fundamental grounds. Towards the end of the nineteenth century, liberalism began to transform itself into a **doctrine** that was far more wide ranging and able to answer the criticisms posed by both conservatives and socialists. To deal with conservative concerns about the creation of disorder by an individualistic society, liberals introduced the idea of social responsibility. In response to socialist claims that the philosophy entailed excessive inequality, liberals developed the principle of equality of opportunity. In this way, liberalism faced its challenges and absorbed criticisms. By the time the smoke of battle had cleared after the First World War, it was clear that the dominant values of liberalism would prevail in most economically developed, non-communist societies. The challenge of fascism in the interwar period was also ultimately a futile threat to liberalism.

Key Term

Doctrine
A doctrine is a strongly held single view or collection of connected views. It is less comprehensive than an ideology in that it does not encompass a complete vision of a desired society. The term suggests that those who hold doctrines adhere to them strongly and that their thoughts and actions are determined by them. For liberals, the desire for freedom in its various forms is a doctrine; for socialists, equality is a doctrine. Liberalism can be described as a doctrine in that it includes closely connected beliefs that all liberals believe in strongly.

The Enlightenment

The Enlightenment period, which roughly corresponds to the eighteenth century, may not have created liberalism, but it certainly made such a movement possible. The new philosophies of the period challenged existing assumptions about the nature of humankind and society, and made unprecedented assertions about the human condition. Among the most significant were the following:

- Each person is born a free, rational individual.

- An individual does not have to accept the judgement of rulers or the established churches to determine what is in his or her own best interest. Rather, each individual is the best judge of his or her own interests.

- An individual is not subject to forces beyond his or her control, including the will of God, but instead possesses free will.

- Society does not have a preordained order that consigns each person to a fixed status. Rather, every individual is free to find his or her own place in society.

- We are born fundamentally equal. Although we may have different powers and potential, we do inherit equal rights.

Key Term

Rationalism
A new mode of thinking associated with the Enlightenment. It proposes that there are rational explanations for all phenomena, including the nature of man, of society and of history.

Today, we take such principles for granted. During the Enlightenment, however, these were truly revolutionary ideas that shook the Western world. A number of celebrated sources illustrate how dramatic these ideas were and how influential they proved to be. In 1689, at the dawn of the Enlightenment, the English philosopher John Locke (1632–1704) wrote in his *Two Treatises of Government*:

> *The liberty of man in society is to be under no other legislative but that established by consent in the commonwealth, nor under the dominion of any will, or restraint of any law, but what the legislative shall enact, according to the true trust put in it.*

Thus, in one statement, Locke dramatically rejects the idea of any form of government established without the expressed consent of the people.

Nearly a century later, the near-opening lines of Thomas Jefferson (1743–1826) in the 1776 American Declaration of Independence widened the debate. This statement established the rights of individuals and so, by implication, asserted the appropriate limits to government power:

> *We hold these truths to be self-evident, that all men are created equal, that they are endowed by their Creator with certain inalienable rights, that among these are life, liberty and the pursuit of happiness.*

The phrase 'the pursuit of happiness' implies that individuals are the only judge of what is best for them.

Jean-Jacques Rousseau (1712–78) had already argued that humankind was being unjustifiably controlled by social and political restraints. In the introduction to his 1762 book, *The Social Contract*, he declared:

Man is born free, but is everywhere in chains.

The 'chains' to which he refers were not merely the restraints imposed by absolute rulers, but any restraint upon the exercise of an individual's rights. He also implies that **natural rights** (e.g. to freedom) exist for all.

What the Enlightenment did, therefore, was to open people's minds to new possibilities. It enabled political movements to challenge the existing order including absolute monarchy and to establish forms of government that would free humankind, rather than enslave it. It made individuals into citizens with rights, rather than subjects with only obligations to obey. It also freed people's minds, enabling them to accept that it was possible to hold different beliefs without necessarily threatening public order and security.

Key Term

Natural rights
This concept was developed by philosophers in the seventeenth and eighteenth centuries. It asserts that all individuals are born with rights that are granted by God or nature. The main natural rights specified are life, liberty and the pursuit of happiness. The theory of natural rights implies that such rights may not be removed or reduced except by the consent of the individual. The English philosopher Thomas Hobbes (1588–1679) is often viewed as the first major theorist of natural rights, but the liberals who followed him (Hobbes was not a liberal), such as John Locke and Thomas Paine (1737–1809), are more closely associated with the concept.

Key Term

Capitalism
Capitalism is the name given to the economic system that emerged in Europe and spread to the developed world during the eighteenth and nineteenth centuries. It describes a system in which entrepreneurs take risks in organising production and extract a profit in return for the risks they take and for their organisational efforts. Under capitalism, goods, labour and finance are all exchanged between capitalists and consumers at values determined by free-market forces. Capitalism, liberals argue, requires a high degree of economic freedom for workers, consumers, financiers and entrepreneurs in order to operate effectively. Most of its aspects are criticised by socialists and anarchists. A more complete description is contained in the chapter on Socialism.

Liberalism and capitalism

Just as liberalism was made possible by Enlightenment philosophy, so it became necessary in order to underpin the development of free-market **capitalism**. Towards the latter part of the eighteenth century, it was clear that a new economic order was emerging in the more developed parts of the world, mainly in Western Europe. Fundamental economic changes were occurring as a result of the growth of international trade and the early stages of the Industrial Revolution. The old feudal order was crumbling and being replaced by a new system. This was spawning new social classes – independent farmers, free traders and merchants, industrialists and entrepreneurs, as well as workers who were free to seek employment by selling their labour to the highest bidder. The effect was the creation of a new dynamic economic structure, characterised by rapid growth and, above all, by freedom of the individual.

The most celebrated observer of the new capitalism was a Scottish economist, Adam Smith (1723–90). Smith's great work, *The Wealth of Nations*, was, by an interesting coincidence, published in the same year as the American Declaration of Independence – 1776. In it, he described how the new economic order was inhabited by individuals with free will, who would pursue their own self-interest as they saw fit. Far from resulting in chaos, the new free economy was forming a cohesiveness and a fresh order of its own. Through what he called the 'hidden hand', the development of free trade and unregulated business would act in the best interests of all. In essence, the 'hidden hand' would regulate the economy. Governments, he asserted, should be restricted to ensuring that all obey the law, and should steer clear of economic management.

Key Term

Laissez-faire
A term referring to a form of governing that interferes to a minimum extent in economic and social life.

Smith and the other advocates of free-market capitalism, such as David Ricardo (1772–1823), saw how vital it had become for individuals to consider themselves to be free, both in their pursuit of self-interest and from over-regulation by governments. The success of new free economies in creating wealth was a testament to how desirable such economic liberalism had become. In the early decades of the nineteenth century, however, liberalism was unable to dominate completely. The forces of conservatism and the interests of the traditional landed gentry opposed it ferociously. As the century wore on, conservatism lost its battle with economic liberalism, but a new adversary emerged to take its place. This was early socialism and, later, radical Marxism.

The development of the concept of liberty

The rationalism of the Enlightenment and the emergence of market capitalism both proved fertile ground for the growth of liberal ideas. One further element was needed in order for such ideas to become a complete philosophy. This was the concept of liberty. The way in which liberty (or freedom – the two terms are used here interchangeably) has been used by liberals is described in some detail below, but the term also has an important role in the development of liberalism itself.

The two great events of early liberal history were the American (1775 onwards) and French (1789) revolutions. In both cases, the revolutionaries were inspired by a desire for freedom. The Americans sought refuge from the increasingly autocratic rule of the British Crown, while the French overturned the old order in the hope of gaining freedom from undemocratic institutions. Most of us are familiar with the great battle cry of the French Revolution, '*Liberté, égalité, fraternité*', which placed freedom as its first goal, as well as with the early words of the American Declaration of Independence (see p. 2). However, despite this, the freedom being promoted here was not quite what we would understand by the term today.

Events in America and France were based on what might be called 'revolutionary liberalism', which used the term 'freedom' to mean escape from existing political authority and the establishment of a new government, a government by consent. The revolutionaries were, in fact, less concerned with individual liberty than with the freedom of the whole people – their freedom from oppression and arbitrary rule. The newly emerging societies of the 1770s and 1780s were not quite ready to deal with widespread individual freedom.

Freedom of the individual was a concept that was developed throughout the nineteenth century. It was the product of a new philosophy, often described as classical liberalism. As we have seen above, it became a necessary companion to the growth of free-market capitalism, but the idea of freedom of the individual was pre-eminent in liberalism for a relatively short time. It was not long before the dangers of excessive amounts of individual liberty were recognised and had to be confronted by liberals.

There were two main responses. First, liberals came to accept that freedom should not be exercised to the detriment of others in society, and that therefore the concept had to be combined with a sense of social responsibility. This can be described as a kind of social freedom, whereby individual liberty is exercised only in a socially responsible way. Second, liberals began to accept that there were two kinds of freedom – now commonly called 'negative liberty' and 'positive liberty'. These are described fully below; it is sufficient to note here that negative liberty refers to the freedom of the individual from external restraints, while positive liberty refers to maximising the individual's choices and opportunities.

By the twentieth century, liberals had moved some distance from their early support for a more general concept of liberty. There had to be a balance between the rights of individuals in society – freedom should be exercised with a sense of social responsibility, and governments needed to promote both positive and negative liberty. The idea of liberty had indeed come a long way from its first practical applications in France and America.

Core values of liberalism

Liberty/freedom

This is the central value for all liberals and therefore worthy of lengthy consideration. There are various different conceptions of liberty, all of which have been used by liberals at different times and in different circumstances. It bears repeating that, in this context, the terms liberty and freedom have essentially the same meaning. We can usefully divide the examination of liberty into three parts, as outlined below.

Political or revolutionary liberty

When the Scottish rebel William Wallace (1272–1305) cried the single word 'Freedom!' before his death on the scaffold in 1305 (at least according to Mel Gibson's film portrayal of the character), he did not mean that the Scottish peasantry should become free from the government and laws of Scotland at the time, or free from the duties that they owed to their landlords. What his futile plea meant was that Scotland as a whole should be free from English domination. Wallace's use of the term expresses its principal meaning over the next 500 years. The only other context in which the term was used in this period was in circumstances where serfs, who were tied to the land and their feudal duties, or in some countries were even slaves, were granted their freedom. This did not imply that they should be 'free' as we understand the word today, but that they be released from their specific feudal or slave duties. They could then become wage earners or independent tradesmen.

As we have seen above, the freedom that the French and American revolutionaries sought was similar to Wallace's idea. For most of the early liberals, political freedom implied the freedom of a people to determine their own form of government and not to be ruled by any external power. This kind of freedom is also often known as self-determination. Throughout the nineteenth century, the word became the rallying cry of many independence movements throughout the Austro-Hungarian, Russian and Ottoman empires, as well as among German and Italian nationalist movements.

Although this particular meaning of freedom is no longer central to liberal thought, it remains true that one of the core values of liberal philosophy is that all peoples should be independent, should determine their own form of government and should be masters of their own national destiny.

Individual liberty

The transfer of emphasis among liberals from political to individual liberty occurred in the early part of the nineteenth century. Writing in 1820, French liberal Benjamin Constant (1767–1830) expressed the transition thus:

The aim of the ancients was the sharing of social power among the citizens of the same fatherland; that is what they called liberty. The aim of the moderns is the enjoyment of security in private pleasures; and they call liberty the guarantees accorded by institutions to these pleasures...Individual liberty is, I repeat, the true modern liberty. Political liberty is its guarantee.

From *Political Writings*, 1815

Before such thinkers as Constant, individual liberty, as a goal, had been the preserve of those philosophers who were considered to be exceptionally radical – for example, Rousseau and the English anarchist William Godwin (1756–1836). From Constant's time onwards, however, it became clear to liberal thinkers that it was a practical aspiration.

The main enemies of liberty, in the view of early liberals, were over-powerful governments. Two main charges were laid against them. The first was that governments were too paternalistic, claiming to understand what was in people's best interests better than the people themselves. The second charge was that governments regulated the behaviour of individuals without just cause – in particular, controlling their actions, even though those actions did not affect anybody else or threaten society. This effectively divides the idea of individual liberty into two categories.

First, the utilitarian tradition of liberalism held, as its fundamental belief, that each individual is the best judge of his or her own interests. For the celebrated English utilitarian Jeremy Bentham (1748–1832), the concept of freedom was relatively simple. As individuals, we are motivated to pursue pleasure and to avoid pain. In other words, we know what we wish to pursue and what we wish to avoid. For Bentham, being allowed to make those decisions for ourselves and to act on them was the essence of freedom. He argued that the role of government should not be to make those decisions for us, nor should government prevent us from following our own self-interest, unless, of course, in so doing we prevent others from pursuing theirs. Hence, the enlightened pursuit of self-interest became a central liberal idea and, of course, one that coexisted well with free-market capitalism.

Second, in England, a follower of Bentham, John Stuart Mill (1806–73), developed a view of 'true' freedom based on the absence of constraint – perhaps this is how most of us tend to perceive the concept. Mill divided our actions into two types. The first were self-regarding actions, i.e. those that do not affect other people. In Mill's day such actions would have been mainly those of religious observance and the development of beliefs and personal morality. In a modern context, they might include recreational drug use, smoking, drinking alcohol, etc. The second type was other-regarding actions that do affect others adversely, such as assault or theft, but also negligent behaviour, cruelty and discrimination.

Mill's explanation of this principle of true freedom has become a motto which all liberals can follow:

John Stuart Mill, the father of classical liberalism

The sole end for which mankind are warranted, individually or collectively, in interfering with the liberty of action of any of their number, is self-protection. That is the only purpose for which power can be rightfully exercised over a member of a civilised society, against his will, is to prevent harm to others. His own good, either physical or moral, is not a sufficient warrant. He cannot rightfully be compelled to do or forbear because it will be better for him to do so, because it will make him happier, because, in the opinion of others, to do so would be wise or even right.

From *On Liberty*, 1859

This famous passage encompasses both Bentham's idea of self-interested freedom and the classical view of liberty as the absence of unwarranted constraints.

Negative and positive liberty

The term 'negative liberty' was not used by Mill himself; the modern philosopher Isaiah Berlin (1909–97) coined the term a century later to describe Mill's view. By 'negative' he did not imply any criticism of the idea but rather that it referred to an absence of restraint. Berlin was concerned to differentiate between negative freedom and another kind of liberty that had been developed by liberals later in the nineteenth century.

Two short passages reveal the differences between negative and positive liberty, as described by Berlin:

Liberty in this [negative] sense is simply the area within which a man can act unobstructed by others. If I am prevented by others from doing what I could otherwise do, I am to that degree unfree.

The positive sense of the word liberty derives from the wish on the part of the individual to be his own master. I wish my life and decisions to depend on myself, not on external forces of whatever kind. I wish to be the instrument of my own, not of other men's acts of will. I wish to be a subject not an object.

Both from *Two Concepts of Liberty*, 1969

We can trace the concept of positive liberty back to the English moral philosopher, T. H. Green (1836–82). Like Mill, Green did not use the term 'positive liberty', but his meaning was close to Berlin's definition. He rejected the classical liberal view of Mill and others that society is made up only of self-interested individuals. Instead, he saw society as 'organic' and its citizens as interdependent as well as independent. In other words, citizens are not merely motivated by self-interest but also by a desire to promote the common good.

It follows from this that individuals achieve self-fulfilment not merely through pursuing their own happiness, but also by pursuing social goods such as the welfare of others. Green's freedom is positive in that we can achieve personal satisfaction by doing good for others as well as for ourselves.

A more modern conception of positive liberty is that there should be the widest possible degree of choice and opportunity for everybody. We can synthesise this with Green's view in that, given freedom and choice, we will exercise a sense of social responsibility by pursuing the common good. This does not make Green a socialist. He still believed that the state should promote individual liberty and that we pursue self-interest, but he asserted that freedom is not one-dimensional: it is both individual and social in nature.

Green's divergence from the traditional, classical liberal view of freedom opened the door for liberalism to expand its political horizons beyond individual freedom. His philosophy ushered in a new liberal age, which was able to embrace equality of opportunity, state welfare provision and even redistribution of income from rich to poor. This also gave rise to the so-called 'enabling state' in the 1990s.

Tolerance

The liberal love of tolerance flows directly from Mill's principles of individual liberty, but it pre-dates him in liberal thought by over a century in the ideas of John Locke. Locke was almost exclusively concerned with religious tolerance, an idea that was relatively radical at the time he was writing. He drew his conclusions from one simple principle: 'That every man may enjoy the same rights that are granted to others.'

Political controversy over religious tolerance raged throughout the eighteenth century and into the nineteenth century. With the arrival of liberals such as Mill, however, the tolerance debate transcended religion and involved every sphere of life. It was in the field of freedom of expression that liberalism campaigned most strongly in the nineteenth century. Toleration of other people's beliefs, values, thoughts and faiths, and their right to express them openly, became one of liberalism's most cherished goals.

In the twentieth century, attention switched to public attitudes towards minority groups. In recent times, liberals have defended and campaigned for the rights of minorities such as gay people and ethnic and religious groups, and have opposed all forms of censorship in the media and the arts.

A well-known liberal expression, dating back to the French philosopher Voltaire (1694–1778), is: 'I detest what you say, but I shall defend to the death your right to say it.' To this, Mill added that to prevent the expression of different beliefs and faiths was an exercise in arrogance. How are we to know, he asked, that our views are correct and those of others are wrong? This principle, nevertheless, needs some qualification.

Liberals will tolerate different beliefs and views but assign limits to this tolerance. If the security of the state or the freedom of individuals is threatened, or if people are being incited to commit crimes, act in a violent way or discriminate against any group, freedom of expression should be curtailed. This brings us back to Mill's view of freedom. We should be free as long as our actions are self-regarding and do no harm to others. Words or actions that adversely affect others should not be tolerated.

Two further modern aspects of liberal tolerance should be considered. First, a typical liberal is sympathetic to the idea that individuals are influenced by their social and economic circumstances. In other words, we are not always responsible for our own actions. It follows that those who become involved in what is considered antisocial behaviour – notably crime, substance abuse and addiction or personal neglect – may do so as a consequence of social circumstances beyond their control. Thus, a liberal tends to be tolerant in his or her outlook and proposes measures to assist individuals in the reform of their behaviour, rather than merely punishing them.

Second, modern liberals have tended to demonstrate greater tolerance than most people over personal morality. On issues such as sexual mores, abortion, homosexuality, same-sex marriage and the like, liberals generally take the view that these are private matters, not the concern of the state or of others in society. Indeed, it is in this area that the divisions between modern conservatism and liberalism are most sharply drawn. Conservatives insist that there is no such thing as entirely private morality; immoral behaviour does threaten the fabric of society and so should be controlled. The contemporary liberal tolerance of varying lifestyles also distinguishes it from various forms of religious fundamentalism.

Equal rights

Liberals disagree among themselves about the existence of natural rights. Locke and Paine certainly based their whole belief systems around their existence. Bentham and Mill, on the other hand, rejected natural rights theory. For them, freedom consisted of the natural inclination of humankind to pursue its own selfish interests. However, this disagreement disguises a principle held universally by all liberals – that we are all entitled to equal rights.

Those liberals who support the idea of natural rights have no difficulty in translating this into support for equal rights. After all, if we all enjoy rights granted to us by God or nature, it must be true that they are given on an equal basis. Other liberals adopt a purely rational position. They can see no reason for inequality. For them it is unnatural, the creation of men in history who have sought to exercise power over others. For a liberal, we are all created equal and so must enjoy equal rights.

However, we must be careful here. A belief in equal rights is not the same as a belief in equality in general. Most (though not all) liberals accept that we have different abilities and potentialities when we are born. What they seek is the equal right to reach our full potential and to seek self-fulfilment.

These positions lead to two further conclusions. First, all distinct groups in society are entitled to the same rights. In other words, discrimination against groups should be outlawed. This has led liberals to advance the causes of full rights for women, gay people, disabled people and minority ethnic groups. Second, we are all entitled to equality of opportunity. This second issue is explored below.

Equality of opportunity

The classical liberals of the nineteenth century proposed a society in which individuals were largely free from restraint and therefore free to succeed or fail, to grow rich or to remain poor, to choose their own occupation and lifestyle and to find their own road to self-fulfilment. However, this philosophy began to present problems for many liberals as the century wore on. It became clear that the doctrines of equal rights and individual liberty were conflicting with each other. Many members of society, through unfortunate circumstances of birth and through no fault of their own, were not blessed with equal opportunity to benefit from such a free society. Early social researchers, such as Charles Booth (1840–1916), revealed to a surprised world that there was such a thing as a cycle of deprivation, that poor families produced poor offspring and that there was little or nothing that could break this cycle.

John Stuart Mill himself, the great champion of individual liberty, late in his life came to accept this as a problem with his own philosophy. At the same time, the newly formed Liberal Party of Great Britain, led by William Gladstone

(1809–98), espoused greater **equality of opportunity** as one of its goals. Thus, elementary education for all was introduced, and entry into the professions – law, government and the army, for example – was opened to a wider spectrum of society. These were small advances in equality of opportunity but they indicated how liberal opinion was changing. The next great advance was promoted by William Beveridge (1879–1963), the creator of the welfare state. Beveridge proposed that the availability of welfare for all, notably education, healthcare and social security, would expand opportunity for all, no matter what their circumstances of birth.

 Key Term

Equality of opportunity
This emerged as a political principle in the latter part of the nineteenth century. It recognises that some individuals are born with disadvantages that cannot be overcome by their own efforts. It is also a moral principle that suggests that all are entitled to equal life chances. Inequality can be justified, argue liberals and conservatives, provided all begin life with equal opportunities. Equality of opportunity is mainly promoted through universal education, but also implies the removal of artificial obstacles and other social problems that could hold some individuals back. It is associated with social mobility – the ability of individuals to move upwards through the class system, and meritocracy, where the most able can rise to the 'top'. It also applies to class differences, gender issues and ethnic diversity.

After Beveridge, the cause of equality of opportunity was largely taken up in Britain by the Labour Party. From the 1960s, the introduction of comprehensive education and the expansion of higher education were the principal measures adopted, with the outlawing of discrimination against women, minority ethnic groups and disabled people coming close behind. Indeed, at this time, the idea of equality of opportunity became part of the British political consensus, with all three main parties supporting, or claiming to support, the principle.

So far we have concentrated on British liberalism, but the discussion would not be complete without reference to the US experience. In many ways the USA can be seen as the natural home of equality of opportunity and, indeed, some might say the whole of its society is based upon it. Education in the USA has long been supplied on a comprehensive basis and there are strong safeguards against discrimination both in the constitution and in the laws. The belief that every individual should have the opportunity to advance in life has become part of the so-called 'American Dream'. Indeed, as in the UK, it has become so much a part of the country's culture that it is no longer associated specifically with liberalism. This should not, however, disguise the fact that it emerged very clearly from the liberal tradition of which Thomas Jefferson, James Madison (1751–1836) and Alexander Hamilton (1755–1804) were founding members.

Pluralism

The term 'pluralism' relates to a modern conception of the truly liberal society. Indeed, the French philosopher Alexis de Tocqueville (1805–59) regarded pluralism as an essential requirement for true democracy. For Tocqueville, pluralism was characterised by a flourishing collection of groups to which people owed allegiance and in which they could freely participate. Such a healthy **civil society** would prevent the state from becoming too powerful. It would also act as a balance against the potential tyranny of rule by the numerical majority.

Tocqueville's vision of pluralism was based upon his observations of the USA in the 1830s, but it was not until the twentieth century that liberals in Europe became concerned with the positive potentialities of pluralist democracy and society in general. The modern conception of pluralism includes a number of aspects:

- The diversity of cultures, religions, ethnic groups and lifestyles in society is tolerated and the rights of such groups protected.

- The state tolerates the expression of a variety of beliefs, philosophies and political creeds, provided they do not threaten the peace and security of the country.

- People are used to participating freely in such groups.

- Groups have access to the political system and therefore the opportunity to influence policy-making.

- The existence of different cultures, values and belief systems helps to prevent domination of society by any single section of society.

In summary, for liberals, a pluralist society enhances freedom, spreads opportunity widely and helps to control the power of the state.

Key Term

Civil society
This expression refers to the wide variety of groups that flourish in pluralist societies. Individuals may be part of such groups naturally, or may choose to join them in order to achieve certain personal goals or aspirations. Families are included as part of civil society, but the term generally refers to such groups as political parties, pressure groups, religious organisations, voluntary groups and charities, trade unions and media organisations. A free and active civil society is now seen as vital to a healthy democracy. It ensures that people become actively involved in society; it can also help to act as a counterbalance to the power of the state.

Government by consent

One of the key elements of the Enlightenment was its questioning of the basis of political societies. Before rational thought was applied to this problem, principles such as the divine right of kings, the sanctity of obedience and the acceptance of the traditional basis of authority were used to explain the legitimacy of government. The new thinking challenged such legitimacy and searched for a new kind of political authority.

The seventeenth-century English philosophers Hobbes and Locke are widely

2·15

acknowledged to have developed, between them, the concept of government by consent. Hobbes imagined a circumstance in which the people would come together in a free compact or agreement to set up a great power over them; this would bring about peace and security. This was not enough for Locke. First, his contract was to be real and not merely a notional device. Second, it would have to be constantly confirmed. This is how Locke described the original contract:

> *And thus every man, by consenting with others to make one body politic under one government, puts himself under an obligation to every one of that society to submit to the determination of the majority.*

From *Two Treatises of Civil Government*, 1690

Nearly a century later, in 1787, the representatives of the newly freed American people came together to make such a contract a reality. The preamble to the US constitution echoes Locke's description of political consent:

> *We, the people of the United States, in order to form a more perfect union, establish justice, insure [original spelling] domestic tranquility, provide for the common defense, promote the general welfare, and secure the blessings of liberty to ourselves and our posterity, do ordain and establish this Constitution for the United States of America.*

Two years later the French revolutionaries followed suit, although the government they established proved to be short-lived. For Locke, the original consent was assumed to be constantly renewed as long as future generations did not dissolve a government. Followers of Locke have argued that consent must be a more continuous process. It follows that by the term 'government by consent' liberals mean that the people should have regular opportunities to express their consent, or indeed to withhold it.

This means more than regular free elections. It implies the use of referendums when any major change to the power or system of government is proposed. On a more general level, we can say that the state must tolerate the free expression of public opinion, even if it challenges the basis of government. Should there be indications that the people, or at least the majority of them, wish to withdraw consent, the whole basis of government would need to be reconsidered.

On a global level, liberals insist that governments, at any time and in every place, should only be considered legitimate if the people have freely given their consent to the system of government. In a UK context, for example, the people of the Falkland Islands, Gibraltar and Northern Ireland have all been offered the opportunity to vote in a plebiscite over whether they wish to remain under British rule. In each case, 'Yes' answers have been enough for liberals.

Limited government and constitutionalism

According to liberals, merely ensuring that government is established by consent is not a sufficient safeguard for the people. It is essential in the interests of liberty that government should operate within strict boundaries. If government is not limited, it is likely to encroach upon the freedom and the private lives of its citizens. Power is a dangerous thing and it must be controlled at all times.

Liberals also fear three other potential consequences of government:

- the exercise of arbitrary power, i.e. power that has no legitimate authority
- the tendency for power to become concentrated in too few hands
- that democratic systems may simply become the tyranny of the majority, to the detriment of legitimate minorities.

Liberals offer a solution to all of these difficulties. This is the imposition of constitutional rule.

A liberal constitution

Typically, a constitution proposed by liberals would enjoy the following features:

- It would be sovereign. Governments would be strictly subject to its terms except in times of national emergency.

- It would define the limits to the jurisdiction of government. This prevents both arbitrary power and any drift towards increased state power.

- It defines the rights of the citizens, which is a further safeguard against encroachments by governments.

- It distributes power among different institutions of government. This prevents the concentration of power in too few hands.

- It would include special arrangements for the amendment of the constitution, ensuring that the citizens themselves are in control of the process. This prevents governments accumulating excessive power without popular consent.

By combining the doctrines of government by consent and constitutionalism, modern liberals have found a way of reconciling effective government with the rights and freedoms of both individuals and intermediate groups.

Justice

There are two aspects of this concept to consider. Legal justice consists of the equal application of the law to all citizens. Clearly, liberals have no difficulty in supporting this principle. It conforms to their attachment to equal rights. The idea of social justice, on the other hand, is more contentious.

Social justice is more closely associated with socialists than liberals. This is mainly because the achievement of a more just society usually requires the intervention of the state. Liberals have traditionally been suspicious of such intervention. Although late-nineteenth-century liberals endorsed the implementation of equality of opportunity – a key element in a just modern society – since then liberals have tended to accept that inequality is natural and, in a genuinely free society, social outcomes are all 'just'. Some contemporary liberals, however, have challenged this position.

Beveridge and others have concluded that deprivation of various kinds curtails freedom just as much as governments and their laws can. It has also been recognised that, even in a free-market system, excessive inequalities cannot be considered just. It may be acceptable to tolerate some degree of inequality in the free market, but not to the extent that the poorest members of society are seriously deprived. Many liberals therefore share with socialism a desire to redistribute some income from rich to poor. A liberal philosophy of social justice was offered by John Rawls (1921–2002). He took the view that some inequalities cannot be tolerated and that the state is therefore justified in intervening. His ideas are explored further below.

Of course, many modern liberals do not accept such intervention in the interests of social justice. They retain the classical, nineteenth-century view that inequalities are justified in the free market, being the result of each individual's own efforts and abilities. It is therefore not without some reservations that this kind of justice is stated as a core liberal value. Liberals would disagree among themselves on this point.

Types of liberalism

Early forms

The first true liberals did not call themselves 'liberals'. They tended to be referred to as 'radicals' or 'republicans', or sometimes even 'rationalists'. In retrospect, however, we may correctly describe them as early liberals. The main principle of the early liberal movement was natural rights. The champions of natural rights theory came from all parts of the Western world and included such historically significant figures as John Locke, Jean-Jacques Rousseau, Thomas Paine and Thomas Jefferson.

The emphasis on natural rights gave rise to the various practical developments given below:

- A government has no authority to encroach upon the rights of its people, unless the people expressly consent to sacrifice some of their rights to that government. Furthermore, even if individual rights have been sacrificed, people must retain the option of reclaiming them by dissolving the government.

- All are born with equal rights (although this perhaps excluded women at this early stage of liberal development). Governments should respect and promote equal rights.

- The most important right that nature grants to all, after the basic right to life, is the right to be free. Freedom in this context means the right to pursue one's own interests. Here again, governments must respect and protect the freedom of its citizens.

- The exercise of power without the expressed authority of the people cannot be justified since it denies fundamental rights.

These were revolutionary ideas and it is therefore no surprise that they gave rise to revolutions. The old world of hereditary rulers, strict social hierarchies and limited individual liberty was either swept away or dramatically reformed by these early radical thinkers.

Jeremy Bentham developed the utilitarian philosophy

Utilitarianism

The concept of 'utility' was developed by early economists in the late-eighteenth and early-nineteenth centuries. The term meant satisfaction or perhaps even happiness – whatever gave an individual pleasure. The utilitarians, led in Britain by Jeremy Bentham, believed it was possible to calculate how much utility each individual could derive from consuming certain goods, and that it was therefore also possible to calculate the total amount of utility a whole society was achieving. However, it was not for external powers to decide what gave people utility. Individuals were to decide what gave them more or less utility for themselves.

The significance of this concept for economists of the period was that if there were free trade within and between countries and if each consumer were able to purchase whatever goods he or she liked within his or her income constraints, total utility in a society would be automatically maximised. Put another way, a free-market economy, inhabited by free individuals, would guarantee the common good.

The political utilitarians agreed, but added a further element. They admitted the possibility that governments could add to the total sum of utility by taking certain actions. Indeed, Bentham argued that all actions by government should be judged on the basis of a kind of algebra or calculus, which would establish whether total utility would be increased or reduced. This implied two principles. First, that governments had to accept what people asserted would give them satisfaction, and second, that government should be limited to providing what the people as a whole preferred. The principle was famously summarised in the idea that governments should pursue 'the greatest good for the greatest number'.

Utilitarians can be described as liberals in that they accepted the freedom of individuals to determine their own best interests and insisted that the role of government should be limited. However, the liberals who followed them identified two main problems with utilitarianism.

The first was that it took a simplistic view of what motivated individuals and what gave them pleasure. For example, the consumption of goods may give pleasure, but it is not as high a form of pleasure as, say, gaining a good education or appreciating the arts. The second objection was that the doctrine opened the door to excessive state intervention. As long as total social utility was increased, the utilitarians argued, the state could take positive action, but early liberals feared that any state activity would threaten the freedom of individuals.

Thus, utilitarianism declined in influence as the nineteenth century progressed. It was replaced in the world of radical politics by a purer form of liberalism known as classical liberalism.

Classical liberalism

The classical liberals were largely inspired by the dominant philosophy of John Stuart Mill, a disciple of Bentham, who took the philosophy of freedom to new heights. For those who later became known as classical liberals, the freedom of the individual was everything. This is how Mill described the scope of liberty:

> [Liberty] comprises first the inward domain of conscience in the most comprehensive sense; liberty of thought and feeling; absolute freedom of opinion and sentiment on all subjects, practical or speculative, scientific, moral or theological... Secondly the principle requires liberty of tastes and pursuits; of framing the plan of our life to suit our own character; of doing as we like... Thirdly from this liberty of each individual follows the liberty, within the same limits, of combination among individuals; freedom to unite, for any purpose not involving harm to others.
>
> From *On Liberty*, 1859

Today we talk of such freedoms as 'civil liberties' and summarise them as freedom of expression, thought, worship, association and movement.

It is important to understand why Mill and the other classical liberals worshipped liberty to the extent that they did. The early liberals derived freedom from natural rights; utilitarians saw freedom in terms of the ability to pursue one's own self-interest. For Mill, individual liberty was associated with higher ideals than these. He believed that freedom would maximise human progress by promoting innovation, creativity and self-fulfilment. It went hand in hand with the entrepreneurial spirit. This is what Mill had to say about his own utilitarian principles:

> I regard utility as the ultimate appeal on all ethical questions; but it must be utility in the largest sense, grounded on the permanent interests of a man as a progressive being.
>
> (Ibid.)

We should note here his use of the term 'progressive being'. Whereas Bentham largely saw self-interest and freedom in terms of the consumption of goods, Mill was interested in human progress. In other words, Mill saw humans as creative individuals, whereas the utilitarians saw them merely as consumers. Thus we can interpret the classical liberal idea of freedom as partly a matter of principle (Mill) and partly a matter of economic wellbeing (Bentham).

The concept of freedom naturally led to an interest in tolerance as a political virtue, i.e. **political tolerance**. Such a progression was utterly logical. The liberals' argument was that our own freedom depends upon all people enjoying the same freedom. In other words, if we expect others to respect our freedom, we must respect theirs. This principle is particularly relevant to freedom of expression, although Mill himself accepted that there were limits to free speech – our words must not be used to harm others or to incite other people to harming others. On the whole, however, we and the law should respect people's right to choose their own beliefs and values and to express them publicly. This same principle has been applied in order to guarantee civil liberties such as freedom of movement, freedom of association and freedom of worship. There is no reason, say liberals, why such freedoms should not be tolerated by the state.

Key Term

Political tolerance

This principle was developed by liberals, notably Locke and Mill. It asserts that the state should tolerate all beliefs and activities that do no harm to the security and integrity of the state, and that do not result in harm to individuals or groups in that society. It mainly refers to freedom of religion, political belief, lifestyle and expression.

Nineteenth-century liberals were concerned by the dangers of rulers accumulating too much power. However, they did not see the growth of democracy as the answer to this. Indeed, classical liberals were opposed to the introduction of popular democracy. For them this meant majority rule and, as both Tocqueville and Mill remarked, this was the tyranny of the majority. For these liberals, universal suffrage was a dangerous idea. The numerical majority formed by the working class would permanently suppress minority groups. Many early liberals therefore supported the retention of the property qualification for voting so as to counterbalance the power of the majority. (Property owners were considered to be more tolerant and responsible in their outlook.)

As for the dangers of powerful government, liberals argued for a minimal state, to be granted only a narrow range of essential functions. The minimal state was to retain responsibility for maintaining order, security and peace in order to guarantee the protection of individual liberties and prevent the formation of monopolies. In a free-market economy, it was understood that some companies might be so successful and grow so large that they would be in a position to exploit both workers and consumers. It was a legitimate function of the state, therefore, to control such economic power. To this day such 'competition policy', as it is now known, has been supported by those who wish to see the deregulation of economic activity in other areas.

Classical liberalism – a summary

We can now summarise the main principles of classical liberals. It is worth adding that they subscribed to the core liberal value that government should only be established by consent, that it should be regulated by a binding constitution and that all citizens should enjoy the benefits of legal justice and equal rights.

The main principles of classical liberalism are as follows:

- Individual freedoms should flourish and be respected.

- The state should be limited to a minimum number of functions, largely confined to protecting people from each other, defending the nation and preventing the accumulation of economic and political power.

- There should be a tolerant society in which behaviour that was not harmful to others would be uncontrolled.

- The economy should be based on completely free markets, except where monopolies were developed.

- The state should be placed in the hands of a representative democracy.

Variations on classical liberalism

One variation of classical liberalism is worthy of note: the Manchester School in England. It was led by two radical politicians, John Bright (1811–89) and Richard Cobden (1804–65). They concentrated on the issue of free trade, although Bright also supported full adult suffrage (unlike Mill). They believed that free trade – national and international – would mean cheap goods, especially food. This development would be the most effective way of improving the conditions of the working classes – more effective, indeed, than state-organised welfare. 'Manchesterism', therefore, looked at liberty from the point of view of the working classes, whereas the Millite liberals were associated with the property-owning and entrepreneurial middle classes.

These ideas remain interesting today, as free trade has returned as a key issue in the modern world, receiving support from liberals and conservatives who consider the interests of Western consumers, and from radicals on the left who believe it can benefit poor countries suffering from excessive protectionism in world trade.

Contemporary neo-liberalism

During the late 1970s and in the 1980s interest in classical liberal ideas enjoyed a major revival. It was not a feature of liberal parties at the time, but of the new style of conservatism known as the 'New Right'. Indeed, Margaret Thatcher (1925–), the British champion of the New Right, was happy to admit that she was 'at heart' a classical liberal. Spurred on by liberal economists and philosophers such as Milton Friedman (1912–) and Friedrich Hayek (1899–1992), she and other disciples of the New Right, including US President Ronald Reagan (1911–2004), Dick Cheney, the Vice President under George Bush junior and one of their economic advisers, Paul Wolfowitz, set about re-establishing free markets in both a domestic setting (though not necessarily in a world setting where the American neo-liberals also tended to favour protectionism for their own industries).

As a conservative development, the classical liberal revival is normally known as neo-liberalism to distinguish it from its nineteenth-century ancestor, but the philosophies of Mill and Bright and Cobden are echoed in this passage from Friedman's work:

> Another essential part of economic freedom as promoted by the neo-liberals is freedom to use the resources we possess in accordance with our own values – freedom to enter any occupation, engage in any business enterprise, buy from and sell to anyone else, so long as we do so on a strictly voluntary basis and do not resort to force in order to coerce others.
>
> From *Free to Choose*, 1980

We must be extremely careful not to imply that neo-liberalism and classical liberalism are the same thing. In terms of their beliefs about free trade they might be, but the New Right neo-liberals had no hesitation in accepting that the state should intervene in people's lives to maintain law and order and to enforce a particular view of personal morality. In other words, for the neo-liberals, the minimal state principle applied to economics but not to politics in general.

After the financial and economic crisis of 2008-09 neo-liberalism became somewhat discredited as the non-interventionist, *laissez faire* policies of Western governments, especially in the USA, were seen as the causes of the recession. The result has been a reaction against neo-liberal ideas and a return to state intervention among most developed economies.

Social Darwinism

In 1859, at the height of the classical liberal era, Charles Darwin (1809–82) published his great work *On the Origin of the Species*. His theories of evolution shook the scientific world and had a dramatic impact on social theory.

A number of thinkers looked at Darwin's discoveries and immediately set about applying them to human society. Herbert Spencer (1820–93) was a leading proponent of a political movement which was later described as 'social Darwinism'. Spencer was already interested in the idea that social justice consists of individuals making whatever they can of their lives, provided (as other classical liberals had insisted) they do not interfere with the freedom of others. Since we are innately unequal in our abilities and our motivation, it is only natural that some will succeed and others will fail. Spencer used the term 'survival of the fittest' to describe this process, even before Darwin's theories were published.

Refining his theories in response to the Darwinian revolution, Spencer argued that it is those who adapt most appropriately to their social environment who will do best. Those who fail to adapt will inevitably suffer. He saw this as the natural order of things, just as it was among animal species. Samuel Smiles (1812–1904), a contemporary of Spencer, turned social Darwinism into a quasi-religion. In his best-known work, *Self Help* (1859), he argued that it is within the capability of all individuals, including members of the working class, to improve themselves through diligent activity and a willingness to set up new economic ventures. Nobody should rely on others, charities or the state to support them. We succeed or fail according to our own efforts. Smiles made this high-minded exhortation:

> *The healthy spirit of self help created amongst working people would, more than any other measure, serve to raise them as a class, and this, not by pulling down others, but by levelling them up to a higher and still advancing standard of religion, intelligence and virtue.*
>
> From *Self Help*, 1859

The fact that *Self Help* sold over 150,000 copies, at a time when a minority could afford books and many were illiterate, bears testament to how strong the entrepreneurial spirit was in mid-nineteenth-century England.

In the 1980s, when classical liberalism was enjoying a revival within the New Right movement, social Darwinism and libertarianism, its close associate, were also enjoying growing popularity. This revival was based on two main beliefs.

First, many conservative and neo-liberal thinkers took their support for free economic markets to extremes, proposing the complete removal of all state restrictions, in particular the removal of nearly all taxation. These followers of libertarianism even proposed that services such as education, law and order and healthcare should be transferred to the private sector and left to market forces. This was linked to social Darwinism, in that it implied the survival of the fittest. In a completely deregulated

society, free rein would be given for able and dynamic individuals to succeed and, therefore, for those who are lazy and fail to adapt themselves to get what they deserve – very little.

Second, there was a growing belief that state welfare had become excessive. What the libertarians (and members of the New Right in general) called a 'dependency culture' had developed, to the detriment of prosperity and human progress. Dependency culture suggested that many people had become used to relying heavily on state support, through social security benefits and the provision of 'free' services by the state. This was sapping people of their dynamism and motivation. Too many individuals, they argued, had grown used to contributing little to society so that growth, innovation and progress were stifled. They therefore proposed the removal of virtually all welfare services. As Samuel Smiles had argued over a century before, people should learn to stand on their own two feet. Furthermore, whatever the outcome of such a free society and however much economic inequality might result, natural justice would be considered to have been done.

Libertarianism

This term refers to an extreme form of liberalism. Libertarianism emerged in the latter part of the nineteenth century and has become more popular since the 1980s. Though they are ideologically closer to liberals, most modern libertarians have seen themselves as part of the conservative movement. They insist that the state is an unwarranted restriction on freedom and its functions should be reduced to a bare minimum. However, unlike anarchists, libertarians stop short of proposing the state's complete abolition. Certainly, they argue, the state should not interfere with economic and social affairs, nor should it become involved in matters of morality. Most social problems can be solved by the free market, even those concerning law and order. The state should therefore do little other than defend the people. Libertarianism's leading modern exponent has been the US philosopher Robert Nozick (1938–2002).

It is a strange irony that libertarianism, considered a 'right wing' ideology, is often also known as anarcho-capitalism and is therefore associated with the most left wing of all philosophies – anarchism. Political ideology appears, therefore, to have come full circle. Nozick argued for the near complete abolition of the state and its functions. This implied no taxation, no welfare and almost no laws restricting human behaviour. Rejecting Mill's principle that our freedoms should not interfere with the freedom of others, Nozick insisted that it was up to individuals to protect themselves from others. They should not rely on the state to do it for them. In other words, Nozick's ideal state was more minimal even than Mill's and Spencer's.

Modern liberalism

After the emergence of new ideas in liberalism after 1870, all liberals are known as 'modern liberals'. The various types of modern liberal are described below.

New liberalism

The term 'new liberalism' is potentially misleading. It does not refer to a contemporary movement. This 'new' philosophy was developed and so named around 1870, the purpose being to distinguish it from the dominant classical-liberal form. The change in liberal philosophy occurred as a result of two developments, one philosophical, the other practical.

The new philosophical perspective was supplied in Britain by T. H. Green (1836–82). Green accepted the liberal belief in the importance of individual ('negative') liberty, but made two observations that were to have a profound influence on the future of liberalism. The first was that we cannot consider ourselves to be completely free merely to pursue our own interests. We also have a social obligation to consider the needs and the welfare of others. Second, he described a further kind of freedom – what Isaiah Berlin was to call 'positive' liberty a

century later. This was freedom in the form of choice and opportunity, the chance to achieve **self-realisation**.

Key Term

Self-realisation
Sometimes also known as 'self-fulfilment', this term describes a situation in which individuals (or sometimes groups) are able to achieve their own aspirations. It is related to the idea of positive liberty, suggesting that individuals obtain freedom by experiencing social conditions that allow them to fulfil their own hopes and goals.

On a more practical level, liberals had to come to terms with the fact that, as the nineteenth century wore on and capitalism and industrialisation intensified, many unpalatable social consequences were emerging. The conditions of the working classes showed few signs of improving, despite the fact that national prosperity, especially in Britain, was growing. Numerous social deprivations were coming to light, notably persistent illiteracy, poor health conditions, bad housing, and recurring unemployment causing economic insecurity. Many argued that these problems were the result of an excessively free market and a lack of positive intervention by the state. Allied to Green's identification of social responsibility as a vital human virtue, the revelation of widening inequality in society caused the liberal movement to re-examine its core beliefs. The result was new liberalism.

The fundamental belief upon which new liberalism was based was that the poorer sections of society were unable to benefit from the economic freedoms that the classical liberals had supported. Society had the potential to progress collectively, provided that all individuals were able to take advantage of their freedom. This implied intervention by the state to provide education in particular, but also a range of other welfare benefits, notably healthcare, pensions and housing. This would achieve two social objectives: greater equality of opportunity and a more humane society in which the benefits of progress would be spread more evenly. Green paid relatively little attention to the practicalities of such welfare. William Gladstone, the great liberal prime minister of the nineteenth century, did attempt to reduce inherited privilege and introduced primary education, but these developments were relatively modest. Gladstone, however, was followed by liberal thinkers and politicians who were prepared to act more decisively.

Elementary education was extended to all in 1901 and the Liberal administration of 1906–11, led by Herbert Asquith (1852–1928) and David Lloyd George (1863–1945), widened the process. It provided the first pensions and state-sponsored insurance schemes for unemployment and sickness. It was not yet a welfare state, but it was a major step in that direction. L. T. Hobhouse (1864–1929) and J. A. Hobson (1858–1940), two major liberal thinkers, argued aggressively that the state needed to take an increasingly active role in creating more social justice. This is how Hobhouse expressed the state's new role:

> *Liberalism is now formally committed to a task which certainly involves a new conception of the State in its relation to the individual life and private enterprise... From the standpoint which best represents its continuity with earlier Liberalism, it appears as a fuller realisation of individual liberty contained in the provision of equal opportunities for self-development.*
>
> From *The Crisis of Liberalism*, 1909

These developments brought liberalism a long way from its classical roots. The new liberals now saw the state as a vehicle for the enhancement of liberty rather than a threat to it. This was a different kind of freedom, effectively positive freedom, represented by equality of opportunity and the widening of choices for all. It was to be achieved by the use of general taxation to provide welfare services and to spread prosperity more widely. Hobson, who was close to the newly formed Labour Party in his views, even proposed some public ownership of major industries.

The problem for the liberal movement in Britain was that the Labour Party, which was formed in 1900, was moving in the same direction. Furthermore, Labour had no qualms about extending the role of the state. Many liberals remained concerned about state power, which inhibited freedom of action, so it was no surprise that Labour effectively annexed most of the new liberal philosophy.

Welfare (social) liberalism

As the liberal movement came to accept the expanded role of the state, it became clear that it needed to respond to the growing popular support for socialist initiatives. In the event, the final acceptance of the state as a vehicle for extending liberty was provided not by a philosopher or a politician, but by a senior civil servant, William Beveridge.

In the 1940s Beveridge was charged by the wartime coalition government with producing a blueprint for social policy after the war had ended. As a liberal, he needed to address the problem of how to propose large extensions to the role of the state without jeopardising people's liberties. He did this by formulating new conceptions of freedom. For Beveridge, such deprivations as poverty, unemployment and lack of education were curtailments of freedom as serious as laws and overbearing governments. By relieving the poorer and needier members of the population from these problems, liberty would be extended, not threatened. He was guided by a Liberal Party report of 1929, which had signalled a new attitude to the state. A key passage read as follows:

> *Liberalism stands for liberty, but it is an error to think that a policy of liberty must always be negative, that the state can help liberty only by abstaining from action, that invariably men are freest when their Government does least.*

Released from the obligation to limit state power, Beveridge was able to consider how an active state could extend freedom. This is how he expressed his fundamental beliefs:

> *To my mind there are three things above all that every citizen of this country needs as*

conditions of a happy and useful life after the war. He needs freedom from want and fear of want, freedom from idleness and fear of idleness enforced by unemployment, freedom from war and fear of war.

From *Why I Am a Liberal*, 1945

Postwar liberals, therefore, came to accept the welfare state that the Labour Government set up from 1945. Although this is seen as the jewel in the British socialist crown, it should be emphasised that it was inspired by a leading liberal figure, namely Beveridge. **Welfare**, especially education, extended equality of opportunity and expanded positive freedom.

Key Term

Welfare

This concept was developed largely in the nineteenth century. It refers to the provision of services and subsidies to individuals and families to help provide them with an acceptable standard of living. Welfare involves the collection of funds – either through taxation or voluntary and charitable contributions – and their distribution in the form of money or services to those who are considered in need. In the case of the welfare state in Britain, some welfare is distributed to all, irrespective of their economic circumstances, e.g. education, state pensions and healthcare. Welfare usually includes provisions such as education, healthcare, pensions, subsidised housing, social services, benefits for the unemployed, disabled, long-term poor, etc.

Meanwhile, another liberal, the economist John Maynard Keynes (1883–1946), felt able to justify extensions in the state's role on the grounds that economic stability could also enhance freedom. He argued that the state needed to engage in positive economic management in order to create an economic environment in which individuals would feel confident in their ability to engage in commercial and industrial enterprises, to pursue their careers with some confidence about the economic future,

to enjoy their private property and to be released from excessive fear of unemployment (the last issue being echoed by Beveridge).

Most of the proposals of welfare liberalism were adopted by Labour governments and, to some degree, were also supported by the Conservatives, with the consequence that the 1950s and 1960s became known as the era of 'consensus' politics. This political consensus over welfare, economic management and equality of opportunity spread to the USA and elsewhere in Europe. There was a pattern of governments extending their role to create the social 'goods' that liberals had promoted. Sadly for the Liberal Party itself, the consensus meant that they were often squeezed out of power by more successful socialist and conservative administrations. It would therefore be true to say that from about 1940 to 1970 liberalism had enormous success in terms of the propagation of its new social philosophies, but was unsuccessful in securing the election of Liberal Party governments.

Contemporary liberalism

Recently, mainstream liberalism has spent much of its time on the fringes of the political arena. In most of the democratic world, governments have been largely dominated either by social democratic or neo-liberal conservative administrations. Liberals have occasionally found themselves in coalitions, for example in Germany, Holland, Japan and Scotland, but have failed to dominate political agendas. This is not to say that liberalism has been totally ineffective. Social democrats, in particular, have adopted many of the core values of liberalism. The US philosopher John Rawls provided a bridge between liberalism and social democracy by developing a theory of justice that combined individual liberty with the provision of social justice. His ideas are described further below (see pp. 26–27).

The most original aspects of contemporary liberalism perhaps lie in its proposals for political reforms. These conform to liberalism's core values. They are designed to protect individual liberties and to preserve the independence of minority groups. The political and constitutional reforms that liberals have supported in recent years include the following:

- decentralising power to regional and local government

- promoting stronger constitutional safeguards against governmental power

- increasing use of referendums to promote popular democracy

- strengthening legal safeguards for individual rights

- promoting freedom-of-information legislation

- safeguarding and extending the rights of women and minority groups.

Some major modern liberal principles and policies

We can now summarise the contemporary position in liberal thought. As we can see there are strong links between the *principles* of modern liberalism and the actual *policies* that have been proposed by liberal parties, including the British Liberal Democrat Party.

- The defence and extension of individual and group rights, e.g. women's rights, and equality of treatment for minority ethnic groups, gay people and disabled people.

- Support for a multicultural society where different ethnic, religious and cultural groups are tolerated and encouraged to flourish together in harmony.

- Campaigns to extend both worker and consumer rights. Liberals recognise the dangers of excessive economic power being wielded by big business corporations.

- Concern for environmental protection.

- Policies to counteract the growth of the inequality that has resulted from neo-liberal, free-market measures introduced by New

Right conservatives. In particular, liberals have increasingly proposed taxation and welfare policies to redistribute income to the poor.

- There should be equality of opportunity. Social class should not be a barrier to individual progress. This implies policies to improve social mobility.

- Efforts to reduce the causes of crime rather than simply relying on punishment, a reaction to hard-line law and order policies.

- Political reform designed to counteract the growing power of the centralised state.

A general overview of contemporary liberalism, therefore, would present the movement as engaging in the defence of groups and in the promotion of policies that have been ignored by other political movements. Put another way, contemporary liberalism can be seen as a reaction against the growth of both state power and the undesirable consequences of free markets. See Table 1.1.

Key liberal thinkers

John Locke (English, 1632–1704)

Locke pre-dates the term 'liberal' and is therefore better known as the father of 'Whig' philosophy. He was part of the political movement that resulted in the Glorious Revolution of 1688. This peaceful revolution replaced the Catholic James II with the Protestant William of Orange but, more importantly, established the sovereignty of parliament over law-making.

Locke took as the basis of his philosophy the twin ideas of natural rights and natural laws. For Locke, government had to be established by consent, respect the natural rights of its citizens and govern according to natural laws. No government could claim its legitimacy either from God or from nature. The only political authority for rulers could come from the people. Such governments should be limited and must respect people's natural rights. He identified

Summary

Classical liberalism	New liberalism	Welfare liberalism	Contemporary liberalism	Libertarianism
● Liberty of the individual ● Individuals free to pursue self-interest ● Tolerance of different beliefs, religions and cultures ● Minimal government ● Free-market economy ● Representative democracy	● Sense of social obligation ● Promotion of positive liberty ● Promotion of choice and opportunity ● Equality of opportunity ● Limited welfare provision	● State-sponsored welfare schemes ● State management of the economy ● Greater concentration on equality of opportunity ● Freedom from social deprivation	● Promotion of greater economic equality or justice ● Political and constitutional reform to control state power ● More popular democracy ● Decentralisation of government ● Environmentalism ● Defence of group rights ● Promotion of worker and consumer rights ● Tolerant social and law and order policies ● Support for a tolerant, multicultural society ● Support for measures to improve social mobility	● A very restricted state, largely confined to defence and possibly regulation of the currency ● Abolition of laws that restrict choice of lifestyles and personal morality ● Minimal law and order protection ● A completely free market economy with no regulation

Table 1.1 Summary of the principal forms of liberalism

these rights as life, liberty, property ownership and the pursuit of happiness. Locke was one of the first philosophers to promote religious and political tolerance; natural law, for Locke, included such tolerance and dictated that man should take into consideration the interests of others when deciding how to act.

The key political concept of the 'social contract' was developed by Locke. Contract theory in politics insists that government should be established by a contract between the government and the governed. The government agrees to govern according to natural law and respect individual rights, while the people agree to accept the authority of the government and to obey its laws. Should the government not govern by natural law or should it abuse natural rights, the people should have the right to cancel the contract and dissolve the government. In practice, Locke proposed a system of constitutionally controlled monarchy, accountable to an elected representative parliament.

Locke can be seen as the earliest proponent of liberal ideas. His influence was felt a century later when both the French and American revolutionaries were chiefly inspired by his philosophy.

John Stuart Mill (British, 1806–73)

The son of the utilitarian philosopher James Mill, John Stuart Mill was a politician and social campaigner as well as a philosopher. He began his political life as a utilitarian, following the teaching of his father and Jeremy Bentham. He took as his starting point the idea that an individual is the best judge of his or her own interests and that no authority has the right to claim a superior knowledge of that individual's interests. However, he soon broke with the utilitarians, claiming that their philosophy was intolerant and inflexible. He also criticised utilitarians' proposals for state intervention in some circumstances to promote the common good; Mill, at least in his early life, saw state intervention as a threat to individual liberty. More importantly, he argued against the utilitarian view that the sole motivation of human beings was the pursuit of material pleasures, claiming that, on the contrary, there were higher goals such as learning and aesthetic appreciation. For Mill, liberty should be used to progress human civilisation, not just to enrich it. He famously expressed this in colourful language:

> …better to be a human being dissatisfied than a pig satisfied; better to be Socrates dissatisfied than a fool satisfied, better to be Socrates satisfied than a fool satisfied.
>
> From *Utilitarianism* 1871

Mill's main contribution to liberal theory was to define the limits of freedom. He divided actions that were self-regarding and that had no effect on others from those that were other-regarding and clearly did impinge on the freedom of others. For example, expressing religious or other beliefs publicly is self-regarding, whereas anti-social behaviour is other-regarding. Governments, therefore, should tolerate self-regarding behaviour but are justified in regulating other-regarding actions. This implies that governments should be limited in their jurisdiction. They should never curtail freedom of thought, religion or expression, nor should they regulate economic activity, other than that which oppresses people, for example monopoly power.

In other matters, Mill was an unusual mixture of radicalism and conservatism. As regards representative parliamentary democracy, which he supported, he hatched a scheme to grant different numbers of votes to people, depending on their level of education. The illiterate would have one vote, while those who could pass tests on political knowledge would have more. This conservative view contrasted with his campaign to extend women's rights, a crusade which he shared with his wife, Harriet Taylor, and his stepdaughter, Helen Taylor. In 1869 all three wrote an early feminist tract together entitled *The Subjection of Women*, which proposed that voting and other rights be granted equally to women.

Towards the end of his life, Mill did modify his views somewhat, accepting that members of the working class required some support from the state. An entirely free society could be unjust, he admitted, and some state interference to correct these injustices could be tolerated.

Mill was one of the greatest English political philosophers. His influence spread well beyond England and remains important today. French and American liberals followed his theories, modern neo-liberals remain inspired by his teachings and even Karl Marx (1818–83) respected his views on the benefits of individual liberty.

Herbert Spencer (British, 1820–1903)

A journalist and philosopher, Spencer wrote at a time when the English state was beginning to engage in an increasing degree of interference and regulation. The era of Mill's classical theories was coming to an end and new liberalism, inspired by Green and Gladstone (see below), was proposing the provision of equality of opportunity by the state.

For Spencer, human society was an evolving organism and therefore subject to natural laws of progress. However, he rejected the emerging notion, shared by new liberals and traditional conservatives, that society is organic and people are interdependent. Instead, Spencer believed that all individuals were free and independent of each other. Indeed, as in the animal kingdom, humankind was in competition for the scarce resources offered by the Earth. This is not to say that he advocated any actions being justified in order to secure an advantage over others; rather he accepted that, within the natural laws, humans are engaged in an economic struggle against each other. He did not suggest that those who are successful should be so at the expense of others. His argument was that those who adapt best to the changing economic environment will move forward, and those who fail to do so will fall back. The term 'social Darwinism' has often been applied to these theories.

Spencer enjoyed widespread but brief popularity in the latter part of the nineteenth century. For most mainstream political thinkers, his beliefs and schemes were simply too extreme at a time when social welfare was becoming popular. In the 1980s and 1990s, however, there was a revival of interest in Spencer among Conservatives and libertarians. In particular, Spencer's opposition to state welfare (and the tax needed to finance it) has proved attractive to those who oppose the so-called 'dependency culture'.

Thomas Hill Green (British, 1836–82)

The moral philosopher T. H. Green (as he is more usually known) made two main contributions to liberal thought. The first was the proposition that we are not merely self-seeking individuals who have no responsibility for others. Rather, he insisted, we do have an obligation to care for the welfare of others. He argued that it is possible to enjoy our own liberty without losing a sense of social responsibility. The second was the concept of the organic society and its application to modern conditions. This was not a new concept. It had become a key part of nineteenth-century German political philosophy, upon which Green based his teaching. Its basic proposition was that society is not merely a collection of unrelated individuals, but a single entity – a living organism with a life of its own, which exists above the consciousness of individuals. This implies that society can have a collective consciousness, dubbed *Volksgemeinschaft* by the Germans.

Green's views on freedom proved to be revolutionary for liberals, forming the basis of what became known as 'new liberalism'. He recognised two senses of the term 'freedom'. One was that of external constraint, as propounded by J. S. Mill. The other was a positive sense of the term, referring to the ability to realise one's own aspirations – in other words, to achieve self-realisation. In a completely free society, with little or no state regulation, self-realisation would be unachievable for most people. Some state intervention was therefore required to promote positive liberty. In practice, Green proposed a narrow range of measures, mainly to reduce inherited privilege and to provide equality of opportunity through education.

At a time when liberalism was in danger of becoming discredited, Green saved the movement from political decline: had liberals continued to support free-market economics and to oppose state welfare, they would have been accused of promoting a heartless and amoral philosophy.

William Gladstone (British, 1809–98)

Gladstone was prime minister four times between 1868 and 1894. He was also, arguably, the founder of the modern Liberal Party. In many ways he was a conventional liberal in that he supported individual liberty, religious tolerance, free trade and independence for Ireland. He also believed that inequality was the natural state of humankind. He can be considered more a follower of Green's than Mill's brand of liberal thought.

In particular, he promoted the introduction of widespread elementary education with the Forster Education Act of 1870. This opened the way for education that was free of Church control. Under his ministries, trade unions were granted more rights, voting was extended to virtually all adults, and the civil service, universities, the army and the legal system were all opened to wider recruitment. Gladstone attacked privilege wherever it appeared to be restricting opportunity and stifling enterprise.

We should not, however, think of Gladstone as a radical. His reforms were relatively modest and many cynics suggest he only adopted his liberal policies in order to attract votes from the newly enfranchised working class. Nevertheless, he was a key liberal figure in that he gave liberalism political coherence. Under Gladstone, liberalism at last achieved its maturity as an ideology.

William Beveridge (British, 1879–1963)

The great liberal prime minister David Lloyd George had already introduced a wide range of welfare services sponsored by the state by the time Beveridge produced his famous report in 1942. Unlike many earlier liberals, Beveridge did not fear the extension of state intervention in society. Nor was he overly concerned by the need to raise finance through taxation (National Insurance payments to be precise), although the idea that the state should take compulsory collections from working people would have been unthinkable for nineteenth-century liberals.

Two main elements of Beveridge's philosophy enabled him to retain his liberal credentials. The

William Beveridge, a liberal whose 1942 report paved the way for the modern welfare state

first was his argument that liberals stand for social justice. It was clear that free-market capitalism could not deliver such justice. The Great Depression of the 1930s had created enormous hardship and resulted in millions of citizens relying on a minimal level of financial support. Inequality grew – and so did inequality of opportunity.

The second was his attitude to freedom. He insisted that liberty was a 'good' that should be available equally to all. The existence of equal legal and political rights, however, was not enough for Beveridge. He believed that various kinds of deprivation were a curtailment to freedom. In particular, poverty and unemployment made the idea of equal rights an absurdity. Poor individuals could not be said to be free to enjoy their fair share of the country's prosperity. Health problems and lack of education similarly narrowed the range of opportunities available to the poor. In 1940 Beveridge addressed the Liberal Party annual conference, describing his new conception of freedom:

A starving man is not free, because, until he is fed, he cannot have a thought for anything but how to meet his urgent physical needs; he is reduced from a man to an animal. A man who dare not resent what he feels to be an injustice from an employer or a foreman, lest this condemn him to chronic unemployment, is not free.

Beveridge's place in the sun was short-lived. He served the wartime government and his report was so eagerly awaited that crowds queued for hours to obtain the first copies. Later, he was granted a peerage and had to watch from the House of Lords while his proposals were implemented – not by a Liberal administration, but by a radical Labour government. Although he spent the rest of his political career in relative obscurity, he remains the principal architect of Britain's much-admired welfare state. The idea that the state should organise a compulsory, publicly funded system of education, healthcare, pensions, social security and unemployment insurance was more at home in socialist ideology than liberal, but Beveridge had at least succeeded in bringing liberalism to the forefront of British politics.

John Rawls (US, 1921–2002)

This enormously influential US philosopher formed a bridge between modern liberal and social democratic thought. His best-known work is a weighty book entitled *A Theory of Justice*, which was published in 1972.

Rawls saw his main task as reconciling the firm liberal belief in freedom with the need to prevent excessive inequality in society. In tackling this, he addressed a problem faced by both liberals and socialists – that measures taken to reduce inequality, or to prevent inequality occurring in the first place, will inevitably involve a loss of liberty for some. For example, if income is to be more evenly spread, there must be higher taxation for the rich and lower for the poor. This clearly represents a loss of liberty. Taxpayers are no longer free to spend their income in the way they wish: the proportion taxed is spent on the individual's behalf by the state. Similarly, any attempt to manipulate wages to prevent poverty among low-paid workers interferes with labour markets and curtails the freedom of entrepreneurs to run their businesses as they wish.

Rawls tackles the problem logically and step by step. His objective is to reconcile individual liberty with social justice and to establish criteria under which inequality or state regulation may be tolerated. He uses a philosophical device, which he calls the 'original position', to develop his conclusions.

The 'original position' and the 'veil of ignorance'

Rawls imagines humankind in the situation that would have existed before society came into being, that is, a natural state, which he terms the 'original position'. If people are to create a society from this state of nature, they need to decide how wealth and goods are to be distributed within society. However, Rawls places a condition upon them before they can make their decisions. People are placed behind what he calls a 'veil of ignorance'. By this he means that they do not know how successful or unsuccessful they are likely to be or where they will end up in the scale of wealth. Life becomes a kind of lottery for them. In these circumstances, he believes individuals would construct a society where the worst off would not be more deprived than they themselves would wish to be if they ended up at the bottom of the scale. They would probably create an unequal society, but one where there was a minimum acceptable standard of living. Nobody should be allowed so much wealth that it would make the worst off in society fall below this minimum.

Applying this philosophical position to the practical, modern world, he suggests that a just society will be one where inequalities do not mean that the worst off are deprived as a result of the wealth of others. If this undesirable position is likely to occur, Rawls argues, the state is justified in intervening in the interests of social justice.

This principle has acted as a guide for both liberals and social democrats who have struggled to determine how much inequality is acceptable.

Rawls's practical principles, in brief, are organised as follows:

- Individuals should be as free as possible.

- Such freedom should only be tolerated if it is compatible with freedom for all. In other words, liberty should not be enjoyed at the expense of the freedom of others.

- Inequalities have to be justified.

- An inequality can be justified if it increases the prosperity of society as a whole.

- An inequality cannot be justified if it results in the poorest in society being made worse off than they were before.

Thus, according to Rawls's 'difference principle', even large inequalities can be justified. Inequality is not an evil in itself, but it cannot be tolerated if it disadvantages those at the lowest point on the economic scale. Similarly, individual freedom cannot be considered to be universally good. It can only be allowed full rein if all are free and have a high enough standard of living to enjoy a reasonable amount of personal liberty.

Rawls's supporters claim that he has provided a firm philosophical justification for a society in which there can be a great deal of individualism and inequality, but within which there can also be said to be social justice and freedom. Cynics suggest his ideas are merely a fudged compromise between socialism and liberalism, but this has not prevented his popularity among politicians of the centre and the centre left. He could certainly count both Bill Clinton (1946–) and Tony Blair (1953–) among his political disciples.

Issues in liberalism

Democracy

Although liberalism is closely associated with the modern development of democracy and democratic institutions, there have been a number of problems in its relationship with democracy. Jean-Jacques Rousseau predicted many of these problems before democracy, as we know it today, had been developed. Rousseau saw democracy as being fundamentally majority rule. While this initially seems to be an acceptable form of government, he points out that there is a key difference between the 'will of the people', which is simply derived from their expressions of self-interest, and the 'general will', which is the collective expression of the common good.

In Rousseau's view, even if 99% of the people supported one course of action, it would not necessarily be for the common benefit if it were simply the sum of the self-interested motives of the individuals who formed the majority. In modern terms, we might say that Rousseau was showing a preference for consensus politics over simple majority rule. He therefore rejected democracy as a satisfactory system of government, except in the unusual circumstance that a small community of enlightened individuals take into account the interests of others as well as their own. Rousseau regretfully rejected democracy with these famous words:

Were there a people of gods, their government would be democratic. So perfect a government is not for men.

From *The Social Contract*, 1762

Since Rousseau, liberals have continued to be suspicious of democracy as majority rule, but for a different reason. It is perfectly acceptable to liberals that individuals pursue self-interest, and that they should use their participation in the political system (mainly by voting) to pursue that self-interest. What is not acceptable, however, is that the majority should govern at the expense of minorities, or of individual rights. Many instances of this happening can be found in places where direct forms of majority-based democracy exist – for example, the persistent discrimination against the Catholic minority in Northern Ireland by Unionists, and the 2005 ban on hunting with dogs, which appears to persecute a minority pursuing a private pastime. Mill's theory of tolerance is relevant here, too – as long as we see hunting with dogs as a self-regarding action.

Democracy therefore emerged as a means by which people could be liberated and free to express their self-interested individualism, and yet excessive amounts of this can result in the oppression of individuals and minorities. This is often said by liberals to be the paradox of democracy. There is no guarantee that the majority is right, or that the outcome of majority rule will be just.

Nineteenth-century liberals were concerned by the tyranny of the majority and recommended a number of remedies. The most common was to retain the property qualification for voting so that the irresponsible majority would be denied political rights. Conservatives insisted that the monarchy and landed aristocracy would govern in the common interest rather than their own; liberals were sceptical of this, but nevertheless many of them believed that property owners would be responsible in their use of political power and not use it to oppress other classes.

Modern liberals could not accept this denial of voting rights to the majority, and social and welfare liberals have been forced to accept considerable extensions in the role and power of the state during the last century. Democracy was essential to control state power, but simple majority rule remained dangerous. The solution was to be found largely by referring to the US experience:

- First, the sovereign constitution of the USA was constructed to protect the people against majority power. By carefully placing controls over governmental power, dividing power among different institutions and including guaranteed rights for individuals and groups, popular democracy could flourish. Inspired by the American experience, therefore, all modern liberals support **constitutionalism** and limited government to protect democracy.

- Second, the political structure of the USA has developed into a pluralist system. Groups have considerable access to decision-making

institutions and have many legal safeguards to protect their rights. Perhaps the most important of these safeguards is freedom of expression and thought, ensuring that a wide variety of views and beliefs may flourish.

Key Term

Constitutionalism
This liberal-inspired principle asserts that modern states and governments must be controlled by a binding constitution that limits their powers and protects the rights of individuals and groups. It also insists that governments cannot set aside constitutional principles for their own purposes. It was first established in the early nineteenth century by the founding fathers of the USA and their first chief justice, John Marshall (1755–1835). Constitutionalism is weak in Britain since there is no binding, codified constitution, although there are constitutional principles by which government is guided.

By adding the ideas gained from the US experience to some of the core principles of the philosophy, we can summarise how modern liberals have been able to offer solutions to the dilemmas and paradoxes of democracy. This is shown below:

- The basis of democracy must be government by consent.

- Government should be limited by a sovereign constitution.

- Individual and group rights must be protected.

- The political system should allow full access to all legal groups.

- There must be freedom of expression.

- Only where a fundamental issue concerning the jurisdiction and system of government arises should direct democracy (effectively a referendum) be used.

- Representative and responsible government is essential in ensuring moderate politics that will mediate between the majority and minorities.

Liberalism and the state

For much of its existence, liberalism has seen the state as a threat to individual liberty and the natural development of society. This was especially true during the classical period of the nineteenth century and the neo-liberal revival of the 1980s and 1990s.

Liberals' original fear of the state, as expressed by Mill in particular, was that it might seek to interfere with aspects of people's lives that were private. Mill also believed that intervention in economic markets would inhibit innovation, enterprise and dynamic progress. The earlier utilitarians had been concerned that government intervention should always consider the best interests of society as a whole, but classical liberals considered only the interests of individuals. For them, if individuals could flourish free of state interference, this would automatically create social progress.

Later in the nineteenth century, the more extreme followers of the classical tradition, often known as social Darwinists, emphasised the dangers of the state providing too much support for people who should take responsibility for their own welfare. Each individual, argued the likes of Smiles and Spencer, is the guardian of his or her own prosperity. He or she should not expect help from the state. They added that individual enterprise is vital if society is to progress successfully. More recently, in the 1980s, the 'excessive' provision of social welfare was seen to be creating a 'dependency culture'. Within this culture, individuals had grown used to relying on the state, so that private enterprise and hard work were stifled. The neo-liberals who opposed the dependency culture therefore proposed the abolition of some social benefits and a reduction in others. In both the UK and the USA, the frontiers of the state were, in Margaret Thatcher's words, 'rolled back'. By this time,

however, traditional liberals were more concerned with social justice and so they had become more tolerant of state activism.

The welfare tradition of liberalism and the liberalism of Green, Gladstone, Lloyd George, Beveridge and Rawls saw the state as an ally rather than an enemy. Of course, all liberals will still seek to protect individual and group rights from the power of the state, but it is felt that, as long as this can be guaranteed, the state should be allowed to pursue liberal objectives. Equality of opportunity requires state intervention in the fields of education and welfare. The more recent pursuit of social justice, too, has implied the redistribution of income and wealth through state policies. The demand for economic stability, which Keynes saw as vital for the maintenance of individual economic enterprise, has meant that the state must intervene whenever the forces of the free market fail to ensure favourable conditions for that individualism.

 Key Term

Keynesianism
A description of the economic views of John Maynard Keynes. He argued, in direct contrast to classic liberal economics, that the state should intervene aggressively to expand an economy suffering from a slump. Keynesian intervention largely involved raising public expenditure, reducing taxes and borrowing to fill the resulting deficit.

Those liberals who supported the positive role for the state in enhancing positive liberty and opportunity had to put their mind to ways in which the potential power of the state could be controlled and restricted to desirable ends only. During the nineteenth and twentieth centuries, therefore, many liberals turned their attention to supporting constitutionalism and the rule of law to achieve this. In the modern era liberals have proposed a wide variety of measures to control the power of the state. Among these have been the following:

- Governments should operate within strict constitutional rules and principles that lay down the limits to their activities and powers.

- The rule of law should operate, ensuring that all are treated equally so that government cannot discriminate against them. The principle also means that government itself must always operate within the law and cannot operate in an arbitrary way.

- These principles should be upheld by a truly independent judiciary.

- There should be a system of internal 'checks and balances' preventing power being concentrated in too few hands.

- As far as possible government should be decentralised to make it more democratic and easier to be controlled by communities.

- Democratic controls, especially to ensure representation and accountability, should be kept strong.

- The rights of individuals and groups in society should be guaranteed by laws that are protected from encroachments by government.

In summary, therefore, the relationship between liberalism and the state has been a variable one. All liberals have a healthy fear of state power, but most liberals have come to accept the state for the benefits it can deliver.

Liberals and tolerance

Tolerance is one of the earliest of all the principles of liberalism. At first it largely concerned freedom of expression, specifically religious expression. John Locke, in particular, had supported religious tolerance and in the early nineteenth century liberals took up the cause of Catholics in Britain, who had been denied the right to hold public office because of their religion.

J. S. Mill saw tolerance in terms of liberty. For him any beliefs, words or actions could be tolerated as long as they did no harm to others. He also asserted that such tolerance of ideas would ensure that society would develop because so many different ideas would enrich social and intellectual life.

The twentieth century brought fresh challenges to the liberal love of tolerance. These have included:

- Political movements, such as those of the radical left and right, have challenged democratic principles. Should such extreme views be tolerated? The liberal answer is to say 'no' if they threaten such principles and will result in losses of rights and freedoms. Extreme political movements, they add, should also operate within the law. Protest must be tolerated, say liberals, but it must be legitimate and principled.

- In the second half of the twentieth century there has been a revolution in moral and social attitudes. Attitudes to sexuality (homosexuality in particular), to family life, to the behaviour of the young and the like have been changing rapidly. Liberals are inclined to tolerate such change but are also concerned that such tolerance may cause deep changes in the nature of society, some of which may be seen as undesirable. Liberals have to make judgements about moral behaviour, deciding whether its consequences are so unacceptable that they should not be tolerated.

- Societies in the West are becoming increasingly culturally varied. Here the challenge lies with the degree of tolerance that should be exercised towards different cultures and religions which may run counter to traditional 'norms'. For example, should groups which favour forced marriage, sometimes of very young girls, be tolerated? Should religions which propose the inferiority of women be allowed to operate freely? Should religions which seem to promote terrorism be allowed to flourish openly? Liberals have tended to suggest that such multiculturalism should be tolerated, but only on the understanding that such minority groups do not threaten the integrity of British culture itself. In other words, as Rawls has asserted, 'all minorities should be subject to the same limitations as the rest of the population'.

Liberals have been criticised by conservatives for being over-tolerant and unprincipled. They suggest that liberals tolerate so much that they have no firm values. Furthermore, they believe that too much tolerance will lead to the decay of society, pointing especially to the rise in crime in the West after the 1960s and the decline of the family, with rising divorce rates as evidence of this. The liberal reply is that social change is inevitable and is a price worth paying for the reservation of freedom. In other words, they insist that the *principle* of individual liberty is as firm as it has ever been.

Liberalism in the UK

Liberalism and the parties

Parties that have called themselves 'liberal' in the UK – the Liberal Party and later the Liberal Democrats – have had remarkably little electoral success since the 1920s. One might, therefore, be forgiven for thinking that liberalism as a political doctrine has been in decline. In fact, the reverse could be said to be true. Liberal ideas now form a large part of the political consensus. In a sense, all mainstream British parties are liberal parties.

The Labour Party in particular has been characterised by its liberal philosophy. Indeed, the moderate nature of British socialism is unique. Many socialists, especially on the European continent, have been notorious for their careless attitude to personal freedom in the pursuit of equality. Labour, in contrast, has always been careful to strike a balance between the two goals. The party was always committed to parliamentary democracy, but from the 1950s onwards it was also associated with pluralist politics and a determination to tolerate alternative doctrines to its own and even varied beliefs among its own members. Labour has also championed the causes of minorities and of civil liberties. In the 1960s and 1970s in particular, Labour governments presided over such liberal reforms as changes to laws on homosexuality, the legalisation of abortion, equal pay for women, the

outlawing of racial discrimination and protection for workers against unfair dismissal. Some of these measures may have been proposed by Liberal politicians, but Labour administrations made them a reality.

The arrival of New Labour in the 1990s introduced more liberal values to the party. Under John Smith (1938–94) and Tony Blair, Labour accepted that the promotion of individualism should be given considerably more prominence, even at the expense of collectivism in some cases. Constitutional reform, a cherished goal of the Liberal Democrats, has formed a central feature of Labour policy. Devolution of power to Scotland and Wales, the incorporation of the European Convention on Human Rights into British law, the removal of most of the hereditary peers from the House of Lords and the introduction of proportional representation for several types of regional election are all liberal aspirations. This is not to say that New Labour is synonymous with liberalism. A number of its key policies have been heavily criticised for being distinctly illiberal, notably in the fields of law and order and security, but the basis of New Labour philosophy has its roots in liberal doctrine.

On a more fundamental level, the Labour Party has come to accept inequality as an inevitable consequence of free-market economics. Like liberals, New Labour believes that, as long as equality of opportunity can be promoted, people should be free to be unequal. The idea that equality can be imposed upon a society has been left far behind by British social democrats. Furthermore, the individual pursuit of self-interest, a throwback to utilitarian liberalism, is now tolerated and even encouraged.

Classical liberalism and social Darwinism enjoyed a revival in the 1980s among New Right, neo-liberal conservatives, but this is not the only sense in which conservatism has been imbued with the liberal spirit. US conservatives, especially, follow doctrines such as limited and decentralised government, constitutionalism, civil rights and economic liberty. The UK Conservative Party has also come to accept the need to safeguard minority and individual rights. Indeed, the Conservatives under David Cameron became more 'liberal' than they have ever been in their history.

Liberal (sometimes called 'social' or even 'Cameronian') conservatism has adopted a number of liberal principles. In particular these conservatives now accept the belief of T.H. Green that all have a moral obligation to care for the welfare of the less fortunate. They insist that society must provide equality of opportunity and that social justice must be established. They are less enthusiastic about multiculturalism, the tolerance of alternative lifestyles and a strict adherence to legal rights for individuals, but accept that Conservative policy must take these principles into account.

Many small parties in the UK have also embraced liberal values. The Welsh and Scottish nationalists base their philosophy upon the principles of government by consent and the self-determination of national groups. These parties have also shown staunch support for human rights and the protection of minorities. Welfarism and equality of opportunity are also key elements in nationalist thinking (excepting, of course, the British National movement and extreme Northern Ireland unionists, who are decidedly illiberal).

Turning finally to the Liberal Democrats themselves, it is clear that liberal philosophy remains at the heart of the party. They place greater stress on state intervention (to create social and economic equality) and on social justice (in the form of the redistribution of income from rich to poor) than most liberals in the past, but individual liberty and tolerance still form their central philosophy. There remains a divide within the party between those who support a wide range of economic liberties and who still praise many of the virtues of classical liberalism, and social liberals who remain committed to the role of the state in promoting welfare and positive liberty.

Liberal democracy in the UK

Although the UK has no codified constitution – a key liberal demand – the story of the development of its political system has been that of the gradual evolution of a true liberal democracy. Without a recognisable constitution the system can never claim to be fully liberal in its inspiration, but it is now true that the vast majority of the UK's political arrangements have become entrenched in law. This may be seen as the next best thing to a real constitution. The 'liberal' elements of the UK political system can be summarised as follows:

- Elections are largely uncorrupted and virtually all adult citizens have the right to vote and stand for office.

- All legal political parties and pressure groups are free to operate within the political system.

- Government is permanently accountable to Parliament and to the people through general elections.

- Important constitutional changes are now subjected to popular referendum and therefore consent.

- National minorities have been granted a large amount of political independence.

- The Human Rights Act guarantees most individual rights.

- Parliament provides a powerful means by which individual grievances can be redressed.

- Parliament – both the Commons and the Lords – sees itself as a mediator between the interests of the majority and minorities.

- The law reflects a high degree of tolerance to minority groups.

- Equal legal and political rights are guaranteed.

- There is a wide variety of social rights accorded to minority groups, to workers and to consumers.

Of course, not all aspects of the political system are liberal:

- The sovereignty of Parliament always threatens individual liberties, especially as the executive branch is usually able to dominate the legislature.

- Much of the prime minister's power remains unchecked and the main electoral system is often considered to be unjust.

- A few unelected institutions have retained a limited political role – mainly the monarchy and the House of Lords – and many public officials are neither elected nor fully accountable to the public.

But despite these reservations, it would not be realistic to describe the UK political system as anything other than liberal in spirit.

Core British values

Finally, the question must be addressed as to whether British political and social culture is liberal in nature. The UK is certainly often praised for its tolerance towards a wide variety of beliefs and cultures. Despite racial tensions, most ethnic minorities live in peace alongside the indigenous population. Even some extreme beliefs – those of the British National Party, for example – are granted freedom of expression. Visitors to the country often speak of the atmosphere of freedom and tolerance that prevails in the UK.

Britain is also said to be notable for its sense of social and legal justice. It is open to question whether it is the mother of modern democracy (the USA and France perhaps have stronger claims), but the common law tradition, which embraces individual rights and protection from excessive state power, is certainly rooted in the UK.

The British media is remarkably free from state influence, as is the broadcasting establishment. Mill's insistence that all reasonable values and beliefs should be tolerated is enshrined in the long-held principles of freedom of speech and of the press. There is widespread artistic freedom and little sense that experimental ideas should be stifled. On the economic front, too, the UK has come (perhaps only recently) to embrace the free entrepreneurial spirit so beloved of nineteenth-century liberals. It is part of the British way of life for a host of intermediate groups to flourish, enabling most citizens to participate in political, social and community-based activities. In other words, the UK has a **pluralist** culture.

✔ Key Term

Pluralism

This term describes a society in which there is tolerance of many different beliefs, movements and faiths. It suggests a political system in which different political parties and pressure groups are free to operate and have access to decision-making processes. Modern liberal democracies are pluralist in nature, while totalitarian regimes inhibit or destroy pluralism.

There is a strong claim to be made that Britain is not just a liberal democracy, but also a liberal society. Neither conservatism nor socialism – both strong British traditions – have ever overshadowed the fundamentally liberal spirit of the country.

Exam focus

Using this chapter and other resources available to you, answer the following questions.

Short questions

Your answers should be about 400 words long.
1 Distinguish between the concepts of negative and positive liberty.
2 Why have liberals supported the idea of individual liberty?
3 Why do liberals support constitutionalism and consent?
4 What is a typical liberal attitude to equality?
5 What part has tolerance played in liberal doctrine?
6 What limits to tolerance can be accepted by liberals and why?

Long questions

Your answers should be about 1200 words long.
1 Why and how did classical liberalism become transformed into modern liberalism?
2 How have liberals proposed that the power of the state can be controlled?
3 In what ways is there a conflict between liberalism and democracy and how have liberals attempted to solve such conflicts?
4 How have liberals reconciled social reform with individual liberty?
5 'All main UK political parties are now essentially liberal.' Discuss.

Further reading

Bellamy, R. (1992) *Liberalism and Modern Society: An Historical Argument*, Polity Press.
Gray, J. (1995) *Liberalism*, Open University Press.
Mill, J. S. (1998) *On Liberty*, Oxford University Press.

Chapter 2

Conservatism

Conservatism is a political tradition that contains both constant and variable principles. A conservative in politics is one who resists the dominance of fixed political doctrines and ideologies. Conservatism prefers the status quo as long as there are no compelling reasons for radical change. When change is needed, conservatives prefer reform to radical transformation or revolution. The nature of conservative thinking depends upon the dominant political ideas of any age or situation; it is in this sense that its principles are variable. The enduring principles of most conservative movements include respect for tradition, a preference for what *is* over what might be and a tendency towards empiricism – basing future action on experience of the past – rather than fixed principles as a guide to action. Conservative views on the nature of society vary, but all conservatives support individualism, i.e. the pursuit of individual goals and fulfilment. Traditions are important to conservatives because they preserve links with the past, which provide a sense of security. Conservatives are pragmatic, not judging political action on the basis of specific principles, but on what is preferable and acceptable to the people at any given time and under those particular circumstances. Above all, conservatives believe that good social order and security are the most basic of human needs. Order is seen as more important than ideas such as freedom, rights and equality.

Introduction

The doctrine of conservatism is perhaps one of the most difficult to pin down. This is because conservatism is, by its nature, a reactionary movement. Its character depends upon what it is reacting against at any particular time. For example, during much of the nineteenth century, conservatism appeared as an antidote to the individualist liberalism that had become dominant in the USA and Europe. By the second half of the twentieth century, conservatives were principally concerned with the progress of socialism. In both cases, the nature of the conservative reaction inevitably varied. In contrast to liberalism, conservatives stressed the collective, organic nature of society. By the 1980s, when collectivist forms of economic and social policy had become popular, conservatives such

as Margaret Thatcher were stressing the importance of individualism.

Conservatism has, however, included a number of constant and enduring principles. These provide a degree of continuity that enables us to differentiate between conservatism and other political movements. Nationalism, opposition to rigid ideology, respect for traditions and a paternalistic view of democracy are all examples of conservative constants.

We must be careful to distinguish between conservatism as a specifically political movement, and a mere state of mind. We often speak of people having conservative tastes in fashion, the arts, food and design. These are merely personal attributes and do not necessarily relate to political principles. We can, also, identify conservative elements in any political movement. For example, Stalinism is often described as a conservative form of communism, and Tony Blair and his close followers are characterised as conservatives within the New Labour movement. This chapter is not concerned with these two types of conservatism, but with a political tradition that has enduring political significance.

One final word of caution: the British Conservative Party is not the same thing as conservatism in general. Naturally most members of the party have been conservatives, but the party has experienced many changes in character and has contained many individuals whose views have been considered un-conservative in nature. Conservatism is an international phenomenon with varying characteristics in different parts of the world. For example, US conservatism tends to have a strong religious element, French conservatives are intensely nationalist, while British conservatives have often been liberal in their outlook. We are therefore justified in considering national variations in conservatism, and should beware of identifying the tradition too closely with particular parties.

The origins of conservatism

The basic nature of conservatism depends upon its reaction to other ideologies. Its origins can therefore be identified in the origins of ideology itself. This approach places the dawning of conservatism, as we understand it today, in the latter part of the eighteenth century. Before that, there were no true ideological movements for it to react against.

The period roughly corresponding to the eighteenth century is now known as the 'Age of Reason' or the 'Enlightenment'. It was an age when many previously held certainties were being challenged by new rational modes of thought. The Enlightenment spread through virtually all aspects of human existence: not only religion, ethics and politics were affected, but also the physical sciences, mathematics, the arts and architecture. Names that are familiar to us today were part of this dramatic new age – Isaac Newton (1642–1727) in science, Wolfgang Amadeus Mozart (1756–91) in music, Robert Adam (1728–92) in architecture and Jean-Jacques Rousseau in philosophy.

In terms of the development of conservatism, however, developments in philosophy, ideology, religion and politics are the most significant. It is useful to consider the ways in which new thinking affected these four fields.

Philosophy

As early as the seventeenth century, René Descartes (1596–1650) proposed that man was capable of rational thought – and indeed was capable of leading a life based on reason. It had previously been taken for granted that man was driven by his physical appetites and emotions. Descartes' proposition had a profound influence on political and religious thought, both of which had been based on the pre-Cartesian view of man. Thinkers such as John Locke, Immanuel Kant (1724–1804) and Jean-Jacques Rousseau converted these rationalistic ideas into political principles, structures and aspirations.

Ideology

Several prominent ideologies owe their conception to Enlightenment thinking. Liberalism and socialism, in particular, were the products of the belief that society and politics could be ordered in a rational way so as to produce predictable and desirable outcomes. Marxism, anarchism and even early feminism can be included among those ideologies that were made possible by rationalism.

Religion

Roman Catholicism had dominated religious thought in Europe for many centuries before the Enlightenment. Leaving aside purely spiritual matters, Roman Catholic Christianity incorporated ideas such as obedience, divine authority, hierarchy and, perhaps above all, the fundamental belief that humankind carried the burden of original sin. This last principle was to become a key aspect of conservative thought in the nineteenth century. Original sin proposes a pessimistic view of human nature, suggesting that each of us is born with a flawed personality and is incapable of throwing this off completely, however well we try to lead our lives.

Rationalism rejected this notion and asserted that human beings are able to order their lives on a moral, rational basis. Enlightenment thought also challenged the traditional, purely spiritual authority of the Roman Catholic Church in general. It opened the door to radical ideas such as free will and individualism and a generally more optimistic view of human nature. The new religious movements that emerged in the sixteenth century became known collectively as 'Protestantism'. To some extent, Protestantism can be seen as a rational form of Christianity. It was strongly linked to liberalism and capitalism, which were both born out of Enlightenment thought. By the eighteenth century, the Protestant creed in various forms had become dominant in northern Europe, significantly in those areas where the Industrial Revolution was also dawning.

In discarding the previously unquestioned ideas that human society naturally falls into an ordered hierarchy and that the traditional authority of monarch and church should be obeyed in all circumstances, political thought and spiritual life were liberated.

Politics
The practical application of the new philosophies and religious thinking arrived in two main stages. The first was the challenge to the traditional or divine authority of absolute monarchy. This occurred as early as the 1640s with the English Civil War, but achieved more permanent forms in the French and American revolutions at the end of the eighteenth century. The second stage was the creation of representative forms of government to replace monarchical authority.

Principles such as government by consent, constitutional government, individual rights and, eventually, universal suffrage naturally followed.

Reaction
So radical was the nature of Enlightenment thinking that it was almost inevitable there would be a reaction. It was the representatives of the social class whose power was threatened by the new order – the aristocracy and landed gentry – who led the way. They owed their economic and political power to the Church and monarchy. When these institutions were threatened, so too was their social dominance.

The conservative reaction, however, was not only self-interested and defensive. As we shall see below, there were principled and pragmatic objections to the new philosophies. It was these empirical and moral objections that created modern conservatism.

Class and conservatism
As is shown above, conservatism, at least in the nineteenth and first half of the twentieth centuries, was associated with class interest. As the Industrial Revolution gathered pace and the economic power of the new capitalist middle classes grew, the landed classes found their position increasingly threatened. Conservatives therefore found themselves in the position of 'conserving' the interests of a particular class. As it became clear that this was merely a cynical exercise in self-interest, conservatives had to develop a more rigorous and justifiable theory of class. Furthermore, the power of the aristocratic ruling class needed more justification than mere tradition. It was the great Tory prime minister, Benjamin Disraeli (1804–81), who expressed this most successfully, developing a quasi-political theory of class known as 'neo-feudalism'. Since the original feudal system had maintained an ordered society for centuries, it was therefore logical that a modern structured class system could continue to maintain that sense of order.

Key Terms

Tory and Toryism

The expression 'Tory' originated in Ireland. It was a term of abuse for a certain type of travelling vagabond or criminal. The early Whigs in England in the late seventeenth century adopted it to describe the royalists, their political opponents. It came into common usage in the nineteenth century as a description of conservatives in general and thus began to lose most of its negative implications.

Today, 'Tory' can have three meanings. First, it is often used, especially by journalists, to refer to any member of the Conservative Party. Second, it can have negative connotations when used by those from the political left. In this sense it suggests a politician who is excessively right wing and out of touch. Third, it can refer to a traditional conservative, as opposed to a modern neo-liberal or neo-conservative. The term 'Toryism' describes the brand of conservatism a traditional conservative would adhere to: one-nationism, inclusiveness, consensus politics and pragmatism.

Disraeli observed that by the 1860s it had become clear that contemporary societies were divided into three great classes. The working class consisted mainly of producers. They could not be expected to exercise power directly, although certainly their interests had to be expressed and represented. The capitalist and commercial classes were the main wealth creators. They could not be entrusted with power since they were self-interested and could not be relied upon to consider the national interest. The landed and aristocrat class was a special case. It enjoyed great privileges and always had done. However, its position now had to be justified; it could not rule simply because it had always done so. It had to accept responsibilities if it were to enjoy privileges. The principle that responsibility comes with power became known as *noblesse oblige*.

Despite this analysis, Disraeli insisted that the traditional ruling class still had a key role to play in politics. Traditional conservatives continued to support this view right up to the 1960s. The great 'father' of English conservatism, Edmund Burke (1729–97), argued that the power of the ruling class could be justified on a number of grounds:

- The traditional ruling class enjoyed great wealth and had no pressing need to toil for a living, so therefore it could govern the country in a disinterested way. The middle and working classes would govern in a self-interested way since they had so much to gain or lose.

- Having governed the country for centuries, the landed class of gentry and aristocracy had accumulated the wisdom of the past. In other words, the ability to govern well was passed down from one generation to the next, each generation learning from the past and adding something to it.

- In a spiritual way, the ruling class was seen by conservatives as superior to all others. Its wisdom would enable it to understand best how to preserve and increase the welfare of the people. This notion came to be described – often by its opponents – as the exercise of paternalism.

For a century after Disraeli, conservatism continued to cling on to ruling-class philosophy, gradually accepting popular democracy and that the authority to govern had to be earned by election.

Class, however, remained an important issue. Conservative movements throughout Europe and the USA became vehicles for the demands of any class with a vested interest in the status quo, or at least with a reason to oppose the new ideologies. Thus, farming groups, especially the small peasant class on both sides of the Atlantic, have tended to be conservative, as have small business owners in general. In Britain, the middle classes have traditionally been conservative, especially those engaged in private enterprise. They hold an interest in the maintenance of order and oppose any ideological change, such as socialism, which would threaten their position in society and politics.

The main practical way in which the conservative attachment to the middle classes in the twentieth century manifested itself was in the movement's support for free-market capitalism. While socialists were arguing for increased state involvement in redistributing income from rich to poor, and liberals supported state welfare provision, conservatives usually opposed excessive state activity. This of course suited the middle-class preference for lower taxation and the free operation of capitalism.

By the 1970s, it was clear throughout the more prosperous Western countries that class divisions were breaking down. People had become less concerned with collective class interests and more interested in their own individual progression. This posed a problem for conservatism since it had always presented itself as a class-based movement. It was, therefore, at this time that New Right conservatism emerged as a new philosophy of individualism, led by Margaret Thatcher and Ronald Reagan. The close relationship between conservatism and class had finally ended.

Conservatism and ideology

As we have seen above, conservatism would probably not need to exist if political ideologies did not exist. Ideologies, by their nature, propose social change. Conservatives are fundamentally opposed to such change when it has not arisen out of natural forces. When change is created by political action motivated by ideological beliefs, conservatives become suspicious and usually hostile towards it.

In opposing ideological change, conservatism has changed its own character in order to provide an effective opposition. The following examples illustrate this:

1 The arrival of liberalism in the nineteenth century gave rise to the protection of individual liberty, human rights, representative democracy and minimal interference by government in the economy or welfare issues. Conservatives responded by stressing the importance of social unity and the need for welfare to combat the divisive effects of free-market individualism. In Britain, this was promoted by Disraeli and became known as 'one-nation conservatism'.

2 With the emergence of socialism as the main opponent of liberalism in the twentieth century, conservatives changed their philosophy. They sought alternatives to the collectivist and egalitarian aspirations of the socialists and thus became the champions of private enterprise and individualism. Excessive action by the state was regarded suspiciously and usually opposed.

3 When fascism began to spread between the world wars, conservatives were at first at a loss as to how to react. This was compounded by the fact that fascism tended to appeal to the same groups in society as conservatism – peasants, small business owners and elements of the disaffected, anti-socialist working class. Once the true nature of fascism was revealed, however, conservatives such as Winston Churchill (1874–1965) began to stress the importance of individual liberty, democracy and firm limits to the activities of the state. In other words, they became more liberal in character.

4 More recently, progressive liberalism has come to the fore. This philosophy supports individual liberty, moral and social diversity and some mild redistribution of income and wealth from rich to poor. In the USA, however, conservatism has developed a more authoritarian position on morality and law-and-order issues in reaction to this permissive philosophy. In many cases, the quest for a more moral society and the restoration of traditional values has given rise to a religious element in conservatism.

Conservatism has often been described as chameleon-like in that it changes its characteristics as its political environment changes. Its objection to ideology and ideological change, however, runs deeper than this, and is further examined later in this chapter.

Core values of conservatism

Conservatism, then, altered its character in the face of two kinds of challenge – that of supporting the dominant social class in any particular age and that of responding to the emergence of new, popular ideologies. This has resulted in considerable variation in the nature of the philosophy. However, conservatism does have enduring values and these are discussed below.

Human nature

Perhaps the most fundamental value of conservatism is its belief about basic human nature. This is more pessimistic in attitude than that of most other ideologies, notably liberalism and socialism. It is demonstrated by the following examples:

- The deepest conservatives take the Roman Catholic view that humankind is born with original sin and must therefore remain severely flawed in character. However much individuals try, they will be unable to achieve perfection. Ideologies such as socialism and anarchism have argued that individuals can be moulded by a just society into more perfect creatures. Not so, say such conservatives, who regard these ideologies as impractical and utopian. The religious nature of modern US conservatism has seen a restoration of this fundamentalist view.

- Individuals are not driven by reason, as Enlightenment thinkers had asserted, but by basic appetites. These include the desire for physical prosperity, for property, for power and to avoid deprivation. The implication is that individuals cannot generally be trusted with government since they will simply use it for their own ends rather than for the welfare of the whole community.

- Human nature is not a constant, but is always changing as the nature of society itself changes. The conservative philosopher Karl Popper (1902–94), for example, criticised all ideologies on the grounds that they have been based on a fixed view of human nature. This was, for him, an error which invalidated all ideologies. Thus, there may be periods when people mostly crave freedom and the pursuit of individualism, while at other times they may be fearful and crave security and welfare.

- It is a conservative tradition to see people as, on the whole, untrustworthy, self-seeking and generally feckless. This leads to the conclusion that humankind is sorely in need of firm government. This should not be government by dictators, who may too easily rise to power since people are readily persuaded by populist figures. Rather, it should be government by benevolent rulers, who need to be firm, but who have the people's general interests at heart. As Edmund Burke observed in the eighteenth century, the relationship between government and the people should be similar to that between a parent and a child. This view is often referred to as **paternalism**.

- We are, say conservatives, basically individuals who are more concerned with our own welfare than that of the community as a whole. As Margaret Thatcher famously asserted in a 1984 television interview: 'There are individuals and there are families. There is no such thing as society.'

The conservative view of human nature has a number of implications, for example in the field of law and order. The causes of crime and disorder, conservatives believe, lie with the individual. Indeed, some have argued that criminal behaviour is the product of humankind's inherent sinfulness. This directly opposes the more liberal view that it is the result of economic and social deprivation. The practical application of these beliefs therefore involves exemplary punishment rather than social remedies.

Key Term

Paternalism

Paternalism is a style of politics usually associated with conservatives, though this is not necessarily always the case. The concept suggests that those who govern claim superior knowledge and judgement over those who are governed. Rulers therefore believe that they understand what is best for the people to a greater extent than the people do themselves. A paternalist may well oppose democracy on the grounds that people will make poor judgements compared with their political masters. The paternalist model derives from the relationship between a parent and a child. This means that it can have positive implications, in that a paternalistic ruler would normally have the best interests of the people at heart, just as parents care for their children. Although mid-nineteenth-century conservatives, such as Peel and Disraeli, adopted a paternalistic approach to politics, in modern political life it has mostly been rejected in favour of popular democracy, whereby the people have a major input into the decisions that affect them.

A further consequence of this conservative philosophy concerns the nature of government. If there is an excess of popular democracy, the country is likely to be poorly governed. As long ago as the 1870s, Disraeli advocated that conservatives accept the need for universal suffrage, but this did not imply that people could be completely trusted with government. The conservative view of representation is that governments should not slavishly follow the fluctuating desires and demands of the people, but should use their wise judgement to serve the best interests of the whole community. In a modern context, this is reflected in the conservative suspicion of the referendum as a governing mechanism. (The British Conservative Party, however, has supported the use of referendums in some circumstances, such as possible approval for a European Union constitution in 2005 – a typical example of conservative pragmatism.)

A more dramatic example of the conservative view of human nature can be found in Margaret Thatcher's policies of the 1980s. She sought to unlock what she saw as humankind's natural desire to be free of the shackles of government (for example, in the form of personal taxation), to pursue individual goals and to compete freely with others in search of prosperity. Her pursuit of free-market policies certainly seemed to tap into the fundamental desires of many people for individualism. Of course, critics have suggested that what she did was to suppress community spirit and the desire for social justice, pandering to those who could benefit from free-market economics and ignoring those who were not in a position to take advantage of it.

Order and authority

In the most basic terms, it could be said that liberals see humankind's most fundamental need, after food, clothing and shelter, as individual freedom. Socialists and anarchists, on the other hand, stress humankind's social nature and its preference for the collective rather than individual pursuit of goals. The conservative view is clear and stands in opposition to these beliefs. Conservatives affirm that humankind's most basic need is for order and security.

We can trace this key aspect of conservative philosophy to two English thinkers, Hobbes and Burke. Thomas Hobbes, writing shortly after the end of the English Civil War in 1651, examined humankind's basic predicament. On the one hand, individuals have a desire to be free and to exercise all their rights. On the other hand, individuals are intensely competitive and self-seeking. This would, if allowed to flourish, lead to an intolerable situation. Life, he famously argued, would become 'nasty, brutish and short' (Leviathan, 1651). In practice, people would consider themselves to be in competition with every other person and therefore live in fear of the results of that restless society. Hobbes believed that, faced with such a dilemma, humankind would choose to sacrifice much of its freedom and rights in favour of a secure existence. The only way to ensure this was to allow an absolute ruler to govern and protect us from each other.

Ever since Hobbes, conservatives have preferred strong authority and have tended to favour the community's need for security over the rights of individuals. Again, we see this philosophy most clearly in the conservative attitude to law and order and its reluctance to champion the cause of civil liberties. Critics have even suggested that traditional conservatives were authoritarian – preferring state power to the freedom of citizens.

Edmund Burke's great work, *Reflections on the Revolution in France*, was written in 1790, one year after the French had dismissed their monarchy and at a time when there was growing hysteria in England over whether revolution would cross the Channel. Starting as a vehement criticism of the actions of the revolutionaries, the book turned into a general manual of conservatism. Above all, Burke's Reflections is a plea for the preservation of order and gradual reform as opposed to the disorder that results from revolutionary change. The French Revolution sacrificed order and security in order to impose abstract theories that were premature, unnecessary and not generally supported by the majority of the people. Since Burke, conservatives have always erred on the side of caution and preserving order – until Margaret Thatcher, that is.

Tradition and preservation

Conservatives' preference for the preservation of tradition is closely related to their desire for public order. When we refer to tradition in this context, we mean both traditional institutions, such as the monarchy, established Church and political constitution, as well as traditional values, such as the preservation of marriage and the importance of the nuclear family, religion and established morality. Again, this is an attitude that traces back to Burke.

The greatest crime of the French revolutionaries, according to Burke, was to abandon traditional forms of authority that had stood the test of time. This is summarised in his

Edmund Burke, whose 1790 critique of the French Revolution became a manual for traditional conservatives

ringing criticism that 'No generation should ever be so rash as to consider itself superior to its predecessors' (*Reflections on the Revolution in France*, 1790). The fact that values and institutions have survived, argue conservatives in general, is a testament to their quality. Furthermore, they carry the accumulated wisdom of the past and should therefore be respected. In a similar way, traditions bring to contemporary society some of the best aspects of past societies. How people thought and behaved in the past can inform current generations. Thus, the nineteenth-century novelist, poet and philosopher G. K. Chesterton (1874–1936) called tradition the 'democracy of the dead', because it allows the wisdom of previous generations to be involved in the activities of current society.

Burke also praised traditions for their ability to provide continuity between the past and present. They give a sense of security and help to prevent violent transformations in society. He described tradition as:

a partnership…between those who are living, those who are dead and those who are to be born.

From *Reflections on the Revolution in France*, 1790

A typical example concerns the monarchy. Elected governments, political ideologies and social change may come and go, but if the monarchy endures in its traditional form the people will retain a sense of security and continuity amid the turmoil. Conservatives take a similar view of traditional morality based around the family. This helps each new generation hold on to a lasting set of values in an ever-changing world, thus giving them a sense of security, which they can pass on to the next generation.

Allied to their theories of tradition, conservatives believe that when institutions and values have proved useful in promoting order and stability in the past, they should be preserved. It is irresponsible, they argue, to reject them for the sake of ideological principles or new theories. This is not, however, a recipe for 'no change'. Rather, it is a tendency to conserve what is seen to be good and to reform what proves to be undesirable.

Despite this, modern British conservatism has largely ignored the importance of tradition, especially since the 1980s. It has embraced new social theories, such as economic monetarism, privatisation and opposition to the dependency culture, and has attacked some traditional institutions, such as the civil service, the Church of England, the legal establishment and the long-standing practices of the financial centre in London. There is still evidence, however, of strong support for traditional institutions and values in US and French conservatism, which have proved resistant to 'excessive' social reform.

Inequality

Until the eighteenth century, the idea that humankind is naturally divided into a hierarchy – that we are born into unequal circumstances, with the few privileged at the top of the hierarchy and the many inferiors at the bottom – was taken as natural and inevitable.

Conservatives gradually modified their view of the natural structure of society during the nineteenth and twentieth centuries. It was becoming clear that society was more fluid than it had ever been and that people had begun to view themselves as individuals rather than as members of a social class (which would give them little chance to progress). By the 1980s, conservatives had abandoned their views of a hierarchical society, but held on to the belief that individuals are unequal in terms of their abilities and potentialities. This is a view shared by both conservatives and liberals.

In particular, conservatives have emphasised their belief in natural inequality in response to socialist ideas. The socialist objective of creating more social and economic equality is seen by conservatives as a completely artificial aspiration, unnatural to society. Furthermore, they suggest that inequality is a positive aspect of society since it creates competition and dynamism.

Organic Society and Hierarchy

The term 'organic society' refers to a belief which became entrenched in traditional conservative thought in the latter part of the nineteenth century. To a great extent it was a reaction against the rise of liberal individualism which had been promoted by utilitarians and classical liberals. It proposes that society is more than merely a collection of free individuals, but it is a single entity, something like a single, living organism. We are connected to each other through our humanity and through common membership of the same community. Put another way, the organic society is seen by many conservatives as a reality which is superior to our own, individual interests. Of course, in the ideal organic society, the goals and aspirations of individuals will coincide with the goals of the society as a whole. In the 1980s Margaret Thatcher challenged this notion, famously remarking that 'there is no such thing as society'. What she was implying was that the goals of individuals are superior to those of society as a whole.

The conservative view of hierarchy may, at first sight, appear to contradict the notion of an organic society. In fact it underpins it. Traditional conservatives believed that there is a 'natural' order into which each individual fits. It is normal and natural that society should be divided into a number of strata. The very rigid feudal system had long since disappeared, but there remained a belief that some kind of class system was inevitable. This hierarchy supports the organic society in that it creates an order and stability which the individualistic society lacks. The different parts of the hierarchy have different roles which complement and support each other. Of course, this also implies inequality, but it is an ordered inequality and one in which those at the upper levels of the hierarchy are expected to take responsibility for the welfare of the lower orders, a principle known as *noblesse oblige*. The idea of hierarchy now largely appears outdated, but the organic society remains a key idea for many conservatives, not least some of the supporters of David Cameron's style of conservatism.

Pragmatism

It would be entirely wrong to suggest that conservatism is a doctrine of 'no change', or that it treats its own principles as eternal and fixed. Conservatives are, above all, pragmatists. Michael Oakeshott (1901–90), a leading conservative philosopher of modern times, particularly advocated a pragmatic approach. He asserted that politics should be 'a conversation, not an argument' (*On Being Conservative*, 1962). What he meant was that political action should never be the result of conflict over political dogmas and theories. Instead, it should be the result of a more gentle relationship between government and the governed. The good conservative politician should engage in a relationship with the people that would allow him or her to reach decisions based on the 'intimations and traditions' of the community.

Pragmatism implies a flexible approach to politics: an understanding of what is best for people, what is acceptable to them and what will preserve a stable society. It is also a rejection of the politics of strongly held ideology and of a dogmatic approach to decision-making. Perhaps the most striking example of pragmatism occurred in the 1950s. A series of moderate Conservative governments in the UK was confronted with a number of radical reforms that

had been implemented by the Labour governments of 1945–51. Should the Conservatives now cancel the widespread nationalisation of major industries, dismantle the newly created welfare state and remove freshly granted powers from local government? In principle, the party was opposed to the reforms, but it had to recognise that they were both popular and seemingly successful. It therefore reached a pragmatic decision to retain Labour's radical initiatives.

Individualism

This is perhaps the most difficult conservative principle to define. It has lost much of its distinctiveness since it is a value that is now shared with liberals, most European democratic parties, both Republicans and Democrats in the USA and the British Labour Party. There is also a problem in distinguishing individualism from individual liberty. Although the ideas are linked, they are not necessarily the same concept, and represent distinct political traditions.

Individual liberty, a fundamentally liberal principle, concerns mainly an absence of external restraint. It refers to the extent to which our activities, as individuals or groups, may be constrained by laws, customs or a moral code. Prominent examples of individual liberty in Western democracies are the right to freedom of worship, thought and expression, freedom of movement and freedom to associate in whatever law-abiding group we wish. Individualism is a more positive concept and refers to choice, opportunity and self-fulfilment.

Conservative individualism has two main elements. First, it suggests that each individual and household should be presented with the widest possible range of choices and opportunities. The state should restrict such choices as little as possible. This provides a link with liberal freedom, but conservative individualism is distinguished from it in that the state can enhance and facilitate choice and opportunity. In other words, the state can play a positive rather than a negative role. Second, individualism implies a sense of privacy. There are many areas where interference by the state may be seen as legitimate – for example, in the fields of law and order, national defence and management of the currency – but there is also an extensive private sphere. For conservatives, private life is not the concern of the state. Matters such as operating private businesses, religious belief, enjoyment of property and family-expenditure decisions are not normally to be interfered with by government. Therefore, it is part of the essence of conservatism that a strong barrier should be preserved between the public and private or individual spheres.

There is one further important implication of the conservative support for individualism. For conservatives, individualism can best flourish in a stable social, moral and economic environment. The continuity provided by morality, law and order and traditions provides the necessary scenery in which individuals can play their roles securely. Indeed, in many circumstances, the excessive exercise of individual liberties, as advocated by pure liberals, threatens individualism. A society that allows too much personal freedom may threaten its own security and stability. Given the choice between a free society and a collectively secure society in which individuals can flourish, conservatives usually favour the latter.

Michael Oakeshott describes such a society as nomocratic, i.e. one where people enjoy shared morality, values and beliefs, thus creating fertile ground for individualism. This, he continues, is preferable to a restless society that is always pursuing utopian goals – he critically refers to this as a 'teleocratic' society. The analogy Oakeshott used in *On Being Conservative* (1962) was that of a ship adrift in an open sea. The ship had no port of departure and no destination, but was constantly faced by crises and dangers which had to be dealt with by its officers. So it is with society, he argued. In the following passage from the work, he expresses the conservative view that society should not be driven towards a preferred goal and that government should confine itself to preventing social conflict:

Government, then, as the conservative in this matter understands it, does not begin with a vision of another, different and better world, but with the observation of the self-government practised even by men of passion in the conduct of their enterprises; it begins in the informal adjustments of interests to one another which are designed to release those who are apt to collide from the mutual frustration of a collision.

Oakeshott's phrase, 'the mutual frustration of a collision', is a telling one for conservatives and sums up why order is so vital for them. Without order, we are liable to be constantly thwarted in our endeavours by conflict with others. For some extreme liberals and New Right conservatives, conflict can be a creative force. For traditional conservatives, however, it is seen as destructive.

Property

For much of the nineteenth century, conservatives (then usually referred to as 'Tories') feared the rise of the property-owning middle classes. This was mainly because they believed the middle classes would sweep away traditional authority by using their vast economic wealth to wield political power. The Whig Party was seen at that time as the promoter of capitalist property. Following the Disraelian era of the 1860s and 1870s, however, the British Tories (who were in the process of turning themselves into the Conservative Party) accepted that they too must incorporate the interests of property owners. Similar stories were unfolding in the rest of Europe and the USA. As the growing property-owning classes required a political force to hold back the rise of working-class movements, mainly socialism, conservatism became a fundamentally middle-class tradition.

The defence of property has included opposition to the introduction of common ownership (i.e. nationalisation), resistance to high property taxes (e.g. Margaret Thatcher attempted to replace local property rates with a non-property-based poll tax in 1988) and heavy stress on law and order since high crime levels tend mostly to affect private property. In much of

Europe, conservative parties also took up the cause of small farmers and business owners. Here again, it was socialist modes of thinking that threatened their enjoyment of their own property.

Perhaps the clearest example of conservative support for private property comes from Margaret Thatcher's time in office. In the early 1980s, shortly after coming to power, she announced an initiative known as the 'right to buy', whereby tenants in council-owned housing would be given the opportunity to purchase their own homes on preferential terms. She saw this as part of a new 'property and share-owning democracy' in the UK. She believed that owning property or shares in businesses (widespread privatisation of nationalised industries gave people the opportunity to buy shares at discounted prices) would give people a stake in society and thus promote a sense of responsibility. This has become a key element in the conservative attitude to property. It was opposed by socialists in the UK, who were strongly attached to collective ownership of low-cost housing. However, ultimately, the popularity of the policy went a long way to eroding socialist elements in the Labour Party. Attachment to private property rights, in other words, became part of a new British consensus.

Opposition to ideology

As has been seen, conservatism changes its character according to the dominant ideology it is resisting at any given time. However, the movement's opposition to ideologies in general runs deeper than merely a suspicion of radical change. It has a number of different aspects:

● Oakeshott's view, described above, that societies should not be directed towards specific social goals has implications for anti-ideology. Most ideologies propose an ideal form of society and are dedicated to working towards it. This is seen by conservatives as contrived and artificial; it flies in the face of both tradition and the need for social stability. They derive no sense of social progress from it.

However, this is not to say that conservatives oppose social improvement. On the contrary, they believe that this is a worthwhile goal, but it should be pursued, they argue, in accordance with the emotions and traditions of the people, not according to an abstract set of political principles.

● Ideological change is normally radical in nature. As far back as Burke's opposition to the actions of the French revolutionaries, conservatives have resisted rapid forms of social revolution or transformation. Reforms, when clearly necessary and desirable, should be gentle and should be carried out with continuity in mind. Burke's warning has remained relevant to conservatives:

[revolutionaries] despise experience as the wisdom of unlettered men, and, as for the rest, they have wrought underground a mine that will blow up, at one grand explosion, all examples of antiquity, all precedents, charters and acts of parliament.

From *Reflections on the Revolution in France*, 1790

● Excessive attachments to ideologies may result in tyranny. There are two main reasons for this. First, ideological leaders tend to become totalitarian in their ruthless pursuit of political goals. Burke observed this in the French revolutionaries; since then, movements such as fascism, communism and even radical feminism have suffered the same fate. Indeed, ideas alone can be tyrannical in nature (a concept that has come to be known as Jacobinism, after Robespierre's revolutionary party in France). The so-called 'political correctness' proposed by militant feminists is seen by conservatism as a form of Jacobinism. Second, the revolutionary change that often results from ideology sweeps away traditional authority and stability, resulting in disorder at best, and anarchy at worst.

● Ideologies have a fixed view of human nature; indeed, several are actually based on such an assumption. Conservatives see human nature as fickle, non-rational and changeable. This makes all fixed political principles fundamentally flawed. The academic conservative Karl Popper further suggested that ideological movements, far from being based on human nature, actually influence human nature. They are not scientific in nature, therefore, but are manipulative. It follows that they create artificial societies and so are doomed to fail. For Popper, the Marxist-inspired communist regimes were a classic example of this. Ideas such as equality and common ownership of property, which communists imposed on their states, were not natural to human nature, so therefore they could not hope to endure.

Scepticism and empiricism

This review of core ideas can be summarised by returning to the typical conservative political state of mind. First, conservatives are, by nature, sceptical of most fixed political principles. As the modern conservative politician Michael Portillo (1953–) stated in a 1996 television interview:

If there were no political nostrums [i.e. fixed beliefs], there would be no need for conservatism.

In fact, conservatives tend to be suspicious of the activity of politics in general. For them it should be a limited activity since they doubt how effective it can, or ought, to be. Another modern British conservative, Lord Hailsham (1907–2001), has gone as far as to say that:

The man who puts politics before his family is not fit to be called a civilised human being.

From *The Case for Conservatism*, 1947

For many traditional conservatives, it is the main role of their philosophy to express reservations and doubts about all political movements.

Second, conservatives are usually empiricists. Empiricism involves judging current actions against the experience of the past. Respect for tradition, pragmatism and suspicion of the new and the untried are all aspects of this empirical approach. The wise politician, it is suggested, builds on the wisdom of the past and is informed by that past. This is a preference for the known (what has gone before) over the unknown (what may be in the future). This view follows Chesterton's concept of the 'democracy of the dead' and respects Burke's plea not to believe that the current generation is wiser than those which have gone before. Critics see this as permanently looking backwards, but conservatives respond by pointing out how much that is positive has been achieved in the past, from which we can still learn.

Box 2.1 gives quotations on some key traditional conservative ideas.

Box 2.1 Some key traditional conservative ideas

'The Tory Party has three great objects…to maintain the institutions of the country…to uphold the Empire of England…and to elevate the condition of the people…'

Benjamin Disraeli, 1872 speech

'Scepticism and empiricism are the foundations of Conservatism.'

'The Tory Party has emotions, but no doctrine.'

Both from Ian Gilmour, *The Body Politic*, 1969

'Moderation is indispensable if passionate men are to escape being locked in an encounter of mutual frustration…'

From Michael Oakeshott, *On Being Conservative*, 1962

'If the main strength of Conservatism is adaptability, its main enemy is ideology.'

From Francis Pym, *The Politics of Consent*, 1984

Types of conservatism

Early conservatism

At the beginning of this chapter, we placed the origins of conservatism at the end of the eighteenth century. The term 'conservatism' itself is probably of French origin, referring to the reaction against the ideals of the French Revolution; at that stage, it represented a movement that hoped to restore the traditional authority of the monarchy and the Church. In the early days of the USA, the conservative elements among the founding fathers wished to see the retention of central authority and the political power of the propertied classes. In England, conservatism was known as Toryism. Its main concern was to hold back the rise of liberal ideas, which prompted such fearful developments as constitutional reform and free-trade policies.

It is tempting, therefore, to see the origins of conservatism in reactionary ideas, and thereby to view it as a wholly negative philosophy. Certainly, there was a powerful conservative movement in the first half of the nineteenth century that challenged all the main ideas of the Enlightenment. Conservatism stood for romantic ideals in preference to rationalism. Politics was seen largely in terms of paternalism and judgement, rather than rational thought and democratic fervour. There were desperate appeals to retain the authority of the Church, the aristocracy and the monarchy.

It was Sir Robert Peel (1788–1850), widely known as the founder of the British Conservative Party, who understood that conservatism would not survive with such a negative philosophy.

The Peelites

Peel recognised that if reform and change were both inevitable and desirable, it was pointless for conservatives to resist it. In his widely acclaimed Tamworth Manifesto of 1834, he insisted that conservatism had to become a pragmatic, rather than a reactionary, movement. By then Parliament had been reformed and there were proposals to introduce free trade in place of the protectionism that served the interests of the great landowners rather than the common people. He urged his party to embrace these changes and to move on to new concerns.

In effect, it was Peel who enabled the British conservative movement to ally itself to free-

Benjamin Disraeli, who developed One Nation Conservatism

market capitalism and so gain the support of the growing middle classes. Peelite conservatism was, therefore, pragmatic, tied to capitalism, protective of property rights and fundamentally middle class in nature. For many of its followers, the movement remained basically Peelite up until the radical reforms introduced by Margaret Thatcher.

One-nationism

After Peel, the next great conservative leader was Benjamin Disraeli. Like Peel, he was a pragmatist and, as such, dealt with the threat posed by the rise of the working classes and their main political tradition – socialism. While Peel had recognised the importance of taking up the cause of the middle class, Disraeli had to decide where to take his party in relation to the working class.

Perhaps Disraeli's main contribution to conservatism – not only in Britain, but also in the rest of Europe and the USA – were his theories about the organic nature of society. What capitalism was doing, he argued, was to create a society of individuals at the expense of a general sense of social responsibility. In other words, the country was in danger of losing its sense of community (what German conservatives were calling *Volksgemeinschaft* – a common feeling of national identity). People who were too busy pursuing their own selfish ends were liable to lose a strong sense of nation and society.

At the same time, the effect of free-market capitalism, which Peelite conservatives had supported, was dividing the country into distinctive groups – the prosperous few and the many poor. Disraeli described this growing phenomenon as two nations. It was a recipe for revolution since it created class conflict. It was the role of conservatives, Disraeli insisted, to unite the nation and create one nation. In order to do this, government should cease to rule in the interests of only one class and, instead, care for the welfare of all classes. R. A. Butler (1902–82), a 'one-nation Tory' and government minister of the 1950s and 1960s, admitted to still being inspired by Disraeli nearly 100 years later. He said in 1954:

> *Underlying all our differences there should be fundamental unity – the very antithesis of class war – bringing together what Disraeli called the Two Nations into a single social entity.*

So, Disraelian one-nation Toryism was a type of conservatism that had as its core aim the unity of the people and the avoidance of social conflict. This was a theme taken up by continental European conservatives at the same time. In Germany in the 1870s, for example, Otto von Bismarck (1815–98) was preaching a similar message to his people.

According to Disraeli, national unity was to be provided by four main forces. These were constitutional unity of the UK (he opposed Irish independence, for example), the maintenance of great traditions around which people could unite, the encouragement of patriotism and the provision of welfare for the poor to prevent excessive inequality and therefore conflict.

One-nation conservatism survives to this day. It formed a powerful opposition from within the Conservative Party to Margaret Thatcher's radicalism in the 1980s. Figures such as Michael Heseltine (1933–), Kenneth Clarke (1940–), Ian Gilmour (1920–) and Francis Pym (1922–2008), collectively and disparagingly known to Thatcher's supporters as 'wets', all claimed to be social unifiers. They criticised the new individualist and free-market policies of the Thatcher era. These new ideas within conservatism were once again, they argued, threatening to divide Britain into two nations – the haves and have-nots. Ultimately, the one-nation group lost the argument and their own positions in the party. It nevertheless remains as a significant minority within the Conservative Party; now often known as 'social' conservatives, the group continues to resist the movement to the right in British conservatism. In the USA, such 'progressive' conservative members of the Republican Party have, by contrast, been completely routed and have moved to the Democratic Party.

The nationalist-authoritarian right

There is a long tradition in Europe of a type of conservatism often characterised as 'ultra right' and, in its most extreme form, even quasi-fascist. A typical example has been the National Front movement in France, led by Jean-Marie Le Pen (1928–), but there have also been popular movements in Austria, Russia, Serbia, Denmark and even in the Netherlands (which has one of the most liberal reputations of the continent).

Ultra conservatives are radical nationalists, placing the national interest above all other considerations. As one would expect, they oppose the activities of the European Union and international organisations in general, and are extremely resistant to immigration into their countries. It would be wrong to characterise this group as 'racist' in outlook, but they certainly do oppose multiculturalism, preferring a 'monoculture' where all citizens are expected to adopt the dominant domestic culture.

It would also be mistaken to describe them as fascists. While they do propose an extremely authoritarian form of state in terms of law and order, morality and national security, they are democrats and support a pluralist society where different groups can be allowed to flourish as long as they do not threaten the national culture or public order. They tend to support free-market economics, insisting that the state, although strong, should be limited to matters of order and security, not industrial and commercial activity.

Few British conservatives have conformed to this model. Enoch Powell (1912–98), a leading politician of the 1960s and 1970s, perhaps came closest to doing so. He was noted for his opposition to immigration on the grounds that it would lead to excessive conflict (he claimed his policy was not racially based), his reaction against the growth of moral permissiveness in the 1960s and his championing of free-market economics (this was well before Margaret Thatcher reintroduced them). Arguably, the emergence of the UK Independence Party (UKIP) in the early years of the twenty-first century marks something of a revival of this political tradition. Although opposition to European integration is the UKIP's emblematic policy, there is no doubt that the party contains many authoritarian-conservative politicians.

The New Right

It is important at this stage to be clear about what is meant by the term 'New Right'. It was coined in the USA to describe a new wing of the Republican Party, represented by Ronald Reagan's presidency, and was imported into the UK to describe the wing of the Conservative Party that gathered around the leadership of Margaret Thatcher. Although it was described as 'new', its main ideas were not new at all. They were, in fact, a revival of a number of past political traditions including classical liberalism, populism, Whiggism and conservatism itself. What was 'new' was that these different strands of thought were brought together into one political movement. In addition, many of the ideas of the New Right were new to the British Conservative Party.

The movement has also been described as 'Thatcherism' or 'Reaganism', or sometimes a blend of 'neo-liberalism' and 'neo-conservatism'. All these terms may prove to be misleading so,

Margaret Thatcher sought to put New Right conservatism into effect in Britain in the 1980s

for the purposes of this book, it will be referred to as the 'New Right'. A second potential confusion arises from the identification of the sources of the movement. It was certainly not developed by Thatcher and Reagan. They were merely the dominant political leaders who were able to put its principles into practice. Our search for its origins are best centred on the USA.

The 'Chicago School' of economists was led by Milton Friedman, who is still seen as the leading figure of the New Right. His great work, *Capitalism and Freedom* (1962), has become something of a bible for New Right thinkers. The Chicago School argued that the rise of socialist thinking had resulted in excessive interference by the state in the workings of the economy. This was holding back progress, stifling enterprise and curtailing individual freedom. Friedman believed that the loss of economic freedom involved in state planning and control would eventually lead to a wider loss of political freedom.

Meanwhile, in Europe, Friedrich von Hayek, the Austrian philosopher, was becoming widely read in conservative circles, notably by Margaret Thatcher and her close adviser, Keith Joseph (1918–94). Like Friedman, Hayek saw the future dangers of the growth of socialism; the pair effectively founded the Chicago School in the 1950s. Hayek's major work, *The Road to Serfdom*, written in 1944, assumed a similar role to that of Friedman's *Capitalism and Freedom* as a source of New Right thinking. For Hayek, the casualty of socialism was individualism and the inevitable result of its progress was a form of totalitarianism. Both the growing power of the state and the influence of organised labour, in the form of trade unions, were identified as vehicles for this new totalitarianism. It existed in full form in the Soviet Union, but Hayek warned that similar states could develop in the West. If we are ever to doubt Hayek's influence we should note the words of Margaret Thatcher in her 1995 memoirs, *The Downing Street Years*:

> *The most powerful critique of socialist planning and the socialist state which I read and to which I have returned so often since is F. A. Hayek's* The Road to Serfdom.

A third key figure of the New Right was Robert Nozick of the USA, whose obsessions with individual liberty and the evils of the strong state are sometimes described as 'anarcho-capitalism'. Nozick had a major influence on US Republicanism at a time when the party was moving towards an anti-government position. Indeed, Ronald Reagan, in his 1981 inauguration speech, expressed the view that 'government is not the solution to our problems, government is the problem'. Thatcher was also prone to describing her policies as 'rolling back the frontiers of the state'. Perhaps Nozick's quasi-anarchist views represent the extreme of the New Right in that he proposed the withdrawal of the state from nearly all activities. Most New Right conservatives limit their anti-state views to the economic sphere.

So the New Right, unlike conservatism in general, does have strong philosophical roots, running through Hayek, Friedman and Nozick. It also draws inspiration from a number of other political traditions. Some of these are described briefly below.

Classical liberalism

This nineteenth-century movement was closely associated with the growth of free-market capitalism. Classical liberals began by supporting extensive individual freedom. This was carried forward into advocating a minimal state, free economic markets, a competitive society and the absence of state-organised welfare. Classical liberals believed strongly in self-responsibility: that individuals should not expect to be cradled by the state but instead must accept that their life circumstances are under their own control. The New Right did not accept the whole of classical liberal philosophy. For the New Right, freedom was to be extended in the economic sphere, rather than in society in general.

Neo-classical economics

The economics of Alfred Marshall (1842–1924) in the early twentieth century were known as 'neo-classical' because they were an adaptation of the economic theories from a century before. In short, this kind of economics included two main propositions. The first was that the state should intervene solely to control the currency and public finances so as to maintain stability (effectively to avoid excessive price inflation). The second asserted that the economy contained internal mechanisms that would always bring it back to full employment and growth. This automatic stabilising system relied upon the state not interfering.

In the 1980s, conservatives rediscovered neo-classical economics and renamed them 'monetarism'. Edward Heath (1916–) had a brief and unsuccessful flirtation with monetarism when he was prime minister at the start of the 1970s, but it was Margaret Thatcher who was the first to dare to experiment with it, when she was faced with a severely depressed British economy in the early 1980s. She argued that high inflation and unemployment resulted from an excess of government intervention, not a lack of it. She refused to intervene and the economy recovered, albeit temporarily. The USA under Ronald Reagan followed suit with the same results. The one-nation conservatives who had opposed such audacity went into retreat and the New Right was well and truly established.

Populism

This political tradition is largely American and French in origin. It is a philosophy and style of politics that is centred on the potential of individuals to succeed as a result of their own efforts. It appeals to individuals who earn their living independently, without the support either of the state or powerful economic interests. It therefore finds supporters among groups such as small independent farmers, shopkeepers, tradespeople and entrepreneurs who run their own small businesses (groups Marx described as the 'petite bourgeoisie'). Populists are suspicious of the power of the state, oppose personal and corporate taxation, seek to control the power of both trade unions and big business and are intensely nationalistic in their outlook. Certainly, it was these petite bourgeois groups that formed the bedrock of support for Margaret Thatcher's brand of conservatism in the 1980s. A remarkable example of a conservative, populist politician is Sarah Palin, the unsuccessful vice presidential candidate in the USA's 2008 presidential election. The message of Palin and other Republican politicians like her, is that government should be carried on in accordance with the basic values of the 'ordinary' people. These, she claimed, include fundamental Christian values, strong family ties, totally free enterprise and rugged individualism, as well as pure 'common sense'.

Right-wing nationalism

The New Right took the traditional conservative philosophy of nationalism and raised it to new heights. As a movement, the New Right was faced by the challenges of both globalisation and the advance of European integration. Its UK supporters reacted strongly by asserting national interests in the face of these threats to the autonomy of nation-states everywhere. Their nationalism was inevitably defensive and, at its extreme, became somewhat xenophobic in nature.

The issue of Europe created a dilemma for the New Right. On the one hand, a single European market with no trade barriers was consistent with its attachment to the importance of free markets. On the other hand, integration threatened the nation's political independence. Ultimately, it was this latter political consideration that prevailed, but not before the Conservative Party in the UK had torn itself apart over the issue.

Neo-conservatism

Although the New Right has been suspicious of state power, it has become equally concerned by the potential social disorder resulting from increased freedom, permissiveness, lack of social responsibility and challenges to authority from alienated sections of society. It has therefore adapted aspects of the origins of conservatism (hence the term neo-conservative) to the modern world. Just as Burke stressed the need for good order and took a paternalistic view of the role of the state, so too has the New Right. A strong stance on law and order issues, attempts to restore traditional values and morality and a firm position on national security have all therefore been adopted. Neo-cons (as Americans call such theorists) also propose the export of the American concept of order and democracy to the rest of the world, no matter what their culture. They belong, therefore, in Burke's tradition of paternalist conservatism. Dick Cheney (US Vice President, 2001–2008) has been a leading exponent of neo-conservatism, a neo-liberal on economic matters and a staunch conservative on social and international affairs.

Putting together the neo-liberal position on the economy and welfare and the neo-conservative stance on law and order, moral values and national security gives a useful summary of New Right philosophy.

Contemporary US conservatism

The rise of the New Right in the USA largely coincided with the movement's success in the UK. Its origins, however, are different. In the USA there was no perceived threat from socialism, as was experienced by British conservatives. It is true that the role of the federal government had expanded considerably in the 1960s and that there was a conservative reaction against this, beginning with the 1968–74 presidency of Richard Nixon (1913–94), but socialism and the expanded state were not the main enemies. For US conservatives, the principal adversary was 'progressive liberalism'.

Classical liberalism and populism had always been important features of US Republicanism, but in the 1980s a new feature emerged. This was a moralistic, religious element. Many of society's problems, especially rising crime rates, public disorder and family breakdown, were blamed on the excessively liberal and permissive culture of the 1960s. The growth of religious observance – mainly Christian – gathered pace in the USA in the 1980s and 1990s. This gave rise to an increasingly moralistic outlook and a stern defence of traditional family values, as well as opposition to feminism and its objectives, such as equal opportunities and abortion on demand. Christianity and a moralistic interpretation of its teachings were now part of the US 'way of life', claimed conservatives. The traditional love of individual liberty in the USA did not, for them, extend to private morality. This was because private moral permissiveness, they suggested, ultimately led to public disorder.

The rise of the 'religious right', represented largely by a movement known as the Moral Majority, coincided with the triumph of the USA and its allies in the Cold War. For US conservatives, this was a victory not just for US economic and military prowess, but also for its traditional values.

The challenge of Islamic fundamentalism has reinforced this belief further and added a new dimension. Traditionally, US conservatives have been isolationist in global terms. They have been reluctant to support foreign adventures and have believed that it is up to other nations to defend their own interests. The Cold War victory and the fundamentalist threat have resulted in a new proactive, interventionist attitude to world affairs. The term New World Order was coined in 1990 by James Baker (1930–), then Republican Secretary of State under President George Bush Senior (1924–). It suggested two main propositions. First, that there was now only one world power able to maintain peace – the USA. The second proposition – essentially conservative in outlook – was that traditional US values were superior to those of other cultures and were, therefore, exportable all over the world. In short, the long-term creation of a stable world order depended on widespread acceptance of those values.

The main elements of contemporary US conservatism can be summarised as follows:

- a religious and moralistic attitude to social issues

- opposition to socially progressive ideas

- deep suspicion of centralised state power

- an attachment to pluralist, decentralised democracy

- classical liberal economic views

- a fixed view of US culture and a sense of its superiority

- a desire to spread US influence and values globally

- a view that democracy is a 'core value' that should be widely exported and applied.

The apparent rejection of American conservatism in the US general election of 2008, and the election of a progressive liberal president (Barak Obama), suggests that the movement may be forced to re-evaluate its principles and it may indeed have entered long-term decline.

Continental European conservatism

It would be a mistake to make too many generalisations about conservatism in Europe outside of the UK. Nevertheless, there are some elements that help to distinguish it from the British tradition.

First, continental conservatives tend to be more nationalistic in their outlook. French

Gaullism is a good example. Inspired by President Charles de Gaulle (1890–1970), Gaullists believe that French national interests are absolutely paramount. This results in French refusal to cooperate fully with international organisations and a monocultural outlook. Like US conservatives, the French are intensely patriotic, especially about French social and political values. They argue that all citizens should support these values.

Second, it is generally true that continental conservatives are less suspicious of state power than their British and US counterparts. They have largely accepted that the state is crucial in maintaining social, political and economic stability. This is probably the result of the greater tendency to revolutionary activity that exists in European countries. The UK and the USA have not come under serious internal threat for more than 200 years. This is not the case in continental Europe: most countries there have turbulent pasts. The interwar fascist regimes are well known. It should also be noted that France suffered violent changes of government as recently as 1958 and 1969; Italy has endured frequent and rapid changes of government since 1945; the Spanish and Portuguese democracies are still in their infancy and Greece was under military rule as recently as the 1970s. For conservatives in these states, liberalism and socialism represent instability. By contrast, the state provides order and security – classical conservative goals.

Third, there is a much stronger element of populism among such conservatives. Many European states have large and influential agricultural sectors. Farmers (especially small, independent farmers, still often described as 'peasants'), are well known for their conservative outlook, as, typically, are small-scale entrepreneurs and the inhabitants of the many thousands of small towns characteristic of continental Europe. Conservatives have appealed successfully to these groups by promoting their independence, adopting agriculture-friendly policies and defending rural causes in preference to metropolitan values. The concerns of the UK's

Countryside Alliance – those of pro-hunting, protectionism against foreign competition, better transport facilities, opposition to excessive environmental interference and support for low taxation, for example – are typical of conservatism in much of the rest of Europe. It is no coincidence that the cross-national conservative group in the European Parliament has adopted the collective name European People's Party. The election of Nicolas Sarkozy as President of France in 2007 demonstrates the strength of this movement, as he represents the tradition very accurately.

Social and liberal conservatism

Although the New Right dominated conservative parties in the USA and Europe, there remained a faction in the conservative movement that is more liberal and progressive in its outlook. Its members call themselves 'social conservatives'. The election of David Cameron to the leadership of the Conservative Party in 2005 elevated social conservatism to a primary position, at least in Britain. For some it even became 'Cameronian conservatism'.

Social conservatives retain some of the values of traditional 'one nation' conservatism. These include:

- A view that society is indeed organic, thus rejecting the New Right neo-liberal perspective that saw society as little more than a collection of individuals. Though social conservatives continue to stress the importance of individualism, they accept that this should not be at the expense of a persistent minority who are denied the benefits of an otherwise prosperous society.

- They retain the principle that families are the cornerstone of an ordered society.

- They remain firm nationalists who promote the best interests of Britain abroad. They therefore remain sceptical of excessive European integration.

- Though they are social reformers, Cameronian conservatives tend to be suspicious of constitutional reform and can be seen as traditionalists where the political system is concerned.

- They remain largely authoritarian in their approach to many, though not all, law and order issues. They place a higher value on order than on personal liberty.

- They do not share the neo-liberal view that welfare benefits are a disincentive to work and self-improvement. Instead, they see a properly targeted benefits system as a means of increasing and spreading opportunities.

Despite these traditional tendencies they do consider themselves to be reformers, notably in the following areas:

- They argue that social reform can be effective and that it is a legitimate function of government to promote such reform. Thus, they support the importance of education, welfare systems and social services in supporting families and promoting equal opportunities.

- They see education as a key element in social reform. In particular they support Labour's policies of providing a wide degree of choice in educational provision, notably secondary schooling.

- They emphasise the need for greater social mobility – the ability of individuals and families to improve their own prosperity and status.

- They have a tolerant attitude to different forms of family and lifestyle. Although they see the traditional family as desirable and superior, they accept that there are many who wish to adopt a different kind of family lifestyle, be it lone parenthood or same-sex relationships.

- While remaining nationalists, the new social conservatives accept the reality of a multicultural society and promote equal opportunities for all minority groups, as long as they are willing to adopt British identity in addition to their own cultural identity.

- Though they fully support the welfare state, they wish to promote further the involvement of the private sector in service provision.

- Social conservatives remain authoritarian in their approach to serious crime, but have come to accept the need for more creative, non-custodial ways of dealing with minor, persistent crime.

The New Right, neo-liberal agenda has not, however, been totally abandoned. Some neo-liberal principles persist:

- Conservatives still firmly believe that free markets are the best way to increase wealth.

- They argue that Britain is still over-governed and there should be less regulation of industry and commerce, as well as our personal lives. This applies to domestic government as well as to the European Union.

- They see taxation as a major disincentive to enterprise and so wish to see much lower corporate taxation.

Key conservative thinkers

Edmund Burke (Irish, 1729–97)

Burke is often described as the father of conservatism and, although he did not coin the term, his best-known work, *Reflections on the Revolution in France*, is certainly one of the first great conservative texts. Burke was born in Ireland and became an MP at Westminster. Confusingly, he described himself as a Whig and associated with other well-known Whigs of his day. His thinking, however, was predominantly conservative. Equally confusingly, he was a supporter of the US revolutionaries and spoke for them in Parliament. He believed that the USA had been hopelessly misgoverned by Britain and that the actions of the republicans were therefore justified. The French Revolution, however, provoked his utter disapproval and prompted him to develop his conservative philosophy.

Burke opposed all rational ways of thinking about political and social issues. Action, he asserted, must always be based on practical experience. Furthermore, it should never threaten the security of a society. 'Good order is the foundation of all good things,' Burke declared; it is the most important good that mankind can enjoy (*Reflections on the Revolution in France*, 1790). He berated the French revolutionaries on the grounds that they had not just threatened order – they had actually thrown society into the melting pot and attempted to reform it along rational lines. In the colourful passage from *Reflections* quoted below, Burke likens the state to a parent and subjects to its children. He expresses horror at the way the children of France have treated their parent:

We are taught to look with horror on those children of their country who are prompt rashly to hack that aged parent in pieces, and put him into a kettle of magicians in hopes that, by poisonous weeds and wild incantations, they may regenerate the parental constitution, and renovate their father's life.

The 'kettle of magicians' undoubtedly refers to the philosophers of the Enlightenment who were proposing a 'renovation' of society along the lines of rational principles.

For Burke, and for all those conservatives who have followed him, social and political change should be undertaken with great caution, and only with reference to the experience of the past and the traditions of the people. Tradition was a key element in society for Burke. He described it as a 'partnership' between 'those who are living, those who are dead and those who are to be born' (*Reflections on the Revolution in France*, 1790). Tradition therefore provided continuity from the past into the future. Furthermore, Burke believed that society was an organic, living thing and as such constantly developing naturally. It was not for humankind to interfere with nature on the excuse that it was attempting to improve it.

Burke is also famous for his view on the nature of representation. The electorate, he announced, should not vote for an MP and then expect him to do its bidding. Instead, it should elect him to use his judgement on its behalf. This extremely conservative view of representation was the result of Burke's fear that politics might become nothing more than a struggle between warring factions and interests. Politics should be a measured activity, based on pragmatism, knowledge of the past and good judgement. In this view he was following the teaching of one of his US associates, James Madison (1751–1836), who attempted to build a constitution for the USA that would not require party activity. Both Burke and Madison were, of course, to be disappointed in this respect.

Although Burke has often been accused of an inconsistent approach to political philosophy, there is a detectable thread that connects his ideas. The key elements of Burkean philosophy were as follows:

- The most important quality of any society is order.

- The people have an obligation to obey the state as long as it provides them with order.

- The affairs of the state should be conducted on the basis of measured judgement and consideration of past experience, not on the basis of abstract theories and principles.

- Traditions and traditional institutions are key factors in the preservation of order and continuity.

- Change in society should only be undertaken when it becomes clear that the existing order is untenable.

Benjamin Disraeli (British, 1804–81)

Disraeli was prime minister twice and, along with his Liberal Party counterpart, William Gladstone, dominated late-Victorian British politics. He rivals his predecessor, Robert Peel, in being credited as the founder of the Conservative Party. Disraeli wrote and worked at a time when there was real danger of social conflict breaking out in Britain. In other words, the greatest of all conservative objectives – the maintenance of order – was threatened.

He saw that Britain was in danger of becoming effectively 'two nations', divided into the rich and the poor. As capitalism flourished, the plight of the working classes and the unemployed worsened. It was for conservatives, or 'Tories' as Disraeli's followers were usually known, to take a paternalistic view and intervene on behalf of the downtrodden masses. Disraeli knew that if the Tories did not take up the cause of the poor, the socialists would. As representatives of the aristocracy and landed gentry, Disraeli believed that conservatives could play a dispassionate, neutral role in the struggle between labour and capitalism. Furthermore, the traditional wealth and privilege that the ruling class enjoyed in society also carried with it responsibility – that of preserving the welfare of the people. The term *noblesse oblige* has often been applied to this concept of the social obligation of the wealthy. Its modern equivalent suggests that those who benefit most from the fruits of capitalism have an obligation to consider the plight of the less fortunate. It is an appeal against a totally self-interested form of economic life. In 1882 Disraeli described the principle of *noblesse oblige* – the principle that the wealthier, landed class should care for the rest of the people:

> *What is the fundamental principle of the feudal system gentlemen? It is that the tenure of property shall be the performance of its duties. Why, when William the Conqueror carved out parts of the land and introduced the feudal system, he said to the recipient, 'You shall have the estate, but you shall do something for it; you shall feed the poor; you shall endow the Church; you shall defend the land in case of war; and you shall execute justice and maintain truth to the poor for nothing'.*

Disraeli and his Tory, one-nation followers sought to preserve national unity by stressing the importance of the great traditional institutions of the country, the Church of England, the monarchy and the Empire, allegiances to which all classes could subscribe. By granting the franchise to a wide section of the population, he believed that people would feel they had a greater stake in their own society.

Many conservatives to this day follow Disraelian principles, albeit updated to suit modern conditions; they are still often described as one-nation Tories. Prominent contemporary examples include Michael Heseltine and Kenneth Clarke. They support tradition, promote policies that unite rather than divide the nation, and wish to see political actions that create **inclusiveness**.

✔ Key Term

Inclusiveness
This concept is associated mainly with liberalism, but is also supported by moderate, one-nation conservatives. It suggests that all sections of the community should be included in decision-making, the enjoyment of rights and in the rewards that society has to offer. Put another way, it implies that no legal groups should be excluded from opportunities or from full participation in society on an equal basis.

George Santayana (Spanish 1863–1952)

Santayana worked largely in the USA and his influence lay mostly in that country. Like most traditional conservatives he saw politics as firmly rooted in society. It should certainly not be the result of rational theories of dogmatic principles. The actual practice of politics should be carried out with full understanding of the feelings of the people and should be more of an artform than a science.

He is mainly known, however, for his empiricism, scepticism and pragmatism. Thus he saw it as vital that political action should be based on a knowledge of the past. Possibly his most famous statement is this:

> *Those who cannot remember the past are condemned to repeat it.*
> From *Life of Reason*, 1905

The ideal political strategy for Santayana should be to consider the experience of the past, to be sceptical of ideological solutions and take into account the belief systems of the people who will be affected.

Santayana, like Burke, insisted that society should be constructed in order to remove insecurity. For him the greatest threat to individualism was disorder rather than a lack of freedom. Individualism consists of the ability to make free choices, and to be able to pursue both economic well-being and personal development in terms of more general happiness and fulfilment. It is the role of the state, said Santayana, to promote such individualism.

Michael Oakeshott (British, 1901–90)

Perhaps Oakeshott's main contribution to conservative thought was to suggest that politics should not have any fixed goals or sense of specific direction. In *On Being Conservative* (1962), he likened the state to a ship afloat on a boundless sea with no origin and no destination (see p. 44). The role of government, which commands the ship, should simply be to keep it on an even keel and care for the welfare of its passengers. The state, therefore, should be governed on a pragmatic basis, taking into account the traditions and 'intimations' of the people. By intimations, Oakeshott meant the general way in which people wish the affairs of state to be run. He was insistent that political action based on fixed theories and principles leads to conflict and takes too little account of the wishes of the people.

In a sense, Oakeshott's philosophy is simple. Governments should merely govern, and that means doing what is right for the people, not what politicians think ought to be right for the people. This is how he sums up his view:

The office of government is not to impose other beliefs and activities upon its subjects, not to tutor or educate them, not to make them better or happier in another way, not to direct them, to galvinize them into action, to lead them or co-ordinate their activities so that no occasion of conflict can occur; the office of government is merely to rule.

From *On Being Conservative*, 1962

In some ways, Oakeshott's philosophy can be seen as a bridge between traditional and New Right, neo-liberal conservatism. In line with traditional conservative thinking, he sees government as a pragmatic activity, free of ideological content. On the other hand, he wishes government to be a limited activity. This is linked with the New Right, which prefers that government disengages from regulation and so restores widespread freedom of action to its citizens.

Karl Popper (Austrian/British, 1902–94)

Sir Karl Popper began life as an Austrian, but fled from Nazi persecution and became a British citizen in 1945. He is mainly known for his opposition to totalitarianism, and was particularly critical of extreme examples of socialism. He based his opposition on what he saw as their flawed view of human nature; in line with other conservatives, he believed that human nature is not a fixed aspect of society, but the product of historical change. Those ideologies that viewed human nature as fixed were therefore in error.

Popper argued that scientific enquiry is based upon the assumption that what has always happened in the past (if it is observed often enough) will continue to happen in the future. He saw this as potentially mistaken. There is no guarantee that what has been happening will continue to happen. Scientific method, therefore, is about proving things to be wrong, rather than confirming that they are right. He called the process of discovering errors in prediction 'falsification'. This theory can also be applied to political action.

We cannot truly predict what will happen in the future, Popper asserted. Human nature and human society are constantly evolving, so society in the past is never like society in the future. For that reason, political theories based on scientific explanations of history and society cannot be proved. They are all utopian in nature. This leads to a rejection of both Marxist and socialist claims that their philosophies are scientific.

In practice, Popper's philosophy suggests that no one has a valid claim to understanding what is best for society in the future. All that politicians can do is attempt to achieve what appears to be in the best interests of the people at any given time. It would be an error for them to claim that they are always right. It follows that good government must be open to criticism and must be removable by the people if it is not acting in their interests. Popper called this 'the open society'. Conservative followers of Popper have used his philosophy to demonstrate the flaws in all ideologies and to justify a pragmatic outlook in politics.

Keith Joseph (British, 1918–94)

Together with Margaret Thatcher, Keith Joseph founded the Centre for Policy Studies in 1975. This think-tank was to become the driving force behind the dramatic change that took place within British, US and European conservatism in the 1980s and 1990s. Indeed, although neo-liberal conservatism became known as 'Thatcherism', it was Joseph who was the ideological inspiration behind it.

Joseph began with the assertion that deprivation in society was inherited from one generation to the next. He called this the 'cycle of deprivation', claiming it was not caused by lack of action by the state, but by too much action. The state was creating a dependency culture in which families had no incentive to better themselves because they had grown used to relying on the state. The answer, therefore, was to create a freer economic society, which would produce more wealth – wealth that would trickle down to all parts of society and so benefit everybody.

Joseph became the main architect of the 1980s programme of liberalising the British state. This involved privatising major industries, reducing the power of trade unions, reducing personal and corporate taxation, deregulating financial markets to make more capital available and reducing the scope of the welfare state, especially social security benefits. When recession struck the UK in the early 1980s, it was Joseph who encouraged Thatcher not to intervene, as so many of her predecessors had done, and to withdraw from economic management and allow the slump to work its natural way through. Many other conservatives lost their nerve, but Joseph and Thatcher stuck to their guns. When the economy eventually recovered of its own accord, Joseph's ideas appeared to be vindicated.

In areas of government such as law and order, immigration and social policy, Joseph was a traditional conservative, but his economic ideas were a throwback to classical liberalism, as he and Thatcher freely admitted. His was a new kind of economic conservatism, dedicated to the free market rather than to state management.

Pat Buchanan (US, 1938–)

Buchanan is one of the most prominent members of the US conservative right (which is seen as more extreme than its British counterpart). He has unsuccessfully challenged for the Republican nomination as presidential candidate and he has also stood for the presidency itself. Although Buchanan attracted the votes of 3 million Americans, he has never looked likely to win office. Nevertheless, his relative success in garnering support has had some influence in shifting the Republican Party to the right.

Like many other neo-conservatives, Buchanan was influenced by the philosopher Leo Strauss (1899–1973), who called for the moral regeneration of the USA and a new sense of shared values, based on a traditional form of Christianity. Strauss saw the world as being divided sharply into good and evil. US citizens must, he insisted, be firmly on the side of good.

Buchanan is the founder of a campaigning organisation known as the American Cause. The 1993 mission statement of the American Cause reveals its aims:

Our mission is to advance and promote traditional American values that are rooted in the conservative principles of national sovereignty, economic patriotism, limited government and individual freedom.

We can certainly recognise limited government and individual freedom as being major features of the conservative New Right, but the inclusion of national sovereignty and economic patriotism demands some explanation. National sovereignty implies that Buchanan's brand of conservatism is determined to protect US interests. It is, in effect, a charter for isolationism, denying that the USA has any global responsibilities or that it should be influenced by any other power or organisation. Certainly, George W. Bush's (1946–) refusal to cooperate with international agreements on global warming and nuclear weapons control are examples of this position.

Economic patriotism is connected to the idea of national sovereignty. It asserts that the USA should be concerned only with its own economic interests. The benefit of world trade is not a consideration. Buchanan has therefore campaigned to protect US industry from competition through the use of tariffs and subsidies. For him, the employment of US citizens is of greater importance than the long-term benefits of international trade. There are echoes of this attitude in the British New Right's opposition to further European economic integration and its suspicion of international trade organisations.

Buchanan and his followers wish to see strict controls over immigration into the USA. They oppose multiculturalism, arguing that there should be one dominant culture in the USA and that all citizens should adopt it. Both these positions are shared by the right wing of the British Conservative Party.

The principal distinction between Buchanan's brand of conservatism and its counterpart in the UK and the rest of Europe concerns religion. For him, religion cannot be separated from politics, and morality is strictly based on a traditional brand of fundamentalist Christianity. European conservatives support the maintenance of traditional values too, but this support has not necessarily been based specifically upon religion. This type of conservatism, which is based on Christian values but is not overtly or exclusively religious, is often described as **Christian democracy**.

 Key Term

Christian democracy
This term refers to a European form of conservatism originally inspired by Christian values; its religious content has since declined. It is similar to the one-nation, social conservatism that flourished in the UK in the 1950s, 1960s and 1970s. Christian democrats support market capitalism, but believe its aim should not be merely personal gain. Its wealth should be spread more evenly, to the benefit of the whole community. The state is therefore justified in intervening to create more social justice and alleviate deprivation. Tony Blair has often been seen as a kind of Christian democrat, rather than a socialist.

The conservatism of Pat Buchanan and others like him somewhat echoes that of early-twentieth-century Republicanism. Indeed, it is so historical in its outlook that it has been described as 'paleoconservatism', a term implying that its views are truly ancient in their origins. Nevertheless, it has gained adherents in recent years, especially after the 9/11 terrorist attack.

Issues in conservatism

Conservatism as an ideology

In essence, the term 'ideology' implies a strong sense of progress towards a specific set of social goals. Ideologies have fixed principles that are coherent and interlocking. They make assumptions about the nature of humankind and develop theories about the true nature of society. Furthermore, ideologies are consistent in their belief systems.

We can now examine the extent to which conservatism conforms to this definition.

Traditional conservatism certainly has no sense of progress. Indeed, Michael Oakeshott specified that true conservatism should avoid adopting any sense of direction. On the other hand, the New Right, as defined by Keith Joseph and Margaret Thatcher, certainly did envisage the creation of a society of free individuals, with wide access to ownership of property and shares in industry and in which each individual was responsible for his or her own welfare.

Similarly, traditional conservatives have tended to avoid adopting fixed principles and have opposed political movements based on such fixed principles. Conservatism has often been described as chameleon-like in that it changes its appearance according to the dominant political environment at any given time. In the nineteenth century, when liberalism was its main opponent, conservatism adopted an organic vision of society, seeing it as a living entity and expecting people to demonstrate a sense of responsibility towards each other. When socialism came to the fore, however, conservatives changed course and began to emphasise the virtues of free markets and individualism to combat collectivist ideals. Such an adaptable movement certainly cannot be described as ideological in nature.

Once again, however, the New Right does not conform. It adopted some fixed ideas that could be described as ideological in nature. In particular, monetarism became its political dogma. This was the belief that the state should confine itself to controlling the currency and public finances rather than attempting to regulate the whole economy. Furthermore, these conservatives, also known as neo-liberals, were inflexible in their attitudes to taxation and welfare, believing both to be barriers to economic progress. There is, perhaps, a case for arguing that the anti-state position of New Right conservatives is an ideological position in that it suggests a fixed view that society will flourish only if it is free of government regulation.

This evidence appears to lead to the conclusion that, while traditional conservatism is very much a state of mind, and a broad and flexible philosophy, the more modern forms of the movement have become ideological in character. The conservative state of mind is to prefer order to liberty, to be suspicious of radical change and to prefer what is known from the past to what is unknown in the future. The New Right, in contrast, has been a radical movement; its adherents have been prepared to reject the past in favour of the pursuit of New Right doctrines.

The paradox of the New Right

The New Right has often been characterised as a synthesis between neo-liberalism and neo-conservatism. This gives rise to an apparently contradictory attitude towards the role of the state.

The neo-liberal aspect of the movement proposes the restoration of free markets, without interference from the state. This echoes the classical liberal era of the nineteenth century. Margaret Thatcher was content to describe herself as a classical liberal at heart and famously claimed that 'there is no such thing as society'. What she meant was that she viewed society as a collection of individuals, not as an organic whole. Taxation and welfare were to be reduced in order to create more individual incentives. The so-called 'nanny state' was blamed for sapping society of its dynamism, for reducing the economic freedom that was necessary for wealth creation and for granting excessive amounts of power to organised labour. As far back as 1968, Margaret Thatcher expressed distaste for the role of the state in a speech she gave to a Conservative Party conference:

What we need now is a far greater degree of personal responsibility and decision, far more independence from the government and a comparative reduction in the role of government.

All these ideas would have been at home in the middle of the nineteenth century, when free-market capitalism was at its height and at its least regulated. Friedrich Hayek and Milton Friedman, both members of the Chicago School of Economics, were the inspiration behind the restoration of classical liberal values. Both these philosophers argued that a lack of economic freedom would entail a loss of political freedom in general. In other words, the heavily regulated and partly government-controlled states run by socialist governments could never be described as 'free' because individuals were not free to pursue their own economic goals.

The main criticism faced by these neo-liberals was that the excessive amounts of freedom and the inequality it generated would threaten the unity of society. The New Right responded by developing a set of policies which became known as 'neo-conservatism'. Recognising that order in society might be threatened by an excess of freedom in the economic sphere, the New Right has emphasised personal morality. It has been relatively intolerant of lifestyles considered to be outside of the 'norm', such as homosexuality. Several attempts have been made (with little success, it has to be said) to return to basic values – for example, the nuclear family, traditional education methods and patriotism. This echoes the principle, dating back to Burke, that respect for traditions stabilises society.

The second strand of neo-conservatism concerns law and order. Again, more traditional methods have been supported, notably the use of prison sentences as a deterrent, a hard line on youth crime and extended powers for an expanded police force.

Conservatives have always accused those on the left of politics of lacking patriotism and paying too little attention to the UK's best interests. With European integration uppermost in their minds, members of the the New Right have stressed national sovereignty and the need to preserve the unity of the UK. They have opposed political integration in Europe and devolution on the grounds that they threaten to remove national sovereignty either upwards to Brussels or downwards to Scotland and Wales. The New Right sees the **nation-state** as the fundamental political community and will resist any threat to its independence.

Finally, the neo-conservative wing of modern conservatism has been concerned with the effects

> ### ✔ Key Term
>
> **Nation-state**
> This term combines the concepts of nation and state. The nation is considered the natural basis for any political community. It is seen, by both conservatives and many liberals, as the most significant binding force for a society since it comprises a people's common circumstances of birth and experience. The state is a political entity. It is the territory within which a single centre of sovereignty can be identified. When the nation is also a state, and the state is based on the identity of a nation, this is a nation-state – the most common form of political society.

of immigration and increasing cultural diversity. Again, diversity is seen as a threat to the unity of a community. The neo-conservative answer is to limit immigration and to insist that all sections of the community learn to conform to a common set of British values.

It should be noted that the British New Right's attitude to the European Union is itself something of a paradox. The movement's neo-liberalism leads it to support the idea of a completely free European market; free trade has always been a goal of economic liberals. On the other hand, the political integration of Europe threatens the integrity of the nation-state and so has been opposed.

Although the blending of neo-liberalism and neo-conservatism in the New Right emerged largely in the UK, it is also a feature of contemporary US conservatism. There, neo-conservative features are underpinned by a strong attachment to fundamentalist religious belief, especially Christianity. Indeed, much of the US style of religion is highly conservative in nature. This has led to a harder line on moral issues, especially abortion and homosexuality.

Table 2.1 summarises the neo-liberal and neo-conservative strands of the New Right.

Neo-liberalism	Neo-conservatism
UK ● Restoration of free labour, product and financial markets wherever possible ● Minimal role for the state in regulating commerce and industry ● Minimal state role in regulating the economy ● Taxation to be kept to a minimum, especially income and corporate taxes ● Belief that welfare is a disincentive to work and enterprise and therefore should be kept to a minimum ● Support for a free market in Europe **USA** As above, plus: ● Preference for power to be reserved for individual states, not federal government	**UK** ● Traditional position on morality and lifestyles ● Authoritarian stance on law-and-order issues ● Heavy emphasis on national self-interest and patriotism ● Opposition to excessive immigration and cultural diversity ● Opposition to European political integration **USA** As above, plus: ● Strong religious element to moral and social issues ● Insistence on protection for US industry from foreign competition

Table 2.1 Summary of the two strands of the New Right

Conservatism in the UK

The crisis of conservatism

In the UK, conservatism has endured a politically difficult period since 1992. To some extent, this is the result of the aftermath of Margaret Thatcher's fall from power in 1990, a blow from which the movement has not fully recovered. In particular, conservatives have been uncertain whether to carry the Thatcher reforms still further or to propose a period of consolidation. Her long political shadow continues to cause controversy. The Conservative Party itself has suffered from a combination of weak leadership, internal divisions and a loss of economic direction, while the wider conservative movement faces longer-term difficulties, which have become so marked that the situation may be described as a crisis.

As a philosophy, conservatism has invariably been a reaction against ideological tendencies that have threatened the order and unity of society and which have been based on apparently 'false' assumptions and principles. In the post-Thatcher era, however, it could be said that a political consensus has descended upon the UK (and indeed the rest of Western Europe). This consensus has been based upon the neo-liberal and neo-conservative principles described above. In some ways, therefore, it could be said that modern conservatism has become the victim of its own success. Its ideas have dominated the political culture to such an extent that conservatism has nothing to react against. At the same time, there are no new political movements threatening the existing order. New Labour and the contemporary Liberal Democrats in the UK may wish to change the emphasis of public policy, but they propose no radical reforms.

Conservatism has also suffered from the legacy of the 1980s – that of being seen as a movement that lacks compassion and which has failed to adjust to the changing social and cultural structure of the UK. Some critics have suggested that the movement has not been true to the traditional principles put forward by the likes of Michael Oakeshott and even Benjamin Disraeli – it has failed to consider the welfare of the whole country and has, instead, concentrated on the interests of one section of the community. There have been many who have benefited from the neo-liberal reforms of the Thatcher era – the business classes, property owners, middle-income families and the like – but there are also many who have suffered – for example, those who rely on welfare, lone parents, deprived ethnic minorities and alienated youths living in depressed regions of the country.

Despite these criticisms, conservatism has not come under serious attack from either the left or the right of British politics. Instead, its philosophy and policies have been absorbed by other political parties. The Conservative Party has tried to respond by supporting multiculturalism and inclusiveness, and by adopting a more compassionate approach to deprived sections of the community, but these causes have already been taken up by liberals and social democrats. They do not represent a distinctive position for conservatives.

The one political stance that does single out modern conservatives as radically different is their attitude to European integration. They have been hampered in this area by internal divisions, and many see their position of supporting a single, free European market while opposing any political integration as illogical, as we have seen above. However, Euroscepticism does resonate with the British people and has been a potential touchstone for a conservative revival. However, on this issue the Conservative Party has been effectively outflanked by the Labour Party. Labour has insisted that any future progress towards integration – mainly entry into the single currency and adoption of a European constitution – should be put to the British people in referendums, thereby taking the whole issue of Europe effectively out of the arena of party politics.

It may be that the UK Conservative Party and the wider conservative movement will suffer the same fate as liberalism did in the 60 years after the First World War. In that period, liberal principles were absorbed by the Conservative and Labour Parties, and liberalism, as a distinctive movement, was squeezed out of the political arena. The Liberal Party found itself in a political wilderness from which it did not emerge until the 1980s. The current Conservative Party is seeking to present itself as the best manager of the post-Thatcher consensus, but perhaps the days of the party being seen as the 'natural party of government' are over.

The impact of Thatcher

Margaret Thatcher became leader of the Conservative Party in 1975. She was a relatively little-known politician at the time, and in many ways a compromise candidate since the party could not agree on any of the more conventional candidates for the office. The party was taking a further chance since it was not clear at that time whether a woman was electable. It is often claimed that the party chose her as a short-term leader while it searched for someone more suitable to fight the 1979 election. Whatever the party's motives were in electing her, there were few clues to the ideological position she was to take up later. Having said that, her close association with Keith Joseph (see p. 59) should have been an indication that she was going to support neo-liberal policies.

She began her premiership cautiously. In this she had little choice, having inherited a front bench full of natural enemies and a country in the grip of economic recession. Over the next few years, however, she replaced most of her opponents with allies and, at the same time, the economy began to recover. She ruffled feathers by insisting that her government would not attempt to 'spend its way out of the recession' – that is, borrow large amounts of money to subsidise failing industries and create jobs artificially. Her neo-liberal instincts, reinforced by Joseph's economic philosophy, told her that if government held on and refused to intervene, the economy would naturally pick up. Traditional conservatives, who were associated with the Keynesian idea that aggressive economic action by government was needed to cure recession, found themselves marginalised and many left the government. The first impact of Thatcher, therefore, was that in times of economic difficulty, governments should do less, not more. This policy was described as *laissez-faire*.

Buoyed up by the success of her economic policies, Thatcher turned to the issue of trade union power. Again, traditionalists warned her against confrontation. They saw the unions as an entrenched and vital part of the economic structure. Attacking them was seen as a radical and dangerous undertaking. But Thatcher once more won her battle with the doubters and embarked on a series of measures to reduce the legal and economic power of the unions. This was the beginning of a series of actions against British institutions. She later turned her attention to the civil service, local government and the financial institutions of the City, reducing their influence and subjecting them to competitive forces. Once again, we can see how her radicalism enabled her to challenge established traditions and the institutions that underpinned them.

The privatisation of major industries was part of her general commitment to 'rolling back the frontiers of the state'. This marked the end of the type of conservatism, dating back to Harold Macmillan (1894–1986) in the 1950s, which accepted the state as a vehicle for providing stability and serving the interests of the community as a whole. The conservative support for the welfare state itself was also shaken under Thatcher. While she preserved the state health and education systems, her governments reduced the size and scope of social security benefits and the old age pension.

Thus, the traditional conservative tendency to paternalism was eroded. The Disraelian view that it was the duty of conservatives to care for the welfare of the people was being replaced by an insistence that individuals should be responsible for their own welfare. Thatcher's attack on the dependency culture flew directly in the face of the traditional Tory sense of social responsibility and its vision of the organic society. For Thatcher, society was made up of self-interested individuals and it was the role of government to provide the conditions where such an individualist community could flourish.

We can see that the impact of Thatcherism and the New Right was considerable and the challenges it posed to traditional conservatism were numerous. These included:

- Society is made up of free individuals; it is not organic.
- Excessive interference by the state is counterproductive, holds back economic progress and inhibits the development of a sense of self-responsibility.
- Traditional institutions may be challenged if they can be shown to be holding back progress.
- Conservative paternalism denies the individual spirit of enterprise and self-responsibility, and so should be curbed.
- Individuals prefer to be granted freedom rather than rely upon the support of the state.
- Radical government can improve society and does not necessarily create unexpected consequences.
- A slavish attachment to traditional modes of thinking prevents original solutions to society's problems.

Conservatism and liberalism

Individualism

What is the difference between the liberal conception of freedom and the conservative notion of individualism? On a simple level, liberal freedom is essentially negative: it proposes a society where there is a minimum of restrictions on the actions of individuals. Conservative individualism, on the other hand, is more akin to positive liberty. It entails the provision of opportunities and choices for individuals and families and the ability of people to achieve their own goals without hindrance. The difference, however, may be more complex in reality.

Individualism is perhaps best viewed as a reaction against collectivism. It is based on the belief that people prefer to achieve their goals individually and not collectively, as socialists insist. Conservatives therefore argue that they have a duty to create the conditions in which such individualism can flourish. This involves economic certainty and stability, low levels of taxation, the protection of private property, low crime rates and a secure international environment. The state has a duty to produce these conditions, but its role should end there. It should not interfere in people's lives directly.

Liberals who promote freedom are also suspicious of state interference, but they concentrate on the need for individuals to enjoy their private lives and to have their rights protected. This kind of free society can, in theory, flourish even in a situation where collectivism is a common method of achieving social goals. This means that, for liberals, there need be no contradiction between a welfare state and a free society. Put another way, freedom requires that the state should guarantee its people's liberties, whereas individualism requires that the state create a stable environment in which people can pursue their own goals. Individualism opposes the idea that the state can achieve goals that individuals could achieve for themselves. Liberals believe freedom need not be compromised by state involvement in society.

One final observation can help to distinguish between the two concepts. A conservative will accept that the state might be justified in curtailing some freedom in society if it can promote individualism by doing so. For example, it may be necessary to reduce the scope of civil liberties in the interests of crime reduction, perhaps by granting extensive powers to the police. Reducing crime in this way might encourage people to feel more secure to enjoy their property and to engage in new economic ventures. Similarly, by removing some of the legal rights and freedoms of workers, entrepreneurs may feel encouraged to employ more labour and so create more wealth to the benefit of all.

Liberal freedom and conservative individualism

At first, these terms seem to be almost identical. Both liberals and conservatives extol the virtues of a free society and tend to be suspicious of the role of the state. However, the concepts do have distinct meanings.

For a liberal, freedom mainly means the absence of restriction. We are free if nobody controls our ability to say what we like, go where we wish and worship whatever gods we may choose. We are also free if the state does not restrict our ability to engage in economic enterprise and does not place too many regulations on our activities.

Individualism is more closely associated with conservatism. The term refers to the ability of the individual to be able to pursue his or her own happiness, to make free choices and to be presented with a wide range of opportunities. It implies too that we will be secure enough to enjoy whatever wealth and property we may possess. Individualism in this sense could only flourish in a society in which each person is free to pursue his or her own goals and is not forced to accept the collective goals of a society. It is therefore associated with free enterprise, the encouragement of the private sector, low taxation, a favourable environment for property owners and minimal regulation of business activities. To secure such freedom necessitates a heavy emphasis on national defence, law and order and property rights.

The main conflict between the two concepts lies in the contrast between the liberal belief that the individual will flourish most successfully in a free society, whereas conservatives typically believe that the individual most needs a secure society. Nevertheless, both philosophies agree that the state should be organised to promote the interests of individuals and individual self-fulfilment; it is about the means to achieve these ends that they disagree.

Property and rights

It is perhaps in their attitudes to private property that conservatives and liberals agree to the greatest extent. When we consider the more general field of rights, however, there are critical points of difference.

The right to private property is one of the original beliefs of liberalism. Figures such as John Locke, Thomas Jefferson and Thomas Paine all saw the possession and enjoyment of property as a basic human right. They believed that the possession of property and wealth is the natural outcome of an individual's pursuit of his or her own interests. This has always remained a liberal aspiration. Liberals are not collectivist by nature and see private property as one of the most important aspects of the individual's fulfilled life.

Conservatism, too, has always been committed to property rights, but for different reasons. For conservatives, property ownership promotes social stability. Those who own property will have a stronger sense of responsibility and will have a vested interest in the preservation of order. It follows from this that all conservatives see the protection of property, both from criminal behaviour and from encroachments by government, as a priority of the state.

The preservation of rights and the guarantee of legal and political equality are fundamental liberal principles. There are very few circumstances in which liberals will accept any compromise in their defence of rights. Conservatives, too, accept that rights are worthy of protection, especially in modern constitutional democracies. There are, however, circumstances in which a conservative would abandon this commitment. Conservatives insist that the community as a whole has rights, not just individuals. There will be occasions when the rights of individuals conflict with the rights of the community. When this happens, the conservative tendency is to consider the community first.

This is most clearly seen in the field of crime. While suspected criminals may expect rights to protect them from injustice, the community also has a right to be protected from criminals. In practice, this might mean that conservatives would support the right of property owners to protect their property over and above the criminal's right to be protected from injury. The clearest example of the conflict between conservative and liberal views concerns the issue of terrorism. While liberals say our rights cannot be sacrificed even in the interests of anti-terrorism measures, conservatives argue that we must be prepared to sacrifice some individual rights in the interests of our security. In short, this means that conservatives revere property and community rights, but their commitment to the rights of individuals remains relatively fragile.

Is the Thatcherite era over?

The financial and economic crisis that emerged after 2007 put into focus the conflict between the neo-liberal ideas of the Thatcherite New Right and the emerging social, liberal form of conservatism, which had been introduced in Britain by David Cameron – in particular the apparent failure of 'laissez-faire' policies and the 'moral crisis' that was identified when it became clear that the quest for ever-greater wealth had not been built on solid ground and had resulted in unacceptable excesses. President Obama's election in the US was a further symptom of this crisis.

The main criticisms of the New Right which appeared after 2007 included the following:

- *Laissez-faire* policies resulted in excessive levels of borrowing and conspicious spending that could not be sustained. Lack of regulation, especially of the financial system, had created a bubble of wealth that was bound to burst. Irresponsible behaviour by unregulated financial institutions led to an inevitable economic recession as the system of credit creation collapsed in 2007–08.

- Despite the growing prosperity from the mid-1990s onwards, there remained a persistent 'underclass' of individuals and families who were excluded from this wealth and lacked the opportunities and means to improve their situation. This underclass was characterised by poor educational attainment, persistent poverty and unemployment, high crime levels and a variety of other social problems. The neo-liberal state that had been created seemed to pay little attention to these groups.

- Lack of support from the New Right for the welfare state and other public services (in the interests of low taxation and sound public finance) had left a legacy of deprivation and poor public services.

- Many argued that the highly individualistic, acquisitive society that had been created lacked a sense of morality and community. This too had led to a growth of social problems, especially among the young who grew up in deprived families.

A consistent theme of conservatism, stretching back to the time of Disraeli around 1870, is that those who enjoy prosperity have an obligation to help the less fortunate (known formerly as *noblesse oblige*). Traditional conservatives also see society as organic and so lamented the loss of sense of community from the 1980s onwards. They also stress the need for good order and security. The highly individualistic policies of the New Right had clearly threatened such order. The lack of morality in economic life seemed to have leeked into social life in general. Margaret Thatcher's well-known assertion that 'there is no such thing as society, there are individuals and families' came back to haunt the British Conservative Party, which went on to lose general elections in 1997, 2001 and 2005. The emergence of Cameron's more social and liberal form of conservatism was the result, as we have seen above.

Neverthless, British conservatives do retain some Thatcherite instincts. There is still a resistence to over-government and excessive regulation; conservatives remain opposed to high personal and corporate taxation; they also see social disorder as largely the responsibility of individuals rather than the circumstances of those individuals. Conservatives also understand where their main support lies – it is among property owners, small business owners and the wealthy. These were the groups to whom Margaret Thatcher and her supporters appealed. The British Conservative Party is, therefore, reluctant to abandon its traditional constituency.

Exam focus

Using this chapter and other resources available to you, answer the following questions.

Short questions

Your answers should be about 400 words long.
1 What is a typical conservative attitude to human nature?
2 Why do conservatives emphasise property rights?
3 What do conservatives mean by individualism?
4 Why do conservatives support tradition?
5 What is meant by the term neo-liberalism?
6 What is one-nation conservatism?
7 Why do conservatives oppose ideology?

Long questions

Your answers should be about 1200 words long.
1 'Conservatism is more a state of mind than an ideology.' Discuss.
2 To what extent have conservatives preferred pragmatism and empiricism to political principles?
3 Is conservatism a coherent philosophy?
4 To what extent has the British Conservative Party abandoned the Thatcherite legacy?

Further reading

Burke, E. (1999) *Reflections on the Revolution in France*, Oxford University Press.
Gray, J. and Willetts, D. (1997) *Is Conservatism Dead?*, Profile Books.
Green, D. (1987) *The New Right*, Prentice Hall/Harvester Wheatsheaf.
Honderich, T. (2005) *Conservatism*, Pluto Press.
O'Sullivan, N. (1976) *Conservatism*, Everyman.
Scruton, R. (2001) *The Meaning of Conservatism*, Macmillan.

Chapter 3

Socialism

Socialism is a political movement, or collection of movements, which advances a number of criticisms of society, particularly the type of society that emerged with the onset of industrialisation and free-market capitalism from the latter part of the eighteenth century onwards. Socialism proposes that humans are naturally sociable, prefer to achieve goals collectively rather than individually and are content to cooperate with others to serve the common good. It also asserts that people are fundamentally of equal worth and should therefore have equal rights and equal opportunities. Extreme examples of socialism argue for total economic and social equality and common ownership of all means of production. More moderate forms of socialism accept less than full equality, replacing it with various ideas of social justice and partial common ownership of property. Modern socialists have accepted a variety of compromises between the pursuit of individual goals and the collective provision of welfare.

Introduction

It is worth beginning a review of this wide-ranging ideology with the words of Jean-Jacques Rousseau, written in 1755:

> *The first man who, having enclosed a piece of ground, bethought himself of saying 'This is Mine', and found people simple enough to believe him, was the real founder of civil society. From how many crimes, wars and murders, from how many horrors and misfortunes might not any one have saved mankind, by pulling up the stakes, or filling up the ditch, and crying to his fellows: 'Beware of listening to this impostor; you are undone if you once forget that the fruits of the earth belong to us all, and the earth itself to nobody.*

From *A Discourse on the Origin of Inequality*

Jean-Jacques Rousseau was an early critic of private property

This is a useful point of departure for a number of reasons. First, and perhaps most importantly, it pre-dates the onset of the Industrial Revolution and the advanced form of capitalism that resulted from it. It has often been argued that socialism should be seen as a reaction to capitalism, but it is clear from this passage that, at least on a philosophical level, a critique of private property and inequality already existed.

Second, it highlights one of the basic assumptions of all socialists: that private property is not natural but a result of the pursuit of self-interest. Third, as Rousseau so colourfully asserts, many of the evils of modern society arise out of property and inequality. It follows that the replacement of private property by common ownership – the natural state of affairs – would alleviate most or all of these problems.

There is no doubt, however, that socialism as a political movement, rather than a collection of philosophical ideas, gained most of its momentum when it became clear that free-market capitalism was creating misery among the poorer elements of society. Furthermore, the gap between rich and poor grew alarmingly during the nineteenth century.

Early socialist ideas

Social anthropologists have discovered in various parts of the world economically primitive tribal societies that practise common ownership and egalitarianism, and there are many examples of small-scale experiments in socialism in Europe's history.

The English Levellers (also known as 'Diggers') mounted one of the first attempts at organised socialism. During the Civil War of the 1640s they flourished within the republican movement and were influential in the army of Oliver Cromwell (1599–1658). They set up a self-governing community, working land collectively and sharing out its produce on an equal basis. This was ridiculed by many, and they were suppressed by Cromwell when it became apparent that they were becoming a dangerous force.

Their leader, Gerrard Winstanley (1609–76), based his ideas on a simple principle – that God had given the world and its fruits to all humankind, but that individuals had exercised greed in order to take as many of those fruits as possible at the expense of others. He described the position thus:

And so, from the thief upon the highway to the king who sits upon the throne, do not everyone strive, either by force of arms or secret cheats, to get the possessions of the earth one from another, because they see their freedom lies in plenty, and their bondage lies in poverty.

From *The Law of Freedom*, 1652

In this passage, Winstanley unwittingly foresaw the battle that was to come between liberal supporters of free-market capitalism and socialism. The advocates of capitalism argued that the pursuit of self-interest was the true nature of freedom. Winstanley agreed that this might be thought to be freedom, but it was not true freedom. For him, true freedom consisted of the pursuit of the common good and general equality.

Some rudimentary ideas about economic equality emerged during the French Revolution. The revolution was inspired by a desire to create equal rights, yet only a few saw equality as an economic and social ideal. The radical Gracchus Babeuf (1760–97) produced a pamphlet entitled the *Manifesto of the Equals*, which attracted the attention of the authorities. Apart from being extremely dangerous for the bourgeois class who had gained power in France, Babeuf's call for economic equality and common ownership of all property was simply too radical to be taken seriously at the time.

A similar fate awaited the radical ideas of the French utopian socialist Charles Fourier (1772–1837). The philosophy behind Fourier's scheme was similar to the kibbutz movement in Israel. He advocated setting up independent communities of nearly 2,000 people, in which all production would be undertaken on a communal basis. (Fourier resisted mass production, insisting that labour should be creative and based on craft skills.) Goods would be shared on an equal basis and all decisions would be made collectively. Had he not also argued for the abolition of marriage and the traditional family, proposing free love instead, his ideas might have been taken more seriously. Fourier was an early influence on all socialists and anarchists, to the extent that Karl Marx (1818–83) and other scientific socialists reserved a good deal of their writings for criticising this kind of idealistic socialism.

The nearest British equivalent to Fourier was Robert Owen (1771–1858), who attempted to set up similar communities in America (but without the free-love element!). Owen took the early principles of socialism a stage further by exploring the nature of human character. Like many anarchists, he believed that human nature could be moulded by society and that nothing was fixed. It appeared logical, therefore, that if a perfect socialist community could be set up on strict principles of equality and community spirit, its people and their descendants would adopt these values as their own, quite naturally.

Key Term

Utopianism

This is generally used as a critical term and has been applied to a number of political movements, including early socialism. The charge of utopianism usually implies that an ideology is not based on rational thought or scientific truths, but on hopes and aspirations alone. It also implies that the goals of such movements are unrealistic and cannot be achieved or sustained. Furthermore, many claim that utopians, such as socialists and anarchists, present their beliefs as rational and scientific but are in fact deceiving themselves and their followers.

Owen and Fourier were both described as utopian in that their schemes were not based on any scientific study of society and economics, and the social and economic systems they proposed were impractical. The true reasons why the utopian socialists were unsuccessful were probably threefold:

- They pre-dated the full development of capitalism. Instead of being a reaction to free-market capitalism, utopian socialism represented an alternative to the early growth of capitalism. In a contest between the dynamic new economic order and idealistic small-community socialism, capitalism was bound to win.

- The social evils of capitalism had not become apparent in the early part of the nineteenth century, which was when the utopian socialists were prominent. It was certainly true that agricultural and craft workers were being forced into factories and mines, but it was not yet clear how much social conflict this would create.

- The utopian socialists, including the later English socialist designer and craftsman William Morris (1834–96), were concerned by the onset of mass production, fearing it would drain working people of their creative instincts. They were, therefore, reactionaries, seeking to hold back the progress of industrialisation. This may have seemed a romantic ideal, but set against the unstoppable force of mass-production capitalism, which could produce cheap goods and provide large-scale employment, it was unlikely to gain many supporters – and in the event it never did.

Socialist reactions to capitalism

Socialism as an influential political movement can best be seen as a reaction to growing unrest over the course that free-market capitalism was taking. The most important reaction was undoubtedly that of Karl Marx, which is described fully later in this chapter. Many other socialist movements were spawned as a direct result of the problems created by free-market capitalism. The nature of these problems provides a useful summary of nineteenth-century socialist issues:

Box 3.1 Key socialist criticisms of nineteenth-century capitalism

- The increasing division and specialisation of labour was creating an army of unskilled workers. Traditional skills were therefore in decline. There was also a marked fall in the number of independent peasants as agriculture became increasingly mechanised.

● Wages paid to the growing unskilled labour force were persistently low.

● Although capitalism was clearly creating great wealth, this was not being shared by the workers. The gap between rich and poor was steadily widening.

● When workers attempted to organise themselves to improve wages and/or working conditions, governments and employers refused to recognise their unions, and even outlawed them. Ruthless methods were used to break strikes.

● There were frequent slumps resulting in unemployment and falling wages.

● With the spread of urbanisation the living conditions of the working class became increasingly squalid. Bad housing, poor health and lack of education were particular problems.

Socialists fell into three main categories with regard to these issues:

1 Scientific socialists, of whom Marx was the most prominent, believed that it was in the nature of capitalism to exploit labour and create inequality. They argued that the problems were insoluble and that capitalism would have to be abolished, to be replaced by a compulsory and exclusively socialist society. This group was typically revolutionary in its methods, believing that the capitalist state would not relinquish its power through peaceful means.

2 Democratic, state socialists saw granting democratic rights to the working class as the answer. If workers could vote and gain office through socialist parties, the worker-dominated state could modify capitalism radically to alleviate the problems described in Box 3.1. This could be achieved by a combination of state control of industry, strong trade union rights and regulation of private enterprises.

3 A further category comprised a collection of socialist movements, which can be described loosely as 'cooperative'. These socialists proposed that the means of production – factories, land, mines, commerce and banking – should be brought directly under the control of workers and peasants, who would run them themselves, in their own interests, and would therefore create economic equality among themselves. The syndicalists, who proposed trade union control of all industry, were the most radical of this group of socialists.

Key Term

Scientism
This term can be applied to a number of political ideologies that claim to be based upon scientific conclusions drawn from an objective and empirical study of history and society. In some ways, scientism stands as an opposite to utopianism. Many socialists – Marxists being a primary example – claim to be scientific in their beliefs and conclusions. They suggest that by understanding the fundamental nature of humankind, the meaning of historical change and the nature of contemporary society (especially capitalism), they can draw scientific conclusions about how society should be changed and ordered. Such thinkers claim that, because they use scientific methodology, their idealised society would be in accordance with natural circumstances and natural justice.

Social class under capitalism

For virtually all nineteenth-century socialists, the defining characteristic of capitalist society was its class structure. They saw class conflict as capitalism's main weakness and the ultimate cause of its demise. Marxist theory is the most important example of a class analysis of capitalism; indeed, for Marxists class conflict was the only significant aspect of capitalism.

The most radical socialists believed that the divergent interests of the working class and the bourgeois or entrepreneurial class could not be reconciled within capitalism. For them, capitalism depended upon the exploitation of one class by another. Class conflict could therefore be resolved only by the victory of the working class and the introduction of a working-class state. There were many more moderate socialists who believed that the way forward lay in striking a better balance of economic power between the working class and the bourgeoisie. These socialists therefore campaigned initially for trade union rights, legislation to improve working conditions, enfranchisement for all adults and a state system of welfare and industrial regulation. The British Chartist movement of the 1830s and 1840s, for example, had these relatively limited aims.

The British socialist movement was especially moderate in its class outlook. Represented largely by the Labour Party, it suggested that the interests of the working class and the capitalist class could be reconciled within a democratic political system. Elsewhere in Europe, socialist parties were more radical and campaigned for a more permanent arrangement to protect the interests of the working class, especially state control of major industries and extensive rights for trade unions.

As the twentieth century progressed, however, the class divide began to abate. Growing affluence among the working classes and the establishment of effective welfare systems rendered the idea of

Key Term

Fraternity
A term, literally referring to 'brotherhood', commonly used in socialism and suggesting that members of the working class have a common bond that is as strong as a family link. Thus, all members of the working class are, effectively, brothers.

Key Term

Social class
At its basic level, social class is a way of dividing society into economic and social groups. It has been used by historians, social theorists and political ideologues as a means of analysing society. The most important class analysis has come from socialists, especially Marxists. They believe that class distinctions are based on specific economic circumstances (e.g. whether one is a wage earner, capitalist, landlord, tenant, etc.) and that they determine the character of society. For socialists, class conflict is the most basic problem of modern societies and needs to be resolved. Other political movements, including moderate socialists, have accepted that class divisions and conflicts are important, but hold that they are not necessarily crucial. Most contemporary social theorists argue that social class is declining in importance as a defining feature of society.

class conflict an apparent anachronism. Many socialists accepted this reality and introduced both pluralism and individualism as core values of the movement. Others remained militant, with communist parties continuing to wield influence into the 1970s. But these radical groups became increasingly marginalised, and social theorists insisted that class divisions were decreasing in importance. Socialism was therefore forced to transform itself into a different movement altogether. At this stage, terms such as 'democratic socialism' and 'social democracy' began to be used instead of socialism to describe political movements on the left of Western politics.

Inequality

Socialism was not only a reaction to the growth of capitalism itself; it was also a response to the increasing levels of inequality emerging under capitalism. Different strands of the socialist movement can therefore be defined not only in their reaction to capitalism and class conflict but also in their proposals to achieve social and economic equality.

Marxists and revolutionary socialists were unequivocal in their attitude to equality. For them, all humans were of equal worth and equally deserving of the rewards of their labour, both physical and mental. Less radical socialists, while abhorring inequality, recognised that our varying abilities and contributions to society might be recognised by differentials in rewards. Some, indeed, recognised the need for incentives to promote efficiency and effort.

Modern moderate socialism has gone a stage further than this. Social democrats accept that inequality is natural. They seek to ameliorate the effects of such inequality mainly in two ways. The first is to ensure that there is equality of opportunity – that all individuals are granted an equal chance to make the most of their abilities. The second is to examine the nature of inequality, judging what can be justified and what cannot. Put another way, these moderates have replaced the pursuit of equality, with the concept of distributive justice. This principle is discussed further on p. 78.

Core values of socialism

Equality

Although equality is seen as the central principle of socialism, it is not a simple issue and has created conflict both between socialists and adherents to other ideologies and within the socialist movement itself.

It is worth beginning with those aspects of equality upon which all socialists, or the vast majority of them, can agree. First, all socialists believe that we are all born with equal rights. Socialists share this belief with liberals. It suggests that we are created equal in terms of our right to both justice and access to power. Second, all socialists reject the idea that society has any kind of natural order. Instead, every individual has the potential to take up any position in society to which he or she may aspire. Third, all socialists believe in equality of opportunity. However unequal people may prove to be, all are entitled to the same life chances.

None of this is particularly contentious, which is why there is unity over these principles among socialists. When we look more deeply, however, fragmentation appears within the movement. Perhaps the issue over which there is most controversy is the extent to which absolute equality should be pursued. This principle is relatively simple – the resources of a society should be distributed equally throughout the community. Whatever contribution is made by an individual, he or she is entitled to an equal share of the rewards. Clearly this presents a number of problems. It eliminates the conventional incentives upon which a modern economy is said to rely and does not acknowledge the variety of contributions that each person makes. It can even be seen as fundamentally unjust, even though many socialists see it as the ultimate expression of social justice.

This problem with equality arises from two differing views of the nature of humankind. Some socialists believe we are all born with equal potential. In other words, we all have the potential to become equal. Others acknowledge that inequality is inevitable, that we have different abilities and potentialities, and that these should be recognised by differential rewards. One way to solve this conflict is to distribute property equally so that each individual has the same opportunity to make what they can of that property. However, although this is feasible in peasant-based societies, it does not appear to be practical in modern industrial society. A further solution could be described as 'equal access to welfare'. This accepts that rewards will be unequal, but asserts that certain basic services and a minimum quality of life should be available for all. In other words, there will be a standard of living below which nobody will be allowed to fall.

Kinds of equality supported by socialists

These include the following:

- **Equal rights** We are all entitled, as a right of birth, to be treated equally by the state and to exercise all our rights as equal citizens.

- **Equality of opportunity** We are all entitled to equal chances to make the best of our abilities. Positive steps should be taken to ensure equal opportunities. There should be no artificial barriers to the progress of any individual or group.

- **Equality of outcome** This is a principle held by more fundamentalist socialists. It proposes that rewards should be based on the value of each person's contribution. This will inevitably mean some inequality, as contributions are bound to vary in terms of both quality and quantity. It also implies that the differences in rewards will not be as considerable as they are in a free-market system.

- **Absolute equality** This is more extreme than equality of outcome. It suggests that all individuals will receive the same rewards, as long as they make a contribution that is to the best of their ability. It is the ultimate goal of Marxist communists and anarchists, but it is assumed that each individual will come to make a broadly equal contribution. Opponents see this as unreasonable utopianism.

- **Equality of welfare** This sees human society as inevitably unequal but argues that everyone should be entitled to an equal minimum standard of living, which can be ensured by the provision of state welfare.

Class conflict

All but the more moderate socialists see social class as a crucial aspect of society. It has been assumed by socialists that most people define their position in society in terms of their social class. This implies that they develop a sense of common interests and common purpose with other members of their class. Marx described this effect as 'class consciousness', but most socialists use the more moderate expression 'common class interest'. Thus, for example, the middle classes feel they have a strong common need to protect private property interests, to promote and protect business and to keep taxes as low as is reasonably possible. The working classes, meanwhile, are more concerned with welfare issues, sympathetic

industrial relations, fair wages, good working conditions and policies that promote greater equality. These two sets of interests conflict with each other. Low taxation combined with high welfare expenditure is not feasible. The business classes normally oppose higher wages since this conflicts with the need to make profits and generate funds for further investment.

Socialist solutions to class conflict

Different strands of socialism produced a variety of responses to growing class conflict in the nineteenth and twentieth centuries. These included the following:

- **Revolutionary socialists**, including Marxists, have argued that the conflict of interests simply cannot be resolved within the context of capitalism. Indeed, they argue that capitalism creates the conflict and that it will intensify as capitalism develops. The answer, therefore, has to be the destruction of capitalism itself and its replacement by a socialist order that will eliminate class conflict altogether.

- **Non-revolutionary socialists**, such as state socialists, have simply sought to form governments that will operate largely in the interests of the working class. Such a working-class state might abolish or dramatically modify capitalism and would certainly introduce a high degree of economic and social equality. The most common form of socialist system that has been promoted by such socialists is one in which most production and distribution are organised by a central state.

- **Democratic socialists** have also sought to modify capitalism, but have stopped short of creating a working-class state. They have instead introduced extensive controls over capitalism, some state intervention in industry and commerce and high levels of state-sponsored welfare provision. The postwar Labour government (1945–51) in the UK and the modern Swedish state provide examples of how democratic socialism can work. Class conflict is suppressed as the state is seen as a relatively neutral arbiter between conflicting class interests.

- **Social democracy**, the dominant form of socialism in Europe since the 1980s, downplays the importance of class. Indeed, many social democrats effectively ignore class as a social or economic phenomenon. The state, therefore, can simply work in the broad national interest, seeking a consensus that is not based on class at all. The apparent fragmentation of the class system and an increase in general affluence have contributed to a decline in the importance of perceptions of class conflict.

In many ways, therefore, changing attitudes to class and class conflict have defined the ways in which socialism has evolved from its predominantly revolutionary character in the nineteenth century to the moderate forms that have proliferated and are now current throughout the developed world. Many commentators, mostly on the left of politics, have suggested that movements that no longer analyse society in terms of class interest should not be described as socialist. New Labour in the UK would certainly fall into this category.

Social justice

Social justice is a difficult concept, not least because it is claimed as a virtue by most mainstream political movements, from Marxism through to contemporary neo-liberalism. The issue to concentrate on here is what meaning the term has for a typical socialist.

This can be simplified if we reduce our discussion to the issue of how the rewards which the economy generates (effectively the national output) should be distributed. Two further questions arise from this.

First, there is the question of what method should be used to distribute the rewards. Marxists and other revolutionary socialists insist that capitalism can never produce a just distribution. They argue that this is because the system contains inequality within its own mechanism. If we attempt to retain capitalism but remove inequality from it, capitalism as a system simply will not work. Capitalism, they assert, relies upon incentives and inequality for its dynamic nature. Therefore, capitalism must be abolished. In its place, some form of rational distribution of rewards should be organised by the state.

More moderate socialists have suggested that social justice can be achieved under capitalism, although different degrees of modification have been proposed by different branches of socialism. Essentially, these proposals have concentrated upon measures such as interference with the wage system to create less inequality (for example, minimum wage legislation), granting significant trade union rights to allow workers to negotiate for more justice, the use of taxation and welfare to redistribute wealth and income from the rich to the poor, and the traditional theme of equality of opportunity. Distribution of rewards is therefore fundamentally determined by the market forces of capitalism, but with the state intervening to a greater or lesser extent to promote social justice.

Second, there is the question of what constitutes a just distribution. Perhaps the best-known formula for a just distribution was provided by Karl Marx:

When labour is no longer just a means of keeping alive but has itself become a vital need; when the all-round development of individuals has also increased their productive powers and all the springs of cooperative wealth flow more abundantly – only then can society wholly cross the narrow horizon of bourgeois right and inscribe on its banner: **from each according to his abilities, to each according to his needs.**

From *Critique of the Gotha Programme*, 1875

There are a number of problems with this apparently simple idea. Marxism itself, of course, has now been discredited. Marx himself also admitted – in the quotation above – that such equality requires 'abundant wealth' and the elimination of scarcity. Many argue that scarcity will never be eliminated, so society will always have to accept some forms of competition for scarce resources. Furthermore, the principle of absolute equality of rewards has been seen as hopelessly utopian and ignores the basic human drive to progress by accumulating more income and wealth.

Most socialists have been forced to find more complex formulae for distributing wealth. Under a state socialist system, it is possible to organise affairs so that each receives rewards according to the value of his or her contribution. This creates some incentives and seems to be naturally just. The problem with this, however, is that it still entails the destruction of free-market capitalism and its replacement by a system of distribution that is bound to be subjective and open to dispute.

Those more moderate socialists who have reached an accommodation with capitalism have had an even more difficult task in defining social justice. They have sought to achieve what has become known as **distributive justice** and have had to face the issue of how much inequality can be tolerated.

Key Term

Distributive justice
This term refers to any conception of justice that seeks to establish a fair and just principle for how rewards should be distributed within a society. It is mainly associated with modern social democracy and especially the US philosopher John Rawls.

Perhaps the simplest conception has been provided by welfare socialists. They seek to establish a minimum standard of living, below which nobody should be allowed to fall. This almost certainly involves considerable redistribution of income from rich to poor through taxation and welfare. Above this base level, there will be inequality within market capitalism. However, as long as workers have strong trade unions and legal protections and there is equality of opportunity, mainly involving education and training, the outcome of capitalism

can be seen as 'just'. The Labour government that came to power in Britain in 1945 and produced the welfare state was based upon these principles.

More recently, social democratic forms of socialism have come to regard inequality as inevitable. They have agreed that there must be a minimum standard of living for all, but that modern society must tolerate considerable incentives in order to ensure dynamic wealth creation. Although the philosopher John Rawls is chiefly associated with liberalism, he did provide a formula of social justice for these moderate socialists that has become widely acceptable:

I shall now state in a provisional form the two principles of justice:

First: each person is to have an equal right to the most extensive basic liberty compatible with a similar liberty for all.

Second: social and economic inequalities are to be arranged so that they are (a) both reasonably expected to be to everyone's advantage, and (b) attached to positions and offices open to all.

From A *Theory of Justice*, 1972

Put another way, Rawls is saying that inequalities are natural and somewhat desirable, but that they must be justified by existing within a just society. For him, a just society provides freedom, equality of opportunity, no barriers to individual advancement and, above all, prevents anybody enriching themselves at the expense of the poorest members of society.

Summarising the socialist attitude to social justice is a difficult task because the concept has evolved so much since its earliest origins. We can, however, make one key generalisation. This is that all socialists, however extreme or moderate, believe that the outcome of a completely free-market system of capitalism cannot be just. They therefore propose some form of intervention to create more just outcomes.

Equality of opportunity

Closely allied to social justice is equality of opportunity. This has already been described as a principle in Chapter 1 on liberalism (pp. 9–10). The difference between a liberal and a socialist attitude is subtle and not extensive, but there are some differences in emphasis.

Before examining the principle within modern socialism, it should be stressed that revolutionary and state socialists have a specific idea of equality of opportunity. For them, equality and equality of opportunity are essentially the same thing. Once a socially just society is established, with the equal distribution of rewards and common ownership of industry, land and so on, all its members will automatically be equal and have equal access to what society offers. Those who accept the maintenance of capitalism in some form, however, do not see equality and equality of opportunity as coterminous.

First, all socialists tend to emphasise the belief that people who live in deprived circumstances do not have equal opportunities. This is not merely a question of education. Socialists believe that there is generalised discrimination against those who come from poorer backgrounds. If living standards can be raised for all, there will also be more opportunities for all.

Second, socialists believe that there are social forces that operate against the interests of some sections of society. In the fields of higher education, the professions, government and business in general, there remains a certain degree of class-based bias, which discriminates in subtle ways against those who come from less-privileged backgrounds. Equality of opportunity therefore demands that such institutions must make themselves open to a wider social spectrum. Members of the middle classes still seem to have advantages in a number of walks of life, especially in university education. Socialists seek to break this cycle of discrimination, either by **positive discrimination** or by introducing laws and codes of practice that outlaw social discrimination.

Third, modern social democrats, along with liberals, have sought to open up opportunities for a wider section of the community to become involved in business and so secure for themselves a greater share of society's wealth.

 Key Term

Positive discrimination
Known as 'affirmative action' in the USA, this term arises from the belief that some sections of society, mainly women and members of ethnic minorities, suffer systematic discrimination. This applies mostly to employment, but also to education and government. In order to counter this apparently unfair treatment, many propose positive discrimination. This gives a positive advantage to such groups in the form of minimum quotas that must be met when people are being recruited or promoted in an organisation. This counterbalances the suspected discrimination and so recreates equality of opportunity. Critics argue that positive discrimination is in itself unfair, as it discriminates against the majority. There are also fears that people who are not suitable will advance simply because they are members of one of the favoured groups.

Collectivism

The term 'collectivism' refers to two main ideas. The first is that people usually prefer to achieve goals collectively rather than independently. The second, and more fundamental, is that action taken by people in organised groups is likely to be more effective than the sum of many individual actions. These ideas stem from the socialist view of human nature, which is that man is a social animal who prefers to live in social groups than alone.

Of course, the degree to which society should be organised on the basis of collectivism varies between different branches of socialism. Marxists and state socialists have proposed that a centralised state should be the vehicle for collective action, organising all or most production and distribution. Socialists who accept some degree of free-market capitalism have promoted collectivism alongside individualism.

Socialist collectivism became the norm for socialists throughout Europe after the Second World War. The collectivist arrangements introduced even came to be accepted by non-socialist governments, albeit reluctantly. Since the 1980s, however, the focus of socialism, and the political consensus in general, has moved away from collectivist ideas. They became discredited in economically developed countries since they appeared to be holding back economic progress, stifling individual enterprise and suppressing individual instincts. As collectivism drifted out of favour, most socialists responded by placing less emphasis on the principle.

Perhaps the clearest way of demonstrating the nature of socialist collectivism is by showing how collectivism has worked in a variety of social contexts and by contrasting it with the individualist approach. This can be seen in Table 3.1.

Common ownership

A feature of socialism that is closely related to collectivism is common ownership of the means of production and distribution. Indeed, common ownership is a form of collectivism. It is perhaps the oldest socialist idea, since it pre-dates the onset of capitalism.

Some socialists have claimed that common ownership of property is a Christian principle, pointing out Christ's insistence that his followers pool their resources and share them out equally. Many movements throughout history – mostly among the poor peasantry – have demanded the seizure of land and its transfer to a communal system of production. In England in the 1640s and 1650s, the Levellers (or Diggers) purchased tracts of land in the south of England and began to farm collectively with the equal distribution of output. It was the development of capitalism, however, that brought about a more complex set of ideas relating to the evils of **private property** and the virtues of common ownership.

As with most socialist principles, there is a great deal of variation in thought in this area. Before looking at common ownership itself, it is useful to consider the variety of reasons why socialists have objected to private property. These have included the following:

- The Earth is given to humankind in general. No individual has the right to claim that any part of it belongs to him or herself.

- Claiming private property deprives someone else of its use.

Context	Collectivist solution	Individualist solution
Industrial relations	Most workers are organised in strong trade unions with bargaining rights.	Free labour markets exist with weak or non-existing unions. Wages and working conditions are determined solely by market forces.
Healthcare	A national health service provides free care according to need and is paid for by general taxation.	Individuals are responsible for their own health provision, probably through insurance.
Housing	Housing is available from local government, subsidised through taxation.	Widespread private home ownership exists.
Key industries	Large industries are nationalised – i.e. brought under government control – so that they operate in the national interest.	All industry and commerce are privately owned.
Education	State education is available to all.	Individuals must buy education privately, possibly with state financial support.

Table 3.1 Collectivism and individualism

- Property gives rise to inequality, especially between those who have and those who lack property.

- Ownership of property, particularly land and capital goods, gives rise to the exploitation by property owners of those who lack property.

By contrast, common ownership can give rise to a number of good outcomes, including:

- The possibility of imposing economic equality, as described above.

- Since many socialists see collectivism as natural, common ownership creates, or recreates, a natural state of society.

- It is possible to direct commonly owned property to serve the interests of the whole community, not just those of fortunate owners of property.

 Key Term

Private property

It is important not to confuse the term 'private property' with the term 'private possessions'. This is especially true in the context of socialist thought. Socialists distinguish between possessions, such as houses, clothes, personal items, etc., and property, which is used in the process of production. Property in this latter sense includes farm and building land, factories, mines, machinery, retail outlets, banks and so on. The crucial distinction is that 'property' can be used to exploit workers and consumers and to promote inequality, in other words, 'to own is to control'. Possessions, on the other hand, are simply those goods that we consider our own and which are not involved in production. Our own homes could be included as a possession in this sense.

Among socialists, the value of common ownership, along with equality, social justice and collectivism, has certainly declined in the modern age. The failure of the socialist 'experiments' that were introduced in the USSR, China, Cuba and much of eastern Europe during the twentieth century served to destroy faith in the idea of common ownership by the state (on behalf of the people). Socialists have therefore tended to modify their attitude to common ownership, seeing it as a complement to private property rather than a replacement for it.

Some socialists have argued that soviet-style socialism failed not as a result of common ownership but because it was based on the centralised state. Syndicalists, for example, have proposed that property should be owned collectively by groups of workers, not by the state. In other words, the workers in each industry should become the collective owners of their own enterprises. This is similar to the cooperative ideal common in continental Europe, whereby independent producers own their own property, but then pool their output and sell it collectively. Such producer cooperatives collectively own the distributional elements of their activities. Similarly, in some parts of Europe, worker cooperatives own individual companies collectively and distribute profits among themselves. In England, a system of consumer cooperatives was developed in the 1840s and has flourished ever since. Under this system, retail businesses are effectively owned in common by the consumers, who then have access to cheap goods.

In recent times, democratic socialists and social democrats have retained some elements of common ownership, organised by the state, but have also encouraged free enterprise when this is seen as the best method of wealth creation and distribution.

Table 3.2 summarises the ways in which different branches of the socialist movement have made use of common ownership.

We can now see that the story of socialism in the modern age is one in which there has been a decline in common ownership as part of the central belief system. The success of private enterprise in creating wealth and promoting innovation has made it difficult for socialists to argue that common ownership is successful or desirable.

Branch of socialism	Form of common ownership
Marxism	All property is common. There is no private enterprise.
State socialism	All means of production and distribution are publicly owned and run by the state. Possibly some small private enterprise is allowed.
Syndicalism	Industries are owned and run collectively by their own workers.
Cooperative movement	Groups of producers distribute their goods in common. Worker cooperatives are owned by their own workers. Retail cooperatives are owned in common by consumers.
Democratic socialism	Welfare organisations, such as for health and education, are publicly owned and state controlled. Some large strategic industries are publicly owned (i.e. nationalised) and run for the public good.
Social democracy (and New Labour)	Welfare services publicly owned. Very few enterprises are nationalised.

Table 3.2 Socialism and common ownership

Types of socialism

Primitive socialism

Primitive socialism can be defined as those forms of the philosophy that existed before the onset of capitalism in the late eighteenth century. Perhaps the best known of these was the imaginary world described by Thomas More (1478–1535) in his *Utopia*, written in 1516. More imagined an island where there was no money or private property and where everybody received goods according to their needs. It was described as a utopia in that it presupposed the elimination of greed and competitiveness. It was, of course, just a fictional creation, but it is possible that More's work inspired a number of socialists who were to follow much later.

In Gerrard Winstanley's Leveller movement in England in the 1640s and 1650s, in particular, can be found echoes of More's Utopia. Winstanley raged against inequality and the iniquities of greed and private property. He believed that the world had become corrupted because people thought that 'their freedom lies in plenty and their bondage lies in poverty' and so sought to take each other's possessions (from *The Law of Freedom*, 1652). The answer for Winstanley and his followers was to abolish private property, work the land cooperatively and distribute its

output equally. In this project, all men (women were excluded from equal rights) would have an equal say in the running of the common property.

Winstanley's movement was crushed by Cromwell and early socialism disappeared until the French Revolution, when some of the rebels hoped to use the upheaval as an opportunity to campaign for economic as well as political equality. These opportunists were also suppressed. The French Revolution was essentially a bourgeois enterprise; the idea that the working classes should be emancipated could not be tolerated. It was another 30 years or so before socialism became a significant movement. Indeed, the term 'socialism' itself does not seem to have existed before the 1830s.

Utopian socialism

The first recognisable socialists came to be known as 'utopian' for a number of reasons. First, they lacked scientific rigour. Second, their ideas were seen as impractical at best, eccentric at worst. Third, the ideas were based on an intensely optimistic and romantic view of the natural state of humankind. All utopians appeared to desire a return to a simpler form of production and social order. In other words, they were reacting violently to the growing problems associated with industrialisation and mass production by attempting to roll back progress. Three prominent utopians are worth describing at this point.

Charles Fourier was an eccentric French social theorist who briefly attracted a following but was ultimately thought to be too outlandish to be taken seriously. This is not to say he was not influential. Marx himself, for example, admitted to drawing some inspiration from his ideas. Fourier was an early communist. He hoped to see the establishment of small, self-supporting communities based on primitive forms of labour rather than the mass production involved in modern capitalism. He was utopian in that it was seen as an unlikely goal to roll back the progress of industrialisation and urbanisation, replacing it with a simpler form of community-based existence.

The second was Robert Owen (1771–1854), who saw himself as a benevolent capitalist. Unlike Fourier, Owen accepted that mass production was here to stay, yet he understood the extent to which workers could be exploited. He therefore was determined to care for the welfare of workers by providing them with housing, education for their children, some health care provision and cheap subsidised goods. He was also instrumental in setting up the retail cooperative movement (which survives to this day), which created a chain of retail shops that sold cheap goods and distributed any profits to the 'members', who were in fact the customers. His utopianism was based on the notion that capitalism, for all its pursuit of profit, could nevertheless avoid excessive exploitation and could ensure a decent quality of life for its employees. His New Lanark Mill in Scotland sought to put this into practice and did indeed flourish for many years. Other similarly benevolent capitalists were to follow Owen's lead later in the nineteenth century, such as Cadbury's (in Bournville, Birmingham) and Lever Brothers (at Port Sunlight, Merseyside).

The third was William Morris (1834–96). His was another form of primitive socialism, based on communities of craft workers and designers who would share equally the proceeds of their labour. Like Fourier he looked back to a former age (in Morris' case to the great days of the craft guilds in medieval England) and despised the brutality of industrialisation. Morris' designs on fabrics and wallpaper can still be bought today.

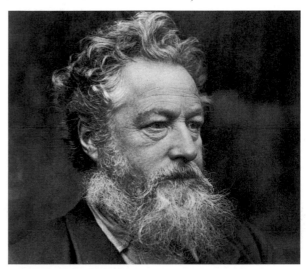

William Morris, interior designer, who combined socialism with a belief in a return to small-scale craft work

All three utopian socialists described above had a common desire to hold back the progress of capitalism and industrialisation. It was this unrealistic aspiration that was their undoing. Those forms of socialism that proved to be successful accepted that economic progress was a fact of life and would have to be accommodated.

Marxism

The Marxist form of socialism and communism is covered in more detail later in this chapter. However, a brief description is useful at this stage in order to place it within the context of the wider socialist movement.

Marx and his close associate Friedrich Engels (1820–95) were among the first socialists to recognise the importance of class conflict in their

Key Term

Communism

This term refers to any social system that is based upon small, independent communities; it is derived from the French word 'commune', which means a small village community. Communists propose not only communal living but also the abolition of systems of money, exchange and competition. Instead, goods are to be produced on a cooperative basis and income distributed equally within the commune. Government of the commune is usually based on direct democracy. The idea of the commune has been shared by utopian socialists, Marxists and anarchists.

Marx – the most celebrated fundamentalist socialist

critique of capitalism. They saw the working class as the only revolutionary class because it was suffering such intense exploitation. Marx and Engels also sought to move socialism away from its utopian roots. They did not merely see a socialist order as a desirable answer to the evils of capitalism: for them socialism, and later communism, were the inevitable consequences of the growing crisis of capitalism. Socialism was therefore a natural development of society, not a political ideology.

They made two further major contributions to socialist thought. First, they were unashamed revolutionaries. They rejected any notion that socialism could be brought about peacefully and/or democratically. Capitalism would have to be smashed by the exploited working class. Second, they understood that industrialisation and mass production were here to stay. A socialist society would have to come to terms with that fact.

Finally, we can compare Marxism with the growing state socialist movements of the nineteenth century. The Marxist idea that a new socialist order should be organised by the centralised state was shared by socialists throughout France, Germany and much of industrially developed Europe. Many socialists

and anarchists in the later nineteenth century proposed the creation of small, independent communities. However, Marx and Engels saw this kind of communism historically, as a later phase of human development. After capitalism, the state would be needed to build socialism. Too much freedom and independence would place the achievements of the **revolution** in jeopardy.

Key Term

Revolution

This term refers to a circumstance where there is a complete (usually sudden) transformation of the whole nature of society. Revolutions are often violent, as in the case of the French (1789) and Russian (1917) revolutions, but are not necessarily so. It is possible to have peaceful revolutions, such as the 'velvet revolution' in the former state of Czechoslovakia around 1990, when the communist system was replaced – without bloodshed – by free-market capitalism and liberal democracy.

Revolutionary socialism

Marxism is, of course, a form of revolutionary socialism. However, in the nineteenth and twentieth centuries there were revolutionary socialist movements that were not completely based on the writings of Marx and Engels.

In France, Auguste Blanqui (1805–81) formed a small socialist party of conspirators and agitators, which he hoped would bring down the capitalist state and replace it with a permanent workers' government. In England, H. M. Hyndman (1842–1921) formed the short-lived Social Democratic Foundation in 1884, an organisation dedicated to the destruction of the bourgeois state by revolution or other means. These two movements were remarkably unsuccessful. They lacked the scientific rigour of Marxism and their ideas on what could replace a capitalist order proved to be too unspecific.

In practice, the most successful revolutionary socialists have been inspired by Marxism. In Cuba, Fidel Castro (1927–) took control after a short guerrilla war in 1959 and set up a centralised socialist state that still endures. Although he drew most of his support from the Soviet Union, Castro was not strictly a Marxist. He did not share Marx's view that the socialist state would ultimately 'wither away' and be replaced by a communist order. However, he did set up an all-powerful state to administer production and distribution and to impose social and economic equality upon Cuban society. Similar regimes were set up, with varying degrees of permanence, in places such as Vietnam, North Korea and a number of former African colonies, e.g. Mozambique and Tanzania.

Fabianism and evolutionary socialism

The Fabian Society was established in Britain in 1884, the product of a group of socialist intellectuals. Notable founders included the playwright George Bernard Shaw (1856–1950), the novelist H. G. Wells (1866–1946) and the academics Sidney (1859–1947) and Beatrice Webb (1858–1943). (The latter couple went on to found the London School of Economics.) All were influenced by Marx, but did not accept his revolutionary theories.

The society was named after the Roman general Fabius, who was said to have won his battles through a gradual war of attrition rather than a single decisive blow against his enemy. This was a conscious indication that the Fabians were opposed to revolution, expecting instead that socialism would come about through a long-term, gradual process. They also developed the idea of the inevitability of gradualism. This doctrine encompassed two main ideas. The first was that socialism would be the inevitable outcome of the development of capitalism. As capitalist enterprises grew and began to dominate the economy, it would become necessary for the state to bring them under its control to ensure that they operated in the public interest. The Fabians believed that working-class demands for social justice and greater equality would become irresistible. The numerical advantage enjoyed by the working class would make the democratic establishment of a socialist state a natural consequence. The second idea was the belief that the transition to socialism would be gradual. The working class would not be ready to administer a socialist state, but would require the leadership of its intellectual superiors. Only when the working classes had become fully educated and informed would they be capable of taking over government. At the same time, it would not be practical to replace all capitalist institutions at once. Socialism would have to be established through a gradual, step-by-step process.

Over the years the Fabian Society (which still exists as an instrument of debate and education among social democrats and as a think-tank associated with New Labour) has become more moderate in its outlook. It has had a profound influence upon the British Labour Party (many of whose members have also been Fabians). The society helped to ensure that British socialism remained a moderate, non-revolutionary

Principles of revolutionary socialism	Principles of evolutionary socialism
• The capitalist system must be destroyed by force as it will inevitably attempt to defend itself • Democracy cannot bring about socialism because democratic institutions are dominated by the capitalist classes • The experience of revolutionary activity will, in itself, create socialist consciousness among the working class • Revolution is essential to prevent counter-revolutionary capitalist forces from re-asserting themselves	• It is feasible that a gradual process can be created whereby capitalism transforms itself peacefully into socialism • The numerical superiority of the working class will enable popular democracy to bring about socialism • The working classes can be educated to achieve socialist consciousness • The decline of capitalism is largely inevitable as its contradictions will undermine it. Revolution is therefore not essential

Table 3.3 Revolutionary and Evolutionary Socialism

movement. It also brought a strongly middle-class, intellectual element into the Labour Party.

In the UK and elsewhere in Europe, the early part of the twentieth century saw the development of an evolutionary form of socialism that rejected the radical, revolutionary nature of Marxism exemplified by Vladimir Ilyich Lenin (1870–1924) and the Russian Bolsheviks. Its leader was Eduard Bernstein (1850–1932). Bernstein argued that capitalism was not going to collapse of its own accord and nor was revolution the way to get rid of it. Like the Fabians, he recommended a gradualist approach and, in so doing, set the tone for mainstream, non-Marxist socialism during the early part of the twentieth century. Socialists, he argued, should not rely upon a revolution created by an alienated and exploited working class. Instead, socialists should adopt a variety of tactics, including the following:

● setting up political parties that would seek representation in parliaments

● working with trade unions to improve wages and working conditions

● pursuing welfare and social justice through democratic means

● advocating state control of major industries in order that they be run in the interests of workers and the community in general.

Bernstein, his close associate Karl Kautsky (1850–1938) and socialist parties all over Europe entered into a struggle against the Marxists, who were insistent that revolution was the only way to introduce socialism.

 Key Term

Revisionism
Originally the term referred to those socialist movements in the late nineteenth and early twentieth centuries that proposed compromises with capitalism and a peaceful transition to socialism. Lenin and his followers were especially critical. Fabianism and the beliefs of Eduard Bernstein were examples. In the modern era, revisionism can refer to any moderate socialist movement that makes compromises with a class analysis of society and with the revolutionary road to socialism. Democratic socialism, social democracy and New Labour would be examples.

Syndicalism

While groups such as the Fabians and evolutionary socialists proposed an alternative to revolutionary Marxism, a different form of socialism was also gaining ground. This became known as syndicalism, a term derived from the French word *syndicat*, meaning trade union.

The syndicalists, who thrived around the turn of the nineteenth century, advocated subversive or outright revolutionary activity by groups of workers, directed specifically at capitalist enterprises. Their objective was that workers would eventually take over their own industries and run them for their common benefit. The bourgeois state would then collapse as the capitalist system that supported it fell into the hands of the working class.

The syndicalists were notorious for their violent methods, especially those promoted by the Frenchman Georges Sorel (1847–1922). Sorel believed that working men formed a heroic class and that their capacity for social solidarity was forged in their struggle against capitalism and the exploitation which it imposed on them. By taking decisive action, the working class would simultaneously defeat capitalism and create new bonds of cooperation and equality. Trade unions provided an ideal structure for this form of socialism, as they were potentially internally democratic and self-governing and gave their members equal status.

Unfortunately for the syndicalist movement, it became closely associated with the fascist ideology that was gaining ground in Italy and Germany. Benito Mussolini (1883–1945) in particular admired syndicalism for its organisation and heroism and used some of its principles in setting up a fascist 'corporate state'. This connection doomed syndicalism to obscurity as its fascist associations alienated most members of the working class. A moderate form of syndicalism, known as 'guild socialism', gained some followers in Britain in the 1930s, but this too had withered away by the 1940s.

Democratic socialism and British Labourism

The British Labour Party was founded at the beginning of the twentieth century. Although technically a product of the trade union movement, its roots lay in a more complex set of influences (see Table 3.4). At first it competed with a party known as the Independent Labour Party (ILP), which was a radical but gradualist

Influence	Manifestations
Trade unionism	British trade unionists are usually moderate, preferring to rely upon collective bargaining, welfare systems and legal rights for workers rather than radical socialism. However, the objective of bringing major industries under state control (nationalisation) was mainly advocated by union leaderships.
Fabianism	This provided the middle-class intellectual element of Labour, concentrating on social justice through the redistribution of income, equality of opportunity and state controls over capitalism.
Nonconformist Christianity	This tradition saw socialism as an ethical issue, based on the idea of a sense of community. It therefore advocated socialist objectives through local government and the formation of consumer cooperatives.
Utopian socialism	Welfare and the welfare state was a key element in this tradition. It stressed the importance of skills training and education to raise the fortunes of the working class. The idea of worker cooperatives was also part of the utopian philosphy, although they failed to achieve popularity or economic success.
Liberalism	The close link between the British Labour movement and liberalism was apparent through the first half of the twentieth century. The liberal wing of Labour therefore promoted the causes of equal rights for individuals and minorities, as well as insisting on parliamentary democracy as the main vehicle for reform.

Table 3.4 Influences on the British Labour Party

Will Hutton
'them & us'

movement of the kind that Bernstein had advocated. However, the Labour Party soon won the struggle for dominance of the left in British politics and the ILP drifted into obscurity.

British socialism, usually known as 'democratic socialism', has a particular character, largely because of the varied nature of its origins and the fact that it was not heavily influenced by Marxism or other movements that based their ideas on the notion of class conflict. European socialists in the modern era have tended to see their role in terms of government on behalf of the working class in order to provide balance with the economic power of the capitalist middle classes. British Labour, while recognising the importance of class differences, has always understood that it would be electable only if it governed in the national, rather than narrow class, interest. In other words, the party has believed that it is possible to serve the interests of both major classes in society.

British socialism has therefore been a relatively moderate movement that has pursued social justice without jeopardising the achievements of market capitalism. A review of its main policies and methods illustrates this. Between 1945, when the first Labour government with an overall majority was elected, and 1979, when the traditional party lost power for the last time, Labour based its socialism on the following principles:

1 Total defence of the parliamentary system of government.

2 The pursuit of equal rights and equality of opportunity.

3 The state control of large strategic interests in order to prevent capitalist monopolies working against the public interest, and to run them instead in the interests of the community and of their own employees. This was known as 'nationalisation'.

4 The provision of a welfare state, with compulsory contributions from all those in work and their employers, and services or benefits provided free on demand for all those in need. This included pensions, healthcare, education and various social security benefits.

5 A range of personal services provided by local government, such as subsidised housing, social services and public health measures.

6 The redistribution of some income through the tax and welfare system.

7 The defence of powerful trade unions and workers' rights in order to promote justice in the workplace between employers and employees.

Traditional Labour policies implied that an accommodation could be reached between free-market capitalism and a just society. European socialists, meanwhile, have tended to oppose capitalism and propose its replacement by some form of state planning. Labour did flirt with the idea of centralised planning in the 1970s and early 1980s, but, true to its moderate roots, it rejected it, preferring instead the maintenance of a mixed economy.

New Labour and modern social democracy and the Third Way

The success of the free-market capitalist, neo-liberal reforms that swept the economically developed world in the 1980s, together with the end of the Cold War and the dismantling of soviet-style socialism, saw the demise of traditional socialism virtually everywhere. Socialist parties throughout Europe went into decline and then transformed themselves into moderate, quasi-liberal reforming parties. They accepted the capitalist system as inevitable and campaigned instead for more social justice, the protection of workers' rights and controls designed to prevent large-scale corporations from exploiting consumers and their own employees. In the UK, this process was seen in its most dramatic and celebrated form in the creation of New Labour as a force for **social democracy** in the UK.

Arguably New Labour is not a form of socialism at all. Indeed, members of the party

Key Term

Social democracy
This term has been used in so many different ways that it scarcely retains any meaning. In the nineteenth and early twentieth century, it was used by revolutionary as well as evolutionary socialists. In the second half of the twentieth century, it came to mean a moderate form of socialism committed to democratic methods and a pluralist political system. Its current usage implies a movement in the centre of the political spectrum that takes a social perspective on many issues and mediates between the demands of individualism and those of the community as a whole. The New Labour version of such social democracy has been called the 'Third Way'.

Key Term

Clause IV
This feature of Labour's history has always assumed iconic status in that it was said to encompass the basis of the party's claim to socialism. Part of the party's constitution, which was first written in 1918, Clause IV was included in the section dealing with the party's political objectives. Its most important clause stated that the party was committed to:

> *secure for the workers by hand or brain the full fruits of their industry and the most equitable distribution thereof that may be possible upon the basis of common ownership of the means of production, distribution and exchange and the best obtainable system of popular administration and control of each industry or service.*

When John Smith and Tony Blair transformed the party into 'New Labour', it was clear that the clause did not reflect modern conditions. It was a key moment when, in 1995, the party agreed to drop the old Clause IV and to replace it with a vaguer commitment to social justice. Labour's traditional claim to be an old-style socialist party was, by that single act, finally laid to rest.

today rarely use the term 'socialism' for fear of appearing to be anti-modernist or frightening the electorate. Despite this, New Labour is included in this chapter for two reasons. First, it still can lay some claims to being a socialist-based movement. Second, it does not belong in any other chapter in this book: it is not liberal nor, despite critical claims to the contrary, is it conservative in nature.

It is now well documented how Labour veered sharply to a left-wing socialist position in the 1980s and, as a result, fell foul of an electorate that was ready for the free-market, individualist policies of Margaret Thatcher. Under three successive leaders, Neil Kinnock (1942–), John Smith and Tony Blair, Labour reinvented itself to the extent that it added the term 'New' to its title. **Clause IV**, which stated the party's socialist intentions, was radically amended and the socialist old guard was marginalised.

The creation of New Labour and its so-called **'Third Way'** was effectively a response to the post-Thatcher consensus that had dominated Britain from the mid-1980s and which had spread to the USA and most of the rest of Europe. The end of the Cold War and the demise of socialism in the communist-bloc countries after 1989 also contributed to the defeat of traditional forms of socialism. All over the developed world, socialist parties were restyling themselves as moderate, social democratic parties.

The main elements of the post-Thatcher consensus and New Labour's Third Way reaction to it are given in Table 3.5.

We can see from the table that many of the key values and institutions of socialism largely disappeared under New Labour. It would be wrong, however, to suggest that Labour moved away from its socialist roots completely. Indeed, there are some examples of New Labour initiatives that could be said to have advanced the cause of socialism.

Consensus issues	New Labour response (the Third Way)
A belief that free markets are the best way of creating wealth and economic progress	Accepting free markets, but control of monopoly power through state regulation
Competition is a useful device for promoting efficiency and innovation	Promoting competition, even within public service institutions such as hospitals and schools
People prefer to own their own homes	Accepting the decline of subsidised rented housing supplied by local government
Privatisation of major industries	Accepting privatisation, but also introducing partnerships between public and private sectors
Withdrawing the state from economic management	No attempt to exercise active control over the economy but introducing measures to ensure stability and discipline in monetary control and the public finances
Weakening the power of trade unions and freeing up labour markets in general	Not restoring unions powers but strengthening the individual rights of workers, mainly through the Social Chapter of the European Union and the national minimum wage
Inequality is a natural and just consequence of free markets	Accepting inequality but establishing a minimum standard of living below which nobody should be allowed to fall
High taxation is unjust and inhibits wealth creation and economic growth	Taxation has drifted up, but taxes on income have been held down and business taxes have been reduced
High levels of social security benefits are a disincentive to work and create a 'dependency culture'	Social security benefits should be targeted at the most needy to ensure a decent standard of living for all, and at those who are working, are seeking work, or are unable to work

Table 3.5 New Labour and the post-Thatcher consensus

In particular, Labour retained the essentials of the welfare state, perhaps the jewel in the crown of British socialism. All sizeable employers and all those in work must contribute to the welfare state. Its provisions remain, on the whole, free at the point of delivery according to need. It is true that some charges have crept in, notably tuition fees for higher education and a range of medical charges, but the welfare state in general is totally funded by taxation. It is still the main vehicle for equality of opportunity and poverty control. Furthermore, education has been stressed as being the most effective way of widening opportunity for all.

There has been an extensive programme of poverty reduction too. Measures such as the national minimum wage, tax credits for working individuals and families, targeted benefits for pensioners and poor families and a new 10% tax band for those on low incomes have all been introduced to take people out of the poverty trap.

Key Term

Third Way

A term coined by the sociologist Anthony Giddens. It refers to New Labour policies after 1992 that steered a path between socialism ('first way') and neo-liberalism ('second way'), so becoming a 'third way' to social justice within a free market, capitalist society.

New Labour accepts inequality and understands its role in creating incentives that promote a healthy and dynamic business environment. However, it also recognises the phenomenon it has dubbed **social exclusion**. This refers to a section of society whose members remain so deprived that they are effectively excluded from mainstream society. The problems of the socially excluded tend to be multiple and can include poverty, low educational attainment, bad housing, crime, poor parenting, drug addiction, etc. The state therefore needs a multi-institutional approach to social exclusion policy.

 Key Term

Social exclusion
This term was created by New Labour and refers to those groups in society that suffer multiple deprivation and therefore do not enjoy the usual rewards, choices and opportunities. They are therefore socially excluded. Social and economic policy should be directed at such groups.

New Labour virtually abandoned its attachment to a class analysis of society. It accepts that we see ourselves mainly as individuals, pursuing our own goals, and that we do not identify strongly with a social class, although we may be members of smaller groups such as religions, campaign groups, sectional interest groups and so on. This carries the danger that society may lose its cohesion as a result of too much individualism. Concern about this is shared by modern liberals and progressive, social conservatives.

The nearest thing New Labour came to an all-embracing term that addresses this concern is 'communitarianism'. However, this term should be used carefully as it has also been used to denote forms of communism and anarchism that propose the establishment of small-scale, autonomous communities. In the context of New Labour, communitarianism is a very different concept. It accepts that society is basically individualist in nature, but also recognises an obligation to maintain the integrity of the community as a social entity. Instead of using the state as the chief method of retaining this community, individuals are expected to take responsibility for maintaining society. This implies taking an active role in the political process, in the promotion of community spirit, in caring for those less fortunate and in caring for the environment. To a large extent it envisages that such active citizenship should take place at a local level. It also implies that if citizens enjoy the rights bestowed on them by the state then they must accept responsibilities for the whole community. The extract from a speech by Tony Blair shown below expressed the communitarian ideals of New Labour, as the party completed its second term of office.

But now, on the foundations of economic stability and record investment, the third-term vision has to be to alter fundamentally the contract between citizen and state at the heart of the twentieth-century settlement; to move from a welfare state that relieves poverty and provides basic services to one which offers high-quality services and the opportunity for all to fulfil their potential to the full.

The values which animated those great reformers of the 1940s – Beveridge, Attlee and Bevan – are our values: equity, solidarity, a society of mutual obligation; the condition of the poor and less advantaged, the test of humanity and decency of the nation at large. Yet the institutions they created 60 years ago were rooted in social conditions and assumptions radically different to those of today. There is a vast agenda of change to bring about...all of it based on a belief that today people want the power to change their lives in their own hands, not those of an old-fashioned state and government. All of it pervaded by a strong commitment to the values of social justice, equality and opportunity for all.

Keynote speech to the Institute for Public Policy Research in October 2004

Here, Blair was summarising New Labour's attempt to combine a free-market, individualistic society, with some of the ideals of social democracy.

Post New Labour

By the time of the 2001 general election it was clear that the Labour Party had moved on from its 'New Labour' period. This is not to say that the party abandoned its attempts to introduce social justice within the context of free-market capitalism. Rather, the party shifted its emphasis. The objectives of the party became clearer when Gordon Brown took over as leader in 2007. The new agenda included the following:

● Although poverty reduction remained an objective, the objective of greater social mobility came to the fore. 'Social mobility' refers to the ability of succeeding generations to move out of deprived circumstances and raise their aspirations and those of their children. Education, training and employment opportunities became the key drivers of this policy.

● Brown re-emphasised the need to target welfare benefits more accurately, concentrating on those in most need. This had two aims. First, of course, to reduce the burden on taxpayers by reducing the welfare burden. In a sense it was an attempt to create better 'value for money'. Second, it would be a more just settlement as it concentrated on those who are most in need – especially poor pensioners and families with children.

● Brown was anxious to involve the private sector as much as possible in the operations of the welfare state and public services in general.

● In general Labour became a more pragmatic movement, less attached to dogmatic 'New Labour' principles.

Of course, the financial crisis and economic recession from 2007 onwards naturally placed new burdens on government, and pragmatism and crisis management inevitably replaced political theory and principles.

Socialism today

It is clear that in the economically developed world the traditional form of socialism is largely a thing of the past. There are some factions and individuals, such as Tony Benn (1925–) and George Galloway (1949–) in the UK, who still believe that socialism can be applied to modern society, but they represent small minorities. In other parts of the world, however, recognisable forms of socialism survive.

Cuba is perhaps the prime example of this. Under Fidel Castro, the country has retained a socialist system since 1959. The state controls most of the means of production and distribution and there is a high degree of economic equality. Great emphasis is placed upon the education and health systems, which are famous for their high quality. In a 1968 speech, Castro set out his vision of socialism:

> It is clear that capitalism has to be pulled out by the roots. We cannot encourage or even permit selfish attitudes among men if we don't want man to be guided by the instinct of selfishness, of individuality; by the wolf, the beast instinct; man as the enemy of man, the exploiter of man, the setter of snares for other men. The concept of socialism and communism, the concept of a higher society, implies a man devoid of those feelings; a man who has overcome such instincts at any cost; placing, above everything, his sense of solidarity and brotherhood among men.

China, however, has abandoned its socialist structure and is gradually encouraging private enterprise and accepting the inequality that inevitably follows. In Africa, a number of quasi-socialist regimes still exist, notably in Zimbabwe and Tanzania, but they have been undermined by the policies of the International Monetary Fund and the World Bank as well as their own corrupt political systems. These international organisations have insisted that, in return for loans and aid, these states must dismantle their socialist systems and introduce free-market policies. It remains to be seen whether such developments can bring these countries significant economic growth or whether there will be a return to socialist ideals if free-market systems fail.

Elsewhere, socialism remains in retreat, being replaced either by neo-liberal, conservative administrations as in France and Italy, or by moderate forms of social democracy as in the UK and Germany. Many argue that socialism was a historical phenomenon that belonged to a specific period in the development of capitalism. The current age is often described as the 'post-industrial' or 'post-capitalist era', in which individualism is firmly established, it is accepted that governments must take active steps to regulate free-market capitalism without controlling it, and most of the infamous evils of industrial society have been reduced. The US philosopher Francis Fukuyama (1952–) has argued that there is now no place for ideologies such as socialism. History has perhaps moved on and the socialist era may finally be over.

Key socialist thinkers

Charles Fourier (French, 1772–1837)

Although his early brand of socialism was short-lived and did not attract a wide following, Fourier is nonetheless an important figure in the history of the ideology. Marx and Engels clearly thought him significant since they spent a good deal of time refuting his utopian socialist ideas. Marx's description of communism, the ultimate goal of his type of scientific socialism, owed much to the community-based ideas of Fourier.

Fourier saw socialism as a means by which people could rekindle the community spirit that had been threatened by the growth of capitalism. His schemes may have been eccentric, but he did understand that socialism is about fellow feeling and social responsibility. He believed that industrialisation was perhaps the worst evil of capitalism in that it drained workers of their creative abilities and drove them into competition with each other. He insisted that in free, small-scale communities, where everybody was guaranteed a minimum standard of living, children were well educated and everybody was well housed, the genuine human spirit could be released. Fourier had an intensely optimistic view

of the potentiality of human nature to create genuine, cooperative communities.

Fourier therefore represents a particular kind of utopian socialism – one that is less concerned with great issues such as class conflict, exploitation and the evils of private property, but rather sees socialism as literally 'social' in nature. It is a tradition that has been followed by such disparate figures as the Victorian designer and craftsman William Morris and the twentieth-century novelist George Orwell (1903–50).

Robert Owen (Welsh, 1771–1858)

Owen has sometimes been called the father of British socialism. This is perhaps an exaggeration, but it is true that he had an immense influence on the movement. He is known as a utopian, but can be described as an ethical or even Christian socialist too. He did not share the class conflict analysis of the Marxists and other revolutionaries, nor did he advocate a state-sponsored system of common ownership. Owen's socialism was, like Fourier's, of a humanist kind, based on compassion, altruism and social responsibility.

Owen set up an experimental ethical capitalist enterprise at New Lanark in Scotland and another experimental community in New Harmony, USA. Neither was especially successful and he was much criticised for his unrealistic schemes, which were based on an over-optimistic view of human nature. He believed that capitalists could be persuaded to adopt a more humanitarian approach to their workers, and that the workers themselves could be turned into creative, enlightened individuals through education and welfare.

It is not, however, for his experiments that Owen is celebrated and revered but for his contribution to the cooperative movement. At New Harmony he set up a cooperative organisation where workers could produce goods on a collective basis and share out the proceeds on the basis of need. The community could operate successfully within a capitalist environment by removing the exploitation of both workers and consumers that the system produces. Owen's principle was a simple one. Capitalism exploits consumers and workers because they are powerless individuals. If both groups can come together as cooperative organisations, they can counterbalance the power of capitalist enterprises. He did not, therefore, advocate the destruction of capitalism, but merely a redressing of the balance of power within capitalism. This turned Owen into the champion of both the growing trade union movement and the developing British cooperative movement, which was set up in Rochdale in 1844.

British cooperative societies have taken the form of consumer organisations selling food, other products and a variety of services, such as insurance, to consumers at low prices. They have achieved this by cutting out most of the distribution chain and by using their collective market power to obtain low wholesale prices. They exist to this day, albeit in a modified form. Members of these societies still elect representatives to Labour Party committees and to the party's annual conference.

Like most of the British Labour movement, Owen represents a complete antidote to the revolutionary, Marxist forms of socialism popular at the time in mainland Europe. He understood that capitalism would probably survive and that therefore the most effective response to its evils was to modify its operation and empower the working class, rather than engage in a futile attempt to destroy it.

Auguste Blanqui (French, 1805–81)

In contrast to Robert Owen, a moderate exponent of socialism, stands the notorious, French revolutionary figure of Auguste Blanqui, a man famous for having spent half his life in various prisons. Like Marx, Blanqui saw society in terms of class conflict. The solution to the exploitation of the working class was to rise up, destroy the capitalist system and the state that supported it and replace it with a workers' state.

Blanqui represented an uncompromising kind of socialism, implacable in its opposition to capitalism. He was even more revolutionary in his outlook than Marx and his followers. He advocated conspiratorial methods among his own followers and set up clubs and societies among intellectuals, students and workers, which were dedicated to revolution and the undermining of the state. Although he stood for election to the French Assembly, he did not approve of parliamentary methods and took advantage of any insurrection that might break out. He was a leading figure in the 1848 revolution in France and in the uprising of 1871 known as the Paris Commune.

In some ways, Blanqui was a similar socialist to Marx, but he had no scientific theory of history and did not attempt a thorough explanation of the true nature of capitalism. He was an emotional socialist who cared only for the emancipation of the downtrodden working class.

Karl Marx (German, 1818–83)

Later on in this chapter we cover Marxism, but Marx's place in the socialist pantheon should be established here too. Marx was the pre-eminent scientific socialist of his day. He was, indeed, the first of the scientific socialists, yet his theories were derived from a variety of sources. His understanding of the nature of capitalism came largely from liberal economists such as David Ricardo, his theories of history were derived from the philosophy of social progress espoused by Friedrich Hegel (1770–1831), and his revolutionary fervour came from figures such as Blanqui. The result, however, bore little resemblance to any of these origins.

After a career as a political agitator and journalist, Marx settled in England. He spent more than 20 years there, effectively in exile, as he was a wanted man in many parts of Europe. His description of capitalism was the result of his own observations of England at the height of the Industrial Revolution. He received help from his lifelong friend and benefactor, Friedrich Engels, who ran his own business and so had an intimate knowledge of capitalism in action.

Marx's socialism was both scientific and idealistic. Although he developed a huge and impressive theory of historical development, his ideas were ultimately based upon a view of the nature of humankind that many have criticised. For Marx, work represents the essence of the human spirit; it is an individual's life force and gives life meaning. His whole theory of human development rested on this assumption. Marx believed alienation was the key feature of capitalism, which would ultimately bring the system down. By robbing workers of their own labour, capitalism was sowing the seeds of its own destruction. This is a critical idea, since it gives rise to the concept that a socialist revolution is, effectively, inevitable. Thus, socialism was not merely an aspiration but the logical outcome of fully developed capitalism.

The idea that socialism is inevitable was shared by the Fabians, but, unlike them, Marx believed that it would not be the outcome of a gradual process, but would result from a hammer blow struck by the revolutionary working class. This was the inevitable revolution.

Marx's critics focus on his assertions about the nature of humankind. He did not allow for the modification of capitalism, which would allow individuals to achieve self-development – even though they might continue to sell their labour in order to live.

Eduard Bernstein (German, 1850–1932)

Bernstein began his active political career as a Marxist sympathiser, but towards the latter part of the nineteenth century he began to lose faith in the ideology and developed a new form of socialism. This would ultimately form the main opposition to classical Marxism during a period when the capitalist structure wobbled and almost collapsed in the early part of the twentieth century. The Marxists turned their fury upon Bernstein, seeing him as a traitor to the cause of socialism. His ideas were branded **revisionism**, the worst kind of insult within the revolutionary socialist world. Bernstein's theories, however, came to dominate European socialism, while Marxism turned into a

Key Term

Revisionism
This term is most commonly used by Marxists to describe, in pejorative terms, the ideas of those followers who have distorted Marxist theory to such an extent that they can no longer be described as socialists at all. Eduard Bernstein was perhaps the most notorious of the Marxist revisionists. The term has also been used by other movements to describe anyone who moves too far away from orthodox beliefs. Anthony Crosland (1918–77) (see below) was often described as a revisionist in the context of orthodox Labour Party policies in the 1970s.

distinct movement far removed from socialist principles. As such, many argued, Marxism became merely a distortion of socialism.

Bernstein was one of the most important early exponents of what became known as 'social democracy'. He rejected Marx's assertions that class conflict would intensify, that this would culminate in revolution and that revolution would usher in a worker's state. He argued instead that socialist principles would be best advanced through democratic, parliamentary means. Furthermore, he rejected the notion that inequality and exploitation would inevitably worsen under capitalism. Within a democratic framework, he asserted, the interest of the working class would receive a fair hearing and capitalism would respond favourably. The appropriate role of socialists should therefore be to form democratic parties, to seek election to power and then to implement reforms in the interests of the working class. Such reforms would include welfare systems, trade union rights and equality of opportunity for all.

Bernstein's brand of socialism successfully opposed Marxism, and social democratic parties sprang up all over Europe (the British Labour Party can be counted as one of these). As communism became a distinct ideology, separate from socialism, the Bernstein position became the heart of non-Marxist socialism.

Anthony Crosland (English, 1918–77)

Crosland's best-known work, *The Future of Socialism*, which was published in 1956, can be seen as the beginning of a process of change in the Labour Party and, consequently, in British socialism; this came to its logical conclusion with the emergence of New Labour in the 1990s. Just as Bernstein was called a revisionist by the Marxists, Crosland was a Labour revisionist.

In particular, Crosland attacked the view that the most effective way of achieving socialist aims was through the nationalisation of major elements of the economy. He argued that capitalism should be allowed to flourish as long as it created wealth effectively and did not exploit workers in the way that nineteenth-century capitalism had undoubtedly done. Under certain circumstances he accepted that nationalisation might be appropriate, as might worker cooperatives, but alongside these two forms of common ownership capitalism would play a leading role. He rejected the idea of centralised state planning, which was gaining favour within the Labour Party in the 1950s and 1960s.

Crosland rejected a wholly class-based analysis of society, arguing that this was outdated in a world that was, in fact, becoming more pluralist and diverse. Furthermore, the working classes themselves were becoming more affluent, so state intervention to create more equality was no longer so necessary.

In essence, Crosland saw socialism as a collection of values rather than a slavish attachment to a set of institutions. Labour had overemphasised the importance of trade unions, state-run industries and taxation at the expense of its general values. For Crosland, socialism referred to ideas such as social justice, equality of opportunity and greater social equality. As capitalism generated increasing amounts of wealth, it was the role of socialists (or social democrats as we now call exponents of this philosophy) to redirect this wealth downwards through taxation and welfare. Crosland wanted to see an end to poverty, poor health provision and lack of education by harnessing the wealth of capitalism, not by taking capitalism over.

Crosland provoked a furious debate within Labour circles that was mirrored within the European socialist movement. In 1959, for example, the German social democrats revoked their Marxist roots and declared a set of principles remarkably similar to those of Crosland. While traditional socialists remained committed to common ownership of the means of production, state planning, powerful trade unions and income equality, the more moderate social democrats were becoming less dogmatic, more tolerant and pluralist in their views and much more accepting of free-market capitalism. The Crosland style of socialism won its final victory when Tony Blair announced that New Labour had arrived and that, as a party, it could occupy the central ground in British and, ultimately, European politics.

> ✔ **Key Term**
>
> **Nationalisation**
> This refers to a device associated with socialism throughout Europe after the Second World War. It involved taking large private enterprises into public ownership. It was also a way of bringing large monopolies under control. The state ran nationalised industries on behalf of the community as a whole. Most of the industries that were nationalised were public utilities, such as gas, electricity, public transport and telecommunications. Some industries producing basic commodities such as coal, iron and steel were also taken into public ownership. These nationalised industries were able to keep prices down since there was no profit motive, and they were able to provide more employment than the private sector. They ran services that might normally be deemed unprofitable and so would have been abandoned by the private sector. Nationalisation became a central part of European socialism, but fell into disrepute; most nationalised industries were privatised in the 1980s and 1990s.

Tony Benn (English, 1925–)

Benn comes from a socialist tradition which can be described as ethical or even Christian. He believes that the principal messages of Christ were equality and brotherhood. Christ condemned the pursuit of wealth and the inequalities that existed even in ancient times. Benn argues that inequality is unethical and must therefore be drastically reduced.

Benn's book, *Arguments for Socialism* (1980), can be seen as a somewhat belated answer to Crosland's 1956 work. In it, he asserted that it was large-scale, monopoly capitalism that was preventing the more even distribution of wealth. Capitalism, he claimed – in direct contradiction of Crosland – would never accept higher taxation as a means of redistributing income. Public ownership of all major industries (what he called the 'commanding heights') was essential, argued Benn, if economic equality was to be achieved.

Benn advocated centralised state planning as a way of running the economy in the interests of the whole community, not just the wealthy few. Production and distribution should be controlled by the state and not left to free markets, he argued. Public ownership and planning, in particular, could eliminate unemployment for-ever. Permanent full employment and economic equality were, for Benn, both desirable and feasible.

It would be wrong, however, to suggest that Benn was advocating a soviet-style socialist workers' state. He has always been a vehement advocate of parliamentary democracy and an opponent of dangerous concentrations of power. Yes, the state should be the vehicle for socialist aspirations, but it should be a highly democratic state firmly in the hands of ordinary working people, not in the hands of a political elite. If Crosland can be described as a social democrat, Benn can be termed a 'democratic socialist'. When asked whether socialists would relinquish power if defeated in an election and allow the achievements of the movement to be dismantled, Benn has always claimed that socialism would

Tony Benn, a leading British democratic socialist

never lose power. Once people experienced a truly democratic socialist state, they would not go back voluntarily.

Today, Bennite socialism has become marginalised and defeated by the moderate form of social democracy that has taken over Labour. Benn is perhaps the last exponent of traditional socialism in the UK and perhaps even in Europe as a whole.

Issues in socialism

The role of revolution

For much of the nineteenth century, divisions within the socialist movement centred largely on the need for, and role of, revolution. Revolutionary socialists, such as Marx and Blanqui, insisted that there could be no compromise with capitalism and the bourgeois state that supported it. They both believed that capitalism would defend itself against socialist attack, so it was almost inevitable that revolution would be violent and bloody. They rejected any notion that socialism could be achieved through peaceful, democratic means. This view was based on the assumption that the state was the agent of capitalism, even though it gave the appearance of democracy and pluralism. Some extremist revolutionaries, such as the Bolshevik Leon Trotsky (1879–1940), went so far as to suggest that the experience of revolution was an important element in the creation of the socialist spirit among the working class.

Of course, revolution need not be violent. The term itself can simply mean 'the complete transformation of society', and this can be by peaceful means. The English socialist H. M. Hyndman, for example, entertained the possibility that capitalism would simply give up under constant attacks by socialists. Indeed, Hyndman's mentor, Marx, admitted that there was a possibility that a socialist state could be established by parliamentary means, but only in Britain where the political system was least class-dominated.

Ranged against the revolutionary socialists were those who believed that socialism could come about by peaceful and gradual means; they became known collectively as 'evolutionary socialists'. To some extent, their beliefs were based on the assumption that, when popular democracy was established, the numerical superiority of the working class would simply vote socialism into power. It was evolutionary socialists such as the Fabians and the revisionists, led by Bernstein, who represented the principal opposition to revolutionary socialism. The Fabians saw socialism as the inevitable outcome of capitalism, largely on the grounds that the evils thrown up by capitalism would become intolerable and all sections of British society would come to realise that socialism was the only answer to these evils. The role of socialists, therefore, was to bide their time, to educate all classes in socialist truths and to wait for the right moment to dismantle capitalism. Named after Fabius, a cautious Roman general, the society's motto includes this exhortation to its followers:

For the right moment you must wait, as Fabius did most patiently, when warring against Hannibal, though many censured his delays.

Meanwhile, Bernstein, at the end of the nineteenth century and beginning of the twentieth, echoed the Fabian non-revolutionary methodology. In his case, he believed that socialism – albeit a more moderate form than that inspired by Marx – could be brought about by purely democratic means.

In the twentieth century, revolutionary and non-revolutionary socialism divided along Marxist and non-Marxist lines. The Marxists remained almost exclusively revolutionary until after the Second World War, when a movement known as Eurocommunism emerged. This shortlived philosophy suggested that Marxist-style communism could be brought about within a liberal democratic environment. Eurocommunists made some progress in France, Italy and Germany during the 1960s and 1970s, but their gains were modest and had withered away by the 1980s. Meanwhile, the non-Marxist socialists were making more significant progress within Western European democracies. Restyling themselves democratic socialists, they fully favoured liberal democratic methods and gradually modified their principles to support a milder form of socialism. This was essential in order to make socialist parties an electable proposition in increasingly affluent societies.

Thus, revolutionary socialism virtually disappeared as a movement after the Second World War. With the exception of a number of quasi-anarchist groups of the 1960s, nearly all socialists – both Marxist and non-Marxist – came to accept that the possibility of revolution had all but disappeared, at least in the affluent West.

The state

The issue of the appropriate role of the state in a socialist society has divided socialists to a much greater extent than the role of revolution. At one end of the spectrum lie the Marxists, whose ultimate goal is the disappearance of the state, while at the other end are hard-line state socialists who see the centralised state as the ultimate vehicle for, and expression of, all socialist ideals and objectives. Between the two exists a wide variety of attitudes. These are explored in detail below, before being summarised later in Table 3.6 on page 102.

Marxism

Marx saw the state as an expression of class rule. The old bourgeois state had to be removed and replaced by a workers' state, a phase known as the 'dictatorship of the proletariat'. The role of this socialist state was to dismantle the capitalist edifice, create a socialist society under the auspices of a central state, engage in propaganda, effect the re-education and socialisation of the people to establish socialist consciousness, and, finally, to create a classless society where the state was unnecessary and could wither away. Thus, the socialist state was to be the architect of its own death. Engels put the state's death in these terms:

> The proletariat seizes political power and turns the means of production into state property. But, in doing this, it abolishes itself as a proletariat, abolishes all class distinctions and class antagonisms, abolishes also the state as state... government of persons is replaced by the administration of things.
>
> From *Socialism, Utopian and Scientific*, 1892

Utopian socialism

Utopian socialists like Fourier and Owen did not see the state as a vehicle for socialism. For them, relatively small-scale, cooperative communities were the way forward in promoting socialist values. Fourier believed that the whole population could come to live in small communities so that the state, in a similar manner to Marx's belief, would become irrelevant and unnecessary. Owen did not see the state as irrelevant, but believed that its role should be minimal and confined to security, defence and the organisation of exchange between communities. The utopian socialists underestimated the extent to which the state was entrenched in modern society and were unrealistic in their belief that small communities could provide all the social and economic needs of the population.

State socialism

The extensive state socialist movements of the nineteenth century saw the central state as playing a major role in achieving socialist ends. Henri de Saint-Simon (1760–1825), who is often associated with the early utopians as well, proposed a state that would govern in the interests of all, not merely the wealthy few, and would take special care to advance the interests of the deserving poor. However, Saint-Simon's state was not to be a great economic institution that would control industry and commerce. Instead it was to be a regulatory body, consisting of the 'great and the good' in society, such as intellectuals, scientists and industrialists. The state would control capitalism so that it created more equality and advanced to the benefit of all.

Auguste Blanqui represented a more orthodox kind of state socialism. For him, the central state was to take over complete control of the means of production and distribution. In this way, complete equality of outcome could be achieved. The state would not be democratic in the traditional sense, but would be run on behalf of the working class. For Blanqui and similar state socialists, the idea of self-governing communities was hopelessly utopian. Social solidarity and economic equality could only be guaranteed if the state became the sole vehicle of common ownership of the means of production and distribution.

Fabianism

The Fabians also demonstrated faith in the state's ability to create socialism, but there were two important distinctions between them and hard-line state socialists. First, they were insistent that the state should be fully democratic. This assumed, of course, that the people of Britain would voluntarily vote for socialism (something Tony Benn asserted later in the twentieth century). Sidney and Beatrice Webb – two of the movement's founders – argued that as long as people were educated in socialist principles, they would be willing to vote consistently for a socialist society. The second distinction was that the Fabians saw local government as an appropriate vehicle for socialism.

'Municipal socialism' was indeed popular at the end of the nineteenth century. This was the theory that some socialist goals, including subsidised housing, public healthcare and education provision, could best be achieved at local level. Ironically, it was a Conservative mayor of Birmingham, Joseph Chamberlain (1836–1914), who pioneered such plans. The attraction of socialism at local level lay in the fact that, by bringing government close to the people, it could also be more democratically based.

Democratic socialism

Like the Fabians, and as their description suggests, this group were convinced democrats. Their position was less clear as to the role of the state in socialist society. In general, they believed that the state had a role, and that the private sector could coexist with it. There should be some kind of state-run welfare system, of course, and taxation would serve to redistribute income.

Public ownership of industry, however, posed a problem. In simple terms, democratic socialists have argued that all major and strategic industries should be under state control to ensure that they serve the community and not merely their owners. By insisting on a democratic political system, state control of these industries effectively becomes popular control. Industries that supply consumer goods, on the other hand, can be left to the free market. The thinking behind this is that, as long as consumers are left with free choices, they will regulate such industries themselves. As for the workers, strong trade unions and employment rights would help prevent exploitation.

Democratic socialists also support state planning. Outside the free market, the state should play some role in planning the output of important goods and services. This is based on the principle that economic development should be carried out in the interests of the community and not merely left to the random, irrational outcomes of a market-based system. Again, democracy would ensure state planning came under popular control.

Social democracy and New Labour

Social democracy entailed a dramatic change in attitude to the role of the state. Control of virtually all industry has been removed from the state and placed into the private sector. There is now a consensus among members of the centre left that individualism should be allowed to flourish and that excessive state power threatens individualism.

The transfer of large sections of industry from state control to the private sector ('privatisation') in the 1980s has been accepted by social democrats and New Labour in the UK. This development has not, however, spelled the end of state involvement. In place of the 'provider state', social democrats have introduced the 'regulatory state'. This state does not control industry and commerce, but does insist on methods of regulation to ensure that the public interest is served. Large utility industries, in particular, have to accept some degree of control over profits, pricing and supply policies.

As well as accepting privatisation, social democrats have supported relatively low levels of personal and corporate taxation, devices that have been used by socialists to redistribute income. Instead of redistribution, therefore, the state has largely been confined to protecting the interests of the poorest sections of society and, where possible, to reducing poverty. Welfare systems have remained a legitimate aspect of state activity, but in general inequality is tolerated.

Perhaps the most important role of the state for social democrats has been to guarantee equality of opportunity. State education lies at the centre of this objective, but state interference and regulation is also tolerated in the interests of broadening and increasing opportunities.

Capitalism and socialism

A historical analysis of socialism can be undertaken by considering its changing attitude towards capitalism. Indeed, it is often suggested that socialism, since its origination, has been fundamentally a series of reactions against capitalism.

The early socialists, of course, did not attack capitalism head on, but instead offered alternatives, which they assumed workers would adopt. The small-community socialism of Owen and Fourier was one such alternative. Saint-Simon, too, did not propose to dismantle capitalism, but rather to control it through an aristocracy of intellectuals, managers and other experts.

The Marxists and fundamentalist socialists, however, did work for the total destruction of the capitalist system. They argued that it was fundamentally exploitative and that the interests of its two great classes could not be reconciled. The Marxists in particular viewed capitalism as an all-pervasive system of production relations that dominated the state, politics, religion, ideology and society as a whole. Those non-Marxist socialists who adopted a less radical view of capitalism nonetheless asserted that equality and social justice could never be achieved within a capitalist context.

In the twentieth century, socialists began to adopt a less radical approach to capitalism. They saw signs that the interests of the working class were being considered by both capitalist enterprises and the state. Trade unions were allowed to be established, wages rose and welfare systems were introduced. Perhaps, they suggested, socialism and capitalism could reach an accommodation. As long as the state ensured that there was oversight of capitalism, and as long as key enterprises and welfare systems remained under state control, there was no reason why socialist values could not coexist with some kind of capitalist organisation.

When democratic socialism was further modified into contemporary social democracy, capitalism and socialism finally became compatible. Two key events in this development were the declaration by the German Social Democratic Party at Bad Godesberg in 1959 that there was no longer a need to destroy capitalism, and the abandonment of Clause IV of the Labour Party Constitution in 1995. Modern social democrats now accept that capitalism is the most effective way of creating wealth. The inequality that results is an acceptable outcome, and it is the role of social democrats to reduce its negative effects.

Table 3.6 compares the attitudes of different groups of socialists towards a range of themes.

Is British Labour still a socialist party?

Although most left-wing critics of 'New Labour' assert that the party has departed from socialism completely, there are some legitimate claims that it remains, at least in spirit, a fundamentally socialist-inspired party. Few would suggest it is actually socialist as such, but the question is whether it retains some elements of socialism. The main evidence in favour of this lies in the following.

Socialist features of Modern Labour

- The party remains committed to the reduction of poverty.

- Social exclusion policy is attempting to create greater social equality.

- The principles of the welfare state have been preserved.

- There is some regulation of large-scale industries in the public interest (notably the banking system following the 2008 financial crisis when the state took considerable stakes in failing banks).

- The Labour government signed the European Social Chapter, which extends considerable employment rights to all workers.

- The rhetoric of New Labour is that the wealth being created in society should be spread more widely.

- The emphasis on education aims to widen opportunity.

Theme	Marxism and revolutionary socialism	Democractic socialism	Social democracy
Capitalism	It must be completely dismantled and replaced by full-scale common ownership	It must be severely modified; ownership of the means of production to be shared between the state and private enterprise	Enterprise mostly private, with large-scale industry regulated, but not run by the state; limited state ownership
Equality	Absolute economic equality should be pursued, with minimal inequalities to create incentives; rewards must be based on need, not contribution	A high degree of equality should exist, but rewards to be distributed on the basis of the value of one's contribution, not merely on the basis of need	Inequality is the natural result of free markets and can be justified; however, a minimum standard of living for all to be guaranteed with some mild redistribution of income
The state	The state to be a workers' state, not necessarily democratic; all production and distribution to be under state control; Marxists aim to create conditions where the state can wither away; non-Marxists see the state as a permanent institution	The state to be democratic and largely pluralist in nature, with the assumption that a democratic state would also be just in its outcomes; large-scale production to be state run	Promotes a pluralist, liberal democracy; the state should not organise production and distribution, but should regulate it to some extent in the national interest and the interests of the less well off
Freedom	Individual freedom seen as a bourgeois concept; collective freedom to be created through equality	Individual liberty to be preserved as long as it does not conflict with socialist objectives	Individual liberty and individualism are to be preserved and guaranteed almost without qualification
Social class	Society is understood in terms of class and class interest; revolutionary socialists seek a state organised exclusively in the interest of the working class; Marxists seek an ultimately classless society	Adopts a class analysis of society; a socialist order would aim to reduce class conflict but balance power in favour of the working class	Social democrats do not analyse society in class terms; they see society as pluralist and class as having reduced importance; the state to be inclusive, protecting and advancing the interests of all groups
Collectivism	A totally collectivist perspective; all important economic and social activities to be collective	A largely collectivist outlook; however, individualism can flourish alongside important collectivist institutions	On the whole, indiduals prefer to pursue their own goals; collectivism largely limited to the welfare state and other public services

Table 3.6 Thematic comparison of socialist forms

Yet there is considerable justification for the view that New Labour has departed utterly from socialism. The principal elements that support this are the following.

Modern Labour's non-socialist features

- The goal of common ownership of the means of production was abandoned when Clause IV was amended.

- The party leaders, and Tony Blair in particular, have praised the virtues of individualism above collectivism.

- The party accepts that a considerable degree of

economic inequality is acceptable.

- New Labour failed to restore the power of trade unions, thus weakening the position of the organised working class against capitalist enterprise.

- Some of Labour's traditional socialist policies have been lost, notably progressive taxation to redistribute income, subsidised council housing, free higher education and generous state pensions.

Socialism and liberalism

Equality

There is considerable overlap between the enduring principles of liberalism and those of socialism. This is especially true of their respective attitudes towards equality. Both traditions have insisted upon the primacy of equal rights and equality of opportunity. Of course, for radical socialists, especially Marxists, these concepts could not be held by capitalists. The socialist movement in general, however, has always seen the creation of this kind of equality as one of its goals.

A useful start in a comparison of socialist and liberal attitudes towards the issue of equality is to consider the perspectives of two radical authorities, that of Marx for extreme socialism and that of Robert Nozick for extreme liberalism:

...from each according to his abilities, to each according to his needs.

Karl Marx, *Critique of the Gotha Programme*, 1875

...from each according to what he chooses to do, to each according to what he makes for himself.

Robert Nozick, *Anarchy, State and Utopia*, 1974

However, when we make more general comparisons between the two ideologies on the issue of equality, we run into some difficulties. Fundamentally, liberals believe that humans are naturally unequal, whereas socialists have argued that the inequality we observe in society is artificial and the product of an unjust society. Thus, while liberals argue that a free society is one where people are 'free to be unequal', socialists seek to create conditions where greater equality can be achieved. In other words, socialists are more optimistic that every individual is capable of becoming equal, as long as he or she has equality of opportunity and society is organised on a just basis. However, when we consider the mildest form of socialism, as represented by New Labour, it is questionable whether there is any real distinction between its outlook and that of liberalism.

Rawls may provide a possible path through this difficulty of uniting both approaches. He suggests:

*All social values – liberty and opportunity, income and wealth, and the bases of self-respect – are to be distributed equally **unless an unequal distribution of any, or all, of these values is to everyone's advantage.***

From *A Theory of Justice*, 1972

This formula appears to be a way of reconciling the socialist insistence on equality and the liberal response that this would be artificial and an infringement on liberty. It is also something of a throwback to utilitarian theory. If inequality can be seen to be for the 'greatest good of the greatest number', and if it does not make the poorest in society any poorer, inequality can be just. When we add that both traditions can agree on equal rights and equality of opportunity, we may have discovered the essence of liberal social democracy.

It should not be forgotten, however, that fundamental socialists still object to inequality, even when it appears to result in greater general prosperity. For them, this is a matter of principle. At the same time, those who are more radical in their liberal outlook still argue that the inequalities thrown up by a free society are all just.

Freedom

The charge that is most often levied by liberals against socialism is that as an ideology it entails the curtailment of liberty. If liberty is fundamental to human existence, attempts to pursue greater equality represent an affront to human dignity.

We can start by turning the discussion round and asking what socialists believe about freedom. Marx provides a critique of the traditional liberal view of freedom, claiming that it is really an illusion:

*In theory, therefore, individuals appear to have greater freedom under the rule of the bourgeoisie than before, in reality of course they are less free, because they are more subject to the **power of things**.*

From *The German Ideology*, 1845

By 'the power of things', Marx meant that individuals were subjected to economic forces beyond their control. They believed they were free because they could sell their labour to the highest bidder and were not subject to undue restrictions on their lives. But the fact was they were not free to decide not to sell their labour at all. They had lost control of their life essence – their own labour.

Yet as capitalism began to modify itself, as workers became free to form trade unions and as working-class parties were formed to represent them, the Marxist view began to appear overcritical. Attention among socialists turned to the charge that freedom itself was unevenly distributed in society. For those with control over their own lives, those who were born with greater opportunities and those with comfortable incomes, there was clearly more positive liberty available. The poorer sections of the community, by contrast, were less free, because they had less income, were subject to more social problems and enjoyed a narrower range of opportunities. Twentieth-century socialists therefore argued that the expansion of opportunities and the provision of welfare, together with some redistribution of income from rich to poor, would result in a more even distribution of freedom. In this sense they followed the philosophy of William Beveridge who, though a liberal, had suggested that social evils were as great a curtailment of freedom as government and its laws.

When liberals and conservatives complained that the expansion of state power after the Second World War was becoming a threat to liberty, the socialist response, typified by Tony Benn, was: 'whose liberty?' The liberty of entrepreneurs and the wealthy may indeed have been narrowing as the state redistributed some of their income, but the liberty of the majority was being expanded.

Turning back to the liberal perspective, however, problems remain. Attempts to create greater economic equality, which means redistributing income and wealth through taxation and welfare, inevitably curtail freedom. This is specifically the freedom to spend one's income as one wishes. There is an additional danger that a society in which there is excessive equality would lack incentives and so progress would be held up; this view stretches back to the beliefs of John Stuart Mill. Inheritance tax, capital gains tax and corporate taxes are all relevant in this context.

Although the liberal suspicion of measures to create economic equality is most at home in the USA, it remains a strong instinct among neo-liberals in the British Conservative Party and a right-wing faction of the Liberal Democrat Party. Mainstream liberals throughout Europe, however, have tended to move towards the social democrat position.

This view is close to Rawls' philosophy. His idea of distributive justice protects the concept of individual liberty, but accepts that the economic liberty of some may reduce the economic liberty of others. Therefore, general liberty remains intact, but economic liberty becomes negotiable. On rational grounds, most liberals and moderate social democrats now accept that the main objective of a liberal society is to be just in terms of the distribution of both goods and freedom.

The Marxist form of socialism

Introduction

Marxism refers to a movement, or series of movements, that owe their existence and take their main beliefs from the work of Karl Marx. All Marxists share the same interpretation of history, the same way of analysing society and a similar critique of capitalism, and propose revolutionary change to bring about a society where there will be both freedom and equality, where private property will cease to exist and, ultimately, where the state will become redundant.

Since Marx's death, there have been a number of different movements that have all claimed to be Marxist, but which have taken different paths towards the ideal society proposed by Marx. The Russian Bolsheviks, who created the first successful communist revolution, claimed to be the purest of Marxists, but there have been significant variations on Marxism, such as in China, in independence movements in poor countries, in South and Central America, and in western European working-class and intellectual movements. The failure of so-called communist regimes and the victory of democratic capitalism in the Cold War led to a dramatic decline in the popularity and application of Marxist ideas, but they remain a major influence on socialism.

✔ Key Term

Fundamentalism

In terms of socialism, fundamentalism refers to those traditions that totally oppose capitalism and are dedicated to its destruction and replacement by a socialist society. Thus there can be no compromise with capitalism. Marxism was the most important, but not the only, example.

There is a great deal of confusion concerning the relationship between Marxism, socialism and communism. This needs to be clarified before proceeding. The term 'communism' pre-dates Marx himself by several decades. It was used by a variety of movements in the nineteenth and twentieth centuries to denote the revolutionary idea that society should be based on small communities; indeed, the term is derived from the French word *commune*, meaning a small village or community. In the middle of the nineteenth century, it was popularly used by both anarchists and socialists.

Marx himself used the term communism to describe the type of society he believed human civilisation was inevitably moving towards. For him this did not necessarily mean small communities, but rather a society in which there would be no state and all goods would be freely distributed among the population according to need. Marx and his followers are therefore often described as 'communists'. It is not necessary, however, to be a Marxist in order to be a communist: the countries that based themselves on Marx's teachings after 1917 are described as 'communist' too. This is somewhat misleading. None of these countries ever achieved communism, or anything like it. They were described as communist because they claimed to be moving towards communism.

Similarly, Marx is often described as a socialist, in particular a 'revolutionary socialist'. This is accurate if socialism is considered to be a social system in which goods are distributed on an equal basis and in which the state organises this process. If there were no state, socialism would effectively be anarchism or communism. Marx argued that, after the anti-capitalist revolution, societies would and should adopt socialism as their system. This was to be an interim stage before communism could be achieved – in other words, before the state could safely 'wither away' without jeopardising equality. This principle was reflected in the names adopted by a number of Marxist-inspired states. Most famously, the USSR stood for the Union of Soviet Socialist Republics, implying that the country was in its interim phase and would move eventually to communism.

It is possible, therefore, to describe Marxism as either communism or socialism, or even both. To avoid confusion, however, it is probably best to describe all those forms of revolutionary socialism and communism that have claimed to follow Marx's teachings as Marxist.

Marxism is unique among the ideologies included in this book in that it takes its name from a single individual. Of course, there have been many individuals and movements that have adapted Marxism in various ways, but as long as they claim to base their ideas upon those of Marx, we can describe them as Marxist. In a way, this makes the study of Marxism fairly straightforward. If we know and understand the works of Marx, it could be argued, we understand Marxism, just as Muslims or Christians may describe their religions in terms of the teachings of Mohammed and Christ respectively. On the whole this is a fair statement. However, the variety of ways in which Marxism has been adapted, interpreted and applied must form part of the study of Marxism too.

The rise of socialism

As capitalism and industrialisation gathered pace in the first part of the nineteenth century, they brought with them a political movement that responded to the social evils and the conflicts they were beginning to cause. This was socialism. It took a number of forms. Some examples of early socialism were relatively mild and peaceful, notably the Chartist movement in Britain, which pressed for the regulation of wages and working hours, better conditions, more protection and, above all, votes for working people. Others were essentially 'ethical' or Christian, for example the beliefs of Henri de Saint-Simon in France and Robert Owen in Britain. Their brand of socialism did not make fundamental challenges to capitalism, but instead proposed more welfare and fair wages for workers, provided either by the state (Saint-Simon's theory) or by capitalists themselves (Owen's theory).

A third type of socialism to emerge was revolutionary in nature. These socialists believed that capitalism at that time was incapable of mere reform. It had to be abolished and replaced by a radically different economic and social arrangement.

Capitalism itself was inevitably exploitative: it was impossible to maintain capitalism without exploitation. Karl Marx was part of this third tradition and became its leading exponent.

By 1848, when many regimes in Europe were threatened by nationalist, democratic or socialist revolutionary activity, socialism was reaching maturity as an ideology. Marx and his radical colleagues were convinced by the experience of 1848 (when most of the revolutionaries were crushed) that capitalism would have to be brought down by violent revolution, and that the working classes must unite to bring this about. Marx's battle cry in the *Communist Manifesto* of that year – 'Workers of the world unite! You have nothing to lose but your chains!' – was an acceptance that it was to be revolution or nothing.

Hegelian philosophy

Marx's theories were derived from those of Friedrich Hegel, whose work dominated European philosophy for much of the nineteenth century, especially in his native Germany. Hegel's ideas are extremely difficult and complex, but can be successfully distilled into some basic principles that influenced Marx.

The dialectic

Hegel did not see history as a series of unrelated events, but as a logical progression. Each historical age was a development from its predecessor. He deduced that historical progress occurred as the result of a process that can be described as dialectic in nature. Dialectic in this context literally means that a proposition is confronted by its own opposite, resulting in a new truth. Thus, each social circumstance will eventually evolve into another when it comes into conflict with its own opposite.

Consciousness and alienation

The dialectic can be explained in more concrete terms. At its height, an age displays a high degree of harmony in which the collective 'mind' or consciousness of the people corresponds accurately with the reality of the world. People experience the world in an objective way and so do not feel alienated. Alienation occurs when people's perception of the world is generally different from the way the world actually is. When this state of affairs occurs, people feel alienated from the world they inhabit.

No age, however, remains in a state of harmony. As the world changes, collective consciousness evolves and moves away from the old perceptions, and therefore no longer corresponds with reality. This leads to alienation and social breakdown and conflict. An example of this is the height of Ancient Greek civilisation. This highly successful society began to break down when its great philosophers – Socrates (?470–399 BC), Plato (?427–?347 BC) and Aristotle (384–322 BC), for example – began to present new perceptions of the world that challenged existing consciousness. Such conflicts result in major social change and a new civilisation – a fresh collective consciousness – emerges. Thus, a new, higher form of harmony is born.

Destination of society

Crucially, Hegel believed that human society was moving towards a destination. This was a society in which there would be no alienation and where the dialectic process would finally end. It was a state of perfect 'freedom' in which people would have the same collective consciousness of the world as every individual's consciousness. It was a collective form of freedom, rather than the individual liberty that liberals were concerned with at the time. This is a difficult concept, which was shared by many conservatives and liberals during the nineteenth century. Put simply, it means that the will of each individual does not conflict with the collective will of all. Social conflict thus ends and nobody feels constricted by the rest of society.

Hegel eventually became controversial as a result of his assertion that the Prussian state of the early nineteenth century had achieved this ultimate Freedom. The combination of capitalism with a constitutional, limited monarchy and the imposition of the rule of law had for him created a state where there was indeed no social alienation.

Hegel's influence on Marx

Hegel's followers divided into 'right Hegelians', conservative nationalists who accepted Hegel's propositions at face value, and 'left Hegelians', who supported his general philosophy but argued with its ultimate conclusions. Marx was one of the 'left' Hegelians and a follower of the radical Ludwig Feuerbach (1804–72). Marx proposed two major modifications of Hegel's philosophy. First, the process of historical change took place within the real world of economics and economic relationships, rather than within human consciousness. Second, history has one further stage to reach. This final stage would be post-capitalist; private property and the state would be abolished and humankind's freedom and personal creativity would be restored.

Those aspects of Hegel's philosophy that particularly influenced Marx, and indeed political philosophy in general, can be summarised as follows:

1 Although Marx made fundamental modifications to Hegel's ideas, he shared his belief that history moves forward in an objectively determined manner. In other words, history can be studied scientifically.

2 The concept of alienation was crucial to Marx. He applied this idea to the state of the working class under capitalism. Workers find that the division of labour, the wage system that exploits them, and the product of their own labour are all alien to them. The world that they inhabit confronts them in a hostile way. This creates the critical conflict within capitalism that ultimately will destroy it.

3 The social phenomenon of consciousness – described by Hegel as 'mind' – plays a key role in Marx's philosophy. This describes a collective way of viewing the world. Marx often spoke of 'false consciousness', by which he meant a distorted view of the world that prevents social progress and promotes the domination by the ruling class. By contrast, consciousness can be positive if it is a true reflection of the world.

Marx the revolutionary

Marx began his political career as a student of German philosophy, along with his lifelong friend and collaborator, Friedrich Engels. He chiefly engaged himself in three activities. He was a journalist and editor of left-wing newspapers, a writer on revolutionary philosophy and a participant in a variety of revolutionary movements throughout Europe. Indeed, the term 'revolutionary' was how Marx preferred to be described. Unsurprisingly, his activities drew him to the attention of the authorities and he spent a good deal of his adult life in exile. He lived in London, then a haven for a variety of political radicals from all over Europe, for the last 20 years or so of his life, and most of his important work was written there.

During the 1840s he became increasingly radical and convinced of the need for a working-class revolution. He was anxious that revolutionary movements were being diverted away from true socialist objectives, and became increasingly radical in his ideas. When revolutionary activity erupted in Europe in 1848, he and Engels rushed out the famous *Communist Manifesto*. This document revealed the truly radical nature of their beliefs. The manifesto urged the working class not to be limited in its aims, but to strike a decisive blow against capitalism and the ruling class that was maintaining it.

The 1848 revolutions were crushed and ultimately failed to advance socialist ideals significantly, so it became clear that a long-term campaign against capitalism was needed. Marx continued to encourage movements that he considered to be genuinely socialist and to warn against those that were making fatal compromises with capitalism. When the Paris Commune was established in 1871, on the whole along Marxist lines, he and Engels believed the communist revolution had finally arrived. When the Commune was crushed after only a brief existence, Marx was once again disappointed, admitting that he had underestimated capitalism's determination to survive.

When Marx died in 1883, his dreams and predictions of the final revolution were still to be realised. His words on his funeral monument in London reveal his attitude to his political life:

> *The philosophers have only interpreted the world in various ways; the point, however, is to change it.*

In the event, it was for others to take up Marx's revolutionary banner. Marx knew that, despite all his scientific theories of history, and despite the apparent certainty of his prediction that capitalism was doomed, it was up to the revolutionary forces of the working class to usher in the new age of socialism and, finally, communism.

Core Marxist ideas

The dialectic and theory of history

Marx's theory of history is crucial to understanding his analysis of the future demise of capitalism. Marx saw history as moving in a specific direction and he shared Hegel's view that the progress of history was characterised by regular processes. However, Marx rooted his historical theory in the real world of economics, rather than the world of ideas, as Hegel had done. His theory of history is often described as 'dialectic materialism, based on economic determinism'.

Marx analysed every age in terms of its dominant economic relations. All other aspects of society – religion, philosophy, ideology, culture and politics – are merely reflections of economic realities. The nature of economic relations is determined by how the means of production are owned, who owns them, how people are employed and what their relationship is to the means of production. For example, under the feudal system, land was owned by the monarch and was leased to a hierarchy of nobles, feudal lords, tenants, subtenants and, finally, serfs. The relationships between these different levels of feudal society determined the political system of monarchy and aristocracy, and were underpinned by Roman Catholicism. The Roman Church was also organised on hierarchical lines and its teachings emphasised authority, obedience and acceptance of one's position in life, however lowly. 'Blessed are the poor' and 'blessed are the meek', Christ had preached.

Under capitalism, the dominant economic relationship is between the capitalists themselves, who own all the means of production, and the proletariat (workers), who exchange their labour for money wages and who own none of the means of production. This relationship gives rise to a corresponding political system (representative democracy), religious tradition (Protestantism) and dominant ideology (based on liberalism).

Whereas Hegel observed that each age begins to change as new ideas challenge the dominant collective consciousness, Marx believed that the dialectic process occurs within the key economic relationships. Marx asserted that in every age there is an exploited class and that the nature of this exploitation always tends to intensify. Under capitalism, therefore, the working class is exploited by the economic system. As the capitalist system developed (faster than any previous system, Marx noted), the exploitation of the working class would grow more marked. This would inevitably lead to conflict, which would eventually bring down the whole structure.

Marx argued that every age progresses in the same fundamental manner. It followed, then, that capitalism would go the way of all past ages. It would create the seeds of its own destruction – an exploited, and therefore revolutionary, working class. As occurred in all other ages, the process would usher in a new age, a new harmony and, eventually, a new dialectic conflict. However, Marx believed that the age that succeeded capitalism would signal the end of historical change and the victory of socialism and communism. The communist age, he confidently claimed, would be like no other, since it would not contain any of the destructive forces (contradictions, as he usually described them) that had characterised all other epochs.

Social class

Marx had a specific understanding of the nature of social class and class structure. Contemporary sociologists have defined class largely in terms of occupation, lifestyle and, to a lesser extent, income. For Marx, however, class was defined in terms of a group's relationship to the means of production. For example, a peasant paid rent to a landlord, but did not own the land. These two facts defined the peasant's relationship to the land and therefore his social class. Indeed, the entire class system under feudalism could be understood in terms of land tenure.

Under capitalism, the bourgeoisie and the proletariat were the two key social classes. The **bourgeoisie** was the class that owned the means of production. The **proletariat**, Marx's term for the industrial working class, owned none of the means of production. Although there were other classes in nineteenth-century industrial society, (notably the petite bourgeoisie of independent craftsmen, shopkeepers and professionals, rentiers (landlords) and peasants), the fundamental

 Key Term

Bourgeoisie and proletariat
Marx defined class in terms of the economic position that people held in the structure of economic relations. It was not a distinction of income, lifestyle or even occupation. Classes were defined in terms of their relationship to the means of production. The bourgeoisie was a small class that owned all the means of production – factories, workshops, mines, etc. This class also included their 'servants', such as professionals, managers and government officials. Those who did not own the means of production and were forced to sell their labour for money wages were the proletariat. The proletariat only included industrial workers; peasants, who worked on the land, were considered to be individuals rather than a cohesive social group. As capitalism developed, Marx argued, virtually everybody would be sucked into one of these two classes, bourgeoisie or proletariat – a process known as 'class polarisation'.

relationship was between bourgeoisie and proletariat.

For Marx, every society could be accurately understood only by reference to its class system. He identified a number of characteristics common to class systems throughout history: there is always a major ruling class and a major exploited class, there is an insoluble conflict between the interests of the two great classes, and ultimately the exploited class will understand its true position and will attempt to overthrow the ruling class. He summarised this theory in the *Communist Manifesto*: 'The history of all hitherto existing societies is the history of class struggle.'

For Marx, a further crucial aspect of class was the concept of class consciousness. Classes are not revolutionary, Marx argued, until they become self-conscious. This entails two developments. First, its members understand that they are part of the same class with the same class interest. This creates the possibility of class solidarity and therefore collective action. Second, in its mature stage, a class comes to understand where its true interests lie. For the exploited class, this consists of the complete overthrow of the existing order. At this point, a class – or at least a part of it comprised of its leading, most conscious members – becomes revolutionary. The process is reinforced by the fact that class polarisation also occurs. This is a process whereby the minor classes in a society become sucked into the two great classes. Most members of the peasantry and petite bourgeoisie, Marx confidently predicted, would therefore be forced to become members of the great industrial army of the proletariat.

The reason the proletariat could not recognise its own interests Marx admitted, was that the ruling class controls the dominant ideology in every age. This ideology tends to distort reality and prevents the exploited class becoming conscious of its true position and its true interests. Only the experience of intensified exploitation creates class consciousness – with help from philosophers such as Marx, of course.

After revolution, at every stage of history, the new age sees the fortunes of the classes reversed.

The exploited class becomes the ruling class and oppresses the former ruling class. Only when the process of revolutionary change is complete can a new age emerge, with a new set of productive relations and a new class system. Crucially, however, the proletarian revolution will be the last. The reason why this dialectic process of history will end is that post-capitalist society will be classless in nature. The imposition of collective ownership of the means of production, together with the equal distribution of income and wealth, will end class-based society. Society will therefore be classless. This is because if everyone has the same relationship to the means of production, there are no class distinctions – effectively, society will contain only one class. Thus, there will be no class conflict. He described this process in the Communist Manifesto of 1848 thus:

Finally, in times when the class struggle nears the decisive hour, the process of dissolution going on within the ruling class, in fact within the whole range of old society, assumes such a violent, glaring character, that a small section of ruling class cuts itself adrift, and joins the revolutionary class, the class that holds the future in its hands.

We can now summarise Marx's position on class, particularly in relation to capitalism:

- The class structure of capitalism is determined by the productive relations of the system.
- The key relationship is that between bourgeoisie and proletariat.
- As exploitation intensifies, leading members of the proletariat become more class conscious.
- Class polarisation then occurs, increasing the size of the exploited proletariat.
- Social conflict intensifies as class consciousness grows.
- The proletariat overthrows capitalism and the rule of the bourgeoisie.
- There is now an interim period, known as the dictatorship of the proletariat, in which socialism is built.

- Ultimately, a classless society will emerge – the end of the dialectic process of history.

The role of the state

As with class, Marx insisted that the nature of a political state cannot be understood except in terms of the system of productive relations and the class structure of the age. In other words, states have always been mere reflections of economic power. He sometimes referred to the state as the 'management committee of the ruling class'. Its role was always to underpin the dominant position of the ruling class, to oppress all those who might challenge the existing order and to control the dominant ideology that seeks to disguise the true nature of productive relations, thereby distorting consciousness and preventing class conflict.

This view is relatively easy to accept when analysing feudal society, for example. The monarchy and aristocracy formed the state and few would argue that these elements also controlled the means of production – land. Under capitalism, the position became more complex, especially as representative democracy started to emerge in Marx's lifetime. The advent of elections and the spread of voting rights called into question the idea that the bourgeoisie controlled the state. Marx had two main answers to this. First, he argued that the political power of elected bodies – e.g. parliaments – is illusory. True political power lies with the permanent apparatus of the state – the bureaucracy, legal system, forces of security and law and order, and so on. Second, the political parties that were fighting out elections were not revolutionary in nature. By supporting or compromising with capitalism, the political parties were also agents of the ruling class, whether consciously or unconsciously. Offering a choice between parties at elections appears to place the state into the hands of the electorate, but this is only an illusion of choice (a common complaint in the UK to this day). For Marx, only revolutionary parties were independent of the ruling class and the state, and therefore capable of challenging the existing order.

Marx and his followers accepted the need to retain the state after revolution. It would remain the agent of the ruling class, but the new ruling class would, of course, be the proletariat. Its role would be to suppress capitalism, preventing any chance of its re-emergence. At the same time, this dictatorship of the proletariat would be building socialism. Once a truly classless society had been established, the role of the political state would cease to exist and it would, in Marx's famous expression, 'wither away'.

The nature of capitalism

Marx spent much of his political life observing and describing the true nature of capitalism. For him, it was different from all past systems of productive relations. It was more dynamic and more exploitative than any system that had gone before. The reasons Marx gave for the rapid success and growth of capitalism mark him out as a great economist as well as a philosopher and revolutionary. It is not necessary to be a radical socialist to accept his analysis of nineteenth-century capitalism. The key aspects that he identified were as follows:

- It was a system based upon individual self-interest. This was a powerful force and gave capitalism its drive. Marx was a student of the liberal economists of the late eighteenth and early nineteenth centuries, notably Adam Smith, David Ricardo and John Stuart Mill. They recognised that capitalism was based on the free interaction of producers and workers, sellers and buyers. As all these agents operated in their own interests, there was a natural drive towards both efficiency and growth. Marx agreed with their conclusions, although, of course, he did not accept their assertions that capitalism could operate to the benefit of all.

- Capitalism was based on the use of capital – the energy systems, plants, machinery and technology that gave industry its productive potential. Unlike land, capital could be constantly increased and improved.

- Capitalism combined this capital with labour power in a unique way. First, it reduced labour to the same status as capital. It dehumanised workers, turning them into objects whose productive output could be purchased for money. Second, it drained human labour of its creativity, forcing workers to undertake mechanical, repetitive work, just as machines did. Indeed, labour became dependent on machines rather than the other way round.

● Most importantly, capitalism extracted what Marx called 'surplus value' from workers. In short, this meant that workers were paid only a fraction of the value of what they produced. No matter how productive labour was, it would be paid only subsistence (i.e. minimum) wages. Thus, as capitalist enterprises become more efficient and productive, the amount of surplus value would simply mount up. The surplus value, controlled by the capitalist owners, would be ploughed back into the creation of more capital, which would in turn become more productive and extract yet more surplus value.

Clearly this is no longer an accurate description of capitalism in the economically developed world (although socialists argue that some of the essential elements are still present). However, many might still claim this to be an image of capitalist production in less economically developed countries.

Marx described how human labour is exploited under capitalism. This extract is taken from an article in the Reinische Zeitung, written in 1849:

The labourer receives means of subsistence in exchange for his labour-power; but the capitalist receives in exchange for his means of subsistence, labour, the productive activity of the worker, the creative force by which the worker not only replaces what he consumes, but also gives to the accumulated labour a greater value than it previously possessed... But it is just this noble reproductive power that the worker surrenders to the capitalist in exchange for means of subsistence received. Consequently he has lost it for himself.

The development of capitalism

Marx was relatively specific about how he believed capitalism would develop from the middle of the nineteenth century, and this analysis formed the basis of his theories. Marx undoubtedly provides the first example of political philosophy and sociology being based upon such empirical research.

At its height, Marx saw capitalism as the most dynamic economic system that had ever existed. The secret of the system's success was its use of **surplus value**. Capitalism produces enormous amounts of surplus value, i.e. resources that are generated well above what is needed to meet the basic needs of the community. Historically, economic systems had failed to produce such surpluses and so their development had been extremely slow. Capitalism was able to reinvest surplus value into the creation of more and more capital. This was the reason for both the quantity of capital – e.g. machines, buildings, transport, mines – and its quality – e.g. new technology.

Key Term

Surplus value

We might simply describe this concept as 'profit', but Marx preferred not to use that expression. He saw surplus value as the portion of workers' time at work that was taken over by the capitalist. To describe this surplus as profit reduced it merely to money; instead, Marx saw it as labour being 'stolen'. Workers are paid considerably less than the value of the hours they work, so that some of the working day does not belong to them and the value of their product is then used by capitalism to exploit those same workers. This occurs when workers are so poorly paid that they cannot afford to purchase what they produce. Furthermore, for Marx, labour represents an individual's 'life essence'. If it is converted into mere surplus value for capitalism, an individual is robbed of much of that essence.

The problem for capitalism, Marx asserted, was how it used its own rapid development. Naturally, profit would be reinvested to make the system more productive. This might be acceptable if the additional wealth created were to be distributed throughout the population, but capitalism, Marx observed, succeeded in keeping wages at 'subsistence level': in other words, just enough to maintain life. It did this by creating a system in which workers were forced to compete with each other for scarce employment. If wages rose, capitalists would lay off workers, thus creating unemployment and weakening the workers' bargaining power. Workers therefore accept lower wages in return for work. At the same time, an army of unemployed, semi-employed and seasonally employed labour (including women, a subject later taken up by socialist-feminists) would be retained to create competition in the workforce.

Thus, capitalism generated increasing amounts of wealth but did not use it to improve the conditions of the working class; instead, the working class was kept in a state of poverty. At first, capitalism's insatiable appetite for new workers was met by draining the population from the countryside and recruiting women and children. Hoards of workers migrated into the growing industrial towns and cities, creating squalor, deprivation, disease and extensive social problems. The gap between the living standards of the bourgeoisie and the proletariat steadily widened and increasing numbers of formerly independent tradespeople and agricultural workers were sucked into the ranks of the unskilled and semi-skilled working class.

Initially, this growing inequality would not create a problem for capitalists, but problems would emerge later. Since capitalism avoided paying workers more than the means of their own subsistence, as the system became increasingly productive capitalists would experience difficulty in finding markets for their own products. The bourgeoisie itself could not continue to consume all the surplus product, so there would be periods of overproduction. Workers would be laid off and economic slumps would result. Wages would then fall and some workers would be re-employed, ending the

slump, but another economic crisis would always be just round the corner. These fluctuations, Marx predicted, would become increasingly dramatic and destabilising.

The next stage in the development of capitalism would be rivalry between capitalist nations as they competed for scarce world markets. The scramble for colonial possessions among developed countries in the second part of the nineteenth century was part of this process. Imperial competition would result in armed conflict, and Marx certainly saw the 1870–71 Franco–Prussian war in these terms. Although the First World War took place long after Marx's death, he would have analysed the conflict as being between advanced capitalist nations essentially fighting for economic dominance over ever scarcer markets.

At the same time as this international rivalry, conflict between the classes would intensify. The exploitation of the proletariat would become greater and more apparent. Workers, who were increasingly affected by urban deprivation, slumps and depressed wages, would develop

 Key Term

Alienation
The full explanation of Marx's analysis of alienation (which he derived largely from Hegel's philosophy) is exceedingly complex. However, it can be considered in simpler terms in relation to the late stages of capitalism. Workers, Marx argued, become alienated in three main ways. First, they are separated from their own labour by the fact that they are forced to sell that labour for money wages. Second, their own workplace is physically alien to them; they become mere accessories to machinery and the production process. Third, the product of their labour, their output, has little or nothing to do with that labour. They do not see their output as a whole – it is often a small part of the production process, owing to the division of labour – nor can they buy most of the objects they help to make.

class consciousness. At the centre of such consciousness would lie **alienation** – an increasing dislocation between the workers' view of the world and the reality of that world. As a result, trade unions would be formed and these would become increasingly militant. Strikes, demonstrations and even revolutionary activity would follow. Indeed, the wave of revolutions that swept Europe in 1848, and which encouraged Marx and Engels to publish the *Communist Manifesto*, was interpreted as a manifestation of growing working-class consciousness.

Marx was convinced capitalism would ultimately collapse, brought down by revolutionary activity. The intensification of the exploitation of the working class made it inevitable that it would become a revolutionary class. This is how Marx described the end of capitalism:

> *The antagonism between the proletariat and the bourgeoisie is a class struggle, whose most complete expression is complete revolution. It is astonishing, moreover, that a society founded on the opposition of classes should end in a brutal contradiction, in a hand-to-hand struggle, as its last act.*
>
> From *The Poverty of Philosophy*, 1847

Marx's description of how he saw capitalism developing and in the end collapsing can be summarised as follows:

1 Capitalism develops and becomes highly productive.

2 The surpluses being generated are reinvested to make capitalism even more productive.

3 The working class grows in size and class polarisation occurs.

4 Capitalism begins to overproduce and economic slumps become regular.

5 Inequality, alienation and socialist consciousness grow among the working class.

6 Rivalry between capitalist countries intensifies, resulting in wars and imperial competition.

7 The class consciousness among the proletariat grows and becomes revolutionary, at which point the working class brings capitalism to an end.

Revolution

The most controversial element of Marx's philosophy was his apparent prediction that capitalism would inevitably be brought down by a violent revolution. Furthermore, this would occur in those countries where capitalism was at its most advanced stage. This is controversial for two main reasons. The first is that the earliest (some argue the only) Marxist revolution occurred in Russia, which was certainly not an advanced capitalist country. Second, revolutions did not occur in advanced capitalist countries such as Britain, Germany and France. If this element of Marx's analysis was wrong, it is argued, his whole theory must be flawed.

The idea that historical change is created largely by the actions of social revolutionaries is known as **voluntarism**, whereas those who suggest that historical forces are outside our control are usually known as **determinists**.

 Key Term

Voluntarism and determinism
These two terms represent alternative analyses of historical development. Voluntarism suggests that people make history and that historical change is not inevitable, but the result of social movements created by people. Determinism suggests that we are slaves to the forces of history, which are out of our control. Major historical changes, therefore, are inevitable. Although most analysts argue that Marx was a determinist, it is more likely that he was a mixture of the two. In other words, he believed that the conditions for change will inevitably arise, but it is up to the actions of men to turn those conditions into tangible reality.

Marx found evidence for the inevitability of revolution in a number of observations. Most importantly, he observed that every age – i.e. every historical economic system – had contained the seeds of its own destruction, which would grow, create conflict and ultimately destroy the very system that had spawned them. Capitalism was no exception to this law of historical materialism. Marx saw revolution as the inevitable result of the progress of capitalism. Because capitalism was the most developed of all systems in history, it would produce the most exploited and therefore the most revolutionary class in history. Finally, Marx claimed that this final revolution would be underpinned by the influence of philosophers (like himself) who would break away from the ruling class – their natural home – and join the socialist movement.

Furthermore, argued Marx, the revolution would probably be violent. The capitalist state was founded upon violence and it would defend itself with violence. Only in Britain, he suggested, might there be a peaceful, democratic transition to socialism. This was because Britain had the most genuinely open democratic system, which might allow for representation of the working class. In this respect, Marx found himself in agreement with the Fabian Society, which was founded in 1884, a year after Marx's death.

The lack of a Marxist revolution

Why then did revolution not occur as Marx apparently predicted? There have been a number of explanations:

- The principal explanation is that Marx's whole analysis was flawed. There are no fixed laws of historical development and therefore no inevitable end to the capitalist era. The twentieth-century conservative philosopher Karl Popper was a leading exponent of this view.

- The Frankfurt School of Marxists, which flourished between the world wars, accepted that socialist revolution would not occur. They believed that capitalism would survive, although some of them, such as Herbert Marcuse (1898–1979), argued that the new exploited class was made up of manipulated consumers rather than alienated workers.

- The Italian communist Antonio Gramsci (1891–1937) argued that capitalism came to understand its own inherent weaknesses and was therefore able to control its own development. It introduced welfare systems and popular democracy, and permitted the formation of free trade unions to prevent the development of revolutionary socialism.

- A plausible analysis suggests Marx was right in that the conditions for revolution did indeed come about much as he had described, but the working class simply failed to topple capitalism, which was more entrenched than expected. After the First World War, there were certainly a number of attempted revolutions, for example, in Germany, Hungary and Italy, as well as in Russia. However, in every case except Russia the revolutions were put down.

- Accepting that revolution will not occur in developed economies, some modern Marxists, such as Frantz Fanon (1925–61), have transferred Marxist analysis to a global scale. They suggest that peasants and workers in less economically developed countries are the current exploited class and that the capitalist world as a whole is their exploiter. The conditions for revolution will arise, but only in such countries.

It must be remembered, however, that there was a revolution – that which occurred in Russia in 1917. The Bolsheviks, who led the revolution, followed Marxist analysis closely. It is therefore important to examine how Marx saw the development of society after the revolution.

The dictatorship of the proletariat

Marx did not suggest that society could move directly from revolution to communism. There would, he insisted, need to be a transition period known as the socialist phase or, more commonly, the dictatorship of the proletariat.

The dictatorship of the proletariat occurs as the product of historical progress. In every age, Marx argued, there will be a ruling class that will control the state and oppress other classes. Once the bourgeoisie has been toppled, therefore, only the proletariat can play the role of the ruling class. This interim phase has a key role to play in the creation of a communist society. Although leading members of the proletariat (the so-called vanguard) might be ready to move towards the purest form of socialism – communism – most of the new society would not. There would therefore have to be a period of preparation, carried out by the dictatorship of the proletariat. This would include the following:

- All private property would be abolished.

- In its place the state would take control of all the means of production and distribution.

- Rewards would be distributed on the basis of 'from each according to his ability, to each according to his contribution'.

- There would be no capitalist forms of enterprise, although the state would offer limited incentives to boost production.

- Information would be controlled by the state to prevent the possibility that bourgeois modes of thought might be restored.

- Individuals attempting to recreate capitalist enterprise or propagate bourgeois modes of thought would be suppressed.

- Consistent attempts would be made by the state to raise the consciousness of the people to pure socialism.

- Although the usual liberal concept of freedom and democracy would be absent, the creation of social equality would effectively liberate the people.

- Ultimately, a classless society would be built, the necessary condition for the end of the socialist state.

Marx gives us few clues as to how long the dictatorship of the proletariat would last. He simply asserted that it would be over when the last remnants of capitalism and bourgeois consciousness had disappeared.

In Russia, under the leadership of Vladimir Lenin and Joseph Stalin (1879–1953), the essential features of the dictatorship of the proletariat were put in place. Arguably the 'dictatorship' element was carried to extremes, and certainly the charges that a new ruling class of party bureaucrats replaced the bourgeoisie can be justified. However, it has to be said that Stalin recognised that the oppressive state could not be dismantled as long as the Soviet Union was surrounded by a hostile capitalist world (something for which Marx had not allowed, since he assumed revolution would spread rapidly). Whatever an accurate analysis of the Soviet dictatorship may be, Marx described the circumstances under which it would be replaced by the final stage of history.

The withering away of the state and communism

According to Marx, the state is an instrument of class rule. If, therefore, a classless society is created under socialism, there would no longer be any need for the state. Having completed its task of building socialism and preventing capitalism from restoring itself, the institutions of the state would simply cease to function. Marx used the term 'withering away' to suggest that the state would simply have no more functions, rather than a conscious process of abolition. The transition to communism would therefore be far from instant. Indeed, in some of his writings Marx suggests a two-stage movement. In the first phase each worker would receive rewards according to the differential value of his or her contribution. This recognises that workers have unequal powers and skills, and so receive unequal rewards. In the second, or 'higher', phase, the inequalities between contributions would no longer be recognised and every individual would receive rewards according to need, not contribution This implies complete equality.

The final transition to communism

In the 1875 *Critique of the Gotha Programme*, a rejection of the anarchist experiments then taking place on the Swiss–French border, Marx presented this colourful description of the transition to communism:

In the higher phase of communist society, when the enslaving subordination of the individual to division of labour, and with it the antithesis between mental and physical labour, has vanished; when labour is no longer merely a means of life but has become life's principal need; when the productive forces have also increased with the all-round development of the individual, and all the springs of co-operative wealth flow more abundantly – only then will it be possible completely to transcend the narrow outlook of bourgeois right and only then will society be able to inscribe on its banners: From each according to his ability, to each according to his needs!

It is possible to piece together how Marx envisaged communist society from elsewhere in his writings. It would be a period of total equality, but other features would also be important, including the following:

- It would be a time of plenty. Presumably this was necessary to avoid competition for scarce resources.

- There would be no money as labour and goods would never be exchanged.

- All production would be placed into a central pool.

- Individuals would draw goods and services from the central pool according to need alone.

- The division of labour would be abolished. Labour would be unspecialised and each individual would freely choose what kind of work he or she would undertake.

- The creative aspect of work would be restored.

- There might be some organisational bodies, but the political state would not exist.

- There would be no laws since social consciousness would prevent the possibility of any deviant behaviour.

This vision, close to the ideas of anarchists such as Peter Kropotkin (1842–1921) and Mikhail Bakunin (1814–76), has been denounced as a utopian dream. Its critics argue that it implies a hopelessly over-optimistic view of human nature and is simply impracticable.

Box 3.2 The stages of history in Marxist theory

1 Primitive societies with no economic organisation
2 Slave societies where slaves are the principal means of production
3 Feudalism with its rigid system of class relations
4 Primitive capitalism, the emergence of small scale capitalist enterprise
5 Capitalism
6 Indications of growing class and socialist consciousness
7 Revolution and the destruction of capitalism
8 The dictatorship of the proletariat
9 The withering away of the state and the emergence of communism
10 Effectively the historical stages come to an end

Marxism in practice

The Russian Revolution

Marx insisted that revolution would occur only in advanced capitalist countries. The Russia of 1917 certainly did not fit this description. It was largely agricultural and only a small proportion of the population were industrial workers and could therefore be described as the 'proletariat'. Yet Lenin, who led the Bolshevik Party that created the revolution, claimed that Russia could conform to classic Marxist ideology.

Lenin's theory of the late imperialist phase of capitalism suggested that the richer and more developed capitalist states would exploit less economically developed countries. Russia was one of the potentially exploited countries. The revolution could, therefore, emancipate the country before it became exploited. Furthermore, Russia contained two exploited classes – the growing proletariat and the peasantry. An alliance of these two classes could build a revolutionary force and begin to construct socialism within the context of a modified dictatorship of the proletariat.

Lenin's main opponents within the Marxist movement were the Mensheviks. They proposed that communists should cooperate with democratic parties to bring about a democratic bourgeois state. This would assist in the development of the economy and then build socialism within the growing proletariat. In other words, they wished to remain faithful to Marx's original analysis of historical development. Lenin, however, was adamant that Russia was in danger of falling into capitalism, from which it might not emerge. He therefore proposed a pre-emptive strike. There was, effectively, chaos in Russia in 1917, as a result of the effects of war, economic crisis and growing unrest among the working class. This led to the overthrow of the tsar in February of that year. If the Bolsheviks seized the moment, they would be able to control the future development of the country.

Lenin's success in first overthrowing the embryonic democratic state, and then bringing post-revolutionary government under Bolshevik control, led, however, to a crisis. Who was to run the new state? The industrial proletariat was clearly not prepared to take over this huge country. At the same time, the Russian economy was in tatters. Soon the euphoria of revolution and the redistribution of property to the state and the people began to wear off. Before he had time to build a socialist state along Marxist lines, Lenin grew ill, and died in 1924. It was left to Stalin to construct the Soviet Union.

The Soviet Union and Eastern Europe

Lenin and Stalin set about constructing the dictatorship of the proletariat along the lines of

Marx's theories. However, they faced two major problems. The first was that the industrial proletariat was underdeveloped and the majority of the population were peasants largely demanding their own land. Second, the country was surrounded by hostile capitalist powers.

Stalin dealt with the problem of the peasantry by turning them into industrial workers. The peasants were not granted their own land. Instead, farms were amalgamated and turned into collectives, with the peasants becoming wage earners – effectively, members of the classic proletariat. Stalin addressed the problem of the hostile capitalist world by cutting off the Soviet Union and instituting an oppressive regime in which information was controlled by the state. The people were subjected to constant socialist propaganda, were unable to travel and were told nothing about the capitalist world, except criticisms.

Stalin claimed to be building socialism from the bottom, completely recreating society along socialist lines. There had to be a repressive regime in order to achieve this, since he constantly feared attempts by the capitalist world to subvert his revolution. The Soviet Union was to be a model of how socialism could be created. When Stalin was able to extend the hegemony of the USSR into Eastern Europe after the Second World War, this model was exported to countries such as Poland, Hungary, Czechoslovakia, East Germany, Romania and Bulgaria.

The great Soviet experiment failed. It was unable to deliver economic prosperity, it could not deal with the implacable hostility of the capitalist world and the people tired of being subjected to a new ruling class – the party bureaucracy and the security services. Instead of creating a classless society, the Soviet leaders and their allies had merely replaced one class structure with another.

China

Following a prolonged civil war, the Communist Party of China, led by Mao Tse-tung (also written as 'Mao Zedong') (1893–1976), seized power in

1949. This was an even more unorthodox revolution than that in Russia. China was an almost completely agricultural society, with little industry and no history of socialist activity. It is true that the Chinese peasantry were ready for revolution, but this was in the hope of throwing off the exploitation of landlords and warlords rather than of creating a socialist state.

Like Lenin, therefore, Mao had to modify Marxist theory. This meant creating a socialist state among the peasantry. As in the Soviet Union, the farms were turned into collectives and production was controlled by the ruling Communist Party. Unlike the USSR however, Mao attempted to avoid the formation of a ruling class, in the form of a powerful bureaucracy, by encouraging the people – i.e. the peasants – to challenge authority and to ensure that the party and its officials remained accountable to them. In this way, he hoped to create a purer form of popular socialism. For about three years from 1966 he instituted the Cultural Revolution – a continuous process by which all figures of authority were challenged by the people. Millions of officials, teachers, intellectuals, magistrates and managers were either killed or forced to work as lowly peasants to teach them humility.

However, this 'continuous revolution' proved to be excessively disruptive. It ensured economic equality and granted considerable power to the people, in contrast to the Soviet Union, but ultimately it failed. Once again, an attempt to adapt classical Marxist theory to particular circumstances had been unsuccessful. Following Mao's death, the regime began to introduce limited free markets, and more recently the country has begun to move rapidly towards full-scale capitalism. All that remains of the old communist regime is the one-party state and its prevention of any form of political opposition.

The Frankfurt School and critical theory

A group of Marxist philosophers who were concentrated in Frankfurt in the 1920s and 1930s sought to explain why Marx's predictions of the final demise of capitalism had not materialised. The group was led by Theodore Adorno (1903–69), Max Horkheimer (1895–1973) and Herbert Marcuse. They developed the term 'critical theory', which they used to refer to a new form of philosophy that had moved away from Marx's traditional methods and was heavily influenced by the ideas of Sigmund Freud (1856–1939), the father of psychoanalysis. They also broadened the analysis of capitalism to include the idea of 'cultural hegemony'. This suggested that capitalism does not merely exploit workers in an economic fashion, but subverts the whole culture. It controls consciousness and all the instruments that control consciousness, such as consumption patterns, education, the arts and the media.

When fascism emerged in Europe, the Frankfurt School explained it as a distorted version of capitalism. It was, in other words, a stage of capitalism that had not been identified by Marx or Lenin. Fascism was for them the political representation of the monopoly power of capitalism. Just as capitalist enterprises had grown in size and power, coming to dominate whole markets, so fascism monopolised the political system for itself. The all-powerful state became the agent of all-powerful capitalism. This is how Marcuse expressed this idea, much later:

> *The turn from the liberalist to the total-authoritarian state occurs within the framework of the single social order. With regard to the unity of this economic base, we can say it is liberalism that produces the total, total-authoritarian state out of itself, as its own consummation at a more advanced stage of development.*
>
> From *Negations*, 1968

In simpler terms, Marcuse claimed that totalitarianism is the inevitable outcome of the development of liberal society. Just as the Fabians argued that capitalism would inevitably develop into socialism, Marcuse asserted that liberalism would become totalitarianism in the modern age. He did not mean the traditional form of totalitarianism, such as the fascist case, but the complete control of the economy, culture and consumerism by monopoly capitalism and its agents.

Having become convinced that fascism and its struggle against liberal democracy marked the final crisis of capitalism, the Frankfurt School was dismayed that capitalism did not collapse after the Second World War, but instead emerged greatly strengthened. The school therefore disbanded and most of its members renounced Marxism. Only Marcuse remained convinced that their analysis was valid. Their influence did, however, extend into the 1960s and became a major factor in the militant New Left movements, which included radical feminism, anti-racism, consumerism and environmentalism.

Contemporary Marxism

Orthodox Marxism is now all but dead. Pockets of the faithful remain in the former Soviet Union and its ex-satellite states in Eastern Europe. Communist parties still exist in most democratic countries but they are small and have become completely marginalised. The end of the Cold War in 1990 and the apparent victory of liberal democracy and capitalism signalled the death knell of orthodox Marxism.

Some former communist regimes remain, but these have become distortions of their original Marxist forms. North Korea, for example, is little more than a dictatorship in which the state controls the economy, but there appears to be no movement towards a genuinely socialist system. The same is true of a number of former Marxist movements in Africa. In Venezuela, the election of Hugo Chavez as president perhaps suggests the possibility of a resurgence of communism, or at least quasi-communism, in Latin America, but, although there is a great appetite for the redistribution of wealth and income in such countries where the distribution of wealth is grotesquely distorted, the likelihood of full-scale Marxist systems remains remote.

In a few countries where there is exploitation of the peasantry, Marxist guerrilla groups still seek revolution in the hope of liberating this exploited class and creating communism in the countryside. Nepal and Columbia, for example, are considerably troubled by their activities. Less economically developed countries were fertile ground for Marxism in the 1960s and 1970s, and these guerilla movements are their legacy. However, the influence of globalisation and the power of international organisations (for example, the World Trade Organisation and the International Monetary Fund) have persuaded these countries that industrialisation and the creation of free-market economies are the answer to their ills, rather than Marxist-inspired socialism.

We do not study Marxism today in the expectation that politics will be seriously affected by it in the future, but because it provides us with insights into how capitalism developed – and how it was indeed able to save itself from the fate that Marx predicted for it. In a sense, therefore, it stands as a warning to current generations of what could happen if we fail to maintain careful controls over the development of capitalism.

Key Marxist leaders

Vladimir Ilyich Lenin (Russian, 1870–1924)

Originally named Ulyanov, Lenin changed his name as part of his attempts to escape the attentions of the Russian state, which saw him as a dangerous enemy. He engaged in revolutionary activity in the late nineteenth century, largely among the peasants, but then became an orthodox Marxist and turned his attention to the industrial proletariat. He spent the first part of the twentieth century agitating among the workers, writing a prolific quantity of books and pamphlets and escaping the attentions of the authorities. He eventually had to flee Russia, spending much of his time in exile.

When the first Russian Revolution occurred in February 1917, Lenin was in exile in Switzerland. However, aided by the Germans (he was campaigning for a peace settlement, so it suited the Germans to have him creating trouble in Russia), he returned from exile. Once back in Russia, he took leadership of a new party, the militant wing of the social democratic movement, known as the Bolsheviks. He persuaded the movement to take the opportunity of chaos in Russia to promote a socialist revolution. He and the Bolsheviks seized power in October 1917, having won the support of much of the disaffected army and working class.

Once in power, Lenin set about creating a workers' state, led by his party. He fought a civil war against the counter-revolutionary 'Whites' and finally claimed full control of the country in 1921. He then turned his attention to his political opponents and established the complete authority of the Communist Party (the new title of the Bolsheviks) by 1922. Lenin fell ill in that year and died two years later without leaving any clear heir.

Lenin claimed to be an orthodox Marxist, but he certainly amended Marx's theories considerably, adapting them to the circumstances of Russia and the state of European capitalism in the early twentieth century. The synthesis of Marxist and Leninist thought was known as 'Marxist-Leninism' and became the ruling ideology of the Soviet Union, its satellite states in Eastern Europe and even of China after 1949. Lenin's contribution to Marxist theory is described below.

History and the revolution
Orthodox Marxist theory stated that revolution would occur only in advanced capitalist societies. Lenin, however, was anxious to create revolution in Russia, where the system would still be described, in Marxist terms, as merely 'primitive capitalism'. How could he justify this?

The basis of Lenin's ideas was a phase of capitalism that he simply called 'imperialism'. In this late stage of capitalism, the advanced countries would begin to exploit the economically undeveloped countries in an imperialist fashion. Russia would be plundered for its cheap natural resources and labour, just as

colonies further away had been for some time. Lenin described the process thus:

The more capitalism is developed, the more strongly the shortage of raw materials is felt, the more intense the competition and hunt for sources of raw materials throughout the whole world, the more desperate the struggle for the acquisition of colonies.
From *Imperialism*, 1919

In order to prevent Russia from falling irrevocably into the capitalist camp, a revolution could be created, after which socialism could be built from the bottom up. Marx had argued that the working class could only become truly socialist as a result of the experience of intensive exploitation. Although such conditions did not exist in Russia, socialism could be built through intense education and propaganda. The peasantry would be recruited to the socialist cause, thereby constructing a new revolutionary class. In effect, Lenin was proposing the acceleration of the historical process described by Marx. If Russia could industrialise rapidly, if socialist consciousness could be created through education rather than experience, and if the Communist Party could lead the people to an egalitarian and classless society, the end result would be the final, communist stage of history.

Lenin's modification of the Marxist theory of historical development proved to be extremely influential upon the growth of communist ideology during the twentieth century. Many other states and revolutionary movements, which did not conform to Marx's classic description of pre-revolutionary society, attempted to create socialism by copying Lenin's model. States such as China, Cuba, Vietnam, Cambodia, North Korea and a number of African countries all sought to build socialism in non-industrial, peasant-based societies.

The Communist Party
Lenin was sceptical of the possibility that the working classes would rise up spontaneously to bring down capitalism and create their own state. He believed that, after the revolution, they would

simply seek to improve their own conditions and would fail to dismantle capitalism and the bourgeois state that supported it. They would therefore need to be led by a small élite party that embodied orthodox Marxist ideology. In this way, the success of the revolution could be assured. This is how Lenin described the danger of spontaneity:

> There is much talk of spontaneity. But the spontaneous development of the working-class movement leads to its subordination to bourgeois ideology... Hence our task, the task of Social Democracy, is to combat spontaneity, to divert the working-class movement from this spontaneous, trade unionist striving to come under the wing of the bourgeoisie, and to bring it under the wing of revolutionary Social Democracy.
>
> From *What Is To Be Done?*, 1902

This lack of trust in the revolutionary instincts of the working class was to last throughout the existence of the Soviet Union. The revolutionary Leninist party turned itself into a dictatorial élite whose pronouncements became iron laws and which would tolerate no opposition. The party's policies became the only 'correct' version of Marxism and all its actions were justified on the grounds of that orthodoxy. Anyone who defied the party was therefore a traitor to the working class and had to be suppressed.

The state

Marx had insisted that the bourgeois state would have to be completely destroyed if socialism were to succeed. Lenin agreed with Marx's view and set about building a new state on the framework of the revolution. At first he tried to make the new state a workers' state, but soon discovered that workers were unable to run their own proletarian dictatorship. He therefore set about creating a new bureaucracy, very much along the lines of the state that had existed under the tsars. The problem which Lenin then encountered was that the revolutionary state, by necessity, would become enormous, since it was charged with the task of organising all production and distribution. This created the danger that such a huge machine would not be kept under political control and would therefore become a new exploiter of labour.

Furthermore, the state was to be the driving force behind the creation of socialism and the classless society. If it became too large and unwieldy, there was a danger that it would lose its sense of mission. To combat this possibility, the state was brought firmly under the control of the Communist Party, which was to give it constant direction. Every section and level of the state was directed by a parallel party committee (the term 'soviet' means committee in Russian). This created the great monolith of the Soviet state, which was to be so beloved of Lenin's successor, Stalin. The system came to be known as **democratic centralism**.

 Key Term

Democratic centralism
The political system developed by Lenin was known as democratic centralism. It was not democratic in the liberal (or 'bourgeois', as Lenin would have it) sense. There was only one party, since there was to be no diversion from the central principles of Marxism, but there was to be open discussion within closed party circles. Once decisions were reached, however, political processes would end and those decisions would be imposed on the party and the state. In theory, any individual who joined the party, and who was willing to work for it and maintain Marxist orthodoxy, could rise through the ranks. Under Stalin, democratic centralism became distorted and turned into the instrument of the rule of Stalin himself and his close advisers.

The communist state could not be pluralist in nature or hold free elections because there could be no variations on Marxist-Leninist orthodoxy. Perversely, Lenin still described his state as democratic, but this was on the grounds that it governed in the interests of the working class and was creating equality. For Lenin, equality and socialist democracy were essentially the same thing.

Joseph Stalin (Georgian, 1879–1953)

Stalin was a close associate of Lenin and one of his inner circle during and after the Russian Revolution. After Lenin's death, Stalin engaged in a struggle for power against the other leading Bolsheviks, especially his arch rival, Leon Trotsky. By 1929, Trotsky was in exile and Stalin controlled the Communist Party and therefore the Soviet state. He proceeded to construct perhaps the most repressive totalitarian regime that has ever existed. When he died, under suspicious circumstances, in 1953, he was still in undisputed control of the all-powerful state he had built.

Stalin accepted Marxist-Leninism as his creed and claimed to be completing the work that Lenin had started. His theories of the state and the role of the Communist Party were essentially the same as those of Lenin, but carried to their extremes. In addition, Stalin added a number of key features to the Soviet state, which are described below.

The peasantry

Stalin did not share Lenin's faith in the peasantry as a socialist class. He believed they were unlikely to develop the necessary consciousness. He therefore sought to turn them into workers by industrialising the land. The farms were taken over by the state and turned into huge collectives where the former peasants worked for wages. The richer peasants were eliminated, either literally, or by forcing them to work in collectives.

In this way, Stalin overcame the problem of creating socialism in a country that had not yet been industrialised. However, as industry developed, many of the agricultural workers were moved into the towns and cities to work in the factories and the mines. Ironically, this process mirrored the effects of capitalist development. The failure of the Soviet Union to generate significant wealth meant that workers' incomes were kept barely above subsistence levels.

Socialism in one country

Because it was surrounded by hostile capitalist countries, some of which adopted fascism in the 1930s and 1940s, Stalin decided that he must cut off the Soviet Union from the outside world. He only traded with other socialist states and would not allow his people to travel to other countries. This isolationism was designed to ensure that socialist consciousness could develop without contamination from the outside world.

Stalin's hope was that the Soviet Union would be economically successful and able to combine prosperity with equality. This would create a perfect model, which other proletarian movements would wish to emulate. Until the time came when capitalist countries were taken over by revolutionary movements, using the USSR as their paradigm, the oppressive state would have to endure. Thus, the withering away of the state would not occur until there was no longer a threat from the antagonistic capitalist world. The attack on the USSR by Germany in 1941 and the later onset of the Cold War were used by Stalin to prove that it was necessary to retain the state as a means of defence.

Economic planning

Stalin accepted that capitalism was an extremely dynamic system and successful in creating wealth, albeit unequally distributed wealth, and he sought to ensure that the USSR could rival the richer countries in terms of productive output. The problem he faced was how to create incentives in a system where economic equality for virtually all workers and managers had been established. Without any profit motive, how was industry and agriculture to develop itself?

Classical Marxist analysis would suggest that, if the proletariat had developed true socialist consciousness, it would not need such 'bourgeois' incentives. Stalin, however, was nothing if not a realist. He recognised that, until true socialism had been built, incentives of some kind would be necessary. He refused to use economic incentives, since this would threaten socialism, and instead developed a system of Five

Key Term

Stakhanovism

Stakhanov was a (probably mythical) worker held up as a model for others to follow. Always exceeding his production targets in the mines, he required no reward other than the knowledge that he had helped to build a socialist future. The principle of Stakhanovism was that if every worker could emulate Stakhanov, the day when the whole world would embrace socialism could be brought forward.

Year Plans with stiff targets for production in all sections of the economy. The rewards for achieving targets were social honour and career advancement. The punishment for missing targets was loss of position and descent into menial forms of work. Stalin even created the myth of a model worker, **Stakhanov**, who always exceeded his targets, to inspire the workers.

Stalin's system of Five Year Plans ultimately failed. The USSR failed to keep pace with the capitalist world. Although Stalinism survived Stalin's death in 1953, it was inevitable that his brand of Marxism could not endure. When the gap between the prosperity of the USSR and that of the capitalist world was fully revealed in the 1980s, the end became inevitable.

Mao Tse-tung (Chinese, 1893–1976)

In the early twentieth century, Mao was a land reformer who campaigned among the peasantry, urging them to overthrow their landlords and redistribute the land. In the 1920s, he became a communist and embraced Marxism. However, although he described himself as a Marxist-Leninist, he was never an orthodox Marxist thinker. He relied heavily on Stalin's support both before and after he took power and so, as a pragmatic gesture, embraced Stalinism. In fact, the two leaders had little in common. Stalin saw progress in terms of the development of industrial socialism, whereas Mao concentrated on the potentialities of the peasantry. After Mao's

death in 1976, China fell into the hands of a small party élite, which ran the country in an extremely authoritarian fashion. Not until the late 1980s did that leadership begin to dismantle the socialist system and to replace it, gradually, with free-market capitalism.

Following a prolonged civil war, Mao took power in 1949, declaring the People's Republic of China and claiming that it was to be a Marxist-Leninist state. But there was a great deal of originality in his thought and action – e.g., Mao saw the peasantry as the principal revolutionary class. He reinterpreted Marx's view that the industrial proletariat was the only revolutionary class by arguing that in China the peasantry were as exploited as the proletariat in capitalist states. This meant that they too could be a truly revolutionary class.

Mao's main original contribution to the Marxist legacy was his insistence that socialism could be built under any economic circumstances, not just in an advanced capitalist state. In order to achieve this, however, it was necessary to destroy the existing culture, so that the new socialist culture could be constructed on a blank society. In the case of China, he instituted

Key Term

Cultural Revolution

The Cultural Revolution was the long-term struggle initiated by Mao and carried out by the Chinese peasantry against all those who claimed to be in authority. It was assumed that all authority figures were likely to abuse their power and exploit the people. Few escaped the campaign – party officials, teachers and lecturers, police chiefs and magistrates were particularly targeted – and many lost their lives through violence or suicide. The main campaign lasted from 1966 until 1969 and left the country on its knees, with few people left who could organise it. Education virtually ceased and agricultural production slumped. The entire administrative system of China had to be rebuilt.

a series of mass campaigns, in particular the dramatic **Cultural Revolution**, to attack aspects of traditional Chinese culture. He encouraged the people to oppose reverence for the aged, the subjugation of women, deference to landlords and local officials, ancestor worship and the rigid class structure of the countryside. Once the existing social order had been destroyed, a pure form of socialism could be created among the peasantry and the growing industrial proletariat.

The Chinese communists under Mao exported their ideas to many other countries that were engaged in anti-colonial struggles or which were recently independent. Mao gave them a blueprint for creating socialism, whatever the circumstances. The most notorious example of this occurred in Cambodia, where the Khmer Rouge movement ruthlessly destroyed existing Cambodian society and replaced it with a totalitarian communist regime in 1975.

In addition, Mao developed the idea of permanent revolution, a theory originally attributable to Lenin's associate and Stalin's main enemy, Leon Trotsky. Rather than building socialism through a static, all-powerful party machine, Trotsky and Mao believed that the people should engage in a constant revolutionary struggle against all unaccountable wielders of power and anyone who seemed to be tending towards a bourgeois mode of thought and action. Thus the people could learn socialism in a practical way, rather than through education and propaganda.

Other Marxists

The contribution made to Marxist thought by a variety of other philosophers and revolutionaries is considered briefly below.

Leon Trotsky (Russian, 1879–1940)

By 1917, Trotsky was already a veteran revolutionary. However, he only joined Lenin's party just before the Russian Revolution. He was thought to be Lenin's natural heir and was therefore Stalin's closest rival. Having lost his power struggle with Stalin, Trotsky spent the rest of his life in exile before being murdered by a Stalinist agent in Mexico. Trotsky argued that the Soviet Union should not cut itself off from the rest of the world but should seek to promote revolution in other countries. He did not believe that socialist states could survive if capitalism were allowed to thrive elsewhere. He criticised Stalin's creation of a state bureaucracy, arguing that it had simply become a new oppressive ruling class and was preventing the development of socialism rather than creating it. Trotsky was certainly one of the most democratic of Lenin's party. He argued that the people themselves should guide government towards socialism and should not be subjected to excessive party control.

Antonio Gramsci (Italian, 1891–1937)

One of the founders of the Italian communist party, Gramsci sought to explain capitalism's success in preventing its destruction by revolution. The system had learned, he argued, to control its own development and so prevent class warfare. In addition, capitalism had developed a hegemony over society that extended well beyond mere economics. Capitalist culture dominated all political, artistic and cultural life. As a result, its control was all-pervading. The only way to combat this hegemony was to undermine capitalism on all fronts. This meant that a 'counterculture' would have to be created among the workers in order to build socialist consciousness.

Gramsci died largely as a result of being imprisoned by Benito Mussolini during the 1930s. His influence extended into the 1960s, when various left-wing movements sought to set up countercultures in opposition to the ruling capitalist ideology.

Frantz Fanon (French, 1925–61)

Born in Martinique, Fanon was a revolutionary and was active in the Algerian resistance movement during the country's fight for independence from France. He focused on the peasantry of the poorest countries in the world, arguing that these were the most exploited class, and therefore the most revolutionary. The peasants must struggle against colonial rule, and having achieved independence, should promote a nationalist–socialist resistance to the economic imperialism of the great capitalist powers.

Herbert Marcuse (German, 1898–1979)

Beloved of the left-wing youth movements of the 1960s and 1970s, Marcuse was by that time the last remaining member of the interwar Frankfurt School of Communism who was still Marxist. He described modern capitalism as a new form of totalitarianism that manipulated the consciousness of the masses. Capitalism, he asserted, created a one-dimensional view of the world, in which people were part of a mass society whose consumption patterns and lifestyles were totally manipulated. We are therefore all alienated as consumers, not as workers, as Marx had observed. The idea of class struggle was outdated for Marcuse. The new struggle concerned the need for people to liberate their own consciousness of the world. He was pessimistic that this could be achieved, but did see some hope among those sections of the community that were excluded from mass society – members of minority ethnic groups, poor people, those who were homosexual, oppressed women and protesting young people. He described the possibility of the downfall of totalitarian capitalism as 'nothing but a chance, only a chance'.

Regis Debray (French, 1940–)

Debray is the principal theorist behind the guerrilla movements that sprang up all over Central and South America in the 1960s and 1970s. He was a particular friend of the Cuban regime led by Fidel Castro. In post-colonial states that were dominated by Western capitalism, he saw small guerrilla organisations as the most effective revolutionary weapon. Broad-based peasant and worker movements were easily infiltrated or diverted from the course of socialism. The oppressed classes were best led by a tight-knit, élite group. The experience of armed struggle by such groups would give them the strength and commitment that would enable them to topple regimes that were much more powerful than themselves. However, the Cuban state remains the only lasting success of Debray's so-called 'revolution within the revolution'. Like Marcuse, Debray became popular with Western New Left resistance groups in the late 1960s and early 1970s.

Issues in Marxism

Was Marx a scientific or a utopian thinker?

The basis of Marx's claim to be scientific was that he relied almost totally upon empirical evidence. In other words, his ideas were developed from the experience of history. A potential weakness arises from this. Marx claimed that all previous versions of history had been corrupted by the ruling ideology of the age. In other words, history was always written by the ruling class to justify its own position. Marx, on the other hand, claimed that his explanation of history was purely scientific, and yet he offered no conclusive proof of this. How can we know that his version is not tainted by the same faults as previous analyses of history?

Marx does have something of an answer to this criticism. He examines history from the point of view of the material conditions of society, asserting that less concrete factors, such as politics, philosophy and religion, are all secondary to economic forces. These material conditions can, he claims, be studied scientifically. For example, the feudal system can therefore be explained in terms of the economic relationships between its various classes. The progress of feudalism towards its own destruction can therefore be explained by changes in the conditions of the real world of productive forces; in other words, by stresses in its economic structure. In the same way, an event such as the French Revolution can be explained scientifically in terms of the growing class struggle that France was experiencing in the eighteenth century. Those who explained the revolution in terms of philosophy – that is, as the culmination of the Enlightenment period – or of politics – as the corruption of the *ancien régime* – ran the danger of corrupting their own analysis by adopting a subjective approach to these developments.

If Marx really did analyse history in an objective, empirical manner, his argument that each age develops in a similar way could be justified. If the oppressed class in every past age did indeed inevitably destroy the system that created it, it seems reasonable that capitalism should behave in the same way and so come to the same end. Critics argue that there is no reason at all why capitalism should behave according to apparently unchangeable laws of history. Why, for example, should capitalism not have characteristics that guarantee its own survival? Marx had, in truth, admitted that capitalism was like no previous system – it was more productive and more dynamic than anything seen in history. There was, therefore, no reason why it should conform to past experience.

The main arguments of Marx and his critics can be reduced to a stark conflict. Marx claimed that there are fixed historical laws that allow us to understand how capitalism will ultimately be transformed into socialism following its catastrophic destruction. Against this is the view that historical laws of this kind do not exist, so the future course of capitalism cannot be predicted. The most cynical of his critics suggest that Marx was a utopian socialist who simply constructed a complex, quasi-scientific theory to justify the apparently inevitable development of a communist society.

Were Leninism and Stalinism distortions of Marxism?

Both Lenin and Stalin accepted that their theories were modifications of Marxist ideology, which they adapted to take into account the conditions of post-revolutionary Russia and the fact that the rest of the world remained capitalist. Since Russia had not been an advanced capitalist state, measures had to be taken to build socialism and industry at the same time.

Having said that, there are still serious criticisms that can be levelled against Leninism and Stalinism in terms of their deviation from Marxism. These accusations are described below.

Leninism

- Marx insisted that socialist consciousness could only be built upon the proletariat's experience of exploitation. Furthermore, that exploitation would have to be widespread and intensive. This was clearly not the case in Russia. Socialism was therefore built on artificial grounds.

- The small, élite revolutionary party that Lenin created excluded large sections of the working class, thus losing the spontaneous development of socialism that Marx had said would spread through the industrial proletariat.

- The state that Lenin built turned out to be similar to the state that it replaced. Indeed, Lenin actually employed many of the bureaucrats, police chiefs and security agents who had served the former Tsarist regime. Marx had stated that the nature of the state would have to be completely transformed and run almost exclusively by the workers themselves, to ensure it would work only in the interests of socialism.

- Lenin employed a large number of bourgeois intellectuals in his new government and party machine. Marx had accepted that some intellectuals would be needed to lead the revolution, but the driving force was to be the proletariat.

Stalinism

- The huge state machine that Stalin built turned into a new oppressive ruling class. Orthodox Marxist theory envisaged a state apparatus which was controlled by the working class rather than by professional bureaucrats and party officials.

- By creating a personality cult around his own leadership, Stalin denied the leading role of the proletariat.

- Cutting the Soviet Union off from other countries meant that Stalin failed to spread revolution throughout the capitalist world. The creation of a world revolution was the first duty of socialist revolutionaries.

- Support for the regime should have been built upon socialist ideology. Stalin, however, appealed to Russian nationalism to achieve this. Nationalism was despised by Marx as a form of false consciousness used to underpin capitalism.

- Above all perhaps, Stalin failed to deal with the problem of scarcity of resources in the USSR. This created competition among its people for those resources. Competition, however, forms the basis of capitalist economic organisation. Thus, Stalinist rule had recreated the conditions that spawned capitalism. This is how Trotsky criticised this development:

The basis of bureaucratic rule is the poverty of society in objects of consumption with the resulting struggle of each against all. When there are enough goods in the store the purchasers can come whenever they want to. When there are little goods the purchasers are forced to stand in line. When the lines are very long it is necessary to appoint a policeman to keep order. Such is the starting point of the power of Soviet bureaucracy.

From *The Revolution Betrayed*, 1936

Marxism today

The end of the Cold War

Although the years 1989–91 can be identified as the end of the great Marxist era, the truth is that Marxist-inspired communism had been in decline for many years before that. Indeed, many have argued that the regimes set up in the USSR, China, Cuba and elsewhere became politically corrupted within a short time of their establishment.

What was remarkable about the end of the Cold War was the rapidity with which Marxist

systems were dismantled. Within a decade, the centralised socialist economies were transformed into free-market systems. Communist parties were quickly marginalised as new parliamentary democracy was introduced, with accompanying multiparty systems. Communist parties either disappeared altogether or transformed themselves into socialist parties, which accepted the existence of mixed economies and pluralist states.

Despite this, the quasi-Marxist regime in Cuba continued and the Chinese state remained officially Marxist, although it was rapidly introducing a free-market system. Currently, small communist guerrilla bands continue to operate in Nepal and various parts of Southeast Asia and South and Central America, but they remain minor remnants of a once mighty ideological movement. There appears to be no way in which Marxism could re-establish itself in the foreseeable future.

A word of caution needs to be added, however. The current world hegemony of Western-style capitalism may not be permanent, particularly where the less economically developed countries of the world are concerned. Just as poor Muslim countries are embracing fundamentalist Islam in their struggle against Western values, other less economically developed countries could adopt Marxist or quasi-Marxist ideologies as a means of rallying the people against economic imperialism. Frantz Fanon's belief that those he called the 'Wretched of the Earth' – the exploited poor peasantry – may yet rise up against their oppressors could still vindicate Marx's analysis.

The relevance of Marx

If Marxism is in such a state of decline or even completely extinct, why should we continue to study it? There are four possible reasons:

1 We could accept Marx's analysis of history as perfectly valid. The fact that the final stage – the destruction of capitalism and its

replacement by a worker's socialist state – has been neither widespread nor successful should not deter us. Marx's dialectic method and his assertion that economic relationships form the basis of any society remain interesting and cogent theories. Although historians are nearly unanimous in their belief that Marx's explanation of historical development is too simplistic and many other factors determine human development, this does not necessarily negate the basic truth that economics and technological change are the main driving forces of history.

Even if Marx's methodology does indeed contain fatal flaws, it is useful in provoking a critical analysis of history. The dialectic method of philosophical inquiry requires that a proposition is confronted by its opposite. Through this, we may hope to arrive at the truth. It is therefore feasible to use Marx's propositions as one side of such a process. In other words, Marx's theories may not contain the truth, but they can help us to unlock the mysteries of historical development.

2 Between 1917 and 1990, a large part of the world was governed by regimes that claimed Marxism as their political inspiration. It is therefore important that we understand the theories that underpinned those regimes. It is interesting to speculate whether these regimes might have endured and been successful had they not become hopeless distortions of orthodox Marxist ideology.

3 In terms of purely historical study, Marx's descriptions of nineteenth-century capitalism, especially in Britain, remain a magnificent body of work, containing insights and analyses that are rooted in empirical, scientific research. Even the most vehement opponents of Marx would have to admit that this aspect of his work informs us in a way which perhaps no other social theorist of the day was able to do.

4 Marx's method of studying past eras can still be useful when applied to the study of contemporary societies. His analyses of class, alienation, surplus value and the dynamic nature of capitalism can still be examined usefully, especially with reference to global forces. We may not accept his conclusions about how capitalism would develop and eventually be destroyed, but many of his insights remain either valid or simply interesting.

Marxism and socialism

It is necessary to clear up a possible source of confusion before making some comparisons between Marxism and socialism. Marx was, in a sense, a socialist. He saw socialism as the system that would succeed capitalism; it was, in essence, the negation of capitalism. Furthermore, he saw socialism as the essential precondition for the final transition of society to communism. The replacement of the capitalist state by the socialist state was the immediate objective of all left-wing revolutionaries in the nineteenth century. Marx numbered himself among these, especially when socialism split from anarcho-communism in 1872. The difference between Marx and other socialists, such as Auguste Blanqui in France and H. M. Hyndman in England, was that Marx believed socialism would evolve into a final historical stage in which the state would become unnecessary. In other words, Marxism, like anarcho-communism, could be described as 'socialism without a state'.

Marxism can be characterised as distinct from socialism in its revolutionary fervour. Marx insisted that socialism would almost certainly come about through bloody revolution. In this sense, he seems closer to anarchism than socialism. He belonged to a European tradition of revolutionary socialism, which included syndicalists, radical peasant leaders and even nihilists.

Indeed, a great deal of Marx's later political thought was directed at leading the opposition to evolutionary forms of socialism. Those who believed that socialism could come about through democratic means, notably Eduard Bernstein in

Germany, and those who thought that capitalism would spontaneously develop into socialism (for example, the English Fabians) represented a huge threat to Marx's hopes for the success of the movement. Marx believed that, without revolution, socialism would become subverted. It would be sidetracked into believing that compromises could be made with capitalism on the road to a workers' state. Marx insisted that such compromises were the greatest danger to socialism. Trade unions, welfare provisions, higher wages and participation in bourgeois democracy would hold back the development of socialist consciousness. The proletariat would be duped into believing they were achieving emancipation, when in fact their cooperation would only help to maintain and strengthen capitalism's hold over society.

Marx was adamant that the capitalist state had to be dealt a shattering blow. No compromises would be successful. The true nature of capitalism could only be fully revealed by revolutionary activity. Without revolution, there would be no socialism.

Marx's followers can certainly claim that, in this respect at least, his fears about the subversion of socialism were justified. In the century after Marx's death, socialism did indeed become largely evolutionary in nature. In the advanced capitalist states – e.g. France, Britain, Germany – the developments that he had feared came to pass. Socialist parties gradually became increasingly moderate as the conditions of the working class were improved. By the end of the Second World War, there were few revolutionary socialists left outside China and the Soviet bloc. Socialism evolved into democratic socialism and then moderate social democracy. Capitalism won its battle against socialism, not by resisting the revolution but by disguising its true nature from working-class movements that preferred compromise to confrontation. At least in this respect, Marx was right.

Exam focus

Using this chapter and other resources available to you, answer the following questions.

Short questions

Your answers should be about 400 words long.

1 Distinguish between revolutionary and evolutionary socialism.
2 What does a socialist mean by the term 'equality'?
3 Distinguish between democratic socialism and social democracy.
4 How do socialists view social class?
5 What is meant by the term collectivism?
6 Distinguish between a socialist and a liberal view of equality.
7 How do socialists reconcile equality and freedom?
8 Distinguish between socialism and communism.
9 To what extent did Marx believe that a communist revolution was inevitable?

Long questions

Your answers should be about 1200 words long.

1 'Socialists have disagreed over means more than ends.' To what extent is this true?
2 'Socialism is best defined in terms of its changing attitude to capitalism.' Explain and discuss this statement.
3 How have socialists disagreed over the role of the state?
4 In what ways has British socialism differed from forms of socialism seen elsewhere?
5 Distinguish between Marxism and other forms of socialism.
6 Why did capitalism not collapse in the West when Marxists had regarded the demise of capitalism as 'inevitable'?
7 To what extent were commmunist regimes in Eastern Europe distortions of Marxist principles?

Further reading

Benn, T. (1980) *Arguments for Socialism*, Penguin Books.
Berki, R. N. (1975) *Socialism*, Everyman.
Bottomore, T. and Rubel, M. (eds.) (1970) *Karl Marx: Selected Writings in Sociology and Social Philosophy*, Penguin Books.
Crick, B. (1987) *Socialism*, Open University Press.
Harrington, M. (1993) *Socialism Past and Future*, Pluto Press.
McLellan, D. (ed.) (2000) *Karl Marx: Selected Writings*, Oxford University Press.
McLellan, D. (1980) *Marxism After Marx: An Introduction*, HarperCollins.
Pimlot, B. (ed.) (1984) *Fabian Essays in Socialist Thought*, Heinemann.
Sassoon, D. (1997) *One Hundred Years of Socialism*, New Press.
Singer, P. (2000) *Marx: A Very Short Introduction*, Oxford University Press.
Williams, B. (2000) *Lenin*, Longman.
Wood, A. (2004) *Karl Marx* (2nd edn), Routledge.
Wright, A. (1987) *Socialisms: Theories and Practices*, Oxford Paperbacks.

Chapter 4

Anarchism

Anarchism refers to a collection of political movements that have emerged at various times and in various circumstances since the end of the eighteenth century. All anarchists are united by the belief that each individual is sovereign, and should therefore be the sole judge of his or her own actions; that no person has the right to exercise power over another; and that the political state is an unnatural institution, which should either be abolished or have a minimal, non-political, non-coercive role. These three beliefs define anarchism.

Anarchists have disagreed about what should replace the modern state and structure of society, and this has given rise to different strands of anarchism with varying objectives. Nihilists oppose any kind of social order and organisation. Syndicalists and communists favour common ownership of property, common norms of behaviour and voluntary communities that are self-governing, directly democratic, and in which all members share a common set of values. Anarcho-capitalists support private property and inequality, but oppose state regulation of any kind. There are a number of other anarchist traditions that combine a variety of beliefs about the best form of society and human conduct.

Introduction

There is a fundamental paradox in the anarchist tradition. On the one hand, all anarchists are united around three basic beliefs – the sovereignty of the individual, that no individual has authority over any other, and opposition to the political state. On the other hand, anarchists are fiercely divided about how these beliefs should be translated into social reality. Put another way, anarchists have agreed about the problems of modern society, but disagreed about how to solve them.

The following ideas are common to all anarchists:

- A belief in the complete sovereignty of the individual.

- A belief that the individual is the best judge of his or her own actions.

- An assertion that no individual or body should exert power or force over any other individual.

- Total opposition to the existence of the political state.

The following are ideas that divide anarchists:

- Most anarchists oppose private property, but some accept limited property as inevitable or a necessary evil.

- Some anarchists are individualists who oppose social organisation; others believe social communities are natural and desirable.

- Some anarchists believe in common ownership and no system of exchange of goods; others propose exchange on the basis of mutual benefit.

- Some, so-called 'anarcho-anarchists' accept that a completely free market economy can have just outcomes.

- Some anarcho-communists propose small, natural communities; others believe communities should be based on industrial or occupational groups.

There can be difficulties in distinguishing between anarchism and communism, between anarchism and socialism, and between anarchism and extreme forms of liberalism (sometimes described as libertarianism). These issues will be tackled later in this chapter; at this stage it is useful to consider anarchism as a distinctive set of political traditions.

A further problem arises from the undeniable fact that there has never been any significant example of anarchism being put into practice on a significant scale. It is true that there have been examples of small anarchist communities, such as the many communes that sprang up among the youth protest movement of the 1960s and 1970s, the 1,000-strong Christiania community in Denmark set up in 1970 (now disbanding), and a brief anarchist period in Barcelona during the Spanish Civil War of the 1930s. However, these experiments have been small and short-lived. The tradition is therefore open to the charge that it is merely a utopian set of ideals, with no realistic hope of practical success. It is hard to counter this criticism.

Why, then, is anarchism so widely studied? The answer is twofold. First, as a philosophy, anarchism has been expounded by many profound and authoritative thinkers, from Jean-Jacques Rousseau, one of the inspirations behind the French Revolution of 1789, to the US philosopher Robert Nozick, a contemporary hero for those who support totally free-market capitalism. In the 200 years between Rousseau and Nozick, many other philosophers and political activists have written or marched under the banner of anarchism. In one way or another, they have had an important impact on the development of political thought.

Second, anarchism provides a comprehensive critique of virtually all aspects of modern society. Anarchists have forced us to question such fundamentals as the nature and functions of the state, the importance of personal freedom, the basis upon which societies are founded, the role of private property and the system by which goods and services are exchanged and distributed. Such a critique can deepen our understanding of how modern society operates and how it is developing. Over the past two centuries, anarchists may have alerted us to the dangers of state power and taught us to guard our personal freedoms with greater determination.

Early developments

As is the case for a number of other ideologies, anarchism, as an influential movement, can be traced back to the time of the French Revolution at the end of the eighteenth century. Like both liberalism and socialism, it can be seen partly as a product of the Enlightenment.

The Enlightenment opened people's minds to the possibility that traditional forms of authority could be challenged. The French and US revolutions were largely the product of such thinking. Yet while these revolutionaries were determined to replace autocratic government with representative institutions, other philosophers and activists were putting forward far more radical ideas. Perhaps, they argued, former examples of political authority could be replaced with no government at all. Or, rather, they could be replaced by the self-government of each individual. Rousseau had already argued that this was the ideal situation, but had reluctantly come to the conclusion that it would be simply impractical. To be capable of self-government, he admitted, every individual would have to enjoy perfect enlightenment. 'Such men are gods', he asserted, dismissing the idea of self-government or direct democracy.

The most important anarchist philosopher of this revolutionary period came, ironically, from England – a country whose traditional forms of authority survived the revolutionary challenge, but produced one of their most effective critics. This was William Godwin, who was arguably the father of philosophical anarchism. He held an optimistic view of the nature of humankind, in direct contrast to contemporary conservatives, such as Edmund Burke. Godwin believed that people were capable of rational thought and moral perfection. Given the correct education and nurturing, coupled with the removal of the evils of the state, everyone was capable of governing his or her own actions, and of considering the wellbeing and feelings of others when deciding upon action. This was an original view of the state of humankind. It opened the door to thinking about government and society in new ways, unhindered by fears of disorder if social discipline were to be relaxed.

Godwin did not recommend revolution as the way to achieve his goals. He believed that education and reasoned debate would eventually lead to a society dominated by rational, moral human beings. They would not need government to direct their actions to good ends: a just, equal and ordered society could emerge naturally from the changes created in the human condition. He described how the state should be as restricted as possible:

> *It is earnestly to be desired that each man should be wise enough to govern himself, without the intervention of any compulsory restraint, since government, even in its best state, is an evil. The object principally to be aimed at is that we should have as little of it as the general peace of human society will permit.*

From *Enquiry Concerning Social Justice*, 1792

This now appears intensely idealistic and utopian. It is true that Godwin did not see his dreams develop to any extent, but he provided a solid philosophical underpinning for the more active anarchists who were to follow.

During the nineteenth century, anarchist ideals gradually caught hold throughout Europe and eventually reached the USA. Anarchism took on different forms, largely depending upon which groups were involved, but all anarchists had an interest in overthrowing the existing order. The most disadvantaged groups were its main standard bearers. It was therefore the exploited peasantry in Russia who formed self-governing anarchist communes, the poorest members of the working classes in France and Northern Europe who supported socialist forms of anarchism, and the independent pioneers of the USA who sometimes became anarcho-individualists in order to preserve their independence from the growing power of federal government.

Revolutionary anarchism

In the middle of the nineteenth century, revolutionary movements of various kinds sprang up all over Europe. Most were socialist in nature and one – Marxist communism – was to become pre-eminent. These developments were a response to the inequalities and deprivations that were seen to be the consequences of free-market capitalism. At the time, there were no clear distinctions drawn between revolutionary socialism, communism and anarchism. They were merely tendencies within the same broad anti-capitalist, anti-landlord movement. As the century progressed, however, the differences between them began to widen, and in 1872, when the leading anarchist Mikhail Bakunin finally split with Karl Marx, anarchism was born as a distinct tradition. In particular, Bakunin and the anarchists differed fundamentally on how society would develop after the downfall of capitalism.

Meanwhile, in those parts of Europe still dominated by agriculture, the final remnants of the old feudal order were breaking down. In some countries, notably Russia, the state remained dominated by landed interests, and anarchism caught hold among those members of the peasantry who were impatient to create social justice. This was mainly to be achieved by seizing land from estate owners and redistributing it among the poorer peasants. Revolutionary anarchism, in these instances, was therefore localised. However, the champions of the peasants, such as Peter Kropotkin, understood that if social justice on the land were to be achieved, the centralised, autocratic state would also have to be destroyed.

Revolutionary socialists and Marxists all proposed that the capitalist state should be taken over by the working class and run by that class in the interests of greater equality and common ownership of the means of production. Revolutionary anarchists shared their hatred of capitalism and the state that supported it, but insisted that the whole apparatus of the state should be completely abolished. While socialists attacked the existing state in order to bring an end to capitalism, anarchists hoped to destroy the state for its own sake. In some ways, the destruction of capitalism was for many anarchists a by-product of the abolition of the state. This was the basis of the Bakunin–Marx conflict referred to above.

Three main strands of revolutionary anarchism emerged. The first was 'nihilism', the most violent and revolutionary of all the left-wing creeds. Its proponents included the notorious Russian Sergei Nechaev (1847–82) and the German radical Max Stirner (1806–56). They wished to destroy the state and set all individuals free without providing any prescription as to how post-revolutionary society should be formed. In practice, they were opposed to social order *per se*. Members of the second strand were known as communists. Many were closely associated with Marx and, later, with Vladimir Ilyich Lenin, disagreeing with them about means rather than ends. The anarchists rejected the Marxist–Leninist insistence that revolution should usher in an interim workers' state; for anarchists, all states are evil. Anarcho-communists, such as Peter Kropotkin and Mikhail Bakunin, wished to move directly from the capitalist state to a no-state organisation of self-governing communities (these were often known as communes, from the French term for a small village or community – hence the term communist). Members of the third strand were known as 'individualists'. These anarchists, many of whom were from the USA, were less concerned with the fate of the state, or with the destruction of private property, than they were with the sovereignty of the individual. They were not revolutionary in the sense of proposing violence, but in that they wished to see individuals withdrawing from the state so that it would become irrelevant to their lives. They preached resistance rather than revolution in its traditional form. Celebrated US pioneers such as Henry Thoreau (1817–62) and Benjamin Tucker (1854–1939) were its leading exponents.

During the nineteenth and twentieth centuries, revolutionary anarchists were responsible for a number of assassinations, insurrections, industrial strikes and violent demonstrations. The philosophy of those who sought to bring down the state by the use of violence – by no means the belief of all anarchists – was that by constantly attacking and undermining the state, it would lose its will to survive and be ripe for toppling by an increasingly exploited working class. During the Spanish Civil War (1936–39), anarchists hoped to fill the void that would be left if the anti-fascist forces were to prevail. (In the event, the fascists under Francisco Franco (1892–1975) took power, and the anarchist movement melted away or moved underground.) As recently as the 1960s and 1970s, anarchist cells have committed atrocities as a means of undermining the state. The Baader-Meinhof Gang in Germany and the Italian Red Brigade are notable examples.

In the event, revolutionary anarchists were unable to attract sufficient support from the working classes to bring down any of the states that they attacked. Successes proved to be both modest and short-lived.

Core values of anarchism

The sovereignty of the individual

Those who treat anarchism as merely a branch of socialism or communism are mistaken, primarily because anarchists insist that each individual is completely independent of all other individuals. For anarchists the individual is sovereign. Socialists and communists, on the other hand, see humankind as essentially social, arguing that there is a natural interdependence among people and that we prefer to achieve goals collectively rather than individually.

A word of caution is needed here. First, the most celebrated of the nineteenth-century anarchists, Mikhail Bakunin, disagreed with this fundamental anarchist belief. He suggested that we are bound by a form of natural law, which dictates that we behave in a social rather than an individualistic manner. He asserted that 'social solidarity is the first human law, freedom is the second law'. By this he meant that, although we are free, sovereign individuals, we do not have the free will to deny our social nature. In other words, we are free individuals within the natural laws of society.

Bakunin, one of the most prominent revolutionary anarchists

Most anarchists, however, are convinced that we are total individuals. Furthermore, they insist that this does not conflict with the needs of society. Given free will, any moral human being will either form natural communities with other people (as the communist Peter Kropotkin argued), or will pursue his or her own self-interest without interfering with fellow individuals (as the individualist anarchist Benjamin Tucker asserted). Rational, moral human beings do not need to be told to behave with sympathy for others, since they will naturally do so. This means that we could live in society, adjusting our conduct to the needs of others, without feeling constrained or controlled.

Bakunin expressed the idea of the sovereignty of the individual in his great work, *Social and Economic Bases of Anarchism* (1872):

> *To be personally free means every man living in a social milieu not to surrender his thought or will to any authority but his own reason and his own understanding of justice.*

Individualist anarchists, for example Godwin, Stirner and Thoreau, stress individual liberty to a greater extent than communists such as Bakunin and Kropotkin. They are less concerned with the need to create a free and just society and more interested in restoring individual liberty. They stress that no individual has the right to exercise power over any other. This eliminates all possibility that we may be governed by any government or by any laws.

The nature of liberty

Perhaps the best way to explain the anarchist view of freedom is to contrast it with the liberal view. Both anarchists and liberals begin with the basic belief that all individuals are born free and ought to remain so. However, liberals concede that freedom cannot be unconditional. If an individual, in exercising his or her freedom, interferes with the freedom of another, this is unacceptable. In other words, we cannot exercise our own freedom at the expense of the freedom of others. This means that we can only be free within laws, for without them we live in fear of encroachments on our liberty by the exercise of freedom by others. It follows from this that we have to submit ourselves to some kind of government and that government's laws. The typical liberal view, therefore, sees freedom in terms of its restrictions (so-called negative liberty). As Rousseau remarked, we may need to be forced to be free.

Anarchists firmly reject this view. They see negative liberty as external restraint and this offends their basic principle of individual sovereignty. How, then, do anarchists avoid the problem that, if everybody considers themselves to be completely free, the world will dissolve into a state of war and of constant fear, the nightmare envisaged by the English philosopher Thomas Hobbes? Their solution is twofold:

1 They have an optimistic view of human nature. (There are some exceptions to this among anarcho-individualists, but they are not in the mainstream.) As long as we are allowed to live a moral and enlightened existence, we will take into account the interests of others. We have a natural empathy for our fellow humans and will adjust our actions accordingly.

2 This positive view allows for the liberal conception of external restraint to be replaced by internal restraint, which William Godwin called 'private judgement'. In a world where we are all returned to our natural state, uncorrupted by the evils of modern society and the repressive state, artificial laws become unnecessary. Bakunin took this view a stage further by asserting that humankind in a natural state is bound by natural laws. These have been replaced in the modern world by artificial, man-made laws. Natural laws govern our conduct towards our fellow creatures. When we obey them, we do not feel constrained since we are acting naturally. For many anarchists, therefore, a new order can be established, governed by natural, rather than state-enforced, laws.

Critics of the anarchist view of liberty concentrate on their assertion that humankind is naturally 'good'. If this claim is mistaken, the whole anarchist conception of freedom fails. Liberals and conservatives have been united in the belief that the natural goodness of people is either an illusion or is, at best, inconsistent. An answer to this was provided by Rousseau, Godwin and Bakunin, all of whom argued that individuals are neither good nor bad; in other words, an individual is not born with any internal moral code. (Bakunin suggested, however, that an individual does soon learn to understand natural law.) Thus, if society could create a community of morally perfect people, humankind could live together without state-enforced laws, because individuals would control their own behaviour naturally.

Rousseau ultimately rejected the anarchist utopia on the grounds that such a society could only be very small-scale in nature. Godwin, Bakunin and others remained more optimistic. The Italian anarchist Enrico Malatesta (1853–1932) expressed the idea of a society of free, caring individuals in sentimental fashion: 'Men must love each other and look on each other as members of one family, if things are to go well with them' (*Anarchy*, 1906).

Critique of the state and consent theory

Although anarchists have disagreed about the precise character of human nature, they have all agreed that the state should be abolished. Their critique of the state offers a number of reasons for this. These are given below.

The state is oppressive

The state is oppressive and represents the few who seek to oppress the many. This is close to the Marxist view, which describes the state as the 'management committee' of the ruling class in any age. Historically, the ruling class was the aristocracy and landed gentry; in the modern age, it is seen as the forces of capitalism, which exploit workers, peasants in less economically developed countries, and consumers everywhere. Enrico Malatesta summarised this view:

The basic function of government everywhere in all times, whatever title it adopts and whatever its origin and organisation may be, is always that of oppressing and exploiting the masses, of defending the oppressors and exploiters; and its principal, characteristic and indispensable instruments are the police agent, the tax collector, the soldier and the gaoler.
From *Anarchy*, 1906

✔ **Key Term**

Autonomy
A term relating to the anarchist view of liberty. Autonomy suggests individuals are free from external restraints, but are also free from internal restrictions created by corrupted societies.

The state removes freedom

The state takes away our freedom. It subjects us to laws and controls that are artificial, offending the basic principle of individual sovereignty. In a colourful diatribe against government, the French anarchist Pierre-Joseph Proudhon (1809–65) expressed this principle as follows:

> *To be governed is to be at every operation, at every transaction, noted, registered, enrolled, taxed, stamped, measured, numbered, assessed, licensed, authorised, admonished, forbidden, reformed, corrected, punished.*
>
> From *General Idea of the Revolution in the Nineteenth Century*, 1846

Like liberals, the anarchists see an incompatability between the power of the state and the freedom of the individual. The more powerful the state, the more liberty is threatened. Furthermore, as the liberal Lord Acton (1834–1902) famously declared, 'Power corrupts and absolute power corrupts absolutely'. Indeed, another of Acton's best-known assertions could easily have been uttered by an anarchist:

> *It is easier to find people fit to govern themselves than people to govern others. Every man is the best, the most responsible judge of his own advantage.*
>
> From *The Study of History*, 1895

The state is corrupting

In common with many liberals, anarchists believe that the act of governing is in itself corrupting. Those who come into government may do so with good motives, but inevitably lose their idealism and become exploiters themselves. The socialist novelist George Orwell (1903–50) satirised the dangers of power in his 1945 work *Animal Farm*, which he mainly wrote as a critique of the Soviet Union – a state that had been born of high ideals but had descended into totalitarianism. In 1870, Mikhail Bakunin wrote a passage that looks as reasonable today as he believed it to be so then:

> *Nothing is as dangerous for man's morality as the habit of commanding. The best of men, the most intelligent, unselfish, generous and pure, will always and inevitably be corrupted in this pursuit. Two feelings inherent in the exercise of power never fail to produce this demoralization: contempt for the masses, and, for the man in power, an exaggerated sense of his own worth.*
>
> From *Federalism, Socialism, Anti-Theologism*

The state is unnatural

Anarchists see the state as an artificial form of society. The anarchist view is either that humankind should be free to form voluntary, natural communities (usually small-scale ones) or that the individual should be free to withdraw altogether from any political organisation. The political state denies this freedom and creates an unnatural community. For this reason, anarchists oppose nationalism, since the nation, although arguably a natural organism, is usually expressed through statehood and so becomes unnatural. Peter Kropotkin was perhaps the most important exponent of the view that humankind should naturally form self-governing communes, arguing that this was how people had organised themselves throughout most of history. Once the state was abolished, he hoped, humankind could return to such an age.

This final critique of the state is central to anarchist belief. If communities are voluntary, they argue, there should be no need for government and laws. If we freely choose to enter a community and support its accepted norms of behaviour, we do not need any compulsion to conform. The state, in contrast, is an artificial organisation. Not everyone will wish to conform and so there must be compulsion.

Anarchist responses to consent theory

At this point, it is useful to confront anarchist opposition to the state with the liberal argument. Liberals understand that states, by their nature, threaten individual liberty. Since the days of the English philosopher John Locke in the late seventeenth century, liberals have developed a theory of political consent to overcome this difficulty. If the people come together voluntarily to set up government over themselves, the state is no longer seen as an imposition. If we consent to be governed, we accept justified curtailments of our liberty. This can be seen most clearly in the philosophy behind the American Constitution, which was written in 1787.

The early liberal view is also known as 'contract theory'. This suggests that the state represents a contract between the governed and the government. The people consent to obey the laws created by the state, while the state is bound to safeguard the liberties of the people as far as possible. If the state fails to honour the contract, the people have the right to dissolve it.

At first sight this seems reasonable. Not so, say anarchists. They offer three main objections:

1 Individuals cannot give up their own liberty in this way if they are to remain true to their real nature. Liberty is a birthright that cannot be conceded. Its abandonment would be a denial of our humanity.

2 Consent theory implies that there will be a majority and a minority. In setting up the state, even by free agreement, the majority oppresses the minority. The US individualist anarchist Henry Thoreau asserted that 'a government in which the majority rule in all cases cannot be based on justice'. Thus, only if all the people offer their consent could the setting up of a state be justified. This seems an unlikely event. In any case, it is invalidated by anarchists' third objection.

3 Even if consent is justly arrived at, it cannot be binding on future generations. For the state to be legitimate, therefore, it would have to be subject to continuous consent. This is clearly impractical, unless the community is extremely small (an Israeli kibbutz might fit the bill). Political states, which force laws on people, can never claim consent unless it is expressly given at all times. In practice, therefore, those anarchists who have made specific proposals for setting up communities suggest that any decisions which have to be made should be reached through direct democracy.

Opposition to property

Not all anarchists have opposed private property. Some contemporary anarcho-capitalists (sometimes known as libertarians), such as the US philosopher Robert Nozick, have asserted that private property is acceptable as long as it has been legally and justly obtained. These thinkers are anarchists in that they believe the state should not be allowed to interfere with the ownership of property and its uses. In addition, the nineteenth-century French anarchist Proudhon reluctantly came to the conclusion that property was a necessary evil in a modern society. As long as the ownership of property was not used to exploit others – either workers or consumers – and the distribution of property was not too unequal, it could be justified. This is explored further in the section on mutualism (see p. 144).

Pierre-Joseph Proudhon, who coined the anarchist maxim 'All property is theft', but recognised property as a necessary evil

Despite these two exceptions, most anarchists believe that social justice can only be achieved if private property is abolished. The inequality it causes is not the only reason for their objection. Many anarchists see the state as the protector of property interests; without a state, property owners feel vulnerable and insecure. Indeed, Rousseau, a precursor of anarchism, suggested that property had been the fundamental cause of humankind's oppression. Kropotkin, who of the great anarchists probably came closest to pure communism, put it this way:

> In common to all socialists, the anarchists hold that the private ownership of land, capital and machinery has had its time; that it is condemned to disappear, and that all the requisites for production must, and will, become the common property of society, and be managed in common by the producers of wealth.

> From *Revolutionary Pamphlets*, 1892

A variety of proposals have been made by anarchists for replacing private property with common ownership. However, they all have one aspect in common that decisively separates anarchism from socialism – that the state should not be the vehicle for common ownership. Communities, trade unions, groups of industrial workers and cooperative organisations might all take over the means of production and use them for the common good, but the idea of public ownership being under the control of the state would clearly offend the core principles of the movement.

Critique of capitalism

As has been noted, some contemporary libertarian anarchists support the maintenance of free-market capitalism, provided it is genuinely free market. However, most anarchists, both in the nineteenth century and today, see capitalism as the root of a number of social ills.

Above all, capitalism is opposed by most anarchists because it exploits, and in doing so negates true freedom. Nineteenth-century anarchists, such as Bakunin and Kropotkin, were like Marxists and other socialists in seeing the working classes and the downtrodden peasantry as victims of capitalist exploitation. They would only be truly free when capitalism was overthrown.

The most vociferous of the anti-capitalist anarchists were the anarcho-syndicalists, who flourished in the late nineteenth and early twentieth centuries. They proposed that the workers should seize control of the instruments of capitalist domination and run them in the interests of all. Georges Sorel, who is often classified as a socialist, led the syndicalist movement in France. For him and his followers, the 'natural' community was the fellowship of workers engaged in the same industry. Such a fellowship should be self-governing and independent of any centralised state. Exceptionally violent in their revolutionary outlook, the syndicalists believed that once capitalism had been undermined and then destroyed, most of the functions of the state would become redundant.

Contemporary anarchists have turned their attention to the ways in which international capitalism is exploiting workers and peasants in poorer countries and exploiting consumers in more economically developed countries. Many, known as 'eco-anarchists', see the degradation of the natural environment as a direct consequence of capitalism. These activists, often seen demonstrating at meetings of world leaders and the World Trade Organisation (WTO), attack both national governments and international institutions, including the WTO itself, the International Monetary Fund (IMF) and the World Bank. These supranational organisations are viewed by anarchists as the heirs of the nineteenth-century capitalist state.

On a more philosophical level, anarchists have argued that capitalism creates inequality. Inequality is, in itself, a threat to freedom, since those who enjoy greater prosperity have the opportunity to dominate the less well off. For most anarchists, social justice is tied up with the concept of liberty, because, they argue, we are all born both free and equal, with equal needs. Capitalism and the state, which supports it, sponsor inequality and, indeed, have celebrated it. Mainstream anarchists therefore oppose both. Anarchists reject religion and nationalism, too; they see both as artificial creations designed to rob people of their personal liberty.

Institution	Reasons for opposition
The state	It oppresses the individual, supports private property and represents the government of the many by the few
Private property	It creates inequality, gives rise to oppressive laws and is a denial of the natural right to the fruits of the earth (though a small minority, including Proudhon, saw it as a 'necessary evil')
Law	Laws are a denial of individual liberty
Capitalism	Goods and services are exchanged on an unfair basis and workers are exploited, creating inequality and giving rise to an oppressive state (though this critique does not apply to anarcho-capitalists)
Religion	Most anarchists argue that it presents a false view of the world. All anarchists argue that it encourages authority to be exercised by some individuals over others
Nationalism	Nations are artificial, not natural, communities. Nationalism leads to conflict and war

Table 4.1 What anarchists are opposed to and why

The reasons why anarchists oppose capitalism, and various other institutions, are summarised in Table 4.1.

Types of anarchism

Anarcho-communism

This has been the dominant form of anarchism. It is sometimes described simply as 'collectivism', or even as 'communism'. However, both these terms have also been applied to Marxism and socialism, which are distinctive movements. The use of the full term 'anarcho-communism' is therefore preferable.

The principal exponents of this branch of anarchism are Mikhail Bakunin, Peter Kropotkin, Elisée Reclus (1830–1905) and Enrico Malatesta, all of whom presented an alternative to socialism and Marxism in response to the perceived evils of capitalism. Anarcho-communists were at the height of their influence towards the end of the nineteenth century and in the early twentieth century – the same period in which Marxism and revolutionary socialism were prominent.

The anarcho-communists proposed dissolving the state – either by violent or peaceful means – and replacing it with small-scale communes (favoured by Kropotkin and Malatesta) or federations of workers (Bakunin's view). Despite differences in emphasis, the various anarcho-communist groups agreed that these communities would display the following characteristics:

- They would be voluntary: each individual would have the right to join a community or to leave it. Communities might vary in their organisation and values, but individuals would not be forced to conform as their decision to join would be taken freely.

- They would be self-governing and there would be no overarching authority to bind them together.

- Internally, they would be governed by some form of direct democracy. This is perhaps the most problematic aspect of such communism. What would happen to minority opinions? Would minorities be forced to accept majority decisions and so become oppressed? This was the very situation anarchists hoped to escape. It is in this context that anarchists can be seen at their most optimistic. They argued that the process of democracy would produce a unanimous conclusion, or minorities would accept majority opinion without feeling oppressed or else leave the community and find another more to their liking. Critics naturally see this as impractical and utopian.

- On the whole, the communities would be self-sustaining. This would avoid excessive need for cooperation with other communities. Too much interdependence, anarchists feared, might result in the restoration of capitalist exchange systems, inequality, rivalry and the need for administration, which might turn into government. Where exchanges were essential, they would take place on the basis of mutual benefit. Instead of the capitalist exchange system, which involves negotiated prices on the basis of supply and demand, mutual-benefit systems would involve exchange being calculated on the basis that both parties to the transaction would benefit fairly. Kropotkin described his own proposals for this kind of system as 'mutual aid', and his vision is perhaps the one most likely to come to people's minds when they think of anarchism. Malatesta was involved in establishing communes based on mutual benefit exchange among the Italian peasantry in the nineteenth century, while Kropotkin was an inspiration behind the Jura Federation in the Swiss–French border country after 1873. Mutual benefit exchange is the basis of the kibbutz system in Israel, the Christiania experiment in Denmark, and many independent subsistence communities in the USA.

- Goods and services would be distributed within the community on an equal basis, according to need. All production and distribution would be organised collectively.

Kropotkin believed that membership of a community should be on the basis of a natural empathy between individuals. Just as prehistoric humans and many species in the animal kingdom naturally formed social, cooperative groups, so should modern humankind. Bakunin, on the other hand, argued that workers in the same industry would have a natural affinity, so occupation would be the most successful basis for cooperation.

The philosophy behind such mainstream anarchist thought is best summarised by Reclus:

But whether it is a question of small or large groups of the human species, it is always through solidarity, through the association of spontaneous, co-ordinated forces that all progress is made... We know that, if our descendants are to reach their high destiny of science and liberty, they will owe it to their coming together more and more intimately, to the incessant collaboration, to this mutual aid from which brotherhood grows little by little.

From *Evolution and Revolution*, 1891

Anarcho-individualism

Although anarcho-communism can be seen as the classical form of anarchism, the individualist movement was also extensive and influential. Its principal authority was the nineteenth-century German radical, Max Stirner. His best known work, *The Ego and His Own*, was published in 1845 and became something of a bible for anarcho-individualists. His main influence, however, was not in Europe but in the USA.

Stirner differed from the anarcho-communists in that he had a specific view of human nature. For him, humankind was driven principally by egoism, i.e. the drive to pursue its own self-interest. He asserted that notions of individuals being naturally sociable and cooperative were false. The state was to be opposed mainly on the grounds that it denied people's egoism, controlling their behaviour and forcing them into unnatural social relations. Stirner summarised this view in a famous and unequivocal passage:

Therefore we two, the State and I, are enemies. I, the egoist, have not at heart the welfare of this human society, I sacrifice nothing to it, I only utilise it.

From *The Ego and His Own*, 1845

Thus Stirner rejected the state and human society as denials of human nature. Josiah Warren (see below), the American anarchist, asserted that any form of social organisation was a denial of individual sovereignty. Having experienced the British socialist, Robert Owen's failed socialist experiment at New Harmony, he complained thus:

> Those who have heard or read anything from me on the subject, know that one of the principal points insisted on is, the forming of societies or any other artificial combinations IS the first, greatest, and most fatal mistake ever committed by legislators and by reformers
>
> From *Manifesto*, 1841

The USA proved to be more fertile ground than Europe for these beliefs, largely because of the deeply rooted sense of human rights, support for individual liberty and suspicion of the state that flourished there. As well as this, socialism, a key opponent of individualist ideas, had made little progress in US society. In Europe, on the other hand, the collectivist movement was well advanced and the state was seen as the main way in which social justice could be delivered.

Three followers of individualism in the USA were Josiah Warren (1798–1874), Benjamin Tucker and Henry Thoreau (1817–62). Warren and Tucker proposed replacing the existing system with cooperative capitalism, which was to be based on two main principles. First, the state would cease to exist and all individuals would be freed from obedience to any laws. Second, individuals should exchange goods and services with each other on the basis of labour value, rather than exchange value. All products would be valued according to the amount and quality of labour that had gone into their production. This would replace the capitalist system, which valued goods according to the forces of demand and supply rather than their intrinsic value. The seller would therefore receive the full value of his or her labour, while the buyer would not have to pay more than a product's true value. This meant that profit would cease to exist.

The schemes of Tucker and Warren were designed to achieve three main objectives. The first was to create social justice without the interference of the state. The second was to create greater (though not complete) social equality. Third, individuals would be truly free, in that

they would no longer be slaves to either the state or to the exploitative nature of capitalism.

Thoreau was less well known in his own lifetime, but was rediscovered by members of the youth-protest movements of the 1960s. His best known work, *Walden*, became a manual for those who opted to withdraw from society and to form self-sufficient, independent communes. Thoreau's opposition to government was less rational than that of other anarchists, but perhaps displayed more common sense. He simply believed that most government was bad government. He admitted that sometimes governments did act in the interests of the people, but this was rarely the case. Therefore, he decided, we should be free to obey or disobey, whichever suited our purpose. This is how Thoreau summed up this view:

> The authority of government, even such as I am willing to submit to, – for I will cheerfully obey those who know and can do better than I, and in many things even those who neither know nor can do so well, – is still an impure one. To be strictly just, it must have the sanction and consent of the governed. It can have no pure right over my person and property but what I concede to it.
>
> From *Walden*, 1854

Unlike Tucker and Warren, Thoreau was not particularly interested in how people might interact. He was solely concerned that the individual should resist the control of the state and, if necessary, withdraw from it altogether.

Although both individualist and communist anarchists oppose the state and capitalism, and both revere individual liberty, the similarity ends there. The anarcho-individualists reject the idea that the state should be replaced by a different kind of social order. For them, there should be no replacement for the state. They also reject the collectivist form of production proposed by the communists, in the belief that this would merely recreate the state by another name. For them, economic and social relations between individuals should be conducted on a free, voluntary basis.

The modern heirs of the egoism of Stirner, the utopian ideas of Warren and Tucker, and the dreamy romanticism of Thoreau, have accepted the need for the restoration of individual self-determination, but have been forced to reach an accommodation with capitalism. For this reason they are often known as 'anarcho-capitalists'.

Anarcho-capitalism

The effects of economic development, increased industrialisation and specialisation of labour in the modern age have rendered the ideas of the nineteenth-century individualists obsolete. Some idealists have suggested turning back the clock and recreating more primitive forms of existence, but they are rare and isolated examples. More commonly, opponents of the state have accepted that the capitalist system of production and exchange is so entrenched that it must be adapted to a circumstance where no state exists.

The most prominent of the contemporary anarcho-capitalists (i.e. modern anarcho-individualists) is Murray Rothbard (1926–95) of the USA, a member of the so-called 'Austrian School' of economics, which proposed a return to completely free economic markets. Rothbard shared Stirner's view that we are all self-interested individuals, but had a more optimistic view of what a world would be like in which everyone is able to pursue that self-interest freely.

Rothbard believed that virtually all the functions of the state can be replaced by the activities of the free market. For example, law and order could be maintained if individuals or groups simply purchased security on the open market. All welfare services could be provided by private enterprise, as could transport, housing and even planning. Furthermore, he argued, if a totally free-market system of exchange were introduced, individuals would become enlightened, understanding that if transactions took place on a fair basis this would benefit everyone in society. When a dispute arose

between individuals, they could resort to private arbitrators with both parties agreeing to abide by the final decision. Why would individuals enter relations with others under such uncertain circumstances? Rothbard's response was that enlightened individuals, with free choice, would only participate if justice were guaranteed. Free-market capitalism is, claimed Rothbard, self-regulating. The state therefore becomes redundant. All that is needed to establish such extreme freedom would be a legal code to which the whole community has consented.

A contemporary of Rothbard, David Friedman (born 1945), takes anarcho-capitalism a stage further. He argues that even law and legal processes could be completely 'privatised'. Indeed, Friedman has argued that virtually all forms of social, economic and political activity can be privatised. A non-revolutionary, Friedman foresees this process as occurring gradually as, one by one, increasing forms of social activity and interaction would be transferred into the private sector. The method of production and exchange would be completely capitalist in nature and the free market would be totally self-regulating. No legal code whatsoever would be necessary.

Anarcho-capitalists are different to other, more 'traditional' anarchists in that they accept the self-interested nature of mankind, recognise our competitive instincts, but also believe that we recognise the need to regulate our own activities in the interests of the successful workings of free markets.

Mutualism

The anarchist doctrine of mutualism, as expounded by Pierre-Joseph Proudhon, bridges the gap between anarcho-communism and anarcho-individualism.

Ironically, Proudhon coined the best-known anarchists' slogan, 'all property is theft', even though he was one of the few anarchists to accept that private property might be tolerated, provided the exploitative aspects of capitalism could be eliminated. He understood that it was essential for small-scale entrepreneurs to own their own means of production. Without this they would lose their independence. Proudhon proposed that peasants should own modest amounts of land, that most workers should be independent, and where large-scale industry was inevitable, that workers themselves should own the means of production. Like the US individualists Warren and Tucker, Proudhon devised a system of exchange that would assign values to goods based on the labour hours used to produce them. Money was to be replaced by 'labour notes' and free credit was to be made available to all, giving individuals the opportunity to set up their own enterprises or to buy land.

Proudhon was not, however, part of the anarcho-individualist tradition. He believed that people should live in small, self-governing communities. As long as the exploitation of workers, peasants and consumers was removed, he argued, people could live in harmony without the need for a coercive state. In this way he attempted to reconcile individual ownership of property with social harmony.

Like the US individualists, Proudhon was an important influence over the establishment of both producer and consumer cooperatives from the 1840s and the commune movements of the 1960s and 1970s. There is even an echo of Proudhon's idea of valuing goods by labour input in the current 'Fair Trade' scheme, which covers a variety of commodities from less economically developed countries where labour has been exploited by the 'unfair' operation of world markets. However, as was the case for much of the anarchist movement, mutualism was swamped in the late nineteenth and early twentieth centuries by the growing popularity of socialism and Marxism among the working classes.

Anarcho-syndicalism

Syndicalism was the name adopted by some revolutionary socialists – mainly French – in the late nineteenth and early twentieth centuries to denote a movement based on the power and organisation of trade unions. Most syndicalists proposed the overthrow of capitalism by workers and peasants and the replacement of the state by a workers' organisation, which would impose worker and peasant ownership of industry and land. In practice, this meant industrial democracy, in which each industry was self-governing on the basis of direct democracy. There would be a centralised state organisation, however, which would organise the distribution of goods and carry out various security functions of government.

The anarchist wing of the syndicalist movement had similar objectives, but opposed the retention of the state. It argued that the self-governing industries and cooperatives would be able to arrange a fair system of exchange, distribution, security and welfare, without the need for a central state. Supporters of this branch are sometimes described as 'radical syndicalists'.

The anarcho-syndicalists gained a reputation as the most violent wing of the anarchist movement. Their French leader, Georges Sorel, asserted that the capitalist state used violence and coercion to maintain its rule and that this should be challenged by even greater violence from the workers. The main weapon they used was the strike – a way of undermining capitalism that it could not combat. Sorel believed that a general strike, in which all workers participated, would actually bring down the state altogether. Such activities became known as **propaganda by deed**.

Key Term

Propaganda by deed
This term refers to the tactic used by the most radical, revolutionary anarchists. When they commit violent acts, the state is forced to respond in an equally violent manner. In this way, the truly oppressive nature of the state is revealed. Anarchists hope that the violent response of the state will persuade people that it is founded on force and so should be resisted.

As the twentieth century progressed, syndicalism began to decline. The violent revolutionary wing was largely absorbed into socialism, while the non-revolutionary part of the movement evolved into a more moderate form, known as 'guild socialism'. The guild socialists took their inspiration from the old craft guilds (metal workers, masons, tailors and so on) that had flourished in the Middle Ages. The guilds were largely self-governing and were granted charters of independence by monarchs over several centuries. This romantic historical image was naturally attractive to anarchists, since it represented a world in which the state's functions were reduced to a minimum and where the collective freedom of natural communities could be safeguarded. However, growing prosperity among the working classes, and the decline of crafts in general, meant that the movement withered away.

Nihilism

The term nihilism is derived from the Latin word *nihil*, meaning 'nothing'. There is no movement as such called nihilism – the term is usually applied to individuals. Max Stirner has been described as a nihilist, as has Sergei Nechaev, an associate of Mikhail Bakunin.

Nihilists believe that all forms of social order are an unjustifiable denial of individual liberty. They have therefore attacked all forms of organisation, not merely the centralised state. Nihilists recommend the completely free exercise of egoism and the unfettered use of **terror**. If the world that results becomes extremely disordered and violent, then so be it, they assert.

In the modern world, nihilism has a good deal in common with the philosophical movement known as 'existentialism'. Existentialists argue that life can only have meaning, and we can only achieve self-realisation, if we throw off society's constraints. Life has meaning for us if we are able to impose ourselves upon it. If we allow society – i.e. its morality and its value system – to impose itself on us, we are guilty of 'bad faith'. Such bad faith is a denial of our humanity. It follows that

Key Term

Terror
When used by revolutionaries, terror might include assassinations, destruction of property and violent demonstrations. In such cases, its purpose is to reduce the will of the state to continue to govern, and of the people to support that state. In reference to the state, terror means the public use of violence to maintain order. This may simply include the regular appearance of police and troops on the streets, but it could also involve public trials and the execution of dissidents.

true existentialists should act according to their own personal will and their own conscience.

However, few existentialists propose the destruction of society and the state. They merely argue that we should impose ourselves on society and the state, not vice versa. Therefore they should not be described as anarchists (even though many may describe themselves as such).

Nihilism has also influenced fascism. In common with existentialists, many fascists argue that it is our destiny and our duty to impose our own will upon society. Decisive action, for fascists, is a heroic enterprise: rational organisations should be challenged for the very reason that they are rational, and therefore lack direction and dynamism; moral and social restraints can be thrown off in the interests of progress. Thus, we come full circle. The most left wing of all political creeds becomes almost synonymous with possibly the most right wing.

Contemporary anarchism

Anarcho-capitalism and libertarianism may be considered modern versions of anarchism, but there are many other activists around today who describe themselves as anarchists and remain anti-capitalist.

The problem with identifying anarchism today is twofold. First, there are no great contemporary anarchist thinkers. The nineteenth century produced a stream of influential anarchists, such as Bakunin, Stirner, Kropotkin, Reclus and the novelist Leo Tolstoy (1828–1910). There have been many contemporary theorists expressing important critiques of the modern state, including Herbert Marcuse, Louis Althusser (1918–90), Jürgen Habermas (1929–) and Noam Chomsky (1928–), but none of them has headed a coherent political movement. Second, the term anarchism itself has been taken over by disparate groups of activists who have specific grievances rather than a comprehensive opposition to the state and attachment to individual liberty. Many environmentalists, feminists, campaigners on behalf of less economically developed countries and radical socialists who have described themselves, or been described, as anarchists, oppose authority largely on the grounds that it stands in the way of their goals.

That said, there is a recognisable world movement that stresses the dangers of globalisation. Just as the nineteenth-century state and the capitalism it sponsored oppressed workers and peasants, so contemporary international bodies (e.g. the WTO, the IMF and the World Bank) and the world trade system they uphold oppress the poor workers and peasants of the less economically developed world. This is the argument of the current radical anti-authority movement.

It is also the case that traditional anarchism proposed alternatives to existing authority systems, even though they were often seen as utopian and impractical. In contrast, modern anarchism is simply anti-authority. Environmentalists, such as Ernst Schumacher (1911–77) and Murray Bookchin (1921–), have recommended a return to more social, small-scale, primitive forms of organisation to preserve the environment, but they are rare exceptions. In practice, modern anarchism is largely confined to the anti-globalisation movement.

The key beliefs of the main anarchist movements are summarised in Table 4.2.

Key anarchist thinkers

William Godwin (British, 1756–1836)

Married to Mary Wollstonecraft (1759–97), an early feminist, and father of Mary Shelley

Anarcho-individualism	Anarcho-communism and anarcho-syndicalism	Contemporary anarchism	Anarcho-capitalism
● Human beings are essentially egotistical ● Society is in general a denial of individualism ● Individuals should be self-sufficient as far as is possible ● Trade between people should be conducted on the basis of mutual benefit, not based on market forces	● Human beings are essentially social ● Free societies enable individuals to achieve true freedom ● Economic cooperation is a natural activity ● Goods should be produced and distributed communally ● Anarcho-syndicalists specifically see social organisation as best based on trade unions	● Human beings are both individuals and have social responsibility ● The human race needs to return to simpler forms of social organisation ● Individuals should be self-sufficient and free to engage in free trade ● Completely free trade is to the benefit of all	● The capitalist system is just in that its outcomes are just ● Capitalism without state intervention gives maximum scope to the individual ● A completely free capitalist system does not need state regulation, it is self-regulating ● All social and economic problems have 'market solutions'

Table 4.2 Summary of key beliefs of the main anarchist movements

(1797–1851), the author of the novel *Frankenstein*, Godwin was an unsuccessful clergyman who turned to philosophy when he became disillusioned with the Church of England.

Godwin rejected the concept of original sin, believing that people are born neither good nor bad. He was optimistic that each individual, through education in morality and rationality, could be made into a perfectly moral human being.

In his main work, *An Enquiry Concerning Political Justice* (1792), he claimed that government would have no purpose in a rational, moral society. Governments have operated in their own interests and have resisted the progress of rationalism to protect themselves. Should a rational society be established, the state would become redundant and disappear. In its place would be left a natural society, dominated by reason and based on benevolent cooperation. Everyone in such a society would understand what actions would be in the best interests of all and behave in such a way as to bring these about.

Godwin's philosophy has been criticised for being over-optimistic and unsystematic in proposing an alternative to the state. He developed vague proposals for small, independent communities, but his theories were relatively unspecific. Nevertheless, he was a key figure who influenced the more extensive anarchist movement that followed.

Mikhail Bakunin (Russian, 1814–76)

A minor aristocrat by birth, Bakunin spent the middle part of the nineteenth century attaching himself to various revolutionary movements before developing his own distinct theory of anarchism. He was closely associated with Marx until 1872, when the two disagreed irrevocably. Bakunin criticised Marx's insistence that, following revolution, a worker's state should be established – the so-called 'dictatorship of the proletariat'. Bakunin, who was by no means implacably opposed to the concept of the minimal state, argued that the continuance of a powerful state would wreck the goals of the revolution. Along with Peter Kropotkin, he became the leading exponent of anarcho-communism.

Bakunin's theories began with the belief that individuals are born neither good nor bad. Their characters are entirely moulded by their experience of life. A perfect society could therefore produce perfect people. A perfect society was, for Bakunin, one in which every individual put the needs of society as a whole above his or her own selfish ends. He believed that humankind could only be free when living in cooperative communities where self-interest did not exist.

His analysis of capitalism and its exploitative nature was similar to that of Marx, as was his vision of the revolution that would come. However, he believed that the state should be abolished immediately and replaced by a federal system of communities, each based on the occupation of its members. These communities would be self-governing and cooperate with others on a mutually beneficial basis.

Bakunin's legacy was to make anarchism an intensely community-based ideal, rather than an individualistic doctrine. Of all the leading anarchists, he perhaps placed the least stress on the sovereignty of individuals and the most on their natural sociability. Before the liberal Lord Acton coined his famous dictum that 'power tends to corrupt, and absolute power corrupts absolutely', Bakunin demonstrated the same principle even more forcefully:

Nothing is as dangerous for man's personal morality as the habit of commanding. The best of men, the most intelligent, unselfish, generous, and pure, will always and inevitably be corrupted in this pursuit. Two feelings inherent in the exercise of power never fail to produce this demoralisation: contempt for the masses, and, for the man in power, an exaggerated sense of his own worth ... If there were established tomorrow a government or a legislative council, a parliament made up exclusively of workers, those very workers who are now staunch democrats and socialists, will become determined aristocrats, bold or timid

worshippers of the principle of authority, and will also become oppressors and exploiters.
From *State and Revolution*, 1870

This passage becomes prophetic when considering the way in which the communist revolution in the Soviet Union became corrupted under Stalin. The causes of Bakunin's break with Marx in 1872, on the issue of the corrupting effects of the state, are clearly illustrated here.

Peter Kropotkin (Russian, 1842–1921)

Like Bakunin, Kropotkin was from an aristocratic background and closely associated with the Marxists. He supported Lenin during the Russian Revolution, but soon became disillusioned and took no part in the Bolshevik government. He was in exile for much of his adult life, the most productive part of which was spent in the Jura region of France. An anarchist federation had been set up there by establishing a series of self-governing peasant communes. It was the traditional peasant communes of the kind Kropotkin observed there, where goods and work were shared on an equal basis, upon which he founded his beliefs.

Kropotkin was perhaps the most scientific of the leading anarchists, and drew inspiration from the animal kingdom when considering human society. In his best-known work, *Mutual Aid* (1902), he argued that humankind, like the higher elements of the animal kingdom, would naturally form small-scale cooperative communities. The modern state had destroyed these natural formations and created an oppressive, as well as unnatural, situation. Kropotkin rejected the Darwinian theory that competition is the normal state of affairs for all species and forms an essential part of their development. Rather, he argued, the more successful species were those that lived in cooperative communities, such as apes, elephants and many types of insect. He supported his call for mutual aid by drawing on the relationship between human and animal environments:

Therefore combine – practise mutual aid! That is the surest means for giving to each and to all the greatest safety, the best guarantee of existence and progress, bodily, intellectual and moral. That is what Nature teaches us; and that is what all those animals which have attained the highest position in their respective classes have done.

From *Mutual Aid*, 1902

Kropotkin's system of mutual aid was based on small, self-governing communities, which would, as far as possible, be self-sufficient. When cooperation between communities was essential, it would be negotiated on a mutually beneficial basis.

He formed close associations with Bakunin, Reclus and Malatesta in the latter part of the nineteenth century. Indeed, their ideals were so similar that they could have formed an anarchist party. However, the notion of a political party offended their anarchist principles. It implied authority and hierarchy, both of which were unacceptable, so they resisted the temptation.

Kroptkin died considerably disillusioned with the state of communism in Russia under Lenin. It is perhaps fortunate that he did not live to see the excesses of the Stalinist regime.

Georges Sorel (French, 1847–1922)

The greatest anarcho-syndicalist, Sorel also had the reputation of being one of the most violent representatives of the mainstream anarchist movement. It is perhaps true that anarchism's reputation for violence (which is not totally justified) was earned largely by him. He believed that the ability of the revolutionary to act in a decisive way was inhibited by traditional morality. It was therefore necessary for the aspiring anarchist to be rid of any moral restraint whatsoever. This provided Sorel with *carte blanche* to carry out any atrocity, no matter how abhorrent. His main work, *Reflections on Violence*, is a clear indication of his priorities.

Sorel is best known in philosophical circles for his theory of the 'great myth'. He ascribed to 'myth' an unusual meaning. For him it was a great dramatic event that would completely transform humanity's view of the world. He therefore referred to the 'myth' of the proletarian revolution or the 'myth' of the general strike. Following these events, the world would never be the same again, and nor would our social consciousness.

Sorel's socialist ideas revolved around his faith in the qualities of the working class, especially the skilled working class. Once freed of oppression by the bourgeois state and monopoly capitalism, this section of the working class was capable, he believed, of striking a decisive blow for liberty and establishing a new age of freedom and social justice.

By a strange irony, Sorel became as popular with fascists as he had been with anarchists and socialists. His rejection of rational philosophy in favour of the efficacy of dynamic action (a view similar to that of Friedrich Nietzsche (1844–1900) appealed to the fascist psyche. He shared their view that power should be obtained through struggle, completely rejecting any notion of democracy.

Sorel was a leading figure within revolutionary socialism and anarchism in the early part of the twentieth century, but his extreme views and espousal of violence eventually alienated most of his supporters.

Henry Thoreau (US, 1817–62)

Thoreau is best known for writing *Walden*, which describes the two years he spent living in a log cabin by Walden Pond in Massachusetts, attempting to be self-sufficient. His experiences there became a model for the hippy communes of the 1960s and 1970s.

Thoreau was a romantic and believed that human fulfilment was best achieved through creative work. He hated both industrialisation and capitalism since they took away an individual's natural creativity. However, by withdrawing from society and becoming self-sufficient, the creative way of life could be restored. He is part of the tradition to which the English socialist and craftsman William Morris (1834–96) and the anarchist poet Herbert Read (1893–1968) also belonged.

Another aspect of Thoreau's anarchism was his hatred of the oppressive state, which removes an individual's freedom. Were the state to disappear, he believed, a natural, individualistic and creative way of life could be restored. However, he had no specific plans for how this could be achieved and remains something of a popular, but impractical, oddity within the anarchist tradition.

Murray Rothbard (US, 1926–95)

Rothbard was a key representative of the modern movement known as anarcho-capitalism or extreme libertarianism. He called his theories 'Austrian Economics' – a revival of ideas that had been developed in the 1930s. Although neo-liberals argue that most goods can be provided by free markets, they accept that the state must exist to provide some services, such as defence and law and order. They also suggest that some social laws, for example concerning morality and drug use, are needed to maintain social stability.

Rothbard and the anarcho-capitalists go a step further than this. Anarcho-capitalists suggest that all services can be provided by private enterprise. There is therefore no need for the state at all. The philosophical basis for this belief lies in natural rights doctrine. If we are born with natural rights, there can never be any justification for the state interfering with our actions. We should be free to exchange goods with whoever we wish, on whatever basis, or with nobody at all. Similarly, the state has no right to intervene in our personal conduct, even if we may harm ourselves. As regards actions which interfere with others, it is up to them to take steps to protect themselves.

In answer to claims that a democratic society and state will also provide all we need, Rothbard asserted that popular democracy is a myth. In reality, as all other anarchists have claimed, government is the exercise of power by the few over the many.

Like Sorel, Rothbard has followers among right-wing as well as left-wing groups. Although he is placed among the anarchists, his views are difficult to categorise accurately. However, some of Rothbard's words are an appropriate summary of the anarchist world view:

My own basic perspective on the history of man is to place central importance on the great conflict which is eternally waged between liberty and power. I see the liberty of the individual not only as a great moral good in itself, but also as the necessary condition for the flowering of all other goods that mankind cherishes: moral virtue, civilization, the arts and sciences, economic prosperity. But liberty has always been threatened by the encroachments of power, power which seeks to suppress, control, cripple, tax and exploit the fruits of liberty and production.

From *Conceived in Liberty*, 1975

Issues in anarchism

Are anarchists utopians?

One of the main charges made against anarchists is that they are unscientific and therefore hopelessly utopian. Their views of an ideal society may well be worthy of support, but they are impractical. The main criticisms are as follows:

- Anarchists have a mistaken and over-optimistic view of human nature. Conservatives, in particular, argue that human nature is at best unpredictable or changeable, and at worst flawed. Humankind is too self-interested for there to be any hope of establishing a society in which there is no political authority. Of course, anarcho-capitalists, extreme libertarians and anarcho-individualists, such as Stirner and Rothbard, accept this view – that individuals should be able to pursue their own interests. They argue that the interaction of free individuals will create its own natural balance,

which does not need regulation. Liberals respond to this by suggesting that no such acceptable balance will exist, and since we will therefore always need to be protected from each other, some kind of state is essential. Thus, both conservatives and liberals claim that anarchism will result in chaos.

- Anarcho-communists have suggested that it is possible to set up a social system based on equality and social justice, in which there will be collective ownership of the means of production. The main criticism of this concerns the nature of property. Conservatives assert that private property is an essential element in a stable society, while liberals have always seen property as a natural right. A system without property, therefore, would be either disordered or unnatural, or both.

- Many critics, from different ideological traditions, have suggested that the drive to power is a natural instinct of humankind. Conservatives, in particular, view people as naturally unequal; there will be some who will succeed and others who will be less successful, some who will lead and others who will follow. Abolishing the state or any other form of political authority is therefore unnatural and will not succeed.

The anarchist response to these criticisms varies. The radical individualists are unconcerned. They believe that individuals should simply be given their liberty, and the outcome of the free exercise of that liberty, whatever it may be, will be natural and can be justified on that basis.

The anarcho-communists, on the other hand, offer a more specific response. The nature of humankind may appear to be inconsistent, selfish and unreliable, but this is because we have been corrupted by a flawed society. If we are indeed the products of our social environment, as Malatesta and Bakunin, for example, claimed, then it is inevitable that a society which lacks morality will produce people who lack morality. If we create a society which is based upon cooperation, morality, justice and liberty, its inhabitants will demonstrate these qualities.

A third view, held by Godwin, for example, is that if individuals are provided with a rational and moral education, they will spontaneously create a just society without the need of government. If individuals can learn to govern their own actions in such a way as to produce good outcomes, then government becomes unnecessary.

William Godwin, the 'father' of individualist anarchism

Can anarchists reconcile individualism and collectivism?

Although anarcho-individualists indeed accept that collectivism and individual liberty cannot be reconciled, thereby rejecting collectivist ideas altogether, mainstream anarcho-communists believe that they can. How can this belief be justified?

The main thrust of the anarcho-communist argument is that free individuals will naturally form themselves into social groups without feeling any compulsion to do so. They will therefore retain their freedom. As long as everyone in society is equally free and equally rational, they will be able to live harmoniously in social groups. Bakunin expressed this idea as follows:

Thus, too, the freedom of all is essential to my freedom. And it follows that it would be fallacious to maintain that the freedom of all constitutes a limitation upon my freedom for that would be tantamount to the denial of such freedom. On the contrary, universal freedom represents the necessary affirmation and the boundless expansion of individual freedom.

From *Social and Economic Bases of Anarchism*, 1872

Kropotkin took this a stage further. He saw human freedom in terms of collective identity, arguing that we are only truly free if we live in natural social units. If we are left to live as individuals, we lose our liberty because we will come into conflict with others. He called this principle 'free communism' to distinguish it from Marxist schemes that involved the enforcement of collectivism.

Finally, Godwin believed that the answer lay in who was doing the restraining. As long as we are rational and moral, we will not need to be compelled to behave in a collectivist, cooperative way. By exercising what he called 'private judgement', we will express our freedom by restraining ourselves, not by being restrained by social compulsion. 'Each man should be wise enough to govern himself', Godwin asserted. Individuals would govern themselves by willing what is for the good of society as a whole, he argued, 'to promote the general happiness'. Thus, we can live in freedom, without government, in a collectivist social environment.

Marx was sceptical of this anarchist argument. After the revolution, the working class could not expect both individualism and socialism immediately. There would need to be a prolonged period of dictatorship by the proletariat until the people's consciousness had changed radically. Eventually, he insisted, the state would wither away and a new communist age of freedom would be ushered in. Unlike the anarchists, he believed that freedom and communism would not be able to coexist for some time to come. The outright opponents of anarchism, of course, claim that communism and freedom will always be irreconcilable.

However, the main objection to anarchist claims that individualism and collectivism can be reconciled is that any form of collectivism inevitably involves a loss of liberty. Collectivism simply cannot work, critics assert, without the need for some system of authority and some sacrifice of individual liberty.

Is anarchism a single ideology?

As is the case with many such questions, the answer is probably 'yes and no'. In short, anarchism is a single movement in that all anarchists share the same basic principles. These are:

1 All individuals have the right to absolute personal sovereignty.

2 No person has the right to exercise power over another.

3 The existence of the political state can never be tolerated.

Individuals who subscribe to these three principles are justified in describing themselves as anarchists.

However, it is impossible to put all those who have described themselves as anarchists into the same political tradition. The following movements can be identified, all of which have described themselves as anarchist:

● nihilism

● anarcho-capitalism or libertarianism

● anarcho-individualism

● anarcho-communism

● anarcho-syndicalism.

Furthermore, there are movements that have added opposition to the state to their primary goals and so have been included in the anarchist tradition. These include feminism and environmentalism. All of these movements propose the abolition of the state but there are fundamental differences in the kind of social order (if any) they would put in its place. For some, there would be no state of any kind; for others, there would be a state that represented a transformed society.

It is also true that different anarchists have even disagreed about **human nature**, from Stirner, who sees us as basically egotistical and self-interested, to Bakunin, who sees us as naturally driven towards social organisation and cooperation. While Sorel and Stirner are pessimistic about human nature, Godwin and Kropotkin are intensely optimistic.

 Key Term

Human nature
All political philosophies and ideologies have developed theories about human nature. This means that they make assumptions about what is the natural state of humankind, i.e. how people behaved before society came about. Some ideologies, such as socialism, have an optimistic view of human nature – they believe we are naturally sociable and cooperative. Others take the pessimistic view that humankind is not naturally social, and may even be excessively selfish. Conservatives have tended to see people as unreliable, and driven by appetites rather than reason. The purpose of developing such theories is to help create a natural form of society suited to humankind's basic character.

To confuse the issue further, anarchists have disagreed over the means of bringing about the anarchist utopia. Most anarchists have been revolutionaries and accept the need for a dramatic, often violent transformation of society into a stateless existence. Some, however, have been pacifists. The most notable example was perhaps the Russian novelist Leo Tolstoy (author of *War and Peace* and *Anna Karenina*), who opposed revolution, preferring instead a gradual, voluntary transition to anarchism. Tolstoy was a wealthy, aristocratic landowner who freed his own peasants and encouraged them to form self-governing communes. Some individualists, such as Thoreau, have recommended that we should simply withdraw from society and so free ourselves from the oppression of the state.

In summary, therefore, anarchists are united on the three basic principles. However, they disagree fundamentally both about the form of social order they would prefer and the means by which this can be brought about.

Anarchism and liberalism

Both anarchism and liberalism were born out of Enlightenment thinking and both place liberty at the centre of their political universe. They also share a strong suspicion of the power of the state. It is therefore interesting to ask whether anarchism is really an extreme form of liberalism. In order to address this question, we need to look at three aspects of the two philosophies:

● Are there fundamental differences in how they view liberty?

● How do they view the state?

● What kind of society do they propose to replace the existing order?

These questions are considered in turn under the three different headings below.

Freedom

In summary, liberals make the fundamental assertion that the most important kind of liberty involves the absence of external restraint. This has become known as 'negative liberty'. Anarchists have no problem in agreeing that this kind of liberty is essential. However, whereas liberals accept that there must be laws and limitations on the individual to ensure that his or her freedom does not interfere with the freedom of others, anarchists say that this will not be necessary. In their idealised, perfectly moral society, each individual will exercise internal restraint, often described as 'private judgement'.

In this sense, the answer to our initial question might be 'yes': anarchism is an extreme version of liberalism in that there would apparently be a greater degree of personal liberty in the anarchist world, although both worlds would be similar in that they would be remarkably free. There is, however, a crucial distinction. Anarchism will countenance no laws. Anarchists insist that all laws are incompatible with freedom, while liberals argue that we cannot be free without laws.

The two philosophies do, perhaps, agree on the form of liberty known as 'positive freedom'. Both claim that the societies they propose would maximise individualism and the fulfilment of personal progress and creativity. The freedom they promote would liberate individuals from the restraints of societies, which restrict choice and opportunity and discourage the achievement of self-realisation. In that sense, therefore, liberation has a positive outcome and the anarchist aim of creating total liberation goes much further than liberalism.

The state

As with freedom, there is an apparent affinity between the two doctrines regarding their view of the state. Both oppose the excessive exercise of power and see the state as the actual or potential enemy of freedom. There is, however, a vital distinction. Liberals see the state as essential to the preservation of liberty (provided, of course, it is a 'liberal' state). It protects individuals from each other and from accumulations of power. Anarchists, on the other hand, insist that all forms of state are unacceptable. It is inevitable, they argue, that states will exercise the power of the few over the many. However benign it may appear, the state must, by its very nature, use force against its citizens. How else is it able to perform its functions? Anarchists reject all forms of power and force, even if the state claims that they are used for good ends.

This is clearly not a difference of degree, but a fundamental distinction. Liberals accept the existence of a limited state, but anarchists will never support any kind of state. They argue that even limited states will eventually become powerful states. Ironically, anarchists find it easier than liberals to support Lord Acton's famous warning about the corrupting nature of power. Acton intended his slogan as a liberal motto.

The free society

The anarcho-individualists and anarcho-capitalists share with liberals a desire to see a society that is as free as it possibly can be. Indeed, classical liberals and social Darwinists share with anarchists the belief that every individual can only reach his or her full potential in a free society. They all believe that the freedom of the individual should stand above social constraints. Of course, anarchists hope and expect that individuals will use their liberty exclusively for 'good' ends, whereas liberals accept that individuals are likely to pursue their own self-interest, and are therefore likely to create a highly competitive world. However, there is certainly a case for arguing that some extreme liberals envisage a society close to an anarchist world of autonomous individuals motivated by egoism. The world of evolutionary competition espoused by Herbert Spencer seems similar to Max Stirner's conception of a complete absence of social order, with individualism being granted free rein.

However, when collectivist forms of anarchism are considered, notably the anarcho-communism of Bakunin and Kropotkin, crucial distinctions between the ideologies emerge. The liberal community comes about through an agreement among the people to set up government over themselves. This community is based on a kind of social contract and usually stems from national identity. Once the community is established, consent is assumed, say liberals, and it is necessary to reserve the use of force against those citizens who defy the restraints within that community. For anarchists, communities must be totally voluntary and therefore natural. The use of force becomes unnecessary because the community comes into

being naturally and not through an artificial contract.

A second key distinction concerns the role of private property. Liberals see the existence of property as a right enjoyed by all individuals. Almost all anarchists (Proudhon being a notable exception) oppose the preservation of private property. They believe that property inevitably creates injustice, inequality and corruption. It also leads inevitably to the emergence of power relationships.

Conclusion

The anarchist principles of the absence of a state and private property, and the voluntary nature of the political community, all make for fundamental and irreconcilable differences between liberalism and anarchism. In terms of values, it may well be argued that anarchism is an extreme form of liberalism, but this is certainly not the case when considering their fundamental beliefs on the nature of freedom and of the free society.

Anarchism, socialism and Marxism

On what grounds do socialists and anarchists conflict?

First, we must eliminate any comparison between anarcho-individualism and socialism. Clearly these two traditions have very little in common and in many ways they can be seen as ideological opposites. Socialists insist that humans are social animals whose instincts for cooperation and mutual sympathy are stronger than their egoism. For socialists, the pursuit of self-interest is unnatural and the result of capitalism rather than a prerequisite for it. By contrast, anarcho-individualists believe that egoism is a fundamental feature of human character, and that any form of social organisation restrains egoism and is therefore unnatural.

However, collectivist forms of anarchism have a good deal in common with socialism, making comparisons between the ideologies more complex. The points of similarity include the following:

- Both traditions see major problems arising from the existence of private property. Indeed, both Marxists and anarcho-communists oppose private property altogether. Less extreme forms of socialism have allowed some scope for the possession of property, but temper this with a need for some common ownership.

- Anarcho-communists and socialists hold similar views of human nature. Both accept that individuals can achieve all or much of their self-realisation, and the fulfilment of their own aspirations, through collective action. In extreme circumstances, this means collectivising all resources. For moderate socialists, it would only involve collectivising some, but not all, of the means of production and distribution.

- Both traditions have a strong sense of equality. They both support equal rights and equality of opportunity, and share a sense that each individual has equal worth. Marxists and quasi-Marxist socialists agree with anarchists that there should be an equal distribution of rewards in society according to need. It is true that moderate socialists accept degrees of inequality as natural, but even they accept that every individual is worthy of equal respect, dignity and opportunity.

Thus, anarcho-communism and socialism have much in common and in many ways they have common roots – in their opposition to capitalism, inequality and the dominance of the state by a ruling class. However, this should not disguise their fundamental differences.

The most striking contrast concerns the position of the state. All anarchists would abolish the state. Whatever its function, the state is always a denial of liberty and individualism. It does not matter to anarchists that a socialist state might abolish private property and impose economic and social equality (as in the USSR or communist China). Once the state's outward

appearance is stripped away it is revealed as the government of the many by the few, say anarchists, whatever its apparent objectives. Furthermore, all states will inevitably become politically corrupt because the exercise of power is as oppressive to leaders as it is to subjects. The leaders of the state become victims of their own drive to exercise power. This drive can be intoxicating and therefore addictive. The experience of the communist-socialist states of Central and Eastern Europe certainly appears to have borne out this anarchist assertion.

In the 1870s, the role of the state split the anarchists and Marxists. Anarchists insisted that the revolution that was to overthrow capitalism would lead immediately to a stateless society and a communist order. Marxists argued that there would need to be an interim phase after revolution in which an oppressive workers' state would be established in order to build socialism and protect the achievements of the revolution. Anarchists predicted that such a state would not wither away, as Marx had declared, but would endure as a new form of ruling class.

So-called state socialists, including the early British Fabians, the French Socialist Party, Eduard Bernstein and Tony Benn, have all seen the state as a vital component in the realisation of socialist goals. They see welfare, equality, common ownership and collective action of all kinds as best organised by the centralised state, as this is the only way of ensuring universal equality. For anarcho-communists, however, equality would naturally follow from the establishment of free, voluntary communities. The state would lead to the negation rather than the facilitation of freedom and equality.

Finally, a more philosophical distinction should be considered. Socialists tend to believe that freedom and individualism are developed by the establishment of equality. This means that the principal enemy of freedom is inequality. This is not acceptable to anarchists. For them, liberty is an individualist concept, which perhaps has more in common with the classical liberal view of freedom. Equality cannot guarantee such freedom; only the complete abolition of the state, its laws and the compulsory herding of people into unnatural communities can do so. Natural anarchist communities can combine individual liberty with both equality and mutual cooperation. Socialism, complain the anarchists, simply involves too much compulsion. On the other hand, socialists argue that anarchism is utopian and unrealistic in believing that equality and collective freedom can be achieved without being organised by some form of state.

Is anarchism merely unscientific socialism?

An important criticism of anarchism in all its forms is that it is an unscientific, utopian philosophy, the product of romantic dreamers or violent revolutionaries who know what they are against, but lack any rigorous conception of how a new social order should be formed. A detailed critique of anarcho-communism, in particular, would include the following features:

- lack of a theory of history

- lack of a coherent view of humankind

- incoherent view of a social order

- lack of a coherent conception of class.

It is certainly true that anarchism does not have its own Marx, a theorist who could demonstrate a natural historical progress towards a no-state society. It is also the case that anarchists differ greatly in their views of human nature. Bakunin believed there was no such thing as human nature or natural morality, and argued that an individual is, at birth, neither good nor bad. Kropotkin and Tolstoy firmly believed that man is naturally sociable, but individualists such as Stirner and Tucker see man as a solitary, egotistical figure. This lack of unanimity over human nature makes it extremely difficult to accept a single ideological position. It certainly weakens any claim that anarchism is a rigorous, rational philosophy.

It is often argued that anarchism fundamentally lacks a scientific explanation of the nature of society and the role of social class in particular. This suggests that anarchists are simplistic in their social vision, looking no further than phenomena such as excessive authority, oppression and exploitation.

This may be overcritical. Most anarchists have shared a set of distinct values with socialists that are fully identifiable. These include equality, community, cooperation, common ownership and mutual respect. In this regard, anarchism, whether or not it is scientific, can be seen as a form of socialism that simply opposes the institution of the state.

Exam focus

Using this chapter and other resources available to you, answer the following questions.

Short questions

Your answers should be about 400 words long.

1 What do anarchists mean by 'liberty'?
2 Distinguish between a liberal and an anarchist view of freedom.
3 Why do anarchists oppose the state?
4 Why do anarchists believe the state unnecessary?
5 How do anarchists view human nature?
6 On what grounds do anarchists oppose private property?
7 Why is anarchism often described as utopian?

Long questions

Your answers should be about 1200 words long.
1 To what extent is anarchism merely a utopian aspiration?
2 'All anarchists agree about ends, but disagree about means.' How true is this statement?
3 Distinguish between individualism and collectivism in the anarchist tradition.
4 Is it possible for anarchists to reconcile collectivism with individualism?
5 Is anarchism merely an extreme form of liberalism?
6 Is anarchism a separate ideology or merely a branch of socialism?

Further reading

Marshall, P. (1993) *Demanding the Impossible: A History of Anarchism*, Fontana.
Miller, D. (1984) *Anarchism*, Everyman.
Nozick, R. (2001) *Anarchy, State and Utopia*, Blackwell.
Thoreau, H. D. (1962) *Walden*, Bantam.
Wolff, R. P. (1970) *In Defence of Anarchism*, Harper and Rowe.
Woodcock, G. (1962) *Anarchism: A History of Libertarian Ideas and Movements*, Penguin.

Chapter 5

Nationalism

Nationalism is a collective emotion felt by groups of people who consider themselves to have common circumstances of birth. Its origins lie in the desire of some eighteenth- and nineteenth-century peoples to create a solid and enduring basis for the formation of a political community. As the nationalist spirit of common identity developed in Europe, it became popular to associate national identity with a need for government by consent. By setting up its own government, it was believed, a nation could confirm its separate identity. When nationalism developed further political aspirations, it became a specifically political movement. The objectives of political forms of nationalism have varied a great deal and have included: a need to protect the nation from conquest or domination by other peoples; a desire to unite a people, thus creating a nation-state as a political reality; a desire for independence of a people; a desire to conquer and/or dominate weaker nations; or simply a desire to protect a threatened culture. Nationalism has been associated with a number of other political movements, notably fascism, liberalism and conservatism. In each case, the dominant values of the political movement in question have been underpinned by the synthesis of political and national aspirations.

Introduction

It is useful to start a discussion of nationalism with an extract from Bernard Crick's (1929–) famous work, *In Defence of Politics*, which was first published in 1962. This is how he expresses the power of nationalist sentiment:

Nationalism is at this time perhaps the most compelling of all motives that can lead men to abandon or to scorn politics. Every feeling of human generosity is stirred by the struggle of an oppressed people to be free. And nothing can argue people who feel themselves to be a nation out of the belief that they are a nation; and that if they are to be oppressed, it is better to be oppressed by their own people than by foreigners.

On this evidence, political movements described as 'nationalist' appear to be straightforward. Nationalists are evidently people who have a strong attachment to the nation of which they are part. Nationalism is therefore an emotion felt by such people. This is clearly true, but it tells us little of nationalism as a specifically political movement.

The early development of modern nationalism is relatively easy to follow. At the end of the Enlightenment period, there was a need to create a basis for the legitimate establishment of new states or new forms of government to replace monarchical authority. If communities were to come together and freely consent to place themselves under a government, there was a need to define such communities. The most obvious solution was to identify national groupings and to agree that each nation should have the right to set up its own state and government. Napoleon Bonaparte (1769–1821) believed that France had achieved this after the 1789 revolution, and he hoped to establish the principle for all the aspiring states of Europe.

Napoleon I, who hoped to spread the model of the nation-state throughout Europe

However, there are a number of problems in following the later development of various types of nationalism. Individuals express their support for, or even love of, their national identity in a number of different ways. For some, nationalism implies a sense of superiority over other nations; for others, it expresses a desire to be free of domination by people of another nation or nations. In some cases, nationalism seeks to unite a people who have become divided by historical circumstances; in other cases, the term may mean nothing more than pride in one's cultural identity and a desire to protect that identity.

Further difficulties arise when we attempt to place nationalism within a conventional political spectrum. It can be an extremely right-wing movement, as was the case with fascism, but there have been left-wing nationalists too – for example, a number of independence movements in Africa and South America. At a more moderate level, there have been liberal nationalists who combine national aspirations with a democratic spirit. Nationalism is also one of the core values of traditional conservatism. In this context, it does not necessarily relate to a desire to conquer other nations, to create an empire or even to

demonstrate a people's superiority, but rather represents a means by which a people can develop a strong sense of unity for the sake of order and security.

Finally, there are problems in distinguishing between nations and races, between nations and states and between nationalism and patriotism. There are even controversies about precisely what constitutes a nation. Are the citizens of the USA a nation, for example? Is the term 'Nation of Islam' anything more than a rallying cry for alienated ethnic groups? Are Jews a nation or followers of a religion? Is there a worthwhile meaning of the term 'British', when most people from the UK prefer to describe themselves as English, Welsh, Scottish, Irish or even Asian?

To find a way through this apparent maze, three objectives must be achieved. The first is to identify some values that can unite all nationalists. The second is to develop a way of categorising different kinds of nationalism effectively. Finally, nationalism must be distinguished from other movements based on different forms of popular allegiance.

Nations and states

Nations

It is important to define what constitutes a nation and to contrast this with the meaning of the term state. It remains true that most nations have formed a state, and that most states are constituted from one dominant nation, but it is important to make some distinctions.

A nation can be defined as a group of people who consider themselves to have common circumstances of birth. These common circumstances are strong enough for them to adopt collective goals based on their national identity. Nationalism is therefore an emotional phenomenon felt by a people. It may be that others will dispute whether such a group constitutes a nation, but this is less important than the fact that the people believe themselves to

Circumstance	Example	Commentary
Single common ancestor	Jewish nation (not necessarily Israel)	Jews share Abraham as a common ancestor with the Arabs, but claim a later division between the two nations
Common historical experience	England	The Scots, Irish and Welsh consider themselves to have different histories and so are separate nations
Common culture	Germany	The German people became divided but were reunited by Otto von Bismarck in 1871
Ethnic identity	China	Although there are different racial groups in China, there is an overarching Chinese ethnic identity
Geographical separation	Malta	The Maltese are an island people with a strong national identity
Religion	Tibet	The Tibetan people, now subsumed into China, all owe allegiance to a single religious leader – the Dalai Lama – who defines their identity
Attachment to territory	France	Although the borders of France have changed frequently, there is a strong sense of 'France' as an historical reality
Language	Wales	The Welsh (although not the whole nation) see their cultural identity in terms of their language and the culture it carries with it

Table 5.1 What constitutes a nation?

be a nation. In other words, a nation may be an objective reality or a subjective emotion.

There are a number of typical circumstances of birth that may give rise to nationhood. In some cases a nation may exhibit more than one at any given time. The scheme shown in Table 5.1 suggests the various criteria and offers some examples. These appear to be fairly clear, but many problems in defining nations remain. For example, is the USA a nation? It certainly tends to call itself a nation and it works hard to create a national identity, even though its people come from a wide variety of ethnic and cultural backgrounds. The key here is whether the dominant US culture is strong enough. Is Britain a nation? The Scots and Welsh would usually disagree, but there remains a strong sense of British national culture. Finally, and perhaps most controversially, are the Arabs a nation? They have a common ancestor in Abraham, but also exhibit a wide variety of cultural identities from the Bedouin in the desert to the city dwellers of Dubai or Beirut. Repeated attempts to unite the

Arab peoples (a movement known as 'Pan-Arabism'), most recently by President Nasser (1918–70) of Egypt in the 1960s, have all failed because internal divisions have proved insurmountable.

What matters most in political terms is not whether we accept objective tests of nationhood, but whether a people consider themselves to be a nation. The Chinese are an example of this. Divided into several ethnic groups, they all owe a strong allegiance to China as a single identity. The Italians, on the other hand, are less sure of nationhood and the Lombard (or Northern) League has been established to campaign for greater autonomy for Northern Italy, suggesting that Italy is an artificial creation dating back only to the 1860s. Unlike the Welsh, many Italians do not believe that a common language necessarily conveys nationhood.

States

A state is a political reality. It either exists or it does not. In contrast to the concept of nation, it does not convey a people's state of mind or emotion. Of course, there are national groupings that aspire to statehood, such as the Palestinians or the Basques of northern Spain and southwest France, but until that aspiration is realised no state actually exists. Nations, on the other hand, can certainly exist even when there is no state representing them.

A state is a defined territory within which there is a centre of sovereignty which is, more or less, in control of that territory. The German sociologist Max Weber (1864–1920) went further, defining a state as a territory within which a central body claims the legitimate use of violence (normally merely meaning force). However, we are not concerned here with whether a state is legitimate, or its borders disputed. What is important is that we can identify political institutions that control the people within a territory. Similarly, the issue is not whether a state is democratic. Even a totalitarian regime, where the people are kept in a state of fear or enforced obedience – for example, the Iraq of Saddam Hussein (1937–2006) – is still a state. A state can also be identified by widespread obedience to a monarch or leader. Possibly the easiest way of defining a state is to give as examples all those countries that are members of the United Nations (UN) – perhaps the only member of the UN whose status as a state remains disputed is Palestine.

There is also a phenomenon known as the 'failed state'. This is a territory where there are no political institutions that can claim to control that territory effectively. Afghanistan has often been termed a failed state, since much of the country has been controlled by warlords. The same analysis has been applied to such countries as Somalia and Ethiopia, where civil wars have raged for many years and the recognised 'state', in each case, has appeared to be at the point of collapse.

The advent of nation-states

The most commonly acknowledged origin of the merging of the concepts of nation and state is the French Revolution. This is because three processes occurred at the same time as a result of the revolution. First, the old state (the *ancien régime*) was dissolved and a new state established. Second, it was declared that the French people were collectively free and had established the right to **self-determination**; the nation was therefore acknowledged to be the basis of the new political community. Third, the new political community was to guarantee individual rights. It was assumed that a state based on the nation would ensure the maintenance of such rights. Thus, the modern concepts of the state and the nation were brought together for the first time in history – see Box 5.1.

Box 5.1 Articles 2 and 3 of the Declaration of the Rights of Man and Citizen by the French National Assembly, 1789

2 The aim of all political association is the preservation of the natural and imprescriptible rights of man. Those rights are liberty, property, security, and resistance to oppression.

3 The principle of all sovereignty resides essentially in the nation. No body or individual may exercise any authority which does not proceed directly from the nation.

Napoleon Bonaparte, who ultimately became emperor of this new nation-state, saw it as a model that the rest of the world could follow. However, for the next 100 years the development of the nation-state as the accepted pattern for a political community was a painful one. Imperial powers, such as the Ottomans and the Austro-Hungarian emperors, denied the right of statehood to many nations. During the same period, peoples who had been divided into imperial territories, kingdoms, principalities and duchies, such as the Germans, Poles, Italians, Hungarians and Serbs, sought independent status. These peoples hoped – as the French had in 1789 – to rid themselves of oppressive, autocratic regimes, and to replace them with democratic institutions based on national sovereignty.

Key Term

Self-determination
This essentially liberal term refers to a principle associated with the concept of the nation-state. It suggests that a people who have a just claim to nationhood should be granted the right to form their own government and to determine for themselves the manner in which they are governed. It also implies that a people cannot hope to claim freedom in general unless they are free to set up their own political institutions.

However, the leaders who gathered at Versailles to negotiate a peace treaty at the end of the First World War sought to establish the nation-state as a fundamental right of all peoples. President Woodrow Wilson (1856–1924) of the USA persuaded the victorious allies to declare that all nations had a right to statehood. Two great empires – the Ottoman and Austro-Hungarian – were therefore dissolved and a number of new nation-states came into existence. Of course, this did not mean that the European powers would relinquish their imperial possessions outside Europe and the Middle East. The issue of the nationalist aspirations of overseas colonies in places such as Africa and the Far East would not be settled until after the Second World War.

Key Term

Culture
This is a difficult concept to summarise. It refers mainly to the dominant historical experience, traditions, values and attitudes shared by a people who consider themselves to have a common identity. At its most basic level, it includes an identifiable 'way of life', artistic activities such as music, literature, dance and costume, and it can encompass national myths and legends (the Knights of the Round Table in England, for example). Language is a key feature, since it is through language that cultural attitudes and identities are passed down from one generation to the next. At a deeper level, however, culture refers to commonly held attitudes about a people's past, present and future aspirations. It may, in a few cases, also refer to a kind of civilisation, which implies the special qualities a people may have, such as organisation, intellect, and artistic or military prowess. This latter sense is especially associated with fascism and other right-wing nationalist movements.

Races and nations

The relationship between the concepts of race and nation often causes confusion. This is not surprising since many nations consider themselves to be a race. This can certainly be said of the Japanese, Jews, Thais and Malays. In general terms, however, a race is not necessarily a nation and, furthermore, nations can contain more than one racial grouping, as is the case with the Chinese and, indeed, the English. The term **culture** helps little as it refers neither to race nor nationhood. Yet we do often refer to 'national' or 'racial' cultures.

The relationship becomes even more confusing when considering the attitude of extreme right-wing fascist or quasi-fascist

movements. The synthesis of race and nation can be seen in the German idea of *volk*. Johann Fichte (1762–1814), perhaps the chief original architect of German nationalism, saw his people as a *volk* in that they were a close-knit culture, based on a narrow racial grouping, which had formed a superior culture and civilisation in the Middle Ages. He believed that the German people, scattered throughout central Europe, retained both their racial and national (or *volkish*) identity. This identity was rekindled by the Nazis in the 1930s with dramatic consequences. In Britain, Oswald Mosley (1896–1980) propagated a similar belief about the British race, although his argument was not that the British had been scattered, but that they had been subverted by capitalist exploitation and weak, liberal democratic politicians.

The idea that common blood ties make up a nation can give rise to a number of problems. It can promote a sense of exclusiveness so that those who cannot demonstrate a blood connection may be excluded from society. This occurred in Nazi Germany and under the apartheid regime in South Africa. It has also been an important factor in inter-tribal warfare in Africa, where in some parts attempts at total genocide have been made in an attempt to create racially pure nations.

In an even more sinister way, it has led to ideas of racial – and therefore national – superiority. This arises from a social Darwinist view of the world, according to which different races are in a struggle for superiority against each other. It has led to quasi-scientific racialist beliefs that a nation can only retain its strength and superiority if it can maintain racial purity. Again, many German Nazis accepted this 'scientific' analysis.

Race as a basis for nationhood should generally be treated with great caution. It is clearly an important factor in some parts of the world, but it is only one of several components of nationalism. Furthermore, the synthesis of race and nation has often led to distorted and dangerous views of the world, based on partial truth and dubious science.

Globalisation, European integration and nation-states

The process of globalisation has been seen as a long-term threat to the future of nation-states. The increasing level of interdependence between states, together with the fact that many global problems do not recognise national borders, has led to a belief that the division of government into many different states is becoming an irrelevance.

As the world moves increasingly towards free trade, the existence of global, rather than national, markets has rendered national governments powerless to control economic forces. Indeed, a good deal of control over trade has now passed to international bodies such as the International Monetary Fund (IMF) and the World Trade Organisation (WTO). The internationalisation of financial markets, too, has marginalised the role of national banking

institutions. Similarly, environmental issues do not respect national borders. The control of emissions, the health of the seas, the protection of endangered species and so on are all international problems. Even separate cultural identities are now threatened by the globalisation of culture and the influence of the internet.

Many liberals welcome these developments. They see globalisation as an opportunity to restore the importance of regional and local government, which they consider to be more democratic and directly accountable to the people. The power of nation-states is often seen by liberals as a threat to democracy and human rights. By reducing their power, globalisation will empower individuals, giving them the potential to be free citizens of the world and not merely subjects of nation-states. This is not to say that liberals would abolish the nation-state altogether; indeed, it was the liberal spirit that first breathed life into the concept of the nation-state. It is simply that liberals favour the dissipation of power into different levels of government, from local to national level.

Conservatives, on the other hand, are staunch defenders of nation-states. They fear the accumulation of power in supranational bodies such as the IMF, the WTO and the European Union (EU). They see democracy in terms of the nation, which is the natural unit of government. They also place greater emphasis upon the importance of the nation as an organic body that represents the culture of its people and its collective identity.

The development of the EU perhaps represents the greatest threat to the institution of the independent nation-state. The champions of European integration argue that economic and political independence must inevitably decline. However, the founder of the European Community – the French socialist Jean Monnet (1888–1979) – did not foresee the demise of the nation-state. Rather, he saw the long-term future of Europe as a single economic and political entity within which national cultures would still exist. For him, the idea of the nation was fundamentally cultural in nature. It could, therefore, survive the inevitable drift towards **supranationalism** in other spheres. Put another way, those who support European integration are happy to weaken individual states, but wish to preserve national identities.

Key Term

Supranationalism
This term refers to a process whereby decision-making power passes upwards from national level to institutions that stand above the nation. Supranational organisations, such as the EU Commission, the European Court of Justice and the World Trade Organisation, look beyond national interests and pursue the interests of groups of nations instead. The principle means that individual nation-states accept decisions made by supranational bodies as binding upon them.

Core values of nationalism

Self-determination

It has become a general principle of democratic politics that a people have the fundamental right to determine how they are governed. This idea, proposed in the late seventeenth century by John Locke, has been enshrined in countless constitutional documents and international agreements. The concept of self-determination, however, contains a problem within itself: that is, what constitutes a 'people'? In other words, how are we to divide humankind into natural units that will express their self-determination? The answer most commonly offered is that the nation is the most natural unit, and so it has proved to be.

The origins and aspirations of nationalism based on this principle have varied according to the circumstances preventing self-determination. In other words, for what different reasons have national groupings been denied self-determination? These can be classified as follows:

1 *Imperialism*
Peoples who have found themselves subject to government by a foreign power will wish to throw off their subjugation and form their own sovereign state. The long struggle for independence from Britain by Indian nationalists and the nineteenth-century nationalist movements in the Ottoman and Austro-Hungarian empires are good examples.

2 *Sovereignty*
There have been national groupings that have enjoyed a degree of self-government, but this has fallen short of full sovereignty. In these cases, nationalists have simply wished to establish full sovereign, independent powers. Examples include Irish nationalism (in both the south and the north), Catalonian nationalism in Spain, Québecois nationalism in Canada and Chechen nationalism within the Russian Federation.

3 *Oppression*
Peoples who have been subsumed into a larger oppressive regime may seek self-determination in order to escape from that oppression. The movements for Bosnian and Kosovan independence from Serbia were classic examples. Other examples include the Kurds in the Middle East and the Tibetans who were annexed by a repressive communist regime in China.

4 *Diaspora*
National groupings that are scattered and subject to rule by many different states are said to have suffered diaspora. In such circumstances, a nationalist movement may seek to achieve statehood both to unite such a people and to achieve self-determination. The Jews in Israel are perhaps the clearest example, with Palestinians and some other Arab groupings finding themselves in a similar position.

5 *External threat*
This concerns nations that do enjoy their own sovereignty but that are in danger of losing it as a result of annexation. Nationalist movements may spring up as a defensive force to guard against the impending loss of

self-determination. Poland has experienced this kind of nationalist surge a number of times in its troubled history, as it has been constantly threatened from both east and west by Russia and Germany respectively; Israel has experienced this as a result of threats from neighbouring Arab states; Korea has responded to threats in this way, historically from Japan.

The desire for self-determination is clearly a strong one. It is therefore unsurprising that an equally strong phenomenon – national sentiment – should have become firmly attached to it. This is how the historian Hans Kohn (1891–1971) expressed the inexorable desire of nations to become states:

> *The condition of statehood need not be present when a nationality originates; but in such a case it is always the memory of a past state and the aspiration towards statehood that characterises nationalities in the period of nationalism.*
>
> From *The Idea of Nationalism*, 1962

It is therefore hardly surprising, if we accept Kohn's assertion, that we have seen so many armed struggles involving nationalists who wish to establish statehood.

Organic society

The concept of nationalism presupposes that a people's common sense of nationality will bring them together into a single entity that will stand above the individual and have a kind of life of its own. This suggests that we all have at least two identities. One is as a sovereign individual; in this case we expect to enjoy rights, liberties and a private sphere of existence. The other is as a member of a nation; in this case we have a higher allegiance, which may, from time to time, transcend our individual identity.

One example of this is times of war. For better or worse, most individuals accept that when their nation is at war they should expect to make some personal sacrifices for the good of the nation as a whole. In extreme cases, individuals may lay down their lives for the national good. Another, more general example is the tendency to feel strong emotional attachments to national symbols and to become extremely patriotic at times of national sporting rivalry, such as during football World Cups and the Olympic Games.

Ukraine's 'Orange Revolution' was a movement to restore self determination for that country against Russian domination

Clearly there are strong emotions at work when the national interest is at stake. This suggests that we are bound together by ties that rival those of families, friendships and occupational units. This sense of 'oneness' is often described as 'the organic society'. On the whole, this concept is seen as a conservative idea. Certainly, it was largely developed by conservative thinkers such as the German philosopher Friedrich Hegel and his fellow-German contemporary, the nationalist Johann Gottfried von Herder (1744–1803). Herder saw the world as being divided up into national cultures, each one of which formed an organic whole. For Hegel, the organic society was more an expression of what he called 'universal will' – that is, a people bound together by a common sense of themselves as a single entity, whether or not this was nationalist in nature. Put in more simple terms, the philosophies of Herder and Hegel suggest that we are bound together by forces that are the result of history, traditions and shared values. The German word *gemeinschaft* expresses this idea better than any English term. Clearly these binding factors are most likely to be found among national groupings.

 Key Term

Gemeinschaft
In a political context, this term refers to the collection of factors that help to make a people think of themselves as a single, separate community. These may include language, history, traditions, institutions and national symbols. The nearest English expression might be 'a common sense of shared identity' or even 'culture', but the German word is perhaps stronger.

Although conservative in origin, the idea of the organic society has come to be shared by liberals – certainly since the end of the nineteenth century, when the Hegelian philosophy of T. H. Green became influential – and even by modern social democrats. As the socialist analysis of a society based on class conflict has declined, a new social perspective has arisen. Social democrats have adopted a more individualistic view of the world, but have also promoted the concept of communitarianism, which is similar to the philosophy of the organic society. The modern concern with 'cultural identity' is a further example of the modern application of the organic society.

The most extreme example of the synthesis between organic society theory and nationalism has been found in fascism. Indeed, Benito Mussolini went a step further by developing the concept of nation into a myth, a creation that would inspire the Italian people to perform great deeds. Furthermore, all individual aspirations were to be sacrificed to the interests of the nation. This is how Mussolini expressed these ideas in 1922, at the dawn of his regime:

We have created a myth. The myth is a faith, a passion. It is not necessary for it to be a reality. It is a reality in the sense that it is a stimulus, is hope, is faith, is courage. Our myth is the nation, our myth is the greatness of the nation. And to this myth, this greatness, which we want to translate into a total reality, we subordinate everything else.

From *The Political and Social Doctrine of Fascism*

Interestingly, and unlike German fascism, this Italian brand of radical nationalism sought to create a sense of national feeling where none existed, or at least where it was relatively weak. This is a more active form of nationalism, which leads its people, rather than follows them.

Whichever ideology embraces nationalism as part of its philosophy, all nationalists accept a general sense of the organic society. For some (e.g. fascists) it is stronger than for others (e.g. liberals), but it is present in all forms of nationalism.

Independence

Although achieving independence from other states is a core value of nationalists, there are some exceptions to this, three examples of which can be found in the UK.

The Welsh are the clearest example. Although some Welsh nationalists do support complete independence from the UK, on the whole the movement exists largely to defend the Welsh culture from dominance by England. The idea of a sovereign Welsh state is supported by a very small group. Most Welsh nationalists simply want to be recognised as a separate culture. Similarly, the Unionists in Northern Ireland wish to remain firmly within the UK. Indeed, their desire to maintain the link with the UK is the reason they exist as a political force. However, there is a sense in which Unionism is a nationalist grouping. Like the Welsh, Unionists seek to defend their own brand of Protestant/Irish/British culture, mainly against the influence of Irish Catholicism.

Lastly, English nationalism is a small movement with virtually no political manifestation. However, as a cultural idea, English nationalism does exist in the minds of its people. Part of the nationalist aspirations of the English is to maintain the United Kingdom of England, Scotland, Wales and Northern Ireland (which is dominated by the English in demographic and economic terms). The desire to separate England from the others and create a new independent state is virtually non-existent.

Having identified these exceptions, we can nevertheless assert that nationalist movements generally seek total political independence. We have already seen that this is particularly important when nations are ruled by imperialist powers. It also applies to nations that feel threatened by other nations or states, for example Israel, Cyprus and several of the Balkan nations. It can be important too in relation to supranational bodies, such as the EU. Many nationalists in Europe oppose further political integration on the grounds that this will threaten national independence. In a less specific sense, but no less powerful for that, many of the poorest nations of the world seek to assert their independence from what they see as the imperialism of international bodies. Thus, the World Bank, the International Monetary Fund and the World Trade Organisation are seen as threats to national independence because their policies demand a large degree of economic control. States such as Venezuela, for example, have sought to free themselves from these kind of strictures. More radical nationalist movements see the USA as being behind such economic imperialism. Nationalist aspirations of this kind can be found throughout Africa (e.g. Tanzania), South America (e.g. Argentina) and Asia (e.g. Indonesia).

Types of nationalism

Liberal nationalism

Although it is arguably the case that a form of cultural nationalism based in Germany pre-dated the French Revolution, it is generally accepted that the earliest effective form of nationalism was linked to the Enlightenment, the development of natural rights theory and the advent of liberalism.

The influence of the Enlightenment led nationalists to believe that the nation-state was the ultimate expression of rational government. Until the nineteenth century, most states owed their existence merely to historical circumstances – they were derived from territories that had been governed by ruling families for centuries. They had originally come into existence through conquest and thereafter the descendants of those original conquerors (although succession was often disputed) continued to rule. Subject peoples accepted this situation, partly out of fear of the disorder that might result if absolute rulers were removed, partly out of respect for tradition and partly out of the absence of any alternative theory of government. Rationalist philosophy provided a new justification for government, an important factor of which was that the natural division of the world into nations could be replicated in sovereign states corresponding to those nations.

The philosophy of natural rights concluded that absolute rulers had denied such rights in the interests of state security. If the rights of individuals were to be restored, there needed to be a contract whereby the people agreed to sacrifice some of their natural rights to government. Thomas Hobbes, the seventeenth-century philosopher, had argued that this sacrifice of rights could be made to any ruler who could guarantee order. However, this was not enough for early liberals. Government needed a stronger basis for its legitimacy than merely the ability to keep the peace, and the modern state needed a firmer basis for its authority. By combining the state with the national identity, these liberals provided such a basis. If the state represented the nation, the social contract became acceptable. Rights could be sacrificed to the manifestation of the nation – the nation-state – in a way that they could not be to an 'external' ruler who did not embody the nation. Thus, the great King Louis XIV of France (1638–1715) was able to declare *'L'état, c'est moi'* ('I am the state'), but he could never have justifiably claimed *'La France, c'est moi.'*

Liberalism demanded simply that every individual should be free, but this could be extended to include the assertion that every nation should be free. If a nation were not free, the individuals who comprised it would also not be free. The freedom of nations and the freedom of individuals were therefore inextricably linked. This is how the nineteenth-century Italian nationalist Giuseppe Mazzini (1805–72) expressed the idea of liberation from autocratic government:

Young Italy recognises therefore the universal association of the peoples as the ultimate aim of the endeavours of all free men. Before they can become members of the great association it is necessary that they should have a separate existence, name and power. Every people is therefore bound to constitute itself a nation before it can occupy itself with the question of humanity.

Quoted in Elie Kedourie, *Nationalism*, 1966

Ever since, liberal nationalists have demanded that every recognisable nation has the right to freedom from subjection to the rule of other nations and states. This demand has manifested itself in a variety of circumstances, examples of which are shown in Table 5.2.

Conservative nationalism

For much of the nineteenth century, conservatives were suspicious of liberal nationalism. They feared that it would lead to the destruction of traditional forms of authority and would therefore threaten order. It implied the demise of imperial power and the risk of civil war in those countries that were multinational in character. However, as more nation-states became established, conservatives began to understand that nationalism could become a force for order rather than disorder.

Movement	Circumstances
Mazzini's 'Young Italy' movement	Established in the 1860s, this was a movement to unite Italian peoples who lived in separate states, some of which were subject to 'foreign' rule. The movement believed that the establishment of an Italian republican state would bring democracy and freedom with it
Irish nationalism	In the nineteenth and twentieth centuries, this movement sought to separate the Irish people from British rule. The movement was also republican in character
Scottish nationalism	In the second half of the twentieth century, this movement grew in the belief that the self-determination of the Scots was essential if true democracy was to be established
Czech nationalism	Having been subjected to the hegemony of the Soviet Union, the Czechs seized the opportunity to establish their independence, individual liberties and democratic rule when the Union began to collapse in 1990. The Czechs asserted their nationalism further when they split from Slovakia in 1993 to form the Czech Republic.

Table 5.2 Examples of liberal nationalism

In this belief, conservative nationalists were inspired by the work of Johann Fichte, for whom the concept of the nation was a cultural idea. Peoples were bound together by their traditions and a common sense of their own history. This united them in a manner more powerful than anything a government could engender. While liberals saw nationalism as a way of creating and maintaining individual and collective liberty, for conservatives nationalism was a means by which societies could be held together.

The binding effect of nationalism could serve two main purposes. The first was to prevent social conflict. This was the motivation behind the nationalism of Benjamin Disraeli in Britain. He understood the dangers that free-market capitalism and the class conflict resulting from it could bring. One of these was the disintegration of society. By appealing to the nationalist instincts of the people, however, social conflict could be prevented. This theme was taken up much later by Margaret Thatcher, who was faced with the class conflict created by her neo-liberal policies of the 1980s. By arguing that her radical reforms served the national interest, and by resisting the increasing forces of European integration, she was able to unite the majority of the nation at a time when class conflict was growing.

The predominantly German form of conservative nationalism, represented by Fichte, and later by Otto von Bismarck as well as Giuseppe Garibaldi (1807–82) in Italy, concentrated more on the development of the nation and the achievement of its historical destiny. Progress depended on national unity. Without it, society would drift aimlessly and without spirit. Of course, as time went by, this conservative form of nationalism was to become more radical in Germany and Italy and contributed to the rise of fascism. The most sinister aspect of this transformation occurred when the fascists saw national destiny in terms of national superiority and the defeat of weaker nations. An exaggerated sense of national superiority of this kind has come to be described as **chauvinism**. A recent example of chauvinistic, conservative nationalism was seen under

Key Term

Chauvinism
Originally a French term, chauvinism refers to a sense of national superiority. It is associated with conservative nationalism, which regards such a sense of superiority as a means of uniting the people. Chauvinism can be displayed in an exaggerated sense of patriotism or as jingoism – a slavish, emotional attachment to nationalist symbols such as flags, anthems and mythology.

President Charles de Gaulle (in office 1958–69). His 'Gaullist' movement led to France leaving the political arm of NATO and blocking British entry to the European Community, both on the grounds of French autonomy.

Conservative nationalism can also be defensive in nature. This occurs when a national identity is perceived to be under threat (even if that threat is illusory). In a British context, the rise of the UK Independence Party (UKIP) can be seen as a typical example. For UKIP, the threat to British national identity is posed by European integration. On a much bigger scale, there has been a recent emergence of Hindu nationalism in India in response to the perceived threat both from Islamic culture and from modernisation.

Right-wing nationalism

Right-wing nationalism includes those forms of nationalism that have gone beyond the type favoured by conservatism. For conservative nationalists, the doctrine's purpose was to maintain order and unity. Right-wing nationalists have developed ideas that are more active and purposeful than those of the conservatives. Some examples are given below.

Imperialism

Some nationalist movements have been overtly imperialist in nature, considering the creation of empires as a key element in the national interest and destiny. During the nineteenth and early twentieth centuries, France, Britain, Belgium, Germany and Holland all displayed imperialist motives. The competition for overseas possessions which resulted can be seen both as a Darwinian struggle for superiority and as a pursuit of national economic interests. In the 1930s, Japanese nationalists wanted to create a Pacific empire for themselves, while the Soviet Union demonstrated imperialist tendencies through most of the twentieth century.

Expansionism

A similar concept to imperialism, expansionism refers to a nation's tendency to expand its territory into neighbouring countries or to exercise political hegemony over them. In recent times, Serbia, Russia and China have all shown a desire to expand their influence over a whole region.

Xenophobia

Xenophobia is the instinct typical of right-wing nationalists to be suspicious of foreigners and to attempt to maintain the exclusiveness of the home nation. It manifests itself in resistance to immigration and, in some more sinister cases, in attempts to impose racial and cultural uniformity. Right-wing movements of this type have been most evident in recent times in France (the National Front movement of Jean-Marie Le Pen), Austria (the Freedom Party) and Holland (the anti-immigration party of Pym Fortuyn (1951–2002)).

Fascism as radical nationalism

All fascists have been radical nationalists. In this context, 'radical' describes a kind of nationalism that is neither liberal nor passive in nature. Instead, nationalism is seen by fascists as a collective and positive movement.

Fascism is obsessed with the idea of uniting people into a single, organic whole. (Indeed, the term 'fascism' is derived from the Latin term for a bundle of rods which is bound together.) Fascists therefore worship any aspect of human life capable of binding people, for which purpose the common circumstances of birth and history that a nation enjoys are clearly ideal. Historically, the concept of nationhood certainly seems to have been the most powerful binding force,

perhaps rivalled only by religion. Indeed, many fascists actively sought to promote nationalism as a kind of religion, or a replacement for it.

A word of caution is needed here. Different fascists have used nationalism in different ways. For the Italian and Spanish fascists, nationalism was merely a vehicle for uniting the state. For them, the state (which expressed the collective will of the people) was paramount. If the promotion of nationalism could safeguard and preserve the interests of the state, then it was a useful political force.

In the Third Reich, however, nationalism took on an altogether more important position. The unification, glorification and final world triumph of the German nation were the ultimate goals of the Nazi form of fascism. The role of the state was to serve the interests of the nation, thus reversing the roles of state and nation as existed in fascist Italy and Spain. Hitler described this view:

The State is only a means to an end. Its end and its purpose is to preserve and promote a community of human beings who are physically as well as spiritually kindred.

From *Mein Kampf*, 1925

Hitler deployed a range of emotional appeals designed to inspire his people. To this end a series of historical myths was a powerful feature of his message. He also played upon the fears and resentments of the German people by claiming that threats to their power and integrity were presented by the other great powers, as well as by Jews and communists. Above all, however, he unveiled a golden future for Germany, in which it would reunite all its scattered peoples, restore its lost territories, conquer weaker peoples and take their land for further expansion. Referring back to a partly factual, partly mythical history, he promised to restore Germany to its former glories. He claimed that Germany had the potential to become the highest form of civilisation the world had ever seen. For many Germans, this proved to have an overwhelmingly attractive appeal. Individuals might not be willing to sacrifice themselves to the abstract concept of the state, but they were willing to

Hitler's Nazi movement laid huge stress on German Nationalism

follow Hitler anywhere in the name of German nationalism.

Fascism and racialism

Before considering this aspect of fascism, two terms need to be clarified. Racism is normally used to denote a particular state of mind rather than a political theory. Racists are prejudiced against certain racial groups and are likely to see their own race as superior to others. Racialism, on the other hand, is a quasi-scientific set of theories about race. It often results in a feeling of racial superiority, and a system of discrimination or worse, but racialist theories claim some kind of rational basis for their beliefs (see p. 178). As mythology played a large part in the appeal of fascism, it was hardly surprising that racialist theories were usually based on such myths. For the purposes of this section, however, we will run together the two concepts of racism and racialism and refer to them as racialism collectively. In other words, fascists were often racists, racialists or both.

It is a common error to believe that fascism and racialism are essentially the same thing. This is not the case. The main reason why the two movements are confused is, of course, that the Nazi regime was intensely racialist in nature. There is, however, nothing necessarily racialist about

fascism. Many fascists movements were scarcely racialist at all. Nevertheless, it would be unrealistic to argue that there is no link between the two, and the reasons for this are outlined below.

First, the National Socialist (i.e. Nazi) movement in Germany was extremely racialist. Hitler and his followers synthesised their fascist creed with an intense form of racialist nationalism. By the mid-1930s, Hitler's Germany had become a model for other fascist regimes to follow, and part of that model was racialism. Mussolini, having met Hitler and fallen under his spell, showed signs of imitating the Nazi regime. As a result, the Italian fascists became anti-semitic and began rounding up Jews and handing them over to the Third Reich. In the UK, meanwhile, the fascist leader Oswald Mosley had shown no particular signs of racialism until he too began to copy Hitler's political style and developed an anti-semitic approach.

The second link is more sinister. As has been shown, nationalism is a key aspect of all fascist movements. Understandably, race is a powerful element in nationalist feeling. Many nations see racial or ethnic identity as the key element in their unity and shared experience. Small wonder, then, that fascists should stress the racial connections among people when seeking to promote social unity. This combination of nationalism and racialism is best expressed by the German term *Volksgemeinschaft*. This is the collective

 Key Term

Volksgemeinschaft
A term usually associated with Nazism. The shorter word '*Gemeinschaft*' suggests community spirit, a shared sense of vision and identity, literally a collective state of mind. The prefix '*Volk*' refers to a description of a people – in this case the German people – united by a common language, culture and attachment to territory. When the two concepts are placed together we have a term that refers to a strong cultural binding force for a people.

expression of nationalism, based on a particular race and its shared history – a potent cocktail, and fascists knew it.

The Nazis carried their racialism several stages further. They adopted a number of 'scientific' theories about race to justify their policies on racial purity, conquest of other peoples and, ultimately, genocide. The two main influences behind fascist racial theories were Arthur de Gobineau (1816–82) and Houston Chamberlain (1855–1927). Both these thinkers considered racial identity to be a key factor in the development of civilisation. Gobineau placed different races into a hierarchy, with the purest and therefore strongest at the top (e.g. Germanic peoples) and inferior races (e.g. Asian peoples) at the bottom. Chamberlain saw the history of modern civilisation in terms of a struggle between Aryan or Teutonic (i.e. North European, Germanic) peoples and the Jews. These theories accord closely with fascist radical nationalism, which was based on racial and cultural superiority. Indeed, Chamberlain was one of Hitler's closest advisers in his early days as a populist politician.

Closely linked to the racial theories of Gobineau and Chamberlain were ideas that emerged from the work of Charles Darwin on evolution, in particular his so-called 'survival of the fittest' analysis. It should be pointed out that Darwin himself firmly denied that his biological theories could be adapted to human society in any strict sense. Nevertheless, many political thinkers of the latter part of the nineteenth century did just that, and created a movement known as 'social Darwinism'. This movement suggested that, as in the animal kingdom, humans were engaged in a struggle for superiority over each other, especially in their economic life and, even more importantly, within capitalism. Far from being a problem, this evolutionary struggle served to strengthen society, just as a similar process did for the genetic lines of animal species. The struggle ensured a dynamic society in which only the strongest would emerge in positions of economic and political power.

However, if fascism is considered as it existed in South America, Spain, the UK and parts of Central Europe, there is no reason to place racialism as one of its more significant aspects.

Rationalism and romanticism

It is difficult to understand the nature of fascism and its relationship to nationalism without first examining the distinctions between rationality and romanticism. These are both ways of thinking and forms of political action. Fascists pride themselves on both their rejection of rationality and their adoption of romantic ideals, which they consider to be vastly superior. Indeed, fascism should be considered in terms of the conflict that existed in politics and philosophy between rationalism and romantic idealism.

The Enlightenment era – roughly corresponding to the eighteenth century in Western civilisation – ushered in new rational ways of viewing the world and society. Rational thought claimed to be able to discover explanations for virtually everything in the world, based on scientific, objective evidence. Alternatives to this rational thought had included explanations that proposed that the will of God was behind most events, or general theories adopted by prominent individuals. It was common to explain the world simply as a reflection of God's grand plan or of his will.

In the Enlightenment age, rationalism was applied to a wide range of areas. In the physical sciences, the ideas of Isaac Newton became dominant; in religion, rational, Protestant thinkers replaced the conservatism of the Roman Church. Rationalism also pervaded artistic fields, such as architecture, painting and even music, where Wolfgang Amadeus Mozart was the primary example.

For the purposes of this book, however, it is rationalism in the fields of philosophy and politics that is of most concern. France spawned a number of celebrated thinkers, many of whom became collectively known as *'les philosophes'*;

Voltaire (the pen name of François-Marie Arouet), Jean-Jacques Rousseau and Charles-Louis Montesquieu (1689–1755) are examples. There were many too in Germany (e.g. Friedrich Hegel), England (e.g. John Locke, John Stuart Mill, Jeremy Bentham), in Scotland (e.g. David Hume (1711–76)) and in the USA (e.g. James Madison). These philosophers and political theorists were largely concerned with the problem of how to set up and run a government along rational lines. There was a pressing need for this since in many countries the traditional form of government – monarchy backed by a hereditary aristocracy – was breaking down as the people sought political power and influence.

Rational government involved such principles and practices as government by consent, democracy (either direct or representative), accountability, the protection of individual rights and constitutionalism. In addition, the objectives of government were to be discovered by rational means. This could mean scientific methods of discovering which actions would be in the best interests of the people (the clearest example of this being utilitarianism) or effective ways of converting the demands and needs of the people into political action – that is, various kinds of democratic arrangements.

The typical fascist of the twentieth century rejected these modes of thinking and forms of action, preferring romantic ideals and actions based on emotion rather than reason – in other words, acting from the heart rather than the head. Two concrete examples of fascist behaviour serve to illustrate this point.

First, there is the fascist response to the problem of how best to serve the interests of the people. Instead of using scientific formulae to do this, fascists favour the inspirational leadership of a single ruler (always a man since fascists were all anti-feminist), who could exercise his superior judgement. He would know what was best for the people better than the people did themselves. The petty self-interests of the people were to be disparaged – far superior to mere economic contentment was the noble cause of the dynamic pursuit of glory for the nation. This was indeed a romantic rather than a rational goal.

Second, there is the fascist objection to democracy. Different kinds of democracy can be seen as the rational means by which political demands can be converted into action. Fascists reject traditional liberal democracy. They believe it is a weak and directionless way of conducting politics. The people – who effectively govern a liberal democracy – are too easily swayed by short-term popular movements. Furthermore, the people are prone to changing their minds and to seeking short-term advantages, often at the expense of long-term ideals.

Again, the power of the romantically inspired leader is preferable to the feckless, unreliable demands of the masses. The leader is likely to be dynamic and determined, and to embody higher ideals than those of the ordinary people. It was clear to many Germans in the early 1930s that the pluralist and chaotic politics of the Weimar Republic, which preceded the Third Reich, was failing them. Instead they chose Hitler, a great orator who had successfully presented himself as a convincing romantic hero. He promised them deliverance from the humiliation of the post-First World War settlement and offered in its place dreams of a return to the past glories of the German nation.

It should be pointed out at this stage that some fascists have argued that leadership-based regimes can be described as broadly democratic. The basis of this argument is that the leader is governing for the people. It is not democracy in the sense of government by the people (as Abraham Lincoln (1809–65) had proposed in his famous Gettysburg Address) but it could be described as government on behalf of the people.

We can thus summarise two very different perspectives on nationalism thus:

Liberals see nationalism in these ways:

● It is a rational concept, based on the assertion that the political community (i.e. the state) should be based on the nation.

- Nationalism and democracy are inevitably linked. A nation-state that is not democratic is a denial of the main objective of nationalism – to promote self-determination.

- All legitimate nations should be granted equal status.

- Nationalism is based upon a neutral version of history.

- The purposes of nationalism are largely limited to the promotion of liberty and democracy for a people.

Fascists see nationalism in these ways:

- Nationalism is a romantic ideal. It is based on the dream that a united nation can achieve heroic deeds. Attachment to one's nation is based on emotion rather than reason.

- There is no necessary link between nationalism and democracy. The aspirations of the nation are best represented by a single, dynamic leader.

- Nations are not equal. Some are superior and others inferior. Furthermore, Nazis in particular see history in terms of a struggle between nations to assert their superiority over inferior peoples.

- The fascist version of history is not neutral and contains myths that are a conscious attempt to promote national unity and to inspire the people to great deeds.

- The aims of nationalism are broad and varied, including expansionism, the conquest of weaker nations, the uniting of a people who have been scattered and the promotion of a strong sense of subservience to the state.

The close adviser to Hitler, Alfred Rosenberg, summed up the philosophy of nationalism, placing it above even religion, thus:

The German people is not marked by original sin, but by original nobility. The place of Christian love has been taken by the National Socialist, Germanic idea of comradeship ...which has already been symbolically expressed through the replacement of the rosary by the spade of labour.

From *The Myth of the Twentieth Century*, 1930

Nazism

National Socialism – or Nazism, as it is commonly known – was undoubtedly the most notorious form of fascism. It was peculiar to interwar Germany and, as such, assumed a character of its own, though there have been imitators since, usually known as neo-Nazis. It is a branch of fascism that is most closely related to nationalism. The Nazis were heavily influenced by two German historian/ philosophers. These were Herder and Fichte. Johann von Herder (1744–1803) saw nationalism in terms of culture and he saw culture largely in terms of language. For him the main purpose of nationalism was to establish national cultures and free them from all forms of oppression. Johann Fichte (1762–1814) also saw nationalism in terms of culture and exhorted the scattered German people to unite and rekindle their cultural history and identity.

Thus, Nazism placed the nation at the apex of human experience. The collective identity of the people (or '*volk*', as they were always termed), its history and its future were all bound up in the concept of nationhood. The state, made up of the political and administrative organs of the country, was secondary to the purposes of the nation. In short, the state served the nation. This was not the case with other fascist movements, which placed the state above the nation. The exercise of power became a political aim for Nazis, rather than a romantic nationalist ideal. For most fascists outside Germany, the nation served the purposes of the state.

Nazism was even more radical than other forms of nationalism for a number of reasons. These included:

- It laid huge emphasis on race as the basis of national identity. Indeed, for Nazis race and nation were indivisible. Furthermore, they believed that the German race was superior to all others in terms of intellect, organisation and purpose. The purity of the racial line was essential to the strength of the nation. Nationalism was therefore a combination of 'blood and intellect'.

● The Nazis were Darwinists who saw history as a struggle between nations (and therefore races). The outcome of this struggle was inevitably that some stronger peoples would triumph and others would be subdued and ultimately conquered.

● They were expansionists, asserting that, as a superior people, the Germans were entitled to more territory into which they could expand.

● German fascists (Nazis) extolled the virtues of warfare. They believed that, in war, the individual could demonstrate his total identification with the purpose of the state and the nation. It was therefore inevitable that Nazism should be extremely aggressive as a movement.

It was Hitler himself who expressed most clearly the aggressive and expansionist nature of Nazism:

When the territory of the Reich embraces all the Germans and finds itself unable to assure them a livelihood, only then can the moral right arise, from the need of the people, to acquire foreign territory. The plough is then the sword; and tears of war will produce the daily bread for generations to come.

From *Mein Kampf*, 1925

Cultural nationalism and volkism

Cultural nationalism often does not include a desire for national independence, but rather a sense of national pride in a distinctive culture and a wish to free that culture from the hegemony of a more dominant neighbour. The classic example of this is Welsh nationalism. Based on an attachment to the Welsh language and the Welsh culture of art, poetry, music and non-conformist religion, this kind of nationalism is a reaction

against the domination of the much stronger English culture. The appeal reproduced below was made in the context of Finland, but its message could be reproduced for several other cultural, language-based movements.

> ### Box 5.2 An appeal to a people with a common language
>
> **The Finnish nationalist Adolf Arvidsson (1791–1858) made this appeal to his people in the early nineteenth century in the hope that they would throw off the hegemony of the Swedish-speaking minority:**
>
> *When the language of its forefathers is lost, a nation, too, is lost and perishes. All speaking the same tongue naturally forms an indivisible whole; they are bound together internally by ties of mind and soul, mightier and firmer than every external bond. For language forms the spiritual, and land the material, boundaries of mankind; but the former is the stronger, because the spirit means more than material.*

Such sentiments could apply to many cultural nationalist movements and were adopted by Julius Nyerere (1922–99), the great African nationalist, in his nation-building efforts.

Rather than striving for independence, Welsh nationalists have campaigned for the teaching of their language in schools, its use in public affairs and the preservation of Welsh literature. Although there is a weak sense of a separate Welsh history, including some struggles against English rule during the early Middle Ages, there is no history of distinct Welsh political institutions (in contrast to Scotland, for example). Thus, Plaid Cymru – the Welsh nationalist party – is more interested in limited autonomy than full sovereign powers. There are Welsh separatists, but they are very much a minority. Movements similar to Welsh nationalism exist in Catalonia in Spain, in parts of the Italian Tyrol region and in French Brittany.

Key Term

Hegemony

This term has a special meaning for Marxists of the Frankfurt School, but in the context of nationalism it refers to the domination of one culture over another. This may have political and economic significance, as in the case of the hegemony of the USSR over much of Eastern Europe, but it is often confined simply to dominant values, traditions, language, media and artistic pursuits. It does not necessarily mean complete political control, but rather irresistible domination. The great powers have often exerted hegemony over whole regions, e.g. the USA in South America and France in North Africa.

Volkism is a more powerful, and in some cases ominous, form of cultural nationalism. The type of cultural nationalism found in Wales is largely benign and non-violent, whereas *volkism* is radical and can lead to armed struggle. It is mostly associated with Johann Fichte, who identified the German people as a classic example of *volk*. By this he meant a people closely bound together by a common culture, language, religion, history and mythology. There is also an element of territorial possession associated with *volkism*. Peoples claim a historical attachment to land, sometimes associated with past conquest of that territory. In some cases, this might become a romantic ideal, a desire either to retain the traditional territory or to regain possession of it after losing it historically. Fichte, for example, believed that the German people had long been deprived of their ancestral lands. In this sense, both the Germans and the Jews could be said to have a *volkish* identity. Zionism is a movement that seeks to restore and retain the historical (and indeed religious) claim of the Jews to the land of Israel.

The idea of *volk*, in the sense of pursuing a historical destiny, reached its height in Nazi Germany. The Nazis, however, added racial exclusivity and superiority to the concept of *volk*. This created an organic and radical form of nationalism that provided justification for conquest and expansionism. (This was known as *Lebensraum* – the right of a superior people to annexe additional territory occupied by inferior peoples.)

Post-colonial nationalism

It is not surprising that many examples of nationalist movements are found in countries that have struggled against colonial rule. When a subject people is fighting for its independence (and when it has achieved that independence), there is an overwhelming need to promote social unity. A strong sense of national identity can provide this. In Africa, where such post-colonial nationalist movements have proliferated, an additional problem has been the existence of tribal loyalties that cut across national identity.

The need to create unity is one of the factors that has led to regimes in such countries becoming highly authoritarian in nature. Were newly independent states to be pluralistic and intensely democratic in character, there would be a danger that the state would fall apart under the strain of internal conflict. The plight of countries such as Uganda, Sudan and Ethiopia, all brought to the edge of ruin by civil war, bears testimony to this problem. By contrast, in Zimbabwe, Robert Mugabe (1925–) – a nationalist freedom fighter – has suppressed tribal rivalry through repressive political methods. Similarly, Julius Nyerere in Tanzania united his country by turning it into a one-party state, although his personal instincts were democratic in nature.

Post-colonial nationalism and anti-colonial nationalism, therefore, are often highly autocratic; many of the examples shown in Table 5.3 are of this type.

Post-colonial nationalist movements have often been socialist. This is the result of a specific set of circumstances and another type of nationalism, which is described below.

Socialist nationalism

Some nationalists – usually in states that were former colonies – adopted socialism or Marxism

Country	Leader(s)	Characteristics
China (1911–49)	Sun Yat Sen (1866–1925) Chiang Kai Shek (1887–1975)	Quasi-democratic
Vietnam (1950s–1970s)	Ho Chi Minh (1890–1969)	One-party communist
Cuba (1959–)	Fidel Castro (1927–)	One-party socialist
Ghana (1960s–1970s)	Joshua Nkrumah (1909–72)	Quasi-democratic
India (until 1947)	Jawaharlal Nehru (1889–1964) Mohammed Ali Jinnah (1876–1948)	Democratic/socialist
Congo (1960s)	Patrice Lumumba (1925–61)	Autocratic
Zimbabwe (1979–)	Robert Mugabe (1925–)	Quasi-democratic/autocratic

Table 5.3 Anti-colonial and post-colonial nationalist movements

as a means of promoting both economic development and independence from world trading systems.

This was done despite the fact that socialism and nationalism are not natural bedfellows. In socialist theory, it is class solidarity which, it is hoped, will replace capitalist individualism. Marxists in particular viewed nationalism as a form of false consciousness, promoted by the bourgeois ruling class to bring together the working classes in the interests of capitalism and to divert their consciousness away from revolutionary activities. It is therefore surprising to find a number of modern nationalists who have also been socialists.

In many cases, the nationalist leaders in question began their freedom fighting activities as socialists or communists. This was true of Ho Chi Minh in Vietnam, Fidel Castro in Cuba and Robert Mugabe in Zimbabwe. It was therefore not surprising that they should synthesise their original socialism with the nationalist desire for independence and self-determination. In fact, a symbiotic relationship developed between nationalism and socialism: nationalism benefits from the imposition of socialism since this enables the country to avoid domination by external capitalist powers. This is most evident in Cuba, where the need to escape from the economic hegemony of the neighbouring USA required that the people of the island should reject free-market capitalism. At the same time, nationalism can assist the building of socialism by creating a sense of solidarity and national purpose. Finally, the social equality that socialism can bring creates a sense of unity through justice.

Racialism

In those states where the basis of nationhood is founded on ethnic identity, there is a synthesis between racialism and nationalism. In extreme cases, such as Nazi Germany, the two concepts can become virtually synonymous. In theory, there need be nothing sinister about such a relationship, but in practice many nations based on race have also adopted a Darwinist view of the world.

The philosophers of racialism who inspired Adolf Hitler (1889–1945), such as Count Gobineau (1816–82) and Houston Chamberlain (1855–1927), adopted a world view which suggested that races are arranged in a hierarchy, with Teutonic (German/Aryan) peoples at the apex of this system and various inferior peoples of Asia and Africa at the bottom. In the great struggles for superiority, those nations that demonstrated the strongest sense of unity and purpose would prevail. What would give them such strength of will? Racial theorists often suggested that it was the purity of the nation's bloodline that would be the decisive factor.

Note that **racialism** should not be confused with **racism**. The distinction is explained below.

Key Terms

Racism and racialism
These terms are certainly contentious in terms of their meanings. For the purposes of this book, however, racism is taken to mean a generalised sense of racial discrimination, prejudice and antagonism; racialism, on the other hand, can mean any form of scientific or quasi-scientific theory about race, the relationship between races and the history of racial development. Thus, those who routinely attack members of ethnic minorities, are prejudiced against them or who discriminate against them in the fields of work and education could be called racists. The theorists who underpinned Nazi theory, however, were racialists.

There have, of course, been a number of race-based national movements that have not engaged in a Darwinian struggle. In Africa, for example, many nationalists have proposed the restructuring of the continent into 'natural' countries based on ethnic groupings. However, there remains a sense of unity within Africa, suggesting that all racial units should be treated as equal. The desire of the Organisation for African Unity (OAU) to recreate independent nations is based on aspirations for mutual respect and peaceful coexistence. Similarly, movements that have sought to unite ethnic groupings, such as Pan-Arabism (aiming to unite all Arab peoples) and Pan-Slavism (aiming to unite the Slavic race), may have proposed racial exclusivity and unity, but included no special sense of superiority. These different types of nationalism are summarised in Table 5.4.

Key nationalist thinkers

Johann Gottfried von Herder (German, 1744–1803)

Herder represents a kind of romantic nationalism that stands in opposition to the rational and liberal forms inspired by Jean-Jacques Rousseau, Napoleon Bonaparte and, later, John Stuart Mill.

Type	Examples	Main characteristics
Liberal nationalism	● 'Young Italy' ● Scotland ● Ireland	Desire for self-determination; creation of democracy; creation or preservation of liberty
Conservative nationalism	● Traditional British conservatism ● French Gaullism	Determination to preserve the national interest; nationalism used as a means of retaining social unity; historically imperialist
Right-wing nationalism	● Fascism ● French National Front	Xenophobic; sense of national superiority; expansionist; totalitarian
Post-colonial nationalism	● Tanzania ● Nigeria ● Singapore	Often socialist, usually autocratic regimes; emphasis on national unity; economic self-sufficiency
Socialist nationalism	● Cuba ● Zimbabwe	One-party, powerful centralised state; opposition to foreign investment; desire for industrialisation
Racialist nationalism	● Nazism ● South African apartheid regime	Sense of racial superiority and racial exclusivity; expansionist; desire to unify the racial group into one state
Cultural nationalism	● Hindu nationalism in India ● Wales	Desire to protect a cultural tradition under threat from another culture; usually politically moderate

Table 5.4 Summary of types of nationalism

His conception of nationalism was based upon culture, and especially language.

In a Europe where various nationalities were mixed up in a patchwork of different states (especially in the region now called Germany), Herder sought to discover how peoples could extricate themselves from circumstances that tend to suppress traditional culture. Historically, civilisations that had retained their own particular culture, and had successfully guarded it against adulteration by other cultures, had retained their own identity and, in doing so, had become dominant.

Since Herder asserted that language was the main vehicle by which culture was transported from one generation to the next, nationality itself could be defined in terms of language. This is how Herder expressed his love of language:

> Has a nation anything dearer than the speech of its fathers? In its speech resides its whole thought-domain, its tradition, history, religion, and basis of life, all its heart and soul. To deprive a people of its own speech is to deprive it of its one eternal good...As God tolerates all the different languages in the world, so also should a ruler not only tolerate but honour the various languages of his peoples...The best culture of a people cannot be expressed through a foreign language.
>
> From *Materials for the Philosophy of the History of Mankind*, 1784

Although Herder was something of a cultural nationalist, it would be wrong to ascribe any of the later German nationalist tradition to him. German nationalism might be concerned with the restoration and preservation of culture, but it was also associated with state power. In other words, the will of the nation was to be expressed through the German state. Herder was less concerned with politics and more interested in the independence of cultures from domination by other peoples. His philosophy therefore had more in common with later Welsh, English and Italian nationalism, which were based upon language, culture and history. Although

twentieth-century fascists drew some inspiration from Herder's thought, this was a distortion of his beliefs. He was a vehement opponent of all forms of tyranny and did not accept that nations were based on racial distinctions.

Giuseppe Mazzini (Italian, 1805–72)

In 1831, Mazzini founded a revolutionary nationalist movement known as 'Young Italy'. Like Herder, he was a romantic figure who saw nationalism in terms of brotherhood and comradeship, the ultimate expression of social solidarity. He linked the idea of uniting the disparate Italian peoples into a free nation with the right to self-determination and liberation from oppressive regimes. He was, in short, a liberal-republican nationalist, the ultimate symbol of the unity of freedom and self-determination. Although principally associated with Italy, he proposed that Europe as a whole should be divided into 12 nation-states, each of which was to be based on a dominant cultural grouping.

The purpose of nationalism and self-determination, Mazzini argued, was to ensure social progress. He likened the division of peoples into natural national groupings to the division of labour under capitalism. Once peoples were free from subjection to tyrannical foreign powers, they would be able to develop their own cultures and experience true liberty.

Mazzini's brand of nationalism became a popular model for other movements that spread through Europe in the nineteenth century, especially among the subject peoples of the Austro-Hungarian Empire. He was also one of the founders of the principle of guerrilla warfare, whereby small conspiratorial groups operated in secret to strike blows against repressive powers, reducing their will to govern and undermining their authority. By waging a war of attrition, the dominating power would ultimately be toppled. Mazzini therefore became an inspiration for later nationalist movements in regions such as Indochina, South America and Cuba.

Alfred Rosenberg (Estonian, 1893–1946)

Like Chamberlain (and indeed Hitler himself), Rosenberg was not born in Germany. He was an Estonian who, as a student, became obsessed with Germany and German civilisation. He was of ethnic German origin, however, along with millions of others of similar heritage who were scattered throughout Eastern and Central Europe in the nineteenth century. Many of these ethnic Germans flocked to the Nazi cause and proved to be even more zealous than those who had been born in Germany itself.

On his return to Germany, Rosenberg threw in his lot with Hitler and the National Socialists, becoming editor of the party's newspaper, the *Völkischer Beobachter* (*People's Guardian*). He collaborated closely with Hitler in the writing of *Mein Kampf* and subsequently established himself as the central philosopher of the Nazi movement. However, as the 1930s continued, his position in the party declined and he spent the war in relative obscurity. He was tried at Nuremberg and executed in 1946. His main influence, therefore, lay in the early development of Hitler's thought.

Rosenberg's main contribution was to the racialist theories of the Nazis. He held similar views to Chamberlain in that he saw European history in terms of a struggle between Aryans and Jews. The Aryans – or Germans, or Nordic people, as he variously described them – displayed superior qualities to all other races. They exemplified honour, intellect, artistic qualities, organisation, action and purity of spirit. For Rosenberg, the pursuit of racial purity and superiority had replaced religion in its ability to inspire men to great deeds. He expressed this view in his best-known work, *The myth of the Twentieth Century* (1930):

The German people is not marked by original sin, but by original nobility. The place of Christian love has already been taken by the National Socialist, Germanic idea of comradeship...which has already been symbolically expressed through the replacement of the rosary by the spade of labour.

Rosenberg can also be credited with developing the notion of *Lebensraum* (literally meaning 'living space'). This theory claimed that if a people could demonstrate superior qualities, they were justified in taking over land occupied by inferior peoples. If blood were spilled in conquering such land, this would give legitimacy to its occupation. Poland and Russia clearly fell into this category for the Nazis.

Rosenberg was the main philosopher of the peculiarly racialist form of fascism developed by Hitler and his party. Ironically, this proved to be his undoing – as has been shown above, fascists tended to despise intellectuals and rationality. Rosenberg was ultimately dismissed by his colleagues for placing philosophy above action. Fascists are pragmatists and resist being bound by rigid social theories of the kind that he promoted.

Charles de Gaulle (French, 1890–1970)

De Gaulle led the free French forces against Germany during the Second World War. After the war, he remained on the fringes of French politics until 1958, when a major political crisis struck the country. The French colonies in Algeria and Indochina were in revolt and the government seemed unable to quell the rebellions. Army leaders in France appeared to be on the point of provoking a *coup d'état* against the tottering French state. The political leadership of France was therefore forced to ask de Gaulle, a figure who enjoyed the same kind of esteem as Churchill in the UK, to form a new government. De Gaulle agreed and took over, writing a new constitution that granted him extensive powers as president and ushered in the fifth French Republic.

De Gaulle was, above all, a French nationalist. His philosophy, which became known as the 'politics of grandeur', was based upon the principle of national self-interest. He sought to reconstruct the French economy so that the country could enjoy greater independence. He pursued an independent foreign policy, withdrawing from NATO in 1966 and maintaining an independent nuclear capability. In the early 1960s, he vetoed the UK's entry into the European Community on the grounds that it represented a threat to French interests. His nationalist credentials were enhanced when he openly supported a movement campaigning for the independence of French-speaking Quebec from Canada.

His brand of nationalism was the pursuit of national independence from growing international forces. The term 'globalisation' was not widely used when de Gaulle was alive, but he certainly wished to maintain an independent status for his people. He refused to accept the dominance of either the USA or the USSR over world affairs. By courting the friendship of China, parts of the Arab world and various other nationalist movements in Africa and Asia, he was able to maintain France's unique position.

Widespread political unrest in France among students and workers and the rejection of his proposed amendments to the French constitution led de Gaulle to resign in 1968 and to retire from politics the following year.

Julius Nyerere (Tanzanian, 1922–99)

The nationalism of Nyerere was typical of a number of African post-independence movements. It synthesised independence, language and socialism as a means of uniting a people and maintaining its autonomy.

Nyerere was the first elected president of Tanzania, a country that was severely divided along tribal and linguistic lines, but which had been artificially thrown together as a single colonial state under British rule. The principle of using common language to unite the people was described by Nyerere as *ujamaa*, which literally

means 'family bond'. He believed he could forge a new nation by insisting that the members of all tribes, who had their own languages, speak a common tongue. This left the problem of how to ensure that, having rid themselves of their former colonial masters, the Tanzanians would not fall prey to the **economic imperialism** of multinational companies and the richer trading states.

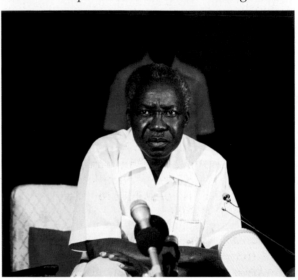

Julius Nyerere, a typical post-colonial African leader

> ✔ **Key Term**
>
> **Economic imperialism**
> We usually associate colonisation with political and/or military control, and the removal of political sovereignty from a country. Economic imperialism, on the other hand, occurs even when states have their own political independence. Richer countries may continue to exercise decisive influence by forcing other states to be dependent on trade, penetrating them with large corporations and creating large quantities of debt. The USA in particular is often accused of exercising economic imperialism over poor states.

Nyerere developed a socialist, self-sufficient system, which he hoped would reduce the need to become economically dependent on the outside world. Unfortunately, the imposition of socialism proved to be unsuccessful. Tanzania became extremely poor and unrest grew. Although Nyerere created a one-party dictatorship, he could not quell the opposition. In 1985, he bowed to the inevitable and resigned as president. During this period, many similar states went through much the same process. Socialist nationalism was failing everywhere and free-market policies had to be introduced.

Issues in nationalism

Conservative and liberal nationalism

The principal question to be asked here is: do these two traditions have anything significant in common, or are they completely different ideologies? It is possible to identify both similarities and differences.

The first feature that both have in common is an overarching aspiration to unite a people who believe that they share a common national identity. Both movements tend to stress characteristics such as common history and traditions, language and culture.

For liberal nationalists, who are invariably struggling against some kind of oppression or foreign hegemony, the need for unity is essential if the people are to throw off the controlling power and thereby restore collective and individual liberty. Mazzini, in nineteenth-century Italy, believed that this meant developing collective, national, revolutionary fervour. In Ireland, a small revolutionary group, Sinn Fein, dedicated itself to armed struggle, but the main thrust of the movement was cultural in nature. Modern Scottish nationalism, on the other hand, is almost exclusively peaceful and dedicated to working through the existing parliamentary system of the UK. It emphasises Scottish history and the traditional Scottish institutions around which the people can unite. The problem for Scottish nationalism was how to place concerted political pressure on Westminster to achieve its aims.

Conservative nationalists have stressed similar symbols of unity. However, the purposes of this type of nationalism are different. On the whole, conservative nationalists operate within a national state that already exists and already enjoys independence. The main purpose is therefore to maintain a sense of unity, which may be under threat. For Disraeli, in the late nineteenth century, the threat to unity was social conflict, mainly between classes. For the French under de Gaulle and his Gaullist descendants, the threat has been mainly from international organisations, such as the European Community and US-dominated institutions.

A second common feature is that both liberals and conservatives – including as disparate a group as Rousseau, Mazzini, Bismarck and the Palestinian nationalist Yasser Arafat (1929–2004) – have asserted that all nations have the right to form their own sovereign state, based largely on nationality.

A third common feature is a concern to unify a people who have become scattered. Such movements can be fundamentally liberal in nature (e.g. nineteenth-century Italy and the Jewish nation in the twentieth century), but can also be conservative (e.g. Bismarck's Germany and some contemporary Islamic 'nationalists'). These movements differ in that the liberal examples seek to emphasise freedom and democracy, whereas the conservative ones stress an organic, common cultural identity.

Notwithstanding the features they have in common, the two types of movement manifest themselves in different ways. At the centre of this distinction lies their differing political attitude towards freedom. For liberals, liberty remains paramount. The purpose of the nation and national independence is to safeguard the freedom of the individual citizen. For conservatives, on the other hand, order and unity stand above individual liberty as the key political objective.

It is normally the case that conservative nationalism is defensive in nature, whereas liberals usually have positive aspirations. Conservatives often emphasise the threats assailing national independence and unity. These may come from excessive immigration, political and military encroachments by a neighbouring power or threats of internal disintegration. Liberals, by contrast, are usually concerned with establishing a state where none exists, or with asserting the right to independence of a national minority that exists within a state. This implies that, once a liberal nationalist movement has achieved its primary objective, it will cease to be a major political force. This was certainly the case after Ireland became independent from Britain in 1921 and once India achieved its freedom from the British Empire (although there has been a recent rise in Hindu nationalism there, as a reaction against Islamic activism).

Nationalism and racialism

It is usually wrong, and sometimes dangerous, to confuse nationalism with racialism. Of course, some nationalist movements have been racialist in character. Nazism is the clearest example (although its racial content was not part of its original appeal to the German people). Another example is the white nationalism of the South African apartheid regime. This movement based its beliefs on the principles that different races could not coexist in the same society and that white races were superior to others. It is also true that many nationalist movements have had a racial element, even if they have not been dominated by racialism. This has certainly been the case in China, Israel and many parts of Africa. The link between nationalism and racialism is not surprising: **race** is a powerful unifying force, and many assume that **nations** are derived from ethnic distinctions.

The truth is, however, that most large nations are multiracial in their origins. We only have to think of the USA, Russia, the UK, Australia, Canada and Brazil – the largest and most powerful states or nations in the world – to appreciate this. All of these countries are multiracial in character and tend to draw strength from this. Admittedly confusion may be caused by the relationship between nation, culture and race. In all of the above examples, there is certainly a discernible common culture. This characteristic – often represented by language – is usually based upon the culture of one dominant race. For example, the USA, Canada and Australia, all former British colonies, can be said to be based on Anglo-Saxon culture; Brazil's character is dominated by its Portuguese features, and Russia is essentially Slavic in nature. But this does not mean that race and nation are synonymous in such cases. Indeed, as time passes, the influence of the dominant culture, and therefore of the dominant race, may weaken.

Right-wing movements, such as the British National Party and the French National Front, continue to emphasise race as the key element in national identity, but the forces of liberalism are ranged against this view. Liberals hold that national culture is a pluralist concept – a synthesis of different traditions, which is constantly evolving. The conservative view of race and nation seeks to preserve exclusivity and so opposes the assimilation of different ethnic identities. However, for conservatives, common national identity is based largely on the development of a single culture rather than on racial purity.

Key Term

Race and nation
The term 'race' refers to a grouping of people based on common ancestry and distinctive racial features, including skin colour and other physical characteristics. The origins of racial distinctions predate the existence of states and so cannot be seen as a political concept. Nations, on the other hand, are based on a people's perception of itself. National identity arises from a variety of common historical circumstances, including history, traditions, culture, language, religion and geographical separateness. Racial distinctions are only one of many factors that might separate one national identity from another.

This is not to say that racialism should be ignored in studies of nationalism. Indeed, racialism and racial perspectives on the world can be key elements in preventing nationalism from taking hold. In Cyprus, for example, campaigners for the creation of a single Cypriot **nation-state** have been constantly thwarted by Greek and Turkish racialism. Similar problems have occurred in states such as Iraq and Sri Lanka. In summary, therefore, any study of nationalism must take race into account, but it would be a mistake to identify race as the key element in the development of modern nationalism.

Key Term

Nation-state
Referring to a reality or an aspiration that all nations should also be states. A nation-state is where nationhood coincides with statehood.

Is the nation-state in decline?

Many modern historians and international relations experts suspect that the nation-state, as a particular political form, is in decline. It must be remembered that the concept is only just over 200 years old. In the context of human history, therefore, the nation-state could be seen as a temporary phenomenon.

The main reason why analysts suggest that the nation-state may be in decline is the development of globalisation. This is because globalisation threatens the basic functions of the state. Let us assume that these are to:

- maintain law and order within the territory
- secure the state against external threats
- develop and maintain useful relations with other states
- regulate the currency, the operation of markets and the economy in general
- maintain the general welfare of its people
- promote economic and social progress
- protect and improve the physical environment of the country.

Bear in mind that these are basic functions. There are clearly other roles played by states, but these vary from state to state and are not usually fundamental activities. We can see how three general world developments have affected these functions:

1 Many of the problems that the nation-state must deal with have become supranational in character. Markets are increasingly international, crime operates across countries, environmental problems do not recognise national boundaries, individual states find it difficult to defend themselves against terrorism and economies in general have become more interdependent.

2 The rapid and extensive increase in international communication, e.g. the internet, and the widespread use of English, may be creating an international culture.

3 Partly because of the development of supranationalism, there has been a huge increase in the power and influence of international organisations, notably the European Union, the World Trade Organisation, the World Bank and the International Monetary Fund.

Therefore, if the nation-state is indeed becoming weaker and less relevant to world problems, it follows that it may well decline in importance and, ultimately, even cease to exist.

On the other hand, there are some reasons for believing that nation-states will endure. If we see the nation as a fundamentally cultural concept, there may be a reaction against the processes we have described above. Put another way, just as nineteenth- and twentieth-century liberal nationalism was largely a reaction against the imperialism of the great powers, so modern cultural nationalism may rebel against the effects of globalisation and the economic imperialism of supranational organisations. If national identity remains a strong enough human emotion, it may well triumph over historical forces.

Is nationalism necessarily expansionist?

Any reading of the previous sections of this chapter will clearly reveal that the answer to this question is emphatically 'no'. But we must first ask why nationalism has attracted such a reputation for aggressiveness. The answer lies with the following factors:

- The overwhelming reputation of radical nationalism represented by Nazism in particularly has understandably led to a belief that nationalism is expansionist in nature.

- Since the late eighteenth century a large number of 'nationalist' wars have been fought, with some nations attempting to spread their hegemony, or defend their existing spheres of influence and other nations trying to thwart them.

- Nationalists have often used expansionist militarism in order to create or preserve a sense of unity. Certainly this was the case in Mussolini's Italy where the aggressive behaviour of the state in the Eastern Mediterranean and North Africa was an attempt to unite the population behind a fragile fascist regime.

- Because many nationalists are essentially 'romantic' in their attitude to the nation, there is a tendency to seek to re-create a glorious history, which often involves struggle against other nations.

The counter view is that there have been many nationalist movements that are without any expansionist motives. These include examples such as the following:

- Defensive nationalists are simply seeking to preserve the integrity of the state and its people. Movements in as disparate countries as Poland and China are clear examples.

- Liberal nationalists are not concerned with national superiority but simply with ensuring that their people are free and can preserve self-determination.

- Post-colonial nationalist movements are usually dominated by the need to build the nation and to promote economic development.

- Although some cultural nationalists have been expansionist and aggressive, notably Nazism, on the whole this kind of nationalism is defensive and pacifist by nature.

- Nationalists who are seeking nationhood where this has been denied to them, tend to make historic claims to territory, but these cannot be seen as expansionist (though their adversaries sometime claim they are). Kurds and Palestinians do not claim territory other than that which they feel has been 'stolen' from them in the past by more powerful forces.

Thus we can see that it is a mistake to take a narrow view of nationalist aspirations and tendencies. Though all nationalists share an exaggerated sense of national community and unity, the safest approach when analysing nationalism may be to study each case as a unique entity.

Nationalism in the UK

The UK is a multi-national state in that it is a single sovereign state with a unitary government, but contains within it several different countries and nationalities. None of these constituent countries, however, enjoys any sovereignty: the UK is not a federal system like that in Germany. Of course, many other countries have strong regional cultures within them – for example, Spain, Italy and Belgium – but these are not individual countries as such. The nearest thing to the British experience is perhaps Switzerland, where peoples of French, German and Italian origin enjoy partial self-rule.

The UK is unusual in another way, too. The types of nationalism that have flourished there have been different from each other in character. The way in which they have pursued their goals has therefore varied considerably (see Table 5.5).

Scottish nationalism

The principal aim of Scottish nationalism is political independence, either in the fullest sense of the word – i.e. separate statehood – or partially, through a federal system, which would grant the country a limited degree of sovereignty. There have been a number of aspirations and grievances that have caused an upsurge in Scottish nationalism since the 1960s. These have included:

- a strong sense of Scottish history, much of which had been characterised by English domination

- the sense that the human and physical resources of Scotland have been consistently plundered by the dominant English. Examples include North Sea oil and gas as well as the potential for wind power and hydro-electricity

- the long history of separate Scottish institutions, such as the Church, universities, the school and examination system, the legal system and tradition, and sporting institutions, but no independent Scottish control over these since the 1707 Act of Union abolished the Scottish Parliament

- a history of strong attachments and alliances with mainland Europe; in some ways, the Scots have felt themselves more continental than the English

- a growing belief that an independent Scottish political system would be more democratic and accountable, prompted by increasing disillusion with politics in Westminster

- as the British economy in general appeared to be stagnating in the 1960s and 1970s, many argued that an independent Scottish economy could be more dynamic.

These beliefs add up to a clear example of a form of liberal nationalism. The Scots have sought both self-determination and a superior democracy. They have wanted control of their own resources and their own government. The devolution settlement of 1998 went some way to satisfying their desire for political autonomy, but, in truth, the powers that were transferred were disappointing for the nationalists.

Welsh nationalism

Unlike the Scots, the Welsh have no tradition of separateness and few distinctive political institutions. However, they have enjoyed a specific culture that is different from the dominant English culture. This is not to say that the majority of the Welsh have supported the nationalist cause. Most see themselves as members of a region of the UK with its own special character, but not distinct enough to suggest political independence.

It is true that a few extreme nationalists in Wales do want full independence, but for most members of the movement the concern is that Welsh culture is being swamped by the dominance of England, and may soon disappear. Language is the touchstone issue for Welsh nationalists. Should Welsh speaking disappear, they argue, the rest of the culture will soon go with it.

Welsh nationalism has therefore been a cultural form of nationalism, seeking a degree of autonomous control over cultural institutions, but not general independence. The Welsh Assembly that was established in 1998 has some control over education, the arts, sporting activities and the promotion of the Welsh language, as well as some responsibility for agricultural and industrial development, and sees itself as the guardian of a distinctive Welsh culture. This has little in common with the aggressive, radical form of cultural nationalism, or *volkism*, that arose in Nazi Germany. The Welsh are not concerned with national rivalry or expansion: their nationalism is defensive.

Ulster unionism

Another form of cultural nationalism can be found in Northern Ireland. There, radical unionism is a synthesis of Ulster (not Irish) nationalism, British nationalism (the Unionists demonstrate a staunch loyalty to the Crown) and Protestantism. It would be wrong to describe Ulster Unionists simply as radical British nationalists; they also feel themselves to be Irish in character, and although they support the jurisdiction of the Queen, they harbour a deep suspicion of British government.

The political aspirations of the Unionists have been to ensure that their kind of culture is defended in Northern Ireland, both from English and Irish Catholic cultural domination. Even more than that of the Welsh, therefore, Ulster Unionism is a defensive form of nationalism. Unionists would ideally like a degree of autonomy for Northern Ireland with its own political institutions, but also a guarantee that the British will defend them from Irish domination. Failing such partial independence, however, they are content to place themselves under the protection of the Crown.

We should perhaps avoid describing Ulster Unionism as a form of nationalism *per se*, but rather as a blend of two brands of nationalism. Thus, in part, Unionists see themselves as loyal Britons, but they are also Northern Irish. They remain determined to protect both these identities for themselves.

Irish republicanism

Once Ireland had achieved its independence from Britain in 1921, Irish nationalism retreated largely into Northern Ireland, where it continued to struggle for the unification of all Ireland. In this respect, it became a republican movement. Irish republicanism has been represented by a radical wing – Sinn Fein – and a more moderate group of nationalists who formed the Social and Democratic Labour Party (SDLP).

Sinn Fein and the radical republicans synthesise nationalism with a degree of socialism. This arises from the belief that Britain was a colonial exploiter of Ireland and that it was the indigenous Irish Catholic population who were the main victims of this exploitation. Certainly,

the followers of republicanism were drawn largely from the Catholic working class. By throwing off British rule and uniting the Irish peoples, radical republicans also hoped to emancipate the working class. Moderate Irish nationalism, represented by the SDLP, can be seen as a more liberal movement, appealing to all classes and to those who have no special religious conviction. Both movements could be said to be cultural in nature, too. Irish national pride is based upon its language (Gaelic), its rich literary tradition, its distinctive music and sport and shared historical experience. Thus, the Irish can be seen as a classic *volk*, with a strong attachment to their own exclusive territory.

British nationalism

During the latter part of the twentieth century, a new nationalist movement emerged in the UK. Of an extremely right-wing character, it has been largely defensive in nature and can be seen as a reaction to a number of developments, including:

- the increase in immigration and the creation of large ethnic-minority populations in British cities

- disillusionment with national politics in general

- the increasing influence of Europe

- a feeling that the UK is in long-term decline, having enjoyed a largely glorious history

- discontent among alienated groups in some regions who have not shared in the increasing general prosperity.

The main standard-bearer of this movement has been the British National Party (BNP), which has enjoyed a steady growth of members in the early twenty-first century. The BNP seeks to restore British 'greatness' and opposes the apparent dilution of the traditional national identity by growing multiculturalism and the decentralisation of government. The party has a distinctly racial character, denying that it is overtly racist but admitting that it wishes to stem the flow of immigration and to 'encourage' peoples of 'non-British' races to return to their countries of origin.

The mission statement of the BNP, part of which is shown below, reveals its attitudes:

Extracts from the BNP mission statement

The British National Party exists to secure a future for the indigenous peoples of these islands in the North Atlantic which have been our homeland for millennia. We use the term indigenous to describe the people whose ancestors were the earliest settlers here after the last great Ice Age and which have been complemented by the historic migrations from mainland Europe.

The migrations of the Celts, Anglo-Saxons, Danes, Norse and closely related peoples have been, over the past few thousand years, instrumental in defining the character of our family of nations...

...The rich legacy of tradition, legend, myth and very real wealth of landscape and man-made structures is one of our island's richest treasures. The men and women of the British National Party are motivated by love and admiration of the outpouring of culture, art, literature and the pattern of living through the ages that has left its mark on our very landscape. We value the folkways and customs which have been passed down through countless generations. We enthuse with pride at the marvels of architecture and engineering that have been completed on these islands since the construction of the great megaliths 7,000 years ago.

This mission statement contains resonances of the Nazi philosophy which flourished in the 1930s and 1940s. This kind of *'volkish'* nationalism is closely connected with attachment to the land, a passion for the history of a people and a sense of racial superiority. This is not to say that right-wing British nationalism is neo-nazism. The main reason is that the BNP deny that they are fascists, possibly having more

in common with socialism. Furthermore the BNP rejects the idea of the *'fuehrerprinzip'* (that all power should lie in the hands of a single leader) which underpinned Hitler's complete control of the German state.

These emotions should not be confused with **patriotism**. The British are known for their patriotism, but this does not denote the kind of outlook demonstrated by the BNP. Such emotions should also be distinguished from English nationalism. Arguably, there is no such thing as English nationalism, and if it does exist, it is not right wing in nature. English nationalism would imply a desire to break away from the UK, relinquishing historic links with Wales, Scotland and Northern Ireland. This is certainly not a significant political aspiration among the English. The nearest English people come to such nationalism is during sporting events, mainly football and rugby. (Bizarrely, the 'English' cricket team is drawn from any part of the UK and has been captained by both a Welshman and a Scot in the past.)

 Key Term

Patriotism
This term is usually used to describe an exaggerated love and support for one's own state and the national culture. It is not a political phenomenon (although political leaders may use it for their own purposes, especially in times of armed conflict) and it does not have specific political aspirations. Nationalism, with which it is sometimes confused, does, on the other hand, have such objectives. A 'patriot' is one who loves his or her country and is willing to make sacrifices for it.

It is therefore useful to accept that there is such a thing as English patriotism (British patriotism is rarer and weaker), but there is effectively no significant degree of English nationalism. The defence of the culture, which goes hand in hand with opposition to European integration, refers to British, rather than English culture.

Nationalism and British conservatism

Traditionally, and certainly as far back as the leadership of Benjamin Disraeli in the 1870s, the British Conservative Party has been intensely nationalist in character. Furthermore, until the 1960s it was also linked to a strong sense of imperialism.

Conservative nationalism served three purposes. First, it encompassed a pride in, and support for, traditional institutions such as the monarchy and the Anglican Church. Second, it promoted a sense of national unity in a country where class distinctions have been traditionally significant and divisive. Third, the determination to retain the integrity of the UK was seen as vital to economic wellbeing.

The relationship between nationalism and the Conservative Party was highly successful. One of the main reasons why so many members of the working class consistently voted Conservative was a belief that the party was best equipped to protect the national interest and preserve the UK's position in the world.

In the 1980s, however, the nationalist element of British conservatism changed character. The New Right, led by Margaret Thatcher, cared less for tradition and more for national interest. This manifested itself in opposition to European integration. As the 1980s progressed, conservative nationalism became xenophobic, campaigning increasingly for the retention of political independence in the face of European integration and globalisation. There was also a growing disquiet within the conservative movement about the effects on the British identity of large-scale immigration. The emergence of the UK Independence Party represents a culmination in the growth of this kind of defensive and isolationist nationalism.

Type	Political movement	Main characteristics and aspirations
Liberal nationalism	Scottish nationalists (SNP)	Independence for Scotland
	Moderate Irish nationalism	Equal status in Northern Ireland for Protestants Possible future unity with the rest of Ireland
Cultural nationalism	Welsh nationalism (Plaid Cymru)	Greater political autonomy Defence of Welsh language and culture
	Ulster Unionism	Defence of the culture against Irish Catholic culture Some autonomy under the British Crown
Socialist nationalism	Radical Irish nationalism (Sinn Fein)	Unity of Ireland Largely in the interests of the Irish working classes
Conservative nationalism	Conservative Party and UK Independence Party (UKIP)	Opposition to European integration Reduction in immigration Determination to maintain the territorial integrity of the UK Encouragement of patriotism
Right-wing nationalism	British National Party (BNP)	End of immigration and some repatriation of past immigrants Opposition to European Union Restoration of strong British industrial base

Table 5.5 Summary of nationalism in the UK

Exam focus

Using this chapter and other resources available to you, answer the following questions.

Short questions

Your answers should be about 400 words long.
1 Distinguish between a state and a nation.
2 Distinguish between racialism and nationalism.
3 Explain the concept of the nation-state.
4 What is meant by the term *volkism*?
5 Distinguish between liberal and conservative nationalism.
6 Why have fascists associated nationalism with racism?

Long questions

Your answers should be about 1200 words long.
1 Is nationalism necessarily right wing?
2 'Nationalism cannot be described as a single political ideology.' Explain and discuss.
3 Assess the extent to which nationalism can be progressive or reactionary.
4 Distinguish between nationalism and racialism, explaining why they are often confused with each other.

Further reading

Alter, P. (1989) *Nationalism*, Hodder Arnold.
Eatwell, R. (1997) *Fascism: A History*, Penguin.
Gregor, N. (2000) *Nazism*, Oxford University Press.
Guibernau i Berdun, M. Montserrat (1996) *Nationalisms*, Polity Press.
Hastings, A. (1997) *The Construction of Nationhood*, Cambridge University Press.
Hobsbawn, E. (1990) *Nations and Nationalism since 1780*, Cambridge University Press.
Kallis, A. A. (2003) *Fascism Reader*, Routledge.
Kedourie, E. (1985) *Nationalism*, Hutchinson.
Passmore, K. (2002) *Fascism: A Very Short Introduction*, Oxford University Press.
Paxman, R. O. (2004) *The Anatomy of Fascism*, Allen Lane.
Smith, A. D. (2001) *Nationalism: Theory, Ideology, History*, Polity Press.

Chapter 6

Feminism

Feminism first became a politically significant movement in the 1960s, although its earliest origins lie in the eighteenth century. It is usually divided into two main 'waves'. The first wave began around the time of the French Revolution and lasted until the early 1920s. It had three, relatively limited, main aims. First, it sought to obtain equal legal and property rights for women; second, to extend the franchise to women; and third, to expand the range of opportunities open to women in fields such as politics, the professions and higher education. The second wave began in the 1960s and was much more ambitious in its aims. Second-wave feminists desire equality (or at least the choice of equality) for all women with men. Liberal feminists have sought to reform society in order to achieve equality, while the various types of radical feminists have proposed revolutionary methods to achieve their aims. The aims of the radical feminists have been far more extensive than those of the liberals on the grounds that patriarchy (i.e. male supremacy) – the principal enemy of feminism – is deeply rooted.

Introduction

Feminism is not like other ideologies. Above all, it is relatively limited in its objectives. Most (although not all) feminists limit their aims to improving the equality and/or status of only half the population. Feminism is an extremely fragmented movement, to an even greater extent than conservatism and socialism. The militant feminists of the 1970s, the period when the movement was at its height, bore little resemblance in their political outlook to the early advocates of women's rights in the eighteenth, nineteenth and early twentieth centuries.

Feminism is one of the most modern of the ideologies described in this book. It is certainly a critique of contemporary society and so could never be accused of being a purely historical phenomenon (as arguably Marxism or fascism have become). Indeed, in its current form, feminism is a challenging and vibrant movement which is relevant to virtually all aspects of contemporary society.

Feminism is unusual too in that there have been no conventional political parties based on the movement; nor have there been organised and influential pressure groups, at least in Europe. Feminism as an ideology has flourished within parties, within intellectual and academic circles, in the media and in popular opinion. Although the superior status of the men who largely run states has been threatened by feminism, the modern state has not been challenged by the movement in the same way as it has been by ideologies such as fascism, communism, socialism and anarchism. It is therefore remarkable that feminism has been so successful. There are many who also argue that we have reached a 'postfeminist' era. This view suggests that most of the main aims of feminism have now been achieved so that the women's movement has moved on to less fundamental issues.

The first wave

Prior to the French Revolution, there were sporadic examples of writers and movements that had proposed equal rights for women, but these were never systematic and were certainly never converted into action. On the whole, the Enlightenment failed to inspire thinkers to consider the inferior social and economic position of women. However, the wave of rationalism and free thinking that swept Europe in the latter part of the eighteenth century, culminating in the French Revolution, did create the possibility for the development of original ideas about women in society.

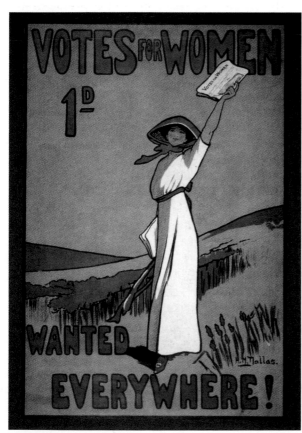

The feminist 'first wave' concentrated on political and legal rights for women

Mary Wollstonecraft (1759–97) was one of a very few thinkers who took the ideas of the Enlightenment and applied them to the status of women. She saw women as naturally equal to men, perfectly capable of rational thought and possessing the same rights. These ideas were explained in her best-known book, *A Vindication of the Rights of Woman* (1792). Wollstonecraft challenged the conservative assumption that women are less rational than men, and that it is, therefore, natural for them to be subordinate to men. This was a radical idea, since the concept of a natural inequality between the sexes was a powerful one in the eighteenth century. That is not to say that Wollstonecraft was herself a militant. Indeed, the rather limited nature of her thought can be seen in this passage, which pleads for greater opportunities for women who wish to choose not to follow the traditional role for their sex:

> *Though I consider that women in the common walks of life are called to fulfill the duties of wives and mothers by religion and reason, I cannot help lamenting that women of a superior cast have not a road open by which they can pursue more extensive plans of usefulness and independence.*
>
> From *A Vindication of the Rights of Women*, 1792

Wollstonecraft's 'road open' clearly referred to education and employment opportunities. But the tone that she struck was a far cry from the more raucous and strident views of the radical feminists of the second wave. As well as Wollstonecraft's ideas, the novels of Jane Austen (1775–1817) satirised the conventional view of women's inferiority, lack of reason and, therefore, lack of potential. However, neither Austen nor Wollstonecraft made any lasting impact in terms of enhancing women's status in society. Their ideas were too advanced and met with little support among women themselves.

More successful was Harriet Taylor (1807–58), wife of the great liberal philosopher, John Stuart Mill. (Ironically, both Wollstonecraft and Taylor were married to more celebrated husbands: Wollstonecraft was the wife of the great early English anarchist, William Godwin.) Taylor and Mill wrote *On The Subjection of Women* in 1869. In this important feminist text, they advocated equal legal rights for women, including the vote. However, Taylor and Mill's main contribution to the advancement of sexual equality was sponsorship of the Married Women's Property Act in the same year. This allowed women to retain their own property even after marriage. The Act had the effect of allowing women much more freedom in determining who they would marry, and gave them the opportunity to separate from unsatisfactory husbands without losing their wealth. In practice, of course, it was significant only to the well-off. For the majority of women, such advances were irrelevant.

Votes for women was to become the principal aim for the first-wave women's movement. In 1869, the National Women's Suffrage Association was formed in the USA. The first realisation of votes for women occurred in New Zealand in 1893 and the British suffrage movement came into existence in 1903. Women over 30 years of age obtained the vote in Britain in 1918, the US constitution was amended in 1920 to enforce women's suffrage, and in 1928 British women were granted the same voting rights as men.

The campaign for women's votes was the key element in First-Wave feminism because it was assumed that, once the vote had been granted, other benefits would follow. Women would, it was hoped, take up positions in legislatures in increasing numbers, and female voters would use their electoral power to demand equality. Although advances of this kind were certainly made, with women gradually being admitted to higher-education institutions and to professions such as medicine and the law, these successes were limited. Why, then, was first-wave feminism so unsuccessful? There are several possible reasons:

- Male pre-eminence in politics was still heavily entrenched.

- Campaigners underestimated the degree to which culture was patriarchal. In other words, the depth of male dominance was not appreciated. Granting women the vote did not scratch the surface of patriarchy.

- The movement was almost completely dominated by the middle classes. Most middle-class women were conservative in outlook and considered feminist ideas too radical, so they limited their demands to the franchise.

- There was still insufficient economic pressure to release women from their traditional roles of wife and mother. A much greater increase in the demand for female labour, especially skilled and educated labour, was required in order to free many women from traditionally inferior roles.

These factors meant that little progress was made until second-wave feminism arrived in the 1960s. This is how Betty Friedan (1921–) described the issue:

The problem lay buried, unspoken, for many years in the minds of American women. It was a strange stirring, a sense of dissatisfaction, a yearning that women suffered in the middle of the twentieth century in the United States. Each suburban wife struggled with it alone. As she made the beds, shopped for groceries, matched slipcover material, ate peanut butter sandwiches with her children, chauffeured Cub Scouts and Brownies, lay beside her husband at night – she was afraid to ask even of herself the silent question – 'is this all'?

From *The Feminine Mystique*, 1963

The second wave

The second-wave women's movement can be seen as part of the wider political phenomenon of the 1960s called the New Left. Radical thinkers were developing a theory based on their observation of the growth of what was to become known as 'mass culture' or 'mass society'. Mass culture had a number of characteristics:

- Consumption was becoming the most significant element in people's perception of themselves. In other words, an individual's consumption patterns had begun to define what sort of person he or she was. This replaced a traditional class analysis of society, whereby people defined themselves in terms of social class, which was largely identified by occupation and income.

● This development meant that producers and sellers in capitalist societies were able to manipulate cultural attitudes and needs in order to promote consumption of their products and services.

● To facilitate their task, it was convenient for producers to create a mass culture. This made it much easier to control that culture and to persuade people to buy mass-produced goods. The media were recruited in this enterprise, especially television, so the whole culture was penetrated.

● Mass culture was aimed at those groups in society which were predominantly white, male, aged over 25, heterosexual and well-off. These groups were the cultural leaders and possessed the most spending power. Other groups were therefore excluded. The poor, black and Asian people, the young, gay people and, of course, women were largely ignored by mass society. Either they had insufficient income to benefit from the new prosperity, or their spending patterns were determined by others. The New Left saw them as being alienated from the mass culture. Radical activists campaigned on their behalf, first helping them to become conscious of their alienation and, having become so, encouraging them to create a counterculture that could liberate them.

Movements that were spawned by the New Left revolution included black rights activists, gay rights campaigners, anti-poverty drives, 'youth in protest' ('yippies') and second-wave feminism.

The key moment in the birth of the second wave was the publication of *The Feminine Mystique* in 1963 by Betty Friedan. This book galvanised the women's movement. It gave rise to a liberal form of feminism and also provided material that was used by a more radical group of writers and activists. Friedan called the position of women 'the problem with no name'. This was to be the case no longer. The problem became known as 'patriarchy' and the women's movement was retitled 'feminism'.

By 1970, feminism had matured as a movement, but it had split into two main branches – liberal feminism and radical feminism. The liberal wing remained firmly within the mainstream of political thought. It proposed reforming society, largely through piecemeal and gradual advances in the women's cause. The radicals, on the other hand, were revolutionary in their thought and aspirations. Shulamith Firestone (1945–) argued that women must throw off the main source of their oppression – their place in the reproductive process – and therefore their reliance upon men. Germaine Greer (1939–) saw women's inferior status in terms of the way in which popular culture portrayed them, while Kate Millett (1934–) argued that male domination did not begin and end with public life, but infected all aspects, both private and public, of the relations between men and women.

Meanwhile, those on the political left were synthesising feminism and socialism. They saw the subjugation of women in economic terms. For them, women would be truly liberated only when class oppression was removed. Indeed, the most extreme of the socialists – the Marxists – supplemented the study Karl Marx had made of developed capitalism by pointing out that female labour had become a vital element in the exploiting process, and that working-class women formed the most exploited of all classes.

Indeed, radical feminism had such a rich variety of perspectives on women's oppression that to talk of one single movement may be mistaken.

Postfeminism

By the end of the 1970s, many of the goals of conventional forms of feminism had been achieved. Women enjoyed legal equality in all economically developed states, male attitudes were finally responding to the constant bombardment of feminist thought and women were making rapid advances towards equal status in fields such as politics, the professions, education, sports, the arts and media and even (albeit more slowly) in business. Discrimination on the grounds of gender was outlawed everywhere in the Western world and a wide range of social and economic legislation was passed to allow women to free themselves from traditional roles. Changing attitudes and new laws in areas such as marriage and divorce, sexual relations, abortion, birth control and state welfare were providing women with life choices and greater freedom to realise self-actualisation – i.e. the achievement of their own chosen goals.

However, rather than resulting in the disappearance of the women's movement, the effect of these developments was to fragment the feminist ideology into many different branches, often described as 'postmodern feminism' or poststructuralist feminism, sometimes even as the 'third wave'. The concept of a single women's liberation movement became outdated. New perspectives on women's conditions were developed and with these came new ideas about how to liberate women. For example, the lesbian movement proposed that all women should abandon relations with men and instead form women-only cultures with no physical relations with men remaining. Matriarchal feminists argued that the male–female hierarchy should be reversed and women should become the dominant gender. The most radical of all the feminists even suggested that technological advances in the procreation of children meant that it might be possible to do without men altogether, so that an exclusively female society could be created.

Postfeminists have concentrated on individual issues as well as the position of women in general. Pornography, for example, has attracted a great deal of their attention, with feminists divided over whether pornography exploits women or men. Others have concentrated on the plight of women in societies where arranged marriages (especially child brides), the denial of women's rights to careers and female circumcision exist. In such societies both first and second wave feminism remain very relevant.

Core values of feminism

As has been shown, feminism became a divided movement in the 1970s. Core values are therefore difficult to identify and limited in number. However, some principles have been shared by all feminists and these are outlined below.

Patriarchy

At its most basic level, patriarchy can be defined as a system of discrimination against women by men. The key word here is 'system'. It implies that a number of different phenomena are connected in some way. The discrimination against women and/or their oppression and exploitation therefore has different aspects, but aspects that are interconnected. The women's movement has always identified individual examples of discrimination – for example, legal inequalities, exclusion from certain activities such as politics and business and unequal rights in marriage. These do not necessarily add up to a system. Radical forms of feminism distinguish themselves by their insistence that there is a whole clutch of aspects that depend on each other.

For example, the traditional (now largely eliminated) discrimination against women in education – i.e. obstacles placed in the way of educational success – underpins male dominance in many occupations. If women are denied education and training in some fields, they cannot challenge men's prominence in those fields. On a more subtle level, sexist attitudes towards women, which suggest that the qualities they typically possess are inferior to the qualities apparently held by men, clearly hinder women's career development. More obviously, the tendency to maintain a female workforce of part-time workers, undertaking menial jobs, ensures that women retain an inferior status in the workplace.

For feminists, patriarchy therefore has a variety of facets, including the psychological, sexual, political, economic and cultural aspects of the relations between men and women. The fact that these features are connected has given patriarchy its strength and endurance. Its all-embracing nature explains the immense difficulty feminists have had in dislodging it.

Although patriarchy is a core value of feminism, different branches of the movement have emphasised different aspects of the concept. Socialist feminists have stressed the economic exploitation of women; liberals have tended to emphasise the political and cultural aspects of patriarchy. Radical feminists have concentrated on sexual and psychological forms of exploitation, particularly emphasising how the role of the father in a typical family is a model for the dominance of men in wider society. This is how Kate Millett described this phenomenon:

Patriarchy's chief institution is the family. It is both a mirror of, and a connection with, the larger society; a patriarchal unit within a patriarchal whole... Serving as an agent of the larger society, the family not only encourages its own members to adjust and conform, but acts as a unit in the government of the patriarchal state, which rules its citizens through the family heads.

From *Sexual Politics*, 1970

Otherness

The idea of the 'otherness' of women is a difficult concept, since it encompasses elements of psychology such as the notion of consciousness. In general terms, it refers to the fact that women are considered to be fundamentally different from men, not merely in the biological sense, but in every other sense too, and economically, culturally and psychologically in particular.

On one level, then, otherness is merely an explanation of the subjection of women to men, but it has a greater significance as well. Women, feminists say, have 'internalised' their otherness. By this they mean that it has not only been imposed on them by men, but they have also come to accept it for themselves. This is largely the result of women's perceptions that they have a separate role as a result of their biological differentness. Men can never understand this otherness since it is a product of biological identity. Note that the biological role of women has been assigned an inferior role in society.

Thus, women are not just inferior in the eyes of men, but are inferior in their own eyes too. Furthermore, otherness is part of a woman's 'unconscious' being – that is, women are not conscious of their own acceptance of their inferiority. It was the French philosopher Simone de Beauvoir (1908–86) who first recognised this phenomenon as long ago as 1949. Betty Friedan, too, argued over a decade later that women's acceptance of their inferior roles is a learned response, which appears in early childhood. This is therefore exceedingly difficult to dislodge. Women must first become conscious of their subjugation before they can begin to struggle against it. This is how de Beauvoir explained women's self-imprisonment in their sense of 'other':

Woman has ovaries, a uterus; these peculiarities imprison her in her subjectivity, circumscribe her within the limits of her own nature.

From *The Second Sex*, 1949

For liberals, otherness can be combated only if the common experience of women changes. For example, when they are granted equal status with men, women will shed their own sense of inferiority. The more radical feminists, however, have been less optimistic. To attack the psychological effects of deep conditioning, it will be necessary for women to set up a complete counterculture against patriarchy. In this way, the consciousness of women themselves can be altered. Indeed, the most radical feminists have insisted that women separate themselves completely from male culture in order to free themselves and take control of their own inner being.

Key Term

The Other

Coined by the French feminist writer and philosopher Simone de Beauvoir in 1949, the term describes the phenomenon that, while the male sex is considered 'normal', women are considered abnormal – different and therefore 'other'. This view of women is created by men, but has become so powerful that women themselves have come to accept it. Thus Simone de Beauvoir described women as *'not man'.*

Gender

Gender refers to the role and consciousness of women, which has been assigned to them by society and which they learn for themselves from an early age. In other words it is a 'social construction' – created by society and not a natural phenomenon. The anthropologist Margaret Mead first brought this to the attention of the women's movement in the 1930s as a result of her studies into traditional, primitive societies in Samoa, but the acknowledged founder of second-wave feminism, Betty Friedan, is largely responsible for recognising the modern importance of **gender**, as opposed to **sex**, which refers to biological distinctions.

Women learn 'womanly' roles from an early age. On a superficial and less significant level, they come to expect that they will fulfil traditional female roles such as child rearing, cookery, housework and caring occupations in general. This is illustrated most effectively by pointing out that, before feminism became influential, women would typically aspire to be nurses, while men might expect to become doctors. On a deeper and more important level, however, the female gender role is considered to be inferior to that of men. Indeed, women used to grow up commonly accepting that they would play an inferior role to men in society. In fields of social power, such as politics and business, it was expected that men would fill the leading positions. It was accepted that the majority of women would not expect to

pursue a career, settling instead for a lifetime of housewifely pursuits.

The process by which women learn to expect that they will play such gender roles, and by which men expect them to conform, is clear. It can be seen in patterns of children's play, in relationships between sons and fathers and daughters and mothers, and in the traditional literature and value systems of every society. Gender roles have been transmitted in the past through educational practice (e.g. domestic science and needlework for girls, woodwork and metalwork for boys) and in the workplace (e.g. male bosses and female secretaries). Feminists have pointed out that gender stereotypes can also be absorbed in more subtle ways – for example, through language and the arts.

But gender is especially important for radical feminists in terms of their revolutionary outlook. They recognise that, as gender differences are deeply rooted in society, society itself must be transformed if gender inequality is to be eliminated. It is not, in other words, sufficient to pursue gender equality; rather, the whole basis of gender consciousness must be removed root and branch.

All feminists, whether they are reformists or revolutionaries, agree that gender is critical to the inequality suffered by women. They therefore

Key Term

Sex and gender

The difference between these two words is crucial to feminists. 'Sex' refers to the biological differences between men and women. These are, of course, natural and unalterable. Women give birth and are physically weaker than men. This produces unavoidable distinctions. 'Gender', on the other hand, refers to typical male and female roles that are the product of upbringing. They are not inevitable and will vary according to the social environment and the consciousness of the individual. Feminists propose changes that could modify or even eliminate such gender differences.

argue that an attack should be mounted on such stereotypes. Liberals argue that women must be given choice and the opportunity to determine their own gender roles, as well as total equality with men. Radical feminists, however, wish to destroy the concept of gender altogether and rebuild women's culture from scratch.

Equality

Equality between men and women should be included as a core feminist value with some caution. While equality is a clear objective for liberal feminists, it is a problematic concept for more radical elements of the movement. However, all feminists agree that, while there are important biological differences between the two sexes, in terms of gender – the learned roles of men and women – there should essentially be no differences. Rather, there is natural equality, and society should reflect this fact.

For liberals, equality means full political, legal, social and economic rights for women, and implies total equality of opportunity. Women should have equal access with men to educational opportunity, public offices and all positions within the economic structure. Success in achieving this has been uneven. In education and employment in general, equality has largely been attained, while in economic life a remarkable degree of male dominance remains.

Although radicals might accept that equality for women is an essential goal, they would see such an aspiration as extremely limited. Some see female culture as superior and would therefore seek to place women in a superior position to men, rather than merely an equal one. Others see superiority and inferiority as irrelevant. These feminists, who include Germaine Greer, have argued that male and female cultures are essentially incompatible and therefore the issue of superiority becomes an irrelevance. Any sense of superiority should be replaced by one of separateness.

Liberation

The women's movement is often described as 'women's liberation' ('women's lib' for short).

This implies that men have somehow kept women in a subservient, even enslaved, position. For liberals, this control is seen as less sinister than the kind of enslavement which many radical feminists have identified; but for all feminists liberation is essential if women are to make significant progress.

Betty Friedan, a liberal, refers extensively to the cultural domination of women by men. It is men who control the culture, therefore women have found it difficult to escape from its clutches since such patriarchy is all-pervading. However, by raising their own consciousness and by liberating their minds, women have found it possible to evade this cultural hegemony. Having liberated their consciousness, women have been able to demand and achieve equality of opportunity and to open up worlds that had previously been closed to them.

It is the radical socialist feminists who hold the most vehement views on liberation. For them, women's enslavement is economic. They are used as a cheap source of labour, both within the home and in the workforce in general. By closing off opportunities to them, men have forced women into inferior, subservient economic roles. This is in the interests of both capitalism and of patriarchy. For women to achieve true freedom, therefore, the economic structure would need to be transformed so that economic exploitation would become unpopular.

Both liberal and socialist feminists, however, would agree that patriarchal capitalism needs to be transformed if women are to be liberated. This is how Kate Millett described women's economic situation:

Since woman's independence in economic life is viewed with distrust, prescriptive agencies of all kinds (religion, psychology, advertising etc.) continuously admonish or even inveigh against the employment of middle class women, especially mothers. The toil of working class women is more readily accepted as 'need', if not always by the working class itself, at least by the middle class. And to be sure, it serves the purpose of making cheap labour in factory and low grade service and clerical positions. Its wages and tasks are so unremunerative that, unlike more prestigious employment for women, it fails to threaten patriarchy financially or psychologically.

From *Sexual Politics*, 1970

Types of feminism

Liberal feminism

This description refers to feminism, or at least the women's movement, as it existed during the 'first wave' – from the eighteenth century to the late 1960s – and to the reformist elements of the movement from the 1960s onwards. The label 'liberal' implies a number of characteristics and principles, which are as follows:

- Liberals do not propose a revolutionary transformation of society. Rather, they would reform some aspects of society in order to achieve their aims. In the context of feminism, therefore, liberals reject the insistence of the radicals and the socialists that there must be a revolution (albeit a peaceful one) if women are to achieve equality and emancipation. The fundamental structures of modern Western societies – capitalism, pluralist democracy, multiculturalism, etc. – do not need to be changed significantly. Women can win equality within these structures.

- There should be a clear divide between public and private life. For liberals, some aspects of our lives are not the concern of the state, the law and public attention in general. If people choose freely to live their lives in a certain way, and this does no harm to others, their lifestyles are of no concern to the rest of us. On the other hand, conduct that does affect others is the concern of society as a whole, and therefore of the state. For example, if employers routinely discriminate against women in recruitment and career promotion, it is a public, not a private, concern. On the other hand, if a woman chooses to play a subordinate role to her male partner, this is clearly private and of no concern to others.

- This distinction between public and private spheres leads to the further conclusion that each individual woman must have the right to decide how she wishes to lead her own life. Betty Friedan, in her book *The Second Stage* (1983), reacted against what she saw as the excesses of the radical feminist movement by insisting that women should feel free to take up the traditional roles of what she described as 'love, nurture, home'. The radicals seemed to suggest that such roles should be forbidden to women.

Liberal feminism has therefore concentrated on reform, largely through the law and changing public attitudes to the position of women. Table 6.1 sets out most of the principal legal and attitudinal changes that liberal feminists have sought, and, to a large degree, achieved.

The liberal issues described in Table 6.1 are not exhaustive. The rights of women with regard to pensions, social security benefits and divorce, for example, continue to exercise the liberal women's movement. There is a continuing struggle to change attitudes towards women too. The idea of 'political correctness' has fallen into disrepute (should we, for example, refer to the 'herstory' of the women's movement, rather than its history?), but the role of language remains important for all feminists. Language transmits cultural attitudes from one generation to the next. For feminists it is therefore vital that stereotypes which suggest female inferiority are eliminated from language.

Liberals have difficulties with women's issues that arise in 'traditional' societies. The apparently inferior position of women in Muslim communities (a view disputed by many Muslims), forced arranged marriages (especially of very young girls), and female circumcision are all examples of such issues. Although modern Western societies object to these practices, liberals find themselves in a dilemma: do we have the right to interfere in the cultural mores of other societies, however abhorrent we may find them? Although there is no absolute solution to this problem, liberals have attempted to solve it by

Legal reforms	Attitudinal changes
Equal pay for women doing work of equal value to men. ● This has been achieved in law in the UK, but has not always been the case in practice. In the USA and elsewhere it is a similar story.	Promoting the belief that women have exactly equal capabilities to men, except in purely physical work. ● There can therefore be no rational basis for discrimination in employment.
Outlawing discrimination against women in employment, education, commerce and other fields.	Raising educational expectations for girls and young women. ● In fact, girls have overtaken boys at most educational levels. However, there is still subject-based bias – for example, boys are more likely to achieve in science and technology qualifications, whereas girls tend to specialise in the arts.
Proposing positive discrimination (known in the USA as 'affirmative action') for women. ● This forces organisations to favour women in some cases. Although voluntary schemes are in operation, especially in the UK, legal requirements remain rare.	Creating a climate of opinion which places women in the workplace in an equal position with men. ● The critical issue is that women should be free from discrimination at work. This is particularly acute when women are considered to be less committed to a career than men.
Legal guarantees for women of maternity leave, childcare facilities at work and help for female lone parents with childcare, enabling them to work.	It should be reasonable for women to choose a professional career over home roles, or to be able to combine the two without being seen as neglectful homemakers.
Legal right to abortion.	Women should have complete control over their own bodies. ● This includes control over contraception and sexual health.
Legal protection against violence and rape in marriage and other relationships with men. ● This includes better safeguards for women reporting rape and fairer treatment for them in court proceedings.	Police and courts' attitudes to rape and domestic violence should be altered so that full protection is afforded to women and more cases are brought to court.

Table 6.1 Some liberal-feminist initiatives

supporting women's movements within the societies affected. This means that reforms would be internal, rather than imposed by external feminist groups.

There are still tasks for the liberal-feminist movement to achieve – full-scale equality and equality of opportunity for women do not yet exist. However, there is no doubt that since Betty Friedan's ideas were first propounded in 1963, huge progress has been made.

Radical and militant feminism

Radical – sometimes described as 'militant' – forms of feminism have their origins in the New Left movement that emerged in the 1960s. The New Left sought to emancipate all alienated groups in society, including ethnic minorities and very poor, gay and disabled people. Women, of course, formed the largest group of all. Although Friedan stimulated the formation of modern feminism, the radicals argued that her views were indeed valid but failed to identify the fundamental causes of women's oppression. Whereas Friedan argued that women were merely suppressed, the radicals declared they were oppressed. While Friedan argued for female emancipation, the radicals were seeking social revolution.

Like all radical political movements, feminism of this kind is highly fragmented. It is therefore important to begin by examining the principles that unite radical feminists. These principles are as follows:

● Patriarchy is extremely pervasive and it exists in all aspects of life, both private and public.

● Although there are important biological differences between men and women, there is no justification for suggesting that gender differences exist, or, if they do, that they are important.

● All relations between men and women are inevitably oppressive.

● The solution to the problems of women in society cannot be achieved by mere reform, but must involve a radical transformation of the structure of society.

Of all the radical beliefs concerning the origins of patriarchy, sexual oppression probably forms the most important critique. Germaine Greer and Shulamith Firestone in particular see sexual relations as the crucial element in the oppression of women. For them, the other aspects of patriarchy are merely reflections of the basic fact that personal relations between men and women involve exploitation and subservience. Furthermore, both men and women have been complicit in this relationship.

It is necessary to refer to Marxist theory for a moment to understand Firestone's thesis. Marx argued that all societies can be understood in terms of the particular class structure and class conflict that characterises them. The dialectic conflict that occurs between the classes is critical and creates its own reflection in terms of politics

and philosophy. Firestone audaciously substitutes sex for class in her analysis of history and claims that it is sexual conflict that characterises every society. The title of her most famous work, *The Dialectic of Sex*, indicates the nature of her philosophy. Clearly the implication is that until sexual equality is brought about, social conflict in general will continue and women will remain an alienated 'class'.

Greer does not share Firestone's scientific analysis of patriarchy, but agrees that sex is the critical factor. For Greer, sexual differences should not be suppressed, but restored and celebrated with mutual dignity. Male dominance has removed female sexuality and subverted it for men's own purposes. If women's identity can be liberated and restored to its genuinely free state, there can be healthier relations between men and women. This is how Greer expressed the importance of sexual difference:

Liberation struggles are not about assimilation, but about asserting difference, endowing that difference with dignity and prestige and insisting on it as a condition of self-definition and self-determination.

From *The Whole Woman*, 1999

Greer believes that a revolution must occur in relations between men and women, so that genuine liberation can be realised and women can achieve fulfilment on their own, and not on men's, terms. She sought to refute the last remnants of **Freudian theory** in this context.

Kate Millett identified the consciousness of women themselves as an agent of oppression and the family as the origin of inferiority consciousness. It is the traditional family unit, Millett asserted in *Sexual Politics* (1970), which is the source of female oppression. Women's consciousness, as well as men's, is conditioned from an early age within the family. Based on what they see at home, children learn that women are subordinate and economically exploited in the home. Once that consciousness is in place, it becomes difficult to dislodge. Furthermore, once men have achieved a dominant role in families, it

Key Term

Freudian theory

Freud's theories are extensive and highly complex, but a key issue in relation to feminism concerns his assertion that women suffer from an undeniable sexual inferiority. This stems largely from 'penis envy'. Women grow up with the belief that men must be more powerful since they possess a penis, while women do not. Most, though not all, feminists reject this analysis, arguing that male superiority arises from social conditioning, not fundamental biological inferiority. Nevertheless, some postmodern feminists have resurrected interest in Freudian theory; they suggest that his beliefs about sexual difference are valid and assist our understanding of patriarchy.

is inevitable that they will achieve dominance in all other walks of life. Unsurprisingly, Millett therefore attacked the institution of the family in her opposition to all-pervasive patriarchy.

It can be seen from this brief review of some of the principal elements of radical feminism that there are a number of different explanations as to how patriarchy has come about. It is therefore inevitable that radical feminists propose a variety of ways of combating the male oppression of women. The proposals of three of the most celebrated radical feminists – Millett, Greer and Firestone – are discussed below.

Kate Millett (1934–): androgynous society

Millett's object was to create an androgynous society in which there would be no significant gender differences between men and women – a state of genuine equality. Of course, sexual differences would remain, but gender would no longer be a significant element in society.

Since the family was the main cause of gender difference and women's oppression, the family would have to be destroyed. In its place, women should form their own communities in which female consciousness would be raised. By

removing themselves from relations with men, women would gradually throw off their alienation and become conscious of their own independent worth. After a long period of consciousness raising, relations between men and women could resume, but on an equal basis. Thereafter, male and female subcultures could exist in some harmony.

Germaine Greer (1939–): sexual liberation

The term 'women's liberation' probably applies more to Greer than any other prominent feminist. Women, she asserts, have been oppressed and rendered powerless by their relentless exploitation by men. The key revolution is therefore not in the structure of society, but in the consciousness of both men and women.

Women must reassert their identity, freeing themselves from all situations in which they fall under the control of men, including in the family, at work, in politics and in social life in general. Above all, however, Greer proposes sexual liberation. The traditional, male-dominated sexual relationship must end and be replaced by relations on a totally equal basis. The family, which she (like Firestone and Millett) sees as a crucial agent of oppression, should be replaced by communal forms of living, or, possibly, women should live alone.

Shulamith Firestone (1945–): removing men's reproductive role

The most modern of the radical feminists, Firestone holds perhaps the most revolutionary beliefs. She sees the family unit, together with the biological differences between men and women, as having made women's inferiority inevitable. She points out that, in the modern world, women can perform their reproductive roles without men. Artificial insemination means that sexual relations are outdated. This, she triumphantly announces, removes the main cause of male control – the reliance women have on men when they are rearing children.

For Firestone, this gives rise to the possibility of a women-only community. Women, she argues, are all capable of forming lesbian relationships, or, short of that, can certainly make a life without men. Firestone's more radical followers have suggested that the need for men will disappear altogether and the world will cease to recognise sex or gender differences. However, for Firestone the vision of a community of free women without the need for men was enough.

Andrea Dworkin, an implacable campaigner against the exploitation of women through pornography, expresses anger as well as a desire for independence. This is how she expresses her scorn for pornography:

In the system of male sexual domination explicated in pornography, there is no way out, no redemption; not through desire, not through reproduction. The woman's sex is appropriated, her body is possessed, she is used and she is despised: the pornography does it and the pornography proves it. The power of men in pornography is imperial power, the power of the sovereigns who are cruel and arrogant, who keep taking and conquering for the pleasure of power and the power of pleasure.

From *Pornography: Men Possessing Women*, 1981

Socialist and Marxist feminism

It is perhaps surprising that one form of Marxist feminism actually pre-dates radical feminism. Friedrich Engels, Marx's collaborator, turned his attention to the plight of women after Marx's death. In *Origin of the Family, Private Property and the State* (1884), he suggests that before the existence of private property there had been a matriarchal society. It was only when private property and a system of exchange of goods emerged that patriarchy came about. More recently, under capitalism, the subjugation of women became more intense, with women being exploited both at home and in the workplace. Women could only be emancipated, Engels argued, when capitalism and private property were abolished. He therefore urged women to join the class struggle, even though revolution appeared to be man's work. He believed that the

raised consciousness of women could help to support the broader revolutionary movement.

The analysis Marxists offered of women's position under capitalism was principally that they had been reduced to the status of an exploited part of the workforce; they were a reserve body of labour that could be brought into action, for low wages, when production levels rose, only to be discarded when the inevitable economic slump followed. Furthermore, those women who remained at home to raise children and do housework were also exploited. At home, women were free labour, releasing men to leave the home and earn wages. Capitalism, Marxists claim, relies upon the exploitation of women to make labour more available.

Many socialist feminists have adapted Marxist analysis in their attempt to understand the subjugation of women. The main thrust of their critique concerns inequality, both in the workplace and in the home. The British feminist Juliet Mitchell (1940–) sought to link the psychological causes of women's inferior status – to be found mainly in the home – to their economic position. By fostering a sense of inferiority in the home, men are able to exploit women in the workplace. The consciousness of women is therefore manipulated in such a way that they are unable to liberate themselves unless the whole capitalist edifice is destroyed.

However, not all socialist feminists have been Marxists. There is a general sense that the creation of socialism – in particular, imposing equality by changing the structure of ownership of the means of production and the system of exchange – will liberate women. Under an economic system that creates equality, women will not only become entitled to equal rewards, but will also cease to be dominated by a patriarchal society. This belief has a long history. It originated in the utopian socialism of figures such as Charles Fourier and Robert Owen (see Chapter 3). Fourier, in particular, argued that a truly socialist society would liberate women altogether from the imprisonment of marriage and the family. Indeed, modern socialist feminists see the family as a model of the exploitation in the wider economic world. For some, the answer lies in paying women (or indeed men) for housework and child rearing as if it were any other professional occupation. As a result, women would not have to face an artificial choice between unpaid housework, which places them under the economic control of men, and a paid career. For more radical socialist feminists, the answer lies in the destruction of the family as an institution.

Table 6.2 summarises the main different types of second-wave feminism.

 Key Term

Essentialism

In relation to feminism, essentialism suggests there are truths about the position of women (for example gender roles) which are permanent and do not change through time or social change. It is challenged by post modernists.

Postmodern feminism and the 'Third Wave'

This is not to be confused with postfeminism, which is described below. Postfeminism suggests that most of the issues concerning the inequaity and exploitation of women have been largely resolved. To understand postmodern feminism we have first to understand postmodernism in general.

Postmodernism is a difficult idea or set of ideas, possibly best exemplified by the work of Michel Foucault (1926–1984). Foucault argues that, in the modern world, we should reject any all-encompassing theories about society or culture or art or any other social or scientific phenomenon. The circumstances in which society and culture are made, he asserts, are constantly changing. We cannot, therefore, find simple theoretical explanations for change. In simple terms postmodernism means that the world is a complex place and human society and culture are also complex; too complex to be explained by theory alone. Instead we should find explanations for social and cultural phenomena (and even for scientific ones) in terms of ever-changing relationships, cultural experience and perceptions of ourselves as individuals and as groups. Another way of explaining postmodernism is to say we should reject any universal theories about issues and problems in society, but instead should view each issue within its own, particular context. Thus, postmodernism in an ideological context, tends to

Liberal feminism	Radical feminism	Socialist/Marxist feminism
● Reforming rather than revolutionary ● Seeking equality of opportunity for women ● Seeking legal, political and economic equality for women ● Accepting that women may choose their own lifestyles and relationships ● Pursuing a number of issues that affect women in general, such as abortion rights, violence in the family, rape ● Campaigning to change attitudes to women which suggest they are inferior	● Fundamental, revolutionary change needed to the nature of society ● Belief that patriarchy does not recognise the boundary between private and public spheres ● Firm rejection of the validity of gender differences, while accepting that biological differences are important ● In order to liberate women, a new society must emerge in which consciousness of gender difference is eliminated	● Belief that the oppression of women is economically based ● Women are used and abused as a source of cheap labour ● The exploitation of women in the family is a model of the wider economic exploitation of women ● Capitalism relies upon the exploitation of women in order to guarantee the superior position of men ● Equality for women relies upon the destruction of capitalist exploitation in general

Table 6.2 Summary of three main types of second-wave feminism

reject such theories as Marxism, radical feminism or traditional environmentalism, and seeks to replace them with explanations that accept the existence of complexity and an ever-changing social and cultural context.

Turning to feminism we can see how postmodernism can be applied to the women's movement. Those radical and socialist feminists who concentrated on one single explanation for the inferiority of women can be described as 'essentialists'. They have proposed one essential theory. Modern feminists thus have tended to concentrate on patriarchy and gender as two over-arching explanations of women's condition. They treat both concepts as a single entity resulting in a general analysis that can be applied in all circumstances. Postmodernism rejects this approach. In the case of gender, for example, they argue that this is not the only feature that defines women and their relationship with men and society in general. Rather, they view women in terms of other cultural aspects. Thus, postmodernists will speak of the position of *black* women, or Asian women, or gay women, or working-class women. For these groups gender does not define them completely enough. The consciousness of women is not determined by gender and patriarchy alone but by a multiplicity of cultural influences.

While postmodernists have been rejecting essentialist models of female oppression, so-called 'third-wave' feminists have been suggesting that the *solutions* to the plight of women must also be viewed in a modern, changing context rather than on the basis of a fixed view of patriarchy and society in general. Modern feminists accept that most of the specific aspirations of women have been achieved, at least as far as liberal feminists are concerned, and therefore seek a new identity for women and the women's movement. To some extent, they are reacting against the revolutionary ideas of the radicals and the socialists. They argue that ideas such as oppression and exploitation can no longer be sustained as criticisms of modern society. Women now have the full range of opportunities for which they campaigned. Although equal pay

has not been achieved, women have been considerably empowered and are moving inevitably towards full equality in the economic structure. What kind of new identity, then, should women be seeking in a postfeminist world?

For many liberal feminists, such as Friedan herself, the postmodernist woman should feel free to adopt the traditional role of mother and wife. This freedom in itself is the main achievement of feminism: women have a voluntary choice in undertaking this role, rather than being forced to do so. Raising children and creating a loving home are dignified and noble occupations. Women, Friedan says, should cease to treat them as inferior to paid occupations.

Other modern feminists declare that women have achieved equality and equality of opportunity, and that they should use their new-found liberation to take a leading role in society. A world in which women can play a leading role is bound to be a better world. Above all, liberated women now have choices that they did not have before. They are in a position to enjoy the fruits of the individualistic world that has been created by social democracy and neo-liberalism.

Lesbian feminism

This has been something of a notorious branch of radical feminism (some American lesbian feminists described themselves as 'radicalesbians') but also one that is much misunderstood. The radical Adrienne Rich in the USA set the scene by arguing that relations between women, whether they were sexual or not, should replace heterosexual relations. Effectively this implies that women should either become lesbians or should at least cease to have relations with men.

Charlotte Bunch ultimately led this movement in the USA, assering that lesbian preference is both a sexual and a political choice. Since, as Carol Hanisch, the early radical feminist, had stated, 'the personal is the political', all relations between men and women are political (i.e. power-based), so they should effectively cease. In practical terms, Bunch and the other lesbian theorists were proposing the setting up of separate lesbian communities. In the early 1970s, she, together with a number of followers, formed the Furies, a women's lesbian commune.

The French radical lesbian feminist, Monique Wittig (1935–2003) – who might be described as 'the Marx of lesbian feminism' – explains why lesbianism is necessary to liberate women in this way:

> *Lesbian is the only concept I know of which is beyond the categories of sex (women and man), because the designated subject (lesbian) is not a woman, either economically or politically or ideologically. For what makes a woman is a specific social relation to a man, a relation that we have previously called servitude, a relation which implies personal and physical obligation as well as economic obligation.*
>
> From *One is not Born a Woman*, 1981

Therefore, at its base, lesbian feminism is proposing to abolish the whole concept of 'woman' as it implies oppression and exploitation. By becoming lesbians, women cease to be women. Just as Marx had foreseen a classless society where there would be no class oppression, lesbian feminists seek to create a genderless society where there will be no gender oppression.

Ecofeminism

As its name suggests, ecofeminism is a synthesis of feminist and ecologist thought. Arguably the movement was founded in the 1970s by the French feminist Françoise d'Eaubonne (1920–2005). She proposed that the earth was in danger of environmental destruction and that women could, by united action, save the planet in a way that men could not. The principal theories of ecofeminism include the following:

- Women are naturally closer to nature, have an affinity with natural things and so are in a better position to empathise with nature's needs. It was Vandana Shiva (1952–) who led the Chipko movement in India where women were encouraged to 'hug trees' in order to prevent forest clearances.

- It is an extension of patriarchy that men should wish to dominate the natural world and exploit it in the same way as they wish to dominate and exploit women. Men, say the ecofeminists, have a natural tendency towards a desire for domination in all aspects of culture and society. Thus, as they wish to dominate women, so they wish to dominate nature.

- Since most land is owned by men, their wish to dominate the natural world is given full scope.

- Over-population is one of the key reasons why the planet's resources are being over-exploited. Since men are seen as responsible for over-population, if women are able to exert greater control over their own fertility, the problem may be reduced or even solved.

- Those ecologists who propose a return to simpler, self-sufficient models of communities as a way of saving the environment are often feminists. This is because they believe that, in such communities, women will inevitably play a greater part than they do in modern, industrialised society where they are systematically excluded from positions of power.

Key feminist thinkers

Mary Wollstonecraft (English, 1759–97)

Married to William Godwin (the early English anarchist) and mother of Mary Shelley (the author of *Frankenstein*), Wollstonecraft died shortly after the birth of her daughter. Her best-known work is *A Vindication of the Rights of Woman*, published in 1792 and one of the earliest feminist tracts.

Nowadays, Wollstonecraft's views would not raise any eyebrows, but in the world of the 1790s she was considered a radical. She was fundamentally a liberal who believed that all people – i.e. women as well as men – are rational beings entitled to rights, freedom and dignity. The women of her day, however, were denied all of these. They were effectively enslaved, as they were tied to their husbands and not allowed any

Mary Wollstonecraft was one of the earliest feminists

legal independence. She observed that the main problem was the lack of true education most women suffered. Education, according to Wollstonecraft, was the answer to women's plight.

Wollstonecraft offered a number of practical measures to counter this inequality. She argued that women should enjoy full civil rights, be entitled to their own property and be allowed to pursue a career whether they were single or married.

Nevertheless, Wollstonecraft was not so radical as to suggest that men and women should be equal in all spheres of life. She recognised that, by virtue of biological necessity, women would be most likely to follow careers as wives and mothers. What she campaigned for was that women should at least have the choice, and, if they chose marriage, that they should enjoy more fulfilled lives as a result of their independence. She saw no reason why women should be considered inferior to men, but at the same time she knew that most women would choose to play a secondary role in society. Should they do so, however, it would make them no less virtuous than men.

John Stuart Mill (English, 1806–73) and Harriet Taylor (English, 1807–58)

Mill and Taylor were husband and wife. They collaborated to produce *On the Subjection of Women* in 1869. Like Wollstonecraft, neither was especially radical by modern standards, but at the time their ideas were extremely controversial.

Their views on the relations between men and women, and on the inferior social status of women, were based on two simple principles. The first was that men and women are born equal in terms of rationality, judgement, intellect and entitlement to rights. Of course, there are biological differences, but there is no evidence for male superiority. The second was that the inferior position of women was based largely upon economic considerations, and that these considerations were designed to retain the superior position of men.

The implications of these principles were that there should be no occupations or any public offices from which women were excluded. In short, women should enjoy full equality of rights and opportunities.

However, it was in the fields of votes and property ownership that Mill and Taylor's beliefs were to have the most significant influence. The Married Women's Property Act, which was passed in 1869, the same year as *On the Subjection of Women* was published, gave women the right to own property even after marriage. Prior to the Act, women effectively passed all their property to their husband on marriage. This situation had had two main effects. First, it made wealthier women vulnerable to fortune-hunting suitors and limited their choice of husband. Second, it made divorce virtually unthinkable for a woman, since she would be left without any property at all: men owned all joint property after divorce.

Mill campaigned for women's suffrage and hoped to have it included in the Second Reform Act of 1867. The failure of his campaign led to the formation of the suffrage movement in Britain, which pressed for votes for women for the next 50 years. This is how Mill expressed his support for female equality and emancipation:

On the other point which is involved in the just equality of women, their admissibility to all functions and occupations hitherto retained as the monopoly of the stronger sex, I should anticipate no difficulty in convincing anyone who has gone with me on the subject of the equality of women in the family. I believe that, there, disabilities elsewhere are only clung to in order to maintain their subordination in domestic life, because the generality of the male sex cannot yet tolerate the idea of living with an equal.

From *The Subjection of Women*, 1869

Betty Friedan (US, 1921–2006)

Friedan is known as the mother of second-wave feminism. Her ground-breaking book, *The Feminine Mystique* (1963), heralded the emergence of modern feminism. She went on to found the National Organisation of Women (NOW) in the USA, which continues to campaign for women's rights and equality.

The basis of Friedan's thought was an attack on Freudian explanations of women's inferiority. Freud had argued that women were inevitably inferior because of their biological distinctions. It was in particular their lack of a penis, and the phenomenon of 'penis envy' women consequently suffered, that consigned them to their inferior role. 'Anatomy is destiny,' said Freud. Not so, replied Friedan. She asserted that women's destiny had been moulded by their long experience of social conditioning. This conditioning had its origins deep in history and was therefore well rooted in society. The typical consciousness of women in 1960, said Friedan, had in fact been developed in the Victorian era. It had nothing to do with biological differences.

Why is it, asked Friedan, that women develop such strong expectations that they will fulfil the limited role of wife and mother? Why do they not expect to pursue careers that will lead them into more fulfilling and public roles? She believed the answer lies in the way girls are raised. Limited expectations are built into their psyche at an early age. Family life, the education system and other cultural institutions, such as religion, reinforce the idea that women should not aspire to be anything more than wives and mothers. Before Friedan, it was commonly believed that traditional female roles were biological in origin. Women gave birth and cared for infant children, the argument ran, so it was natural that they should remain in the home. Challenging this assumption was a radical act in Friedan's day.

The process whereby a male-dominated culture propagates assumptions of women's inferiority has become known as **sexism**. In order to combat it, Friedan recommended a sustained campaign by women's groups to open up opportunities for women, change public (i.e. both male and female) attitudes towards women, challenge male domination everywhere and obtain legal and political equality. Friedan was therefore a liberal: she did not propose a revolutionary transformation of society, but, rather, reforms within the existing social structure. In other words, she believed that the relationship between men and women could be fundamentally changed without making significant changes to society in general.

> ### ✔ Key Term
>
> **Sexism**
> This is a collective term for the range of ways in which men propagate the inferiority of women. It particularly refers to cultural attitudes that tend to perpetuate the belief that men are superior. Sexism exists in cultural fields such as education, language, the media, the arts and psychology. Feminists argue that sexist attitudes are based purely on myths and have no objective basis.

Friedan later demonstrated her liberal outlook still further by arguing that women should feel sufficiently free to choose the more traditional role of wife and mother. Indeed, she accepted that many women do possess a deep need to nurture children and to provide a loving home for a male partner. Although feminism had made great advances, she argued, it was dangerously close to losing sight of some women's genuine desires.

This is how she expressed her concern:

> In the first stage, our aim was full participation [of the women's movement], power and voice in the mainstream. But we were diverted from our dream. And in our reaction against the feminine mystique, which defined women solely in terms of their relation to men as wives, mothers and homemakers, we sometimes seemed to fall into a feminist mystique which denied that core of women's personhood that is fulfilled through love, nurture, home.

From *The Second Stage*, 1983

Kate Millett (US, 1934–)

The 1970 publication of Millett's book, *Sexual Politics*, sent shock waves through the feminist movement, and indeed through all radical political communities. Millett agreed with Betty Friedan that the roots of patriarchy lie in the traditional structure of the family, but she went much further than Friedan in her analysis. She argued that patriarchy had invaded the whole of human culture and society, so that it existed in politics, business, the arts, the media and all aspects of social life.

Millett claimed that the relationship between men and women is a power relationship. It is therefore political in nature, because politics is about power. Men exert power and oppression over women everywhere. They use this power to place women in inferior roles. The biological differences between the sexes are exaggerated and distorted by men in order to suggest that their dominant role can be justified by such differences. Furthermore, Millett asserted that men exert psychological control over women. In doing so, they have been able to persuade women to accept their inferiority as though it were true. Women learn that if they are to survive in the male-dominated world, they need to adopt a 'feminine' attitude, which is determined by men.

Millett declared that patriarchy is not restricted to public life. It exists in private relations between men and women, including their sexual relations. Men do not just seek to dominate in the workplace, but in the home and

Kate Millett, one of the most radical of modern feminists

the bedroom too. There is no escape for women: patriarchy is everywhere and has invaded women's minds, taking a firm hold over their consciousness.

What is the answer to this patriarchy? Unsurprisingly, Millett offers a radical solution. Women, she argued, must develop their own consciousness, which should be completely separate from men. They must have no relations with men, including sexual relations, and must instead form their own communities. (Millett herself was bisexual or lesbian and recommended that women should follow her lead or be celibate.) Rather like the anarchist communes that were formed in the late 1960s and early 1970s, the female commune was to be self-sufficient.

In Millett's ideal, **androgynous** world, power relationships between the sexes would come to an end and true gender equality would emerge. The characteristics of men and women, having become identical, would lead to the end of patriarchy, or indeed any relationship of power. Male–female relations could then resume on the basis of true equality.

Key Term

Androgyny

This term literally refers to a state in which an individual is neither exclusively male nor female. In radical feminist thought, notably that of Kate Millett, the term is used to describe a world in which gender differences are abolished, and the consciousnesses of men and women are identical. This would result in the end of patriarchy.

Germaine Greer (Australian, 1939–)

It would perhaps be wrong to suggest that Germaine Greer has been a major contributor to feminist thought, but she deserves consideration on the grounds that she has done a great deal to popularise feminist ideas. She has been accomplished in using the media to put across feminist ideas and even once posed nude (an obviously ironic gesture) to publicise her views.

Greer's emphasis has been on sexuality. Male domination, she claimed, has repressed female sexuality and prevented women from being able to express themselves and achieve self-realisation. Greer argues that the unsatisfactory nature of male-dominated sexual relations is bad enough in itself. However, more importantly, it is symbolic of the way in which oppression prevents women from developing. The term 'women's liberation' can be applied most appropriately to Greer's thought – her belief was that liberation of the mind could be achieved if women could free themselves from exploitative relationships with men. She also turned her attention to the radical belief that '**the personal is the political**'.

A major problem for Greer lay in the fact that she was heterosexual and therefore not willing, as Kate Millett suggested, to give up relations with men altogether. Furthermore, like Friedan, she recognised that childbearing and homemaking were reasonable occupations for women. Greer

proposed two solutions to these problems. The first was to recommend sexual freedom, which would avoid the potential enslavement involved in an exclusive relationship. Second, she addressed the stifling effect of the traditional nuclear family. To avoid this, she recommended a form of group living that would be close to the idea of the extended family. This arrangement would mean that children could be raised and relationships freely engaged in without the dangers of subjugation by dominant males.

Key Term

'The personal is the political'

This term was developed by the radical feminist Carol Hanisch (1941–) in 1970. It suggests that the dominant position of men and the political power they exert over women are not confined to public life alone. All relations between men and women are political, Hanisch argued. Family life, sexual relations, work relations and politics itself are all aspects of the politically based power relationship between men and women. The concept is also associated with Kate Millett and Germaine Greer.

Shulamith Firestone (US, 1945–)

Firestone's principal work, *The Dialectic of Sex*, which was published in 1970, centred on the significance of biological differences between men and women. What she attempted was a Marxist analysis of history, in which sex was substituted for class. Firestone saw the alienation of women as solely the result of sexual oppression. The economic, political and physical oppression of women by men emanated from biological differences and the assumption that male sexual characteristics were superior.

Just as Marx had predicted that the oppressed class would rise up against its capitalist oppressors, so Firestone assumed that the oppressed sex would rise up against men. The catalyst for this was to be technology. With the possibility that women could reproduce without the active involvement of men came the possibility of a world without sexual conflict.

Taking her quasi-Marxist analysis to its logical conclusion, Firestone foresaw the emergence of a sexless (her substitute for classless) society, which she referred to as androgyny. This was a society without significant gender differences, in which no individual could therefore suffer inferiority or claim superiority on the grounds of biological difference. Women would have the choice of whether to form completely separate communities or to coexist with men on an equal basis.

Firestone was not a Marxist as such, but rather adapted Marxist historical analysis to suit feminism. She can therefore be seen as a feminist-Marxist, instead of a Marxist-feminist – in other words, a true radical, but not a pure socialist. Her ideas found relatively little support within the women's movement, partly because they were simply too radical and partly because her use of Marxist philosophy was considered both artificial and unsustainable.

Andrea Dworkin (US, 1946–2005)

Dworkin was perhaps one of the most militant and extreme of all the radical feminists. She is best known for her war on pornography, though she also campaigned vigorously against prostitution. She saw both as the clearest manifestations of the exploitation of women by men.

For her, virtually all forms of heterosexual intercourse were violent and were used by men to exert their dominance over women. Citing the use of rape in warfare, she insisted that men used sex as a means of subjugating women. The use of so-called 'date-rape' drugs was the most recent example of this exploitation. Not surprisingly, therefore, Dworkin proposed that women should consider becoming lesbian and that a separate lesbian state should be set up. She saw parallels between the oppression of women with the experience of the Jews. She was criticised by many feminists for the extreme nature of her views and her violent antagonism towards men.

Her philosophy virtually eliminated the possibility of heterosexual relationships that might not be violent or exploitive. Critics claimed that Dworkin's personal experience of abuse as a child and later in marriage had excessively influenced her outlook.

Monique Wittig (France, 1935–2003)

Wittig was possibly one of the most important members of the lesbian school of feminism. She argued that the women's movement has made the mistake of concentrating on *men's* view of women. Instead she insisted that women should be concerned with their own view of themselves. The male view is determined by heterosexuality and women's child-bearing role. If women can engage only in lesbian relations, therefore, they will free themselves from this form of consciousness. To illustrate this, Wittig stated that the term 'woman' is a negative expression, whereas the term 'lesbian' is positive. It implies that women take control of their own lives and do not define them in terms of relations with men.

It is not sufficient, argues Wittig, along with fellow radical lesbian feminists, such as Charlotte Bunch and Ti-Grace Atkinson, for women to refrain from heterosexual relations. They must become lesbians in order to create new relationships with other women that will, effectively, bind them together and create a new collective consciousness.

Wittig followed Simone de Beauvoir's maxim that women are not born, but that they are made women by society. In order to combat this, therefore, Wittig suggests that lesbians should be the product of a new society that does not include men. She expresses this thus:

Thus a lesbian has to be something else, a not-woman, a not-man, a product of society, not a product of nature, for there is no nature in society.

From *One Is Not Born a Woman*, 1981

An additional feature of Wittig's thought was to describe women as a 'class', rather than merely a gender. Indeed, she criticised Marxists on the grounds that 'class' is only defined in economic terms, so women cannot, collectively, be a class. Women are a class for Wittig because they are collectively oppressed and will ultimately achieve class consciousness, at which point they will become revolutionary. By synthesising lesbianism with this kind of class consciousness a very powerful movement can be created.

Issues in feminism

Distinctions between liberal and radical forms of feminism

This is perhaps the most common issue encountered by students of feminism. It might initially seem relatively simple, and possible to understand in the same way as the distinctions between socialism and social democracy, or between liberal and conservative forms of nationalism. In reality, however, it would be a mistake to assume that there is a clear distinction between the two sets of beliefs.

It is true that radical feminists have sought to stress that there is little in common between their analysis and that of the wider women's movement, which began in earnest with Mary Wollstonecraft, and was transformed into a full-scale political organisation by Betty Friedan nearly 200 years later. From the liberal perspective, however, there has been a good deal of common ground which all feminists have shared. It is therefore useful to list the aspirations and values that unite *all* feminists. These have included the following:

Common principles and beliefs
- The inequalities women have endured are not based on any natural inferiority. There are certainly differences between men and women in society as a result of biological reality, but these do not imply that men are superior in any way.

- Male dominance originates in the early social conditioning of both men and women. It is therefore the task of all feminists to alter social consciousness so that the equality of women is accepted.

- Women must be able to take control of their own circumstances of life, rather than allowing men to determine them on their behalf. In other words, what and who women are is the business of women themselves.

- All aspects of male–female relations that exploit, degrade or control women should be eliminated. Women must be emancipated so that they can make their own choices and never fall under the control of male-dominated social structures.

- The status of women as 'victims' must be combated. This raises issues such as rape, violence in marriage, prostitution and pornography.

This impressive range of issues add up to a major area of common ground. However, a casual observer in the 1960s and 1970s might have failed to realise that the huge increase in activity by women and women's groups disguised a fundamental fracture in the broader movement. By 1970, it was becoming more clear that the women's movement had indeed broken apart, and while liberal feminists were claiming victory after victory, the radicals were warning against such triumphalism. They believed that the fundamental causes of women's oppression had not been addressed. The principal ways in which radical feminism has been distinct from liberal feminism are as follows:

Key distinctions of radical feminism
- Patriarchy does not distinguish between public and private spheres. The liberals had certainly made many gains in public life, but they left the private circumstances of women to individuals. This was a mistake, the radicals argued. The roots of exploitation lie in private life, families and the sexual relations between men and women. They must be addressed first if true emancipation is to be achieved. This means that the most basic

building blocks of society and its structure must be dismantled and reformed.

- Radical feminists warned that by failing to transform society, the liberals were winning illusory victories. Without dramatic changes in consciousness of sex and gender differences, there can never be true freedom for women.

- The economic exploitation of women does not stand in isolation from other forms of exploitation. Whereas liberals see economic equality and freedom as the key to all other forms of women's liberation, radical feminists argue that all forms of exploitation are interconnected and should not be treated separately. For example, the exploitation that is entailed by pornography and prostitution, or suffered by women who find themselves trapped in violent and alienating relationships with men, are part of the same system of patriarchy. Granting women economic independence alone will not bring them true freedom.

- On the whole, radical feminists believe that women will only achieve true consciousness of their role and genuine self-realisation if they separate themselves from male-dominated culture. By contrast, liberals aspire to achieving all their objectives within the existing culture.

Why are sex and gender so important to feminists?

Before Betty Friedan published *The Feminine Mystique* in 1963, the issue of sex and gender was either ignored or confused. It is true that the early French feminist Simone de Beauvoir had declared that 'one is not born, but becomes a woman' in the 1950s, and that her assertion made a firm distinction between sex, which is biological, and gender, which is socially determined. However, de Beauvoir did not mean to make this distinction for its own sake. She was more concerned with the superiority of men and the inferiority of women being an artificial social creation rather than a natural state of affairs. It was Friedan and the later feminists who took de Beauvoir's assertion and then used it to define sex and gender.

Early feminists, such as Wollstonecraft and Taylor, believed that gender distinctions arose directly from biological differences between men and women. They therefore saw them as natural. Women would inevitably have to play a different role from men in society because they were the natural raisers of children. They did not see gender roles as a separate problem, created by men for their own purposes.

However, modern feminists have identified gender differences as a product of men's attitude towards women, rather than as merely a product of women's attitude to themselves. They argue that they have therefore been able to envisage the true liberation of women. Such an analysis has created horizons for women well beyond anything that had been expected before the 1960s.

Once gender had been identified as a social product, the way was cleared to understanding how women could realise their true potential. For liberal feminists, developments such as economic equality and equality of opportunity would mostly eliminate gender differences. Radical feminists did not oppose these aspirations, but argued that there would need to be a revolutionary change in consciousness itself if gender were to be abolished completely as a social phenomenon.

Sex, on the other hand, would continue to differentiate between men and women for all but the most radical of feminists. For liberals, it should be a matter of choice as to whether the biological distinctiveness of women is important to individuals. For radical thinkers, there is less clarity over this issue. Some radicals have argued that women can play a superior role by virtue of their sex; for others, it simply implies 'otherness', i.e. recognition that women will inevitably have a different consciousness of the world. The idea of androgyny goes even further, proposing that there could be a world in which men and women become elements of the same gender.

Despite these different responses to gender within feminism, there is no doubt that when sex and gender were identified as separate concepts, the women's movement attained a new, higher level of ambition after the 1970s.

Can a conservative be a feminist?

At first sight, conservatism and feminism appear to be utterly incompatible. Indeed many conservatives call themselves '**anti-feminists**'. While nobody would deny that there is a consensus among all but the most trenchant neo-conservatives and reactionaries that women deserve economic equality, and should not be subjected to discrimination, there seem to be clear conservative objections to the more fundamental feminist beliefs. These are as follows:

● Feminist beliefs threaten the traditional family structure. Conservatives see the conventional family as an essential foundation of a stable society.

● Conservatives argue that social change should be natural and evolutionary. Feminists, by contrast, have sought to promote social change on the basis of fixed principles and utopian dreams. Conservatives insist that if women are to achieve liberation and equality, this should occur naturally.

● Most conservatives insist that the biological circumstances of women are natural so the role of wife and mother is also natural. By challenging this fact, conservatives suggest that feminists are defying nature.

● It has always been a conservative value that individuals should be free to lead their own private lives as they wish. Many feminists, especially the radicals, seek to dictate to women how they should conduct themselves and even what consciousness of the world they should adopt. Conservatives have always resisted Jacobinism – the tyranny of ideas – and they see the more militant forms of feminism in this light.

Despite these apparent objections it would be wrong to deny dogmatically any possible connections between the two movements. It is certainly reasonable for a conservative to believe that society can embrace female equality and the reduction of gender differences without risking disintegration. It is even conceivable that a conservative could accept that there are valid forms of family other than the standard nuclear model. It is also true that there has been something of a conservative reaction within the feminist movement against radical perspectives. These conservative feminists wish to restore women's ability to choose a traditional role for themselves. They admit that it might be reasonable to propose that women may be more appropriate homemakers than men, given their biological status. Conservative feminists insist, in common with other feminists, that women should have free and informed choices, the resources and opportunities to choose for themselves, and must not allow themselves to be governed by patriarchy.

> ✔ **Key Term**
>
> **Anti-feminism**
> A largely conservative belief that feminism is both unnecessary and subversive. It suggests that the condition of women should develop naturally as society evolves.

Have we entered a postfeminist or postmodern era?

This question has three very different elements. First, has feminism succeeded in its main, fundamental aims and can therefore move towards more specific issues affecting women? This is known as postfeminism. Second, have the traditional radical and militant versions of feminism served their purposes and now need to be replaced by more specific critiques and a more focused approach to the problems of women in modern society. This is often decribed as the 'third wave'. Third, have the main doctrines and beliefs of feminism been finally discredited and therefore need to be replaced by a new 'postmodern approach' to the problem of the status of women.

Postfeminism

This describes a belief that feminism has essentially succeeded in achieving its fundamental aims. It should be seen in two ways. First the term 'postfeminism' is often used critically of modern feminists. Opponents of feminism argue that, as women have, by and large, achieved equality in modern society, the continuing 'postfeminist' demands for further change are misplaced and unnecessary.

A more benign version of postfeminism says that women have achieved fundamental reform and there is more to achieve, but that one basic principle has been established – that women now have sufficient equality and equality of opportunity to be able to make their own choices, rather than have choices made for them by men. In other words, postfeminism in this sense is the liberal feminist's typical attitude to the women's movement today. In the postfeminist era women can choose most career options, can compete with men on more equal terms and can choose to play a more 'traditional' female role of caring for children and homemaking. What makes this postfeminist is that it is women who may freely choose to be 'homemakers' or 'housewives'. As they have now been released from cultural pressures that lead them to make no choice at all, it is no longer a feminist concern.

The third wave

This movement, largely a product of the early 1990s, was seen as a natural extension from the second wave. In contrast to postfeminism, the third wave suggests there remain many fundamental problems that women must attack. Unlike the second wave, however, these modern radical feminists concentrate on specific issues to a greater extent. Whereas second-wave feminists such as Millett, Mitchell or Firestone were revolutionary and concentrated on patriarchy as a complete 'system' of exploitation, the third wave is radical in its objectives, but cannot be described as revolutionary. A useful description of the third wave is, therefore, that it is a radical, but not a revolutionary movement.

The aims of the third wave are perhaps best summarised in the thirteen-point *Manifesta*, produced by two leading modern feminists, Jennifer Baumgardner (1970–) and Amy Richards (1970–), in the USA in 2000. The points can be summarised briefly thus:

- Young women should be *re-politicised* into the feminist movement.

- Women should have complete rights to choose whether or not to bear children.

- Gay couples as well as single women should have the right to have children.

- Men should be forced to take a more active role in preventing sexual disease.

- To raise awareness of the history of radical feminism.

- Lesbian and bisexual women should be encouraged to take a leading role in the women's movement.

- To encourage feminist activism.

- Women must have equal access to health care.

- Women should be able to play an equal role to men in the military.

- Adolescent girls should be protected from sexist behaviour in schools.

- To give equal opportunities for all women at work.

- The women's movement should unite its activists, however liberal or radical they may be.

- The US Constitution should be amended to include guaranteed equal rights for women.

What is interesting about the *Manifesta* above is that it contains elements that would, in the past, have been described as both radical and liberal. This suggests that the third wave is actually a synthesis of radical and liberal feminism. The third wave is not a united body, but its supporters share a view that less emphasis should be placed on the *difference* between men and women. Certainly they all believe that women have equal potential, but others still argue that there are important differences between men and women that should not be ignored.

Postmodern feminism

Postmodernism in general is a reaction against essentialism. Essentialism is a philosophy or outlook that assumes that people all have essential characteristics that define them and we can therefore draw conclusions from those characteristics. In the case of feminism, the radical movement had made a number of essentialist assumptions about women, not least that they may indeed be 'superior' in some ways to men. Radical feminists also made assumptions about the nature of men too. These essentialist ideas led to 'discourses' that defined the feminist movement. Discourses involve a language which is derived from essentialist assumptions. Thus, when Carol Hanisch asserted 'the personal is the political' she created a feminist discourse that was locked into the idea that all relations between men and women were political relations, involving the exercise of power.

Postmodernists seek to escape from these discourses, which are based on fixed assumptions. The nature of women and their relationships to men and society in general, they argue, has infinite variety. Put simply, every individual woman's situation is unique to the woman in question. It is therefore up to each individual to find her own way to equality and liberation. This may involve solutions that are every bit as radical as those of second wave feminism, but they are not limited by a reliance on inflexible feminist values.

A further critque of feminism by postmodern thinkers is that they see women *merely as women;* in other words their whole circumstance is seen in terms of their femininity. Instead, postmodern woman is seen in terms also of her social class, ethnic origin, sexual orientation, etc. In order to seek liberation and end alienation, therefore, the oppressed woman must act across a number of different fields.

There is one common theme adopted by postmodernists, however, and this is the importance of language. The influence of language is stressed by all postmodern thinkers, and feminists are no exception. The argument here is that attitudes towards women are partly determined by language. This has given rise to the much derided drive towards so-called 'political correctness' in language. A simple example is the prevalence of the term 'he', especially when discussing individuals who hold positions of power or high status and whose gender is not specified. By using the masculine form, an assumption is propagated that high status roles *should* be held by men (critics argue that this practice is merely a reflection of what is, rather than what ought to be). Perhaps the clearest example of the postmodernist attack on the role of sexist language in oppressing women is their support for *The Women's Bible,* produced by Elizabth Cady Stanton as long ago as 1898. This version of the Judao-Christian Bible was a rewriting of scripture, removing what were seen as false representations of women as inferior to men. Though *The Women's Bible* itself did not suggest it, it did inspire the postmodern feminist assertion that 'God is a woman.'

Exam focus

Using this chapter and other resources available to you, answer the following questions.

Short questions

Your answers should be about 400 words long.
1 What do feminists mean by the term 'patriarchy'?
2 Why do feminists say 'the personal is the political'?
3 What are the main distinctions between liberal and radical feminism?
4 Why do some feminists relate Marxism to feminism?

5 How and why do feminists distinguish sex and gender?
6 What is meant by the term 'postfeminism'?

Long questions

Your answers should be about 1200 words long.
1 'Feminism is not a single movement, but a loose collection of doctrines and beliefs about the problems faced by women.' Discuss.
2 'All feminists are radical and none is conservative.' To what extent is this true?
3 On what grounds have radical feminists criticised liberal feminists?
4 Has feminism achieved most of its aims?
5 In what ways, and to what extent, are we now in the postfeminist era?

Further reading

Beasley, C. (1999) *What is Feminism? An Introduction to Feminist Theory*, Sage.
Dworkin, A. (1981) *Pornography: Men Possessing Women*, Women's Press.
Firestone, S. (2003) *The Dialectic of Sex*, Farrar Strauss Giroux.
Freedman, E. (2007) *The Essential Feminist Reader*, The Modern Library.
Freedman, E. (2002) *The History of Feminism and the Future of Women*, Ballantine.
Friedan, B. (1963) *The Feminine Mystique*, W. W. Norton.
Humm, M. (2003) *The Dictionary of Feminist Theory*, Harvester Wheatsheaf.
Kemp, S. and Squires, J. (1998) *Feminisms*, Oxford University Press.
Randall, V. (1987) *Women and Politics*, Palgrave Macmillan.
Segal, L. (1999) *Why Feminism? Gender, Psychology, Politics*, Polity Press.
Tong, R. (1989) *Feminist Thought: A Comprehensive Introduction*, Routledge.

Chapter 7

Ecologism

Before examining the issue of the environment as it exists within politics, it is necessary to define the terms 'environmentalism', 'ecologism' and 'green politics'. These terms have been used in a variety of ways and contexts, so there are no precise, universally accepted definitions. However, the following will suffice for the purposes of this book.

'Environmentalism' refers to a general political concern for the environment that stops short of being ideological. Environmentalists may be moderate or radical. They do not believe that society needs fundamental transformation for them to achieve their aims. This is often referred to as 'light green ecologism'.

'Ecologism' refers to a movement that seeks to change the nature of humankind's relationship to its physical environment. It is largely based on the science of ecology, which suggests that it is an ideology in the full sense of the word: it is built on solid scientific evidence, not merely an arbitrary set of goals: that is, ecologists propose fundamental changes to the nature of society in order to bring about equally fundamental changes in humankind's relationship to its environment. This is often described as 'dark green ecologism'.

'Green politics' refers to the wide variety of political issues that relate to environmental considerations. Green parties seek to influence public policy, secure the election of representatives, and may even aspire to share power with broader-based parties (as is the case in Germany). The terms 'greens' and 'green politics' do not necessarily suggest an ideological approach to the environment. Green politics is ideological for some people, of course, but for most it includes a range of issues, such as conservation, emissions control, genetically modified food production, and preserving areas of outstanding natural beauty, rather than presenting a single unified vision of a reformed society. In practice, the green movement is now a collection of both political parties and pressure groups. The most important of the pressure groups, Friends of the Earth and Greenpeace, have become international, but every country has spawned its own environmental campaign groups.

Introduction

None of the three movements outlined above existed in any coherent form until the 1960s. Before then, concern for our physical environment and our relationship to it had been expressed in a variety of contexts, but no systematic form of environmental politics had been developed. During the nineteenth century, for example, rapid industrialisation caused anxiety about the destruction of the natural environment and the deteriorating quality of air and water. But these remained marginal issues in politics and failed to exercise the interest of policy makers. Indeed, it was not until 1956 that the Clean Air Act was passed in the UK to control the production of air pollution. By the 1960s, however, a growing number of environmental issues were beginning to emerge. These are examined below.

Biodiversity

One of the earliest environmental concerns of the 1960s was the threat posed to many animal and plant species by a number of developments, including industrialisation, urbanisation, rapid population growth, intensive agriculture, industrial methods of whaling, fishing and poaching, and the degradation of natural environments. On one level, this threat was seen as a general quality-of-life issue, but later, as environmentalism developed into a deeper political philosophy during the 1970s, it became a **biodiversity** issue. Biodiversity was also associated with ecologists who took a holistic view of the living world, seeing all species as interconnected. Should the variety of species decline, it was argued, the whole of nature, including humankind, would be adversely affected. It was therefore a mistake to think of conservation in terms of individual species, argued ecologists: the threat to biodiversity was a crisis for nature itself.

Key Term

Biodiversity
This term refers to the belief that the fullest possible range of the Earth's plant and animal species should be preserved. There are two main bases for this view. The first is that biodiversity is desirable for its own sake (a shallow ecology view). Life will be enriched by the existence of many different living species. The second is the more radical view that life is one single web (a deep ecology perspective). If parts of the natural world are lost, the whole of nature suffers. This is part of the holistic attitude to the environment.

Holism

This refers to the view, largely associated with Fritjof Capra (1939–), that the natural world is a single, organic whole. All aspects of nature are interconnected, so change or damage to some parts will affect the whole. Capra insisted that we will not necessarily find conventional scientific solutions to environmental problems. So-called 'new physics' suggests that we cannot be sure how natural phenomena are connected. When one part changes, we are unable to predict how the rest will be affected. From this belief in uncertainty, it follows that we should avoid interfering with any part of nature because we cannot be certain of the consequences of our actions.

Air and water quality

As the quality of air and water declined, a trend that occurred especially in urban regions and those parts of the world experiencing rapid industrialisation, the problem was seen largely in terms of human health. Water pollution was a direct threat to people's wellbeing, because it led to widespread disease, while poor air was identified as a cause of longer-term health problems, such as cancer, asthma and respiratory ailments in general. However, both types of pollution were having an increasing impact on plant and animal populations too.

The problem of air quality took on a new, more frightening dimension in the 1980s, with the realisation that the ozone layer had been damaged by chlorofluorocarbon (CFC) emissions, and that the release of 'greenhouse gases' – as a result of industrial processes – was causing global warming. Widespread concern over these developments, fuelled by increasing numbers of scientific studies that confirmed the damage and its long-term effects, led to environmentalism entering the world stage. Water and air pollution do not recognise national borders, and the ways in which countries behave affect the rest of the world. Transnational agreements and organisations are therefore required to combat pollution. This has proved to be the greatest of the challenges facing the movement in general.

Destruction of habitats

The best-known example of this phenomenon is the ongoing destruction of the world's rainforests. The southward expansion of the Sahara desert is viewed with similar alarm, as is the gradual shrinking of the Caspian and Aral Seas in Central Asia. The destruction of habitats has three main consequences. First, rainforest loss has adverse effects on the atmosphere – it exacerbates the greenhouse effect, leading to global warming and rises in sea levels. Second, the destruction threatens the traditional habitats and ways of life of local human populations. Third, many animal and plant species have become endangered by the loss of their natural habitats. Note that environmentalists are as fearful of the loss of traditional human communities as they are of the loss of plant and animal species.

Resource depletion and sustainability

Global economic growth has led to the rapid depletion of a wide variety of the world's resources. Dwindling energy supplies have been the primary concern, but the supply of other commodities is also threatened. Attention has focused on fossil fuels, mainly oil, but minerals, timber and other natural products are running out alarmingly quickly as well. Fear of such a dramatic depletion of physical resources is exemplified by 'spaceship Earth' theory. Environmentalists have argued that we cannot rely for ever on discovering new resources or improved technology in energy production. The answer lies, they argue, in dramatic reductions in

Key Term

Spaceship Earth
This phrase refers to the belief held by most environmentalists that the resources of the Earth are finite. Just as a spaceship uses its supplies which will inevitably run out, so too will the Earth run out of resources. In order to prolong the Earth's life, therefore, we must use up its resources more slowly. Some campaigners, such as James Lovelock (1919–), have questioned this analysis, suggesting that we can rely upon renewable sources of energy in the future and ought to be developing them as quickly as possible.

our resource use. At the same time, resources should only be used where they can be replaced, a principle known as 'sustainability'. The more radical elements in the environmental movement, including the anarcho-environmentalists, have argued that a completely new attitude to economic growth must be developed. The socialist and anarchist wings of environmentalism see capitalism itself as the culprit, given its insatiable desire for growth, and have therefore campaigned to replace it with new economic structures that limit growth.

Core values of environmentalism and ecology

It is difficult to identify the core values of environmentalism and ecologism because in each case there is more than one tradition to consider. However, there are a small number of ideas that are shared by all or most environmentalists and ecologists.

Key Term

Anthropocentrism
This term describes the placing of human beings at the centre of the natural world. It implies, therefore, that humans are superior to the other aspects of the world. In terms of green politics, anthropocentrism suggests that humans are 'stewards' of the Earth and have a duty to care for it.

Opposition to anthropocentrism

Anthropocentrism refers to the notion that humankind is the centre of the natural world and that the human species may therefore use nature for its own purposes. This is seen as being largely the result of the belief held by Abrahamic religions – Judaism, Islam and Christianity – that God created the world mainly for man's benefit and gave him 'dominion … over all the Earth' (Genesis 2:26).

This is seen as false consciousness by most ecologists. For them, humankind is simply a part of nature as a whole, with no special status above that of all other living things. This view is not confined to ecologists. Hindus and Buddhists, for example, see humankind as part of the eternal circle of nature. Humans come from nature and will return there in a constant cycle of death and rebirth. The Jains, a Hindu sect, particularly emphasise this perspective on human life; they insist that all living things should be protected and respected, as humans are part of the same living organism as all other forms of life.

If we can free ourselves from our anthropocentrist obsession, therefore, we will learn to respect our natural environment. The depletion of resources is a classic example of this objection to anthropocentrism. Humans assume that the Earth's resources belong to them and that they may therefore use them as they wish. Environmentalists argue that we are not entitled to view them in this way. The Earth's resources are part of the whole of nature, so we are depriving nature itself when we selfishly deplete them.

Natural quality of life

The issue of what constitutes a good quality of life is highly contentious. Critics of modern international capitalism argue that the system sees quality of life largely in terms of the consumption of goods and services. In crude terms, the more we are able to consume, the better off we consider ourselves.

Environmentalists have two objections to the consumption model. The first is that the constant desire for increased material wealth is depleting the world's resources too rapidly and threatening the natural environment. In this sense, the price that must be paid for consumerism is simply too high. The second objection is that quality of life does not consist solely of conventional forms of wealth. Instead, they argue, the state of the natural environment is a key element in the quality of life. If, therefore, we curb our desire for consumption, we will reap great rewards in environmental terms.

Anti-industrialisation

It would be wrong to suggest that all environmentalists and ecologists are opposed to industrialisation. However, to varying degrees, environmentalists have seen industrialisation and economic growth as fundamental threats to the natural environment. The most liberal of these campaigners have proposed compromises with industrialism. They see industrial development as inevitable and believe that it is utopian to expect humankind to control it.

At the other end of the spectrum are those groups who wish to see the tide of industrialisation turned back. Indeed, for many radical, deep ecologists, industrialisation is the main cause of our environmental problems. They propose a return to simpler ways of life; self-sufficiency and the curbing of constantly rising levels of demand would lie at the centre of this new world. As is explained in more detail below, anarcho-environmentalists see political institutions as accomplices in the relentless capitalist process of exploiting the world's resources, without concern for the future or for the health of our 'biosphere'. For anarchists, we will not be able to protect our environment unless the political structures that underpin capitalism are destroyed.

Perhaps the leading exponent of this concern with industrialisation was the radical economist Ernst Schumacher, who coined the term 'small is beautiful'. Schumacher argued that the scale of production was considerably too large and human communities had become oversized. Humankind must therefore return to a more appropriate scale of living and production. Schumacher also challenged the notion that human wants are infinite and will therefore always grow. We can, he asserted, curb our insatiable desire to consume more and more. We can return to a more natural way of living in small communities, which are integrated with the natural world rather than merely exploiting it.

Types of environmentalism and ecologism

Liberal environmentalism

Liberal environmentalism can be defined using the same approach as that taken with other ideologies. This means that the 'liberal' elements of the environmental movement are among those that do not propose revolutionary change and which believe that their objectives can be largely achieved within existing social and economic structures. Of course, any distinctions between the liberal and radical wings of an ideology are bound to be blurred, and environmentalism is no exception. For our purposes, it is sufficient to include those environmental issues that constitute the mainstream green movement in a review of liberal environmentalism.

Moderate environmentalism of this type generally places humankind at the centre of the natural world. The concerns that these environmentalists express mainly relate to the future of humanity. If the environment is degraded, this will threaten humankind and its future development. Unlike the deep ecologists, the liberal green movement tends to see environmental issues in isolation from each other. The holism that characterises the more ideological elements of green politics is largely absent. The main issues that concern liberal environmentalism include the following:

- biodiversity and species preservation

- preservation of areas of natural beauty

- pollution control

- habitat protection

- organic farming

- opposition to genetically modified foods

- opposition to nuclear energy

- concentration on the use of renewable resources

- protection of the habitats of traditional societies.

Although liberals in general have a wide range of global concerns, the moderate (or shallow) green movement has tended to concentrate on what the individual can do in his or her own home and personal life to alleviate environmental problems. Typical examples of this are recycling, energy-saving consciousness, 'green' houses with a variety of devices for conserving energy, and natural forms of gardening.

Of course, the deep ecologists criticise this kind of environmentalism as tinkering around the edges. They argue that it fails to deal with our relationship with the Earth. Such measures merely treat the symptoms of the problem; deep ecologists say that we must identify and deal with fundamental causes, which concern humankind's basic relationship with the natural environment.

The Green Party principles, shown below, are anthropocentric. The protection of the environment is seen in terms of the welfare of the human race and future generations. Indeed, many of these principles can be seen as ultra-liberalism. They are as much about how humans should live together in harmony as about how we can live in harmony with nature. The principles are also relatively moderate in their tone. The Green Party urges us to adopt a new mode of living and looks forward to a more localised and direct form of democracy, but it suggests nothing that would shake the existing social and political structures. This is the essence of the liberal agenda – recognition that conventional politics does not take enough account of environmental concerns, but expressing no desire to rebuild society from the bottom up and to develop new kinds of human consciousness. The next section shows the core values and beliefs of the Green Party. It should be noted that some of the values are not directly related to the environment, as the Greens have policies across a wide range of issues.

Core principles of the British Green Party, issued in 2001

Life on Earth is under immense pressure. The environment around us is faced with massive destruction. Conventional politics has failed us because its basis is fundamentally flawed.

The Green Party is not just another political party. Green politics is a new kind of politics guided by these key principles:

1 *Humankind depends on the diversity of the natural world for its existence. We do not believe that other species are dispensable.*

2 *The Earth's physical resources are finite. We threaten our future if we try to live beyond those means, so we must build a sustainable society that guarantees our long-term future.*

3 *Every person should be entitled to basic material security as of right.*

4 *Our actions should take account of the wellbeing of other nations and future generations. We should not pursue our wellbeing to the detriment of theirs.*

5 *A healthy society is based on voluntary co-operation between empowered individuals in a democratic society, free from discrimination, whether based on race, colour, sex, religion, national origin, social origin or any other prejudice.*

6 *We emphasise democratic participation and accountability by ensuring that decisions are taken at the closest practical level to those affected by them.*

7 *We look for non-violent solutions to conflict situations, which take into account the interests of minorities and future generations in order to achieve lasting settlements.*

8 *The success of a society cannot be measured by narrow economic indicators, but should take account of factors affecting the quality of life for all people: personal freedom, social equality, health, happiness and human fulfilment.*

9 *Electoral politics is not the only way to achieve change in society and we will use a variety of methods to help to effect change, providing those methods do not conflict with our other core principles.*

10 *The Green Party puts changes in both values and lifestyles at the heart of the radical green agenda.*

Shallow and deep ecology

The term 'ecologism' can be used in two contexts. It may refer to the science of humankind's relationship with other humans, the animal world and the physical environment. Its other meaning is as a collection of interconnected beliefs about what humankind's relationship to the natural world ought to be. It is therefore a political and a quasi-ideological movement. Ecologism in this sense can be further divided into two branches – shallow ecology and deep ecology.

Shallow ecology

Shallow ecology can be treated as mainstream. It is characterised by a number of beliefs:

- Humankind should consider itself a 'steward' of the natural world. Rather than simply exploiting the world for its own purposes, humankind has a duty to protect the Earth and ensure its survival.

- Humankind must protect the Earth and its resources for future generations. In other words, we must not ignore the consequences of our exploitation of the Earth. In political terms this implies energy conservation, use of renewable resources and protection of natural habitats.

- The richness and diversity of the plant and animal world are ends in themselves. They do not merely exist on Earth to serve us; their life has value in itself.

- Although shallow ecologists do not share the holistic view of their more radical colleagues, they understand that humankind's manipulation of the Earth for its own purposes may have consequences far beyond what can be perceived. The depletion of the ozone layer is an example of this.

- Whereas liberal environmentalists treat various issues separately, shallow ecologists have a sense that the environmental movement should be all-encompassing. Ecologism is a state of mind which can be applied to all issues that affect the natural world (deep ecologists take this further by seeking a new consciousness). Thus, we should not separate issues such as emissions control, biodiversity and habitat protection from each other, but treat them as a single problem.

- Shallow ecologists use science to develop and reinforce environmental theories. However, you should note that they do not tend to apply philosophy or religion to their belief system, as deep ecologists do.

Jonathon Porritt, one of the pioneers of the green movement in the UK, made a useful distinction between liberal environmentalism and ecology. He accepted that for most liberals (who are usually middle class), environmentalism exists to support humankind's own self-interest. In other words, we will care for the environment if this will be to the benefit of humankind. For genuine ecologists ('deep greens', Porritt called them), concern for the environment should not be self-interested. We should consider the welfare of the natural environment for its own sake.

> ✔ **Key Term**
>
> **Light Green**
> A term that is applied to the beliefs of so-called shallow ecologists. It suggests an anthropocentric approach to ecology and sees environmental issues in terms of human-centred reforms rather than any deep change in relationships between humans and the Earth.

Deep ecology

The first distinction between shallow and deep ecology was made by the philosopher Arne Naess (1912–2009), who articulated the idea in 1972. While not disparaging the efforts of shallow ecologists to raise awareness of issues such as biodiversity, air quality control and protection of the oceans, Naess argued that these were 'shallow' concerns, which failed to appreciate

that ecologism was a philosophy that should exist for its own sake. Although the shallow ecologists wished to see a better balance between the natural world and humankind's needs, Naess claimed that they still placed humans on a higher level than the rest of the Earth. Ecologism, Naess insisted, must consider the natural world as a system within which humankind has equal status with other species. Environmental protection is worth doing simply because it is worth doing, not merely because it satisfies humankind's desire to live in a more pleasant world. Instead of thinking about humankind's relationship with the natural world, we should see ourselves as part of a single whole.

The animal rights movement, although not necessarily part of the environmental mainstream, demonstrates a deep ecological attitude. By seeing animals as part of our own natural world and deserving of as much respect as we expect to have for ourselves, the movement has reached a deep level of consciousness. It has, in other words, freed itself from anthropocentrism.

Murray Bookchin (1921–2006), an anarcho-environmentalist whose views are explored further below, deploys a similar argument. For him, all life on Earth is part of a single web in which every part is equal in importance to every other part. Thus, it is not acceptable for humans to consider themselves to be superior to the rest of nature any more than it is correct to consider elephants to be superior to micro-organisms just because they are larger.

> ✔ **Key Term**
>
> **Dark Green**
> A term used to describe the beliefs of deep ecologists. They generally take an ecocentric, rather than anthropocentric, approach, seeing the Earth as a single organism, all of whose parts are interrelated. They propose fundamental changes in the relationship between humans and the rest of the Earth.

Bookchin's view involves a radical change in human consciousness – one of the defining features of deep ecology. Naess expressed the idea of developing a deeper consciousness by identifying different levels of involvement with ecology. At the lowest level (which he termed level 4), we are merely concerned with environmental issues on an individual basis, perhaps concentrating on those aspects that we meet in our own lives. We do what we can at this level but make no fundamental changes to our lives. At the highest level (level 1), we can achieve self-realisation. This means that our whole lives can be conducted in accordance with the philosophical principles of ecology. We immerse ourselves in consciousness of the natural world and see no separation between it and ourselves. Naess' contribution is summed up in his eight-point platform, shown below:

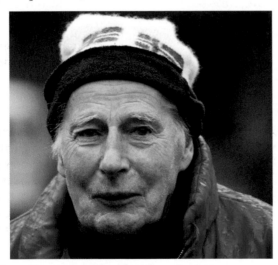

Arne Naess, leading 'deep' ecologist

The eight-point platform

Written in 1984, and largely the work of Arne Naess and George Sessions, the eight-point platform is a kind of deep ecology manifesto and statement of principles:

1 *The wellbeing and flourishing of human and non-human life on Earth have value in themselves. These values are independent of the usefulness of the non-human world for human purposes.*

2 *Richness and diversity of life forms contribute to the realisation of these values and are also values in themselves.*

3 *Humans have no right to reduce this richness and diversity except to satisfy vital needs.*

4 *The flourishing of human life and cultures is compatible with a substantially smaller human population. The flourishing of non-human life requires a smaller human population.*

5 *Present human interference with the non-human world is excessive, and the situation is rapidly worsening.*

6 *Policies must therefore be changed. These policies affect basic economic, technological and ideological structures. The resulting state of affairs will be deeply different from the present.*

7 *The ideological change will be mainly of appreciating life quality (dwelling in situations of inherent value) rather than adhering to an increasingly higher standard of living. There will be a profound awareness of the difference between bigness and greatness.*

8 *Those who subscribe to the foregoing points have an obligation directly or indirectly to try to implement the necessary changes.*

James Lovelock, a scientist, represents a part of the deep ecology movement that can be characterised as 'Earth first'. This places the whole of the Earth, both animate and inanimate parts, above the interests of humankind. In some ways, Lovelock is not as radical as Bookchin and Naess – for example, he argues that nuclear energy is to be tolerated and even encouraged – but he does represent an important branch of the deep ecology movement. This branch accepts that technology can be harnessed to serve the interests of the planet as a whole. Indeed, to a certain extent, Lovelock suggests that the Earth is capable of making its own adjustments to humankind's influence. What matters to Lovelock and his supporters is that we understand that everything on the Earth is

Liberal environmentalism	Shallow ecology	Deep ecology
Concern for the environment is centred upon the interest of humankind	Humans should care for the environment for its own sake	Humans must develop a new consciousness that sees humankind as an intrinsic part of the natural world
Environmental issues can be treated separately	Different aspects of the natural world are interconnected, so our treatment of nature should take this into account	The Earth is a single, complete organism. Humans are part of that whole
Environmental problems can, in theory, be solved within existing political and economic structures	Existing political and economic structures must be transformed so that they place environmental issues at the centre of their concerns	There must be a total change in all economic, social and political life so that humankind can be placed more naturally within its physical environment
Most environmental issues are fundamentally economic in nature	Ecology is largely scientific in nature	Ecology is a synthesis of science, philosophy and, in some cases, religion or even mysticism

Table 7.1 Summary of mainstream environmentalism and ecologism

interconnected. Furthermore, we cannot possibly know how these interconnections work, and so must avoid activities whose consequences for the Earth are uncertain, and possibly irreversible.

 Key Term

Gaia

Gaia was the Greek goddess of the Earth. James Lovelock used the name to describe his understanding of the Earth. Lovelock sees the Earth as a single entity with all its parts interrelated. Both animate and inanimate (i.e. the rocks and minerals) parts of the Earth a part of the same whole. Humans are merely one equal part of the Gaia.

Although deep ecology is not a cohesive, united movement, it does have one element that brings together all its members. This is that humankind must be prepared to change its whole consciousness if the environment is to be saved. It is not sufficient merely to be aware of environmental issues and place them at the centre of the political universe: our whole being must become one with nature.

The key beliefs of liberal environmentalism, shallow ecology and deep ecology are summarised in Table 7.1.

Anarcho-environmentalism

Although there are active groups of feminists and socialists who have synthesised their primary ideological position with an environmentalist stance, it is perhaps today's anarchists and quasi-anarchists who form the main group of 'specialised' environmentalists – that is, those who see no barrier between their specific political aims and a radical attitude to ecology.

The main thrust of modern anarchism – whether environmentally based or not – has concentrated on anti-globalisation. Anarchists argue that the problems created by globalisation are various. Their beliefs include the following:

● Opposition to the behaviour of multinational and transnational corporations. Anarchists accuse these organisations of destroying traditional cultures, exploiting cheap labour forces through low wages and bad working conditions, and destroying local environments and community-based forms of self-sufficiency. The incident at Bhopal in India in 1984 is perhaps the most notorious example of such exploitation and has acted as a touchstone issue for many anarcho-environmentalists. The Union Carbide Company's chemical plant exploded, causing at least 20,000 immediate deaths and many more subsequently, with hundreds of thousands suffering illness and homelessness. Bhopal became a symbol of multinational exploitation of the developing world. Several instances of badly maintained and managed supertankers running aground, causing huge damage to wildlife and natural habitats from oil pollution, also illustrate a lack of consideration for the environment. The same is true of the activities of oil companies in Alaska.

- Opposition to the policies of international organisations such as the World Trade Organisation, the International Monetary Fund and the World Bank. These organisations stand accused of forcing poor countries to restructure their economies in order to ensure that such states can boost export earnings. Anarcho-environmentalists argue that this has had a disastrous effect on both traditional communities and the ecology of such countries. Forests have been cut down, intensive agriculture has caused deserts to expand and native plant and animal populations have come under pressure.

- Attempts to reach international agreements on environmental control have been blocked by the influence of multinational companies. The USA's reluctance to comply with such agreements has been singled out as the critical factor in its resistance to cooperation. Anarcho-environmentalists recognise that environmental issues have to be dealt with on an international basis, but argue that agreements can never be successful as long as the governments of the main industrial countries are dominated by business interests.

It should be stressed that these concerns are not the monopoly of anarchist groups. Many liberal environmentalists are also critical of international organisations and corporations, but propose reforms rather than revolutionary methods to change the way in which environmental issues are solved.

Social ecology

The anarchists' case rests on their assertion that humankind must adopt a simpler, more natural way of living and producing. This involves the withdrawal of giant corporations from the world stage and the replacement of international political organisations with community-based social structures. Much of the inspiration for these ideas can be traced back to the nineteenth- and early twentieth-century anarchist Peter Kropotkin and his modern US counterpart Murray Bookchin.

Bookchin's ideas centre on the destruction of all forms of social hierarchy. For him, humans are naturally equal and society should reflect this equality. He argues that by forming small, self-sufficient communities similar to those proposed by Kropotkin, such equality can be achieved. However, he extends his ideas into humankind's relationship to the natural world, rejecting the notion of hierarchy here, too. All living things, he insists, have equal status in nature. Thus, if there are no hierarchies in nature, humans cannot claim to be superior. Life, he says, is a web, not a pyramid. Bookchin's holistic and egalitarian view of nature is illustrated by the passage from his work shown below:

If we recognise that every ecosystem can also be viewed as a food web, we can think of it as a circular, interlacing nexus of plant–animal relationships (rather than a stratified pyramid with man at the apex) that includes such widely varying creatures as micro-organisms and large mammals. What ordinarily puzzles anyone who sees food-web diagrams for the first time is the impossibility of discerning a point of entry into the nexus. The web can be entered at any point and leads back to its point of departure without any apparent exit. Aside from the energy provided by sunlight (and dissipated by radiation), the system to all appearances is closed. Each species, be it a form of bacteria or deer, is knitted together in a network of interdependence, however indirect the links may be. A predator in the web is also prey, even if the 'lowliest' of the organisms merely makes it ill or helps to consume it after death.

From *The Ecology of Freedom*, 1982

In many ways, Bookchin is perhaps the deepest of deep ecologists. His ideas are inspired by science, philosophy and religion, as well as by his anarchist politics. Although he can be seen as an anarchist, his theories can be applicable to all radical ecologists.

Ethical ecology (ethical environmentalism)

We can realistically trace the origin of environmental or ecological ethics to the writing of Aldo Leopold (1887–1948). Leopold's best-known work is A *Sand County Almanac* (published posthumously in 1949). In it he proposed a completely new relationship between man and nature. He described his views as 'land ethics'. This brief extract from that work summarises his view:

That land is a community is the basic concept of ecology, but that land is to be loved and respected is an extension of ethics.

Leopold, and those who have followed him, mostly deep ecologists, suggest that environmentalism must take a different perspective. In particular it must abandon anthropocentrism (see above). Shallow or liberal environmentalism has seen environmental protection in terms of the welfare of humankind, and ultimately of its very survival. Thus, such light green thinkers have argued that it is necessary to preserve resources, habitats and species diversity because it will be to the long-term benefit of humankind, not because they simply *ought* to be protected and nurtured. This anthropocentric view has strong philosophical and religious underpinning. In *The Politics Book 1*, Aristotle had clearly stated, 'nature has made all things specifically for the sake of man', over two thousand years ago. Perhaps more powerful, the Old Testament book of Genesis, to which Jews, Muslims and Christians all subscribe, states unambiguously that man is superior to nature:

God created man in his own image, in the image of God created he him; male and female created he them. And God blessed them, and God said unto them, Be fruitful, and multiply, and replenish the earth, and subdue it: and have dominion over fish of the sea, and over fowl of the air, and over every living thing that moveth upon the earth.

From Genesis, 1:27–8

The ethical approach to ecology largely rejects the anthropocentric approach. It suggests that nature and the Gaia as a whole has intrinsic value. That is, it is worth protecting because it has value in itself, not because it can serve the interests of humankind. Thus, for example, we should preserve rain forests not simply to reduce global warming and so prevent a future ecological disaster, which will in turn cause major problems for human populations, but because the rain forests are part of nature and so have their own value. Similarly, we should protect endangered species not because we, as humans, are superior to them, but because they are all of equal value to us.

We can also say that ethics involves morality. Put simply, this suggests that we have a 'moral duty' to protect the environment. This morality may have a number of features:

- As humans have been granted, by God or nature, an ability to control nature, we have a moral duty to protect nature. This is also described as 'stewardship'.

- We have a moral duty to protect the environment for the sake of future generations. If we have a moral duty to care for our own children, we must therefore have the same moral duty to care for all children of the future.

- If animals and humans are indeed equal, we, as humans, have a moral duty to care for them in the same way that we have a moral duty to care for each other.

- Nature, both living and inanimate, may be considered to be sacred (whether or not we take a religious view). If it is sacred, we must have a moral duty to protect it.

Ethical ecology and 'instrumental' (i.e. environmentalism for the sake of humankind) environmentalism come together in Lovelock's concept of the Gaia. As Lovelock argues, if we are all part of one single organism, Mother Earth, if we damage the Gaia, we also damage ourselves. But, in addition, the Gaia stands above humankind, and is therefore sacred and deserving of love, respect and protection.

Ecofeminism

Ecofeminism is also described in the earlier chapter on feminism. The movement is a synthesis between radical feminism and radical ecologism. Its leading exponent has been the French feminist, Françoise d'Eaubonne (1920–2005).

At its base, ecofeminism believes that environmental science has been patriarchal in nature. The link between patriarchy and environmental degradation is that men have a natural disposition to see themselves as superior to nature. Women, by contrast, are free of this patriarchal consciousness. They see themselves as a part of nature, not above it. Important manifestations of ecofeminism have been seen in protests concerning the use of nuclear energy and the development of genetically modified crops. Women also blame patriarchy for such environmental problems as over-population, habitat destruction and the over-exploitation of natural resources. It therefore follows that the destruction of patriarchy is a prerequisite for a radically new attitude to ecology and to humans' relationship to the Earth.

Ecofeminism naturally falls into two main strands of thought. One is that there is a natural affinity between women and nature. This stems from the biological role of women as the givers of life and a key role in nurturing new life. The second strand is political rather than biological. Here it is proposed that capitalism is patriarchal in nature, that capitalism inevitably leads to the over-exploitation of the natural world and that therefore men are responsible for environmental problems. Thus for these radical, highly ideological and left-wing feminists, the destruction of both capitalism and patriarchy are essential if the environment is to be protected and if our relationship to the Earth is to be fundamentally changed.

An important example of ecofeminism has been the Third World movement led by Vandana Shiva (1952–). Shiva, who is also an anti-globalisation campaigner, sees the importance of women in ecologism in two senses. First, they see the answer to the processes of both globalisation and environmental destruction to be a return to simple, self-sufficient forms of production. Second, women, who have a special affinity with land and nature in general, are more suitable in the creation of such communities. Men are seen as naturally acquisitive people and so capitalism is natural to them. By contrast, women see production in terms of maintaining a 'good life' rather than simply acquiring ever more wealth and property. Thus, self-sufficiency is natural to women, and less natural to men.

Right-wing ecology

So far we have assumed that all theories of the Earth and man's relationship to it are radical and either liberal or left-wing in nature. However, there have been some right-wing movements that have taken on aspects of a kind of ecology.

The best known, perhaps, is the Nazi doctrine of the Earth in the 1930s and 1940s. Tied to their theory of the land was the concept of the 'Volk' and Volksgemeinschaft. For the German Nazis the Volk was more than merely a national group or a race. The Volk also enjoyed a special relationship with the land that they occupied. Furthermore there was an historical relationship, which could take on a sacred characteristic. But, while the Nazi doctrine of Blut und Boden (Blood and Soil) is best known for its association with the idea of Lebensraum or living space for the 'superior' German race, the link between race and the land had a more mystical significance. On a practical level, this largely meant that the land should be respected and even worshipped. However, Nazism pre-dates the principal modern concerns about the environmental so it is doubtful whether the movement would ever have sacrificed progress for environmental protection.

The Hitler Youth movement, for example, were encouraged to take hiking and camping holidays in order to bring them closer to the sacred land. Culture and the land were seen as inextricably tied together so that the relationship was to be constantly renewed. The modern British National Party has also developed the idea of this relationship. The party sees the unique landscape of Britain as a part of its also unique history. The shape of the land is therefore seen as part of the 'genius' of the British people. Indeed, even the BNP claims to be an environmentally friendly party on the grounds that a betrayal of the natural world is also a betrayal of the British people.

Having said that extreme right-wing philosophy does propose a sacred relationship between man and the land, it would be an error to see right wingers as some kind of deep ecologists. Indeed, less extreme right-wing conservatives have traditionally placed environmentalism low on their scale of priorities. On the whole, right-wing ideologists see man as being superior to nature and that there will ultimately be technological solutions to environmental problems. If man has created environmental problems through technology and industrialisation, his 'genius' will also find solutions.

A very different form of 'right wing' ecology is associated with neo-liberalism. This suggests that there is no need for government or international action to deal with environmental problems. Instead, the free market will provide solutions. That is to say, if there is a great enough demand for emissions control, resources preservation, solutions to climate change or habitat preservation, the free market will supply solutions as it always does. This is connected to US President George W. Bush's early environmental policy, which was based on technology. He proposed that the answers to environmental problems were all capable of being solved by technology and, once the demand existed, technology would be developed as it would enjoy the prospect of an economic return on its investment.

Under the leadership of David Cameron the UK Conservative Party has advocated green policies, though whether this is 'real' or merely 'opportunism' remains to be seen.

Left-wing ecology

Socialist and Communist regimes have a poor record in environmental protection. Indeed, the USSR became notorious for its poor environmental record. But there is no intrinsic link between socialism and communism and anti-environmentalism. However, there is some historical evidence of an early synthesis between socialism and ecology.

William Morris (1834–96), the English socialist, is an example of a romantic thinker who believed that the Earth was threatened by the onward rush of industrialisation. Morris believed that both the alienation of workers, and the degradation of the environment could be eliminated if simpler, more traditional forms of production were to be introduced. These simple modes of production would be organised along socialist, egalitarian lines – on the grounds that this would remove the natural tendency of capitalism to grow and industrialise in an uncontrolled fashion.

In a modern context, left-wing ecologists (also called 'eco-socialists') have adopted a number of criticisms of the relationship between capitalism and economic degradation. Among them are these:

● Some Marxists have suggested that capitalism has not one, but two contradictions. The main analysis suggests that capitalism exploits its workers and that this exploitation will inevitably intensify. To this they add the belief that capitalism also exploits the environment and will do so more intensively as it seeks out new resources in order to expand. Not surprisingly, and following Lenin's analysis of the exploitation of poor countries by advanced capitalism, the environments of Third World countries will become the target for growth once the resources of the West have been used up.

● Naturally Marxists believe, in the light of the analysis described above, that only revolution can reverse this otherwise inevitable development.

● Other socialists have concentrated on the tendency of capitalism towards consumerism. The need to maintain ever-expanding markets makes the exploitation of the world's resources inevitable. Capitalism cannot, it seems, survive, unless it grows and it must therefore eat up increasing amounts of the Earth's resources.

● It is clear to most socialists that the elitist nature of capitalist society inevitably leads to environmental problems. This is because elites become detached from the lives of the ordinary producers and consumers and so lose any contact with the environment that their activities threaten.

● Socialists who are close to the anarchist movement advocate a return to subsistence forms of simple production, which will re-connect producers directly with the environment.

Perhaps the leading advocate of eco-socialism, however, is the American Joel Kovel (1936–). Kovel campaigns against both uncontrolled capitalism and globalisation. The elites who control transnational corporations and international financial institutions will not relinquish their economic control of the environment and so they must be removed by revolutionary means. Unlike eco-anarchists, who advocate the dismantling of capitalist production and its replacement by simpler forms of self-sufficiency, and unlike traditional state socialists, Kovel supports a cooperative approach. The means of production should be returned to cooperative groups of workers. This will result, he argues, in the removal of the inevitable exploitation of the environment by unaccountable elites.

Key environmentalist and ecologist thinkers

Arne Naess (Norwegian, 1912–2009)

Naess is possibly the most philosophical of today's leading ecologists. His belief system, which has become known as deep ecology, has three fundamental bases. These are romanticism, science and philosophy.

Naess' romantic view of nature has led him to understand that humans have a deep spiritual relationship with nature, which has largely been lost in modern, complex civilisation. His theme, which is echoed by writers, musicians and religious traditions such as Buddhism, involves the natural affinity that all living creatures have for each other and for the physical landscape which surrounds them. In the high mountains, where Naess has spent much of his life and from which he draws most of his inspiration, this oneness with nature is most apparent.

As regards science, Naess' theories are closely related to Lovelock's 'Gaia' thesis (see pp. 226–27). The Earth, says Naess, is a biosphere – a single living organism in which all parts of it are interrelated biologically and spiritually. As humans, we must develop a deep understanding of both the relationships between the different parts of nature and our own personal relationship with the biosphere.

It is in the field of philosophy that Naess' contribution to the ecology movement is perhaps most original. Indeed, it has been ascribed its own name – **ecosophy**. He argues that on a personal level we seek to achieve self-realisation – that is, the fulfilment of our deepest desires for harmony within the world that surrounds us, both human and physical. Philosophers of many kinds, including Marxists, anarchists, existentialists and feminists, have sought to explain how best we can achieve such self-realisation. Naess emphasises the search for total harmony with the natural world we inhabit; for him, the highest level of human consciousness is

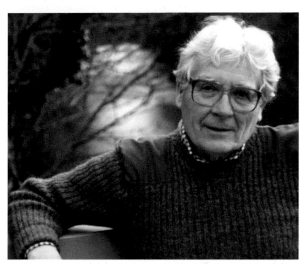

James Lovelock, who developed the concept of 'Gaia'

to reach an understanding that we have relationships with the whole of nature and that all parts of nature itself are interconnected. What affects nature, for good or ill, also affects us. Once we achieve self-realisation, Naess declares, we will also have developed a full understanding of how we must interact with the natural world.

However, Naess' beliefs are not purely philosophical. Having achieved self-realisation, he says, we can better understand the practical ways in which we, as individuals, can protect and nurture the environment. In the case of a farmer, for example, this will involve emphasising natural methods, avoiding pesticides, protecting wildlife and recycling materials. For an individual involved in business, it will mean conserving energy, avoiding pollution and caring for the physical environment. For a feminist, it may mean exploring feminine consciousness in order to discover ways in which women can contribute to the environmental movement both practically and politically.

James Lovelock (English, born 1921)

A scientist by calling, Lovelock developed his theories while working on the NASA space programme in the USA during the 1960s and 1970s. His particular field was the assessment of whether life existed, or had existed, on other planets. He is best known for his development of the concept of the Gaia. Gaia was the Ancient Greek goddess of the Earth, and it is upon the Earth as a whole that Lovelock bases his ideas.

He sees the Earth (and indeed any planet) as a single, organic, living whole. Most interestingly, Lovelock includes the inanimate parts of nature – even the rocks – among that whole. Humankind is but a part of the organic Gaia. We are not separate from it, nor even passengers on it. However, human society has developed its own consciousness of the world, believing that as a species it is superior to all the other parts of the whole and that the Earth can be manipulated for humankind's own benefit.

Lovelock argues that the Earth is a self-regulating organism. If any part begins to change significantly, the rest of nature will adjust itself in order to recreate a balance. For example, if temperatures began to rise for some reason, the plant life on the planet will adjust in order to change the composition of the atmosphere and restore temperatures to their normal level. A second example of this mechanism concerns the salinity (salt concentration) of the seas. From time to time this may rise or fall, threatening sea life, but there will be an adjustment to restore salinity to a compatible level.

The processes that maintain the Earth's balance are exceedingly complex, something on which all environmental scientists and theorists agree. Lovelock therefore asserts that humankind should resist the temptation to interfere with natural processes since it can have no idea of the consequences of its actions. As he says: 'We'll never know enough...hands off!' Although to some extent the Earth will be able to adjust itself to human interference, we have become so intrusive that eventually this will not be possible. In particular, the tiny micro-organisms that make up life on Earth are affected by human action so fundamentally that the very basis of life may be threatened.

The implication of Lovelock's theories is that we must avoid taking any actions (including towards inanimate objects) that will affect the balance of the Earth. We must be sensitive to natural processes and allow the Earth to find its own balance. In particular, Lovelock considers energy production to be the most damaging human activity of all. He recognises that humankind needs energy to sustain itself and argues that nuclear energy is the way forward – rather than renewable forms, which will never satisfy our growing needs. Whereas most environmentalists oppose the use of nuclear power, on the grounds that it produces waste products that will remain a threat for thousands of years and because of the ever present danger of a catastrophic accident, Lovelock believes that this is the price we have to pay. Nuclear fission produces virtually no interference with the balance of the Earth, so its long-term consequences are less severe than those of any other known method of energy production.

Fritjof Capra (Austrian, born 1939)

Of the three thinkers discussed in this section, Capra is perhaps the one most inspired by the physical sciences, especially physics. Like Naess and Lovelock, he is closely associated with Schumacher College, a centre for environmental research in England. Capra's science is complex, but some accessible conclusions are described below.

Capra challenged the explanations of the biosphere offered by traditional forms of science. Since science had suggested that the different parts of the natural world could be studied separately and that they could therefore also be manipulated separately, fundamental errors were made in our understanding of the natural environment. The alternative to these scientific models offered by Capra was 'holism'. The holistic approach asserts that all living organisms are interconnected and form one great whole. Furthermore, Capra says, this does not just occur on a macro level – e.g. the seas, atmosphere, animal and plant species – but also on a micro level. The building blocks of life, including micro-organisms, cells and, indeed, parts of cells, are all interconnected and communicate with each other in ways that we have not even begun to understand.

The idea of the Earth as being a single entity with interrelated parts was held by the ancient world in the form of mysticism and religion. Although ancient people had little science as we understand it today, they had a fundamental understanding that all life is part of a single whole and that energy flows through all of it in a continuous stream. These ideas can still be seen in traditional medicine (e.g. acupuncture and reflexology), in religions (e.g. Buddhism, Jainism and Taoism), and in a mystical understanding of the energy forces that pass through the Earth (e.g. lay lines).

Capra accepts that science will probably never be able to fully make sense of all these interconnections. Similarly, many astrophysicists assert that we will never fully understand the workings of the universe. However, an understanding that the Earth is a single organism must inform the way in which we treat our natural environment. Above all, Capra attacks anthropocentrism – the belief that humankind is at the centre of nature and is separate from and superior to it. We must replace this belief with ecocentrism – the reality that nature, as a single whole, dominates all life, and that we humans are merely a part of that whole and equal to all other parts.

Issues in environmentalism and ecologism

Are environmentalism and ecologism ideologies?

An ideology is a set of ideas that have coherence and are therefore interlocking. These ideas propose the transformation of society in a fundamental way. Ideology therefore involves revolutionary rather than evolutionary change, which is created by positive, purposeful actions, rather than being gradual and natural, without any specific political aims.

According to these criteria, liberal environmentalism cannot be seen as an ideology. The environmental movement as a whole certainly shares a common value – that our physical environment should be protected and that humankind must readjust its relationship to the natural world. However, liberal environmentalists do not believe that any transformation of society and its structures is necessary. For example, there is no need to reform capitalism in any fundamental way. Capitalism, liberals argue, can be regulated and moderated in order to take environmental concerns into account. Similarly, liberal environmentalists have no specific political goals other than a desire to place environmental concerns high up or even at the top of the political agenda.

Evidence of liberal environmentalism's lack of ideological credentials is that it does not seek to change the relationship between humans and nature in any fundamental way. In short, it remains anthropocentric. By retaining humankind's place at the apex of the natural world, liberals are failing to propose revolutionary change. The fundamental structure, or 'hierarchy', as Bookchin would call it, remains unaltered. Liberal environmentalism is therefore better described as a political movement rather than as an ideological one. Despite this, it is worth noting that it is an extremely coherent political movement, far more unified in its principles and objectives than mainstream, democratic political parties.

When we turn to the radical ecologists the picture changes considerably. The deep ecologists, led by Capra and Naess, criticise the shallow ecologists on the grounds that they are not sufficiently ideological. The key reason for this concerns human consciousness. At the deepest level of ecologism (Naess' level 1), humankind achieves self-realisation through the development of a complete subjugation of human consciousness into the continuous flow of natural forces. This can be compared with the Marxist concept of total socialist consciousness, which can become so deep-rooted that no alternative form of consciousness is possible. The shallow ecologists, on the other hand, do not seek such depth of consciousness, but merely modify anthropocentrism in the interests of the natural world. This can arguably be described as radical, but shallow greens remain reformers rather than revolutionaries.

Deep ecologists certainly demonstrate values and principles, as well as a liberated consciousness, that give their movement an ideological coherence. This coherence is evident in two senses. First, their philosophy involves a fundamental change in social structures. Industrialisation must be firmly controlled and even turned back; capitalism must be replaced by simpler forms of production and distribution; the acquisitive, consumer society must be turned into one that caters for needs, not wants. Second, it proposes a completely new attitude towards nature. Humankind must not be separated from nature, but must see itself as part of it, equal to its other parts and part of nature's wholeness. For Capra, this relationship is a flow of energy, whereas for Bookchin it is a web; but in both cases, humankind becomes part of nature, not separate from it. These characteristics seem to be both coherent and purposeful.

Similarly, those who combine environmentalism with other ideologies – anarchists, socialists and feminists in particular – can be seen as ideologues. They are ideological in the sense that they have adopted an ideological approach to social transformation in general, and have linked social revolution to fundamental changes in humankind's relationship with the natural environment.

The answer to this question must therefore be that liberal environmentalism is not in any sense ideological; that a weak case can be made for describing shallow ecologists in such terms; but that deep ecology certainly is an ideological movement.

Is ecologism merely a utopian philosophy?

Many deep ecologists, especially Arne Naess, would be proud that their beliefs might be described as a 'philosophy', but would object to them being termed utopian. This is because the term 'utopian' implies 'unrealistic'. In other words, are the radical ecologists merely romantic dreamers?

Certainly, there is a strong case to be made for describing ecologism as a philosophy rather than a political movement. We should, perhaps, separate 'green politics' from 'green philosophy'. Such a philosophy need not have highly specific ends and might have unforeseeable consequences for society. The Enlightenment of the eighteenth century can serve as a model for this idea. The original Enlightenment philosophers, most notable of whom was René Descartes, were not ideologues in the sense that Marxists or anarchists have been. Rather, they changed our consciousness of the world in fundamental ways without specifying any political objectives. The philosophical developments they made gave rise to specific political movements at a much later stage in human social progress. Yet we would not describe the Enlightenment period as utopian in character. In fact, the contrary is true – it is seen as an age when new truths were revealed to us, which led humankind to a 'higher' form of civilisation. It may be that deep ecology will one day be recognised as a similar philosophical revolution, whose consequences may prove to be as fundamental and significant as those that followed the ideas of Isaac Newton, Descartes and Darwin.

However, the problem of where to place deep ecology in human consciousness has been exacerbated by the fact that its adherents have associated themselves with mysticism and religions like Buddhism and Taoism. The latter have been seen as little more than philosophies of individual self-realisation, rather than social religions that provide ethical codes. To make matters worse, mysticism is often criticised as 'quackery', with no basis either in science or the human imagination.

A specific charge that can be levied against Naess, for example, is that he proposes to turn back progress and return to simpler ways of living that do not acknowledge industrialisation and technological advances. He goes so far as to assert that the 'natural' human population of the Earth is only 100 million, a tiny fraction of its current number. Clearly this 'natural' level cannot be achieved and must therefore be viewed as intensely utopian. Admittedly, the notion of returning to simpler forms of community and economic organisation has long been explored by anarchists, and may therefore be seen as a perfectly reasonable alternative to modern, complex societies. Such communities can be created within existing human society (like the Israeli kibbutzim, for example). However, the ecology movement demands that all humankind would have to eschew progress, dismantle most industry and adopt simple technologies. Since the aim of the movement is environmental, it would be futile if only some people adopted new forms of communal living. In order to make an environmental impact, we must all make fundamental changes to our way of life.

However, the picture is perhaps not so stark for deep ecologists. We could, for example, take one basic principle from the movement — that humankind is part of nature and not superior to it or merely separate — and adopt it as a fundamental consideration in all our activities. If we change our consciousness, seeing ourselves as interdependent organisms within the total Gaia, and understand that we must avoid taking actions the environmental consequences of which we cannot predict, it may be possible to sustain lifestyles that modern humankind can find acceptable. We could therefore continue to engage in industrial processes, provided we only use non-polluting, renewable forms of energy. We could retain sophisticated economies while always replacing any resources we take from the Earth. Agriculture could develop in such a way that the rest of the living world remains unexploited. Respect for all life forms cannot be seen as utopian, nor need the retention of biodiversity be viewed as revolutionary.

The most powerful claim that ecologists can make is that humankind really has no alternative. The inevitable result of our present attitude towards the natural environment is disaster. They can therefore say that it is utopian to believe that humankind can survive without a fundamental change in consciousness. The ecologists are, in fact, the realists; it is the rest of humanity that is utopian.

What is the impact of globalisation on the green movement?

In some ways, globalisation has had the effect of bringing the green movement to the forefront of international ideology. When environmentalists were nationally based, their concerns seemed parochial. The emergence of truly global environmental issues, such as ozone depletion, global warming and biodiversity, forced the movement to itself become global in nature. This has chiefly occurred in two ways.

First, the two main organisations that campaign on environmental issues – Greenpeace and Friends of the Earth – have become global organisations. Their campaigns are international and they have increasingly focused their attention on international organisations and conferences. The great environmental conferences of recent times – Rio (1992), Kyoto (1997), Johannesburg (2002) and Kobe (2008) – were characterised by intense lobbying on the part of both organisations.

Second, a new quasi-anarchist, anti-globalisation movement has grown up separately from the more conventional environmentalist lobby. The groups that make up this movement, whose philosophy and aims are varied, argue that conventional methods of campaigning are futile. They believe that an anthropocentric and exploitative attitude to the environment is so entrenched within international organisations and multinational companies that radical methods must be employed. Such methods have included mass demonstrations and even attacks upon property, especially where international conferences are being held.

The main problem for environmental groups is that, no matter how much influence they may have over national governments, environmental problems are now so extensive that only global action can be effective. Furthermore, the administration of the most influential country, the USA, has shown relatively little interest in green issues, and the US Green Party, led by Ralph Nader (1934–), has made virtually no impact on electoral politics.

Globalisation has therefore been a two-edged sword for the green movement. On the one hand, it has united environmentalists throughout the world (a development facilitated by the internet) and has prompted enormous amounts of scientific research into issues such as climate change, movements in animal populations and habitat degradation. On the other hand, it has presented environmentalists with a host of new problems. The power of large corporations and international financial organisations is immense. Their interests in trade, technology, energy resources, development and industrial issues have pushed environmental considerations to one side. For such groups, short-term gains take precedence over the long-term dangers of adverse environmental impacts.

There is also a considerable amount of tension concerning the issue of the economic development of poor countries. The green movement has argued for genuinely sustainable development in such countries. They should, greens say, be presented with opportunities to develop their own natural and organic economic systems. If this can be done, these countries will retain a vested interest in environmental protection. Self-sufficiency and traditional social structures will mean that natural habitats will be protected and the damaging effects of rapid industrialisation will be avoided. For example, if India had developed its own chemicals industry, using its own technology controlled by local communities, Bhopal would never have occurred. If the native peoples of South America were given the opportunity to exploit the rainforests in a sustainable way, their traditional way of life would be protected, their natural habitat would survive and the problem of global warming would be reduced.

Against this view is ranged pressure from international economic organisations for rapid economic development to bring less developed countries out of poverty. Saddled with huge debt and massive social problems, together with fast-growing populations, the temptation for these countries is to take the short-term view and accept aid that will create immediate growth. This has a seriously damaging impact on natural environments.

Thus, environmentalists have had to become concerned with issues of economic development. It could be argued, however, that global ecology issues cannot be separated from economic considerations since they are essentially the same thing.

Is ecologism science or politics?

As has been shown, the origins of both deep and shallow ecology are both scientific and philosophical. Indeed, leading authorities such as Arne Naess and Fritjof Capra would argue that no meaningful distinction can be made between science and philosophy. Such a distinction is historical, they argue, and has no place in modern ecological thinking. Furthermore, these ecologists have rejected the conventional science, especially physics, of Newton and his followers. Newtonian science presents the world as a kind of machine,

the workings of which can be discovered by observation and empirical research. If a part of the machine is damaged, it can be repaired in isolation from the rest of the machine.

Instead, deep ecologists propose an alternative philosophy of science which challenges the basis of known physics. No part of the natural world, they argue, can be seen in isolation from the whole. At the same time, the natural world is constantly experiencing instability; every time it does so, new elements enter the system to change its dynamics. It is therefore mistaken to adopt a fixed view of how nature works, which is what conventional science does. We must instead adopt a new synthesis of philosophy and science that accepts the instability of nature and the unknowability of all the implications of humankind's impact upon it. Whether we accept Capra's idea of nature as constant energy and matter flows, or Bookchin's idea of it as an enclosed web of life, we must adopt new methods of studying and understanding the complexity and inherent chaos of the natural world.

Deep ecology is therefore neither science nor philosophy in isolation. If it is not a science in the usual sense of the word, can it be seen as political? If philosophies are political in nature, the answer is 'yes'. However, politics suggests more than this. Philosophy forms the basis of political development, but does not replace it. Deep ecologists propose new forms of consciousness and attempt to educate us into thinking about the relationship between our lives and the natural world, but this does not translate as politics. It may be left to others to create the specific forms of action that can facilitate this new consciousness. The French Revolution is a model for this. It was certainly inspired by Enlightenment thinkers such as Jean-Jacques Rousseau, Thomas Paine and Voltaire, but it was the revolutionaries themselves who translated their philosophy into political action.

The liberal environmentalists and shallow ecologists, as represented by green pressure groups, Greenpeace and Friends of the Earth, are

Greenpeace believes in militant action in the environmental field

clearly political. They have developed manifestos for action and seek to influence decision-makers in specific ways. This is uncontroversial. However, the deep ecologists have challenged these groups on the basis that they remain anthropocentric. Without changing fundamental human consciousness, attempts to salvage the planet from environmental disaster will be unsuccessful. In other words, by making compromises for the sake of political gain, such pressure groups fail to confront the real, profound issues.

To summarise this discussion, therefore, it can be said that ecologism is certainly a science, but one that is based on a completely new philosophy. It is not political in the conventional sense, since it proposes changes to the basis of our ethics and our relationship with nature, and is unspecific about its precise political objectives. The liberal environmentalists, by contrast, are intensely political, but are criticised by their radical colleagues for failing to understand the importance of the new philosophy of science. Thus, they cannot claim to be true ecologists. They are simply well-meaning liberal campaigners.

It is worth finishing with the words of Aldo Leopold, who wrote *A Sand County Almanac*, published posthumously in 1949. This passage from his work does not propose political action, new science, or even philosophy, but a new system of human ethics:

All ethics so far evolved rest on a single premise: that the individual is a member of a community of interdependent parts. His instincts prompt him to compete for his place in that community, but his ethics prompt him also to cooperate (perhaps in order that there be a place to compete for). The land ethic simply enlarges the boundaries of the community to include soils, waters, plants, and animals, or collectively: the land.

Exam focus

Using this chapter and other resources available to you, answer the following questions.

Short questions

Your answers should be about 400 words long.
1 What do environmentalists mean by 'anthropocentrism'?
2 Outline the meaning and importance of the term 'Gaia'.
3 To what extent are there important distinctions between deep and light green ecology?
4 What is meant by the term 'deep ecology'?
5 Why are some environmentalists also anarchists?
6 Why are some feminists also ecologists?

Long questions

Your answers should be about 1200 words long.
1 What are the main distinctions between liberal environmentalism and the different forms of ecologism?
2 'Anthropocentrism is the main enemy of environmentalism.' Explain and discuss.
3 Explain the importance of holism in the ecology movement.
4 Distinguish between anthropocentrism and ethical ecology.

Further reading

Baxter, B. (2000) *Ecologism: An Introduction*, Georgetown University Press.
Capra, F. (1997) *The Web of Life*, Flamingo.
Dobson, A. (2000) *Green Political Thought*, Routledge.
Goodin, R. (1992) *Green Political Theory*, Polity Press.
Merchant, C. (2005) *Radical Ecology*, Routledge.
Naess, A. (1990) *Ecology, Community and Lifestyle*, Cambridge University Press.
Radcliffe, J. (2002) *Green Politics*, Palgrave.
Young, S. (1993) *The Politics of the Environment*, Baseline.

Websites

Greenpeace: www.greenpeace.org
Friends of the Earth: www.foe.co.uk
The UK Green Party: www.greenparty.org.uk
Schumacher College: www.schumachercollege.org.uk

Chapter 8

Multiculturalism

Multiculturalism is a movement and a set of beliefs that grew in Western society after the 1960s. It arose partly as a result of the increasing levels of immigration into Western European countries, including Britain, as well as into Australia and Canada. It also gained strength from other movements that became prevalent from the 1960s, notably civil rights movements, liberal ideas of tolerance and an increasing belief that all cultures were of equal value. Thus, multiculturalism was both a reaction to demographic changes and part of a wider, liberal-inspired movement that promoted respect for different groups in society. It found itself growing alongside 'liberationist' movements such as racial equality, gay rights and radical feminism. Multiculturalism stresses the importance of 'culture' and asserts that the key element in the identity of each individual is their cultural background and heritage. Though race, nationality, religion, gender, sexual orientation, etc. remain important, multiculturalism sees them as secondary to specific cultural identities. Some, though not all, have claimed that multiculturalism became so embedded in Western thought after the 1960s that it almost became an ideology in itself, though others have merely placed it as a contemporary element of a wider liberal tradition.

Introduction: The nature of culture

Race and culture

After the Second World War there was a renewed interest among anthropologists and sociologists in the idea of culture as opposed to race. The Nazi/fascist conception of race had stressed the biological nature of racial differences and had ascribed a number of different characteristics to racial groupings. In addition, the Nazis had placed racial groups into a hierarchy in which, not suprisingly, the white, aryan peoples stood at the apex. With the defeat of Nazism and the large-scale movement of peoples from the 1950s onwards into Europe, the USA, Australia and Canada, resulting in racial mixing of a kind never seen before, the issue of racial differences had to be placed into a new context.

The response was to de-emphasise the biological differences between races and instead to suggest that racial groupings had distinctive *cultural* characteristics. Of course, race continued to play some part in cultural identity – for example, in the black consciousness movement of the 1960s and 1970s, but it has ceased to be the only significant factor (as had been the case in racialist theories). Instead it is religion, traditions and ethnicity (meaning nationality and historical roots rather than merely biological race) that increasingly define the term 'culture'.

There remain a number of movements, mostly of a 'right-wing' character, that consider race and culture to be virtually coterminous. The British National Party is a clear example, as are both black and white supremacists in the USA and parts of Europe. Like the pre-war Nazis, these groups believe that culture is racially determined and that even skin colour can define one's identity in as fundamental a way as gender or nationality. But such right-wing conceptions of culture need not concern us here as they have played no significant part in the development of multiculturalism (though they have remained firm critiques of the movement, as one would expect).

A neutral conception of culture

The term 'culture' is often used in a purely neutral way to describe the customs and traditions of a specific community. Such conceptions have no political significance and are purely descriptive. They reject the notion that any one culture might be superior to others. They often refer to religious practices that are purely private in nature. Thus, for example, one may speak of Muslims fasting during Ramadan, Jewish families gathering to eat Friday evening dinner together and observing certain historical rituals, or the practice of Christians to exchange gifts at Christmas time. On an even less fundamental level, culture may refer to music, dance or costume which some groups emphasise to a greater or lesser extent. They may be important pastimes for a community, but they are not used to distinguish one community from another in any significant or *political* way.

Language can present more difficulty. For some communities a distinctive language may mean little more than the retention of literature, folk dances and songs. For others, however, language can become an issue of great political significance. Certainly this is the case with militant Welsh nationalists or with Catalonian nationalists in Spain. Indeed, the cultural characteristics of language can illustrate well the distinction between culture as a neutral concept and its role as a political vehicle. Language may be retained by some groups in order to preserve that group's literary or musical traditions (as with moderate Welsh language groups). Sometimes the preservation of a language that has been threatened by a large dominant culture can become a symbol of a wider political struggle. The Basque people of Northern Spain and Southern France, for example, seek political autonomy as their primary goal and use their distinctive language as a means of establishing their separate identity.

We can dispense with such neutral conceptions of culture here as they play little or no role in the political movement known as multiculturalism. Certainly liberals may wish to encourage cultural traditions and may seek to nurture and protect them, but they do not form any part of the conflict over the political significance of cultural identity.

Culture and identity politics

Here we are considering culture in a more fundamental way. Culture can be used as a means by which a community asserts its identity and especially its sense of 'differentness' from other cultures. More specifically, if a group feels it suffers from discrimination, oppression or persecution, it may use its distinctive culture as a force for asserting itself and seeking liberation. It is widely acknowledged that **identity politics** has its modern origins in Canada. Here a long struggle by the minority French population, concentrated largely in Quebec province, became a *cause célébre* both in Canda and France in the 1950s. Ultimately, the Canadian government was forced to accept that French-Canadian identity should be recognised positively by granting some political autonomy to Quebec (short of full independence) and by giving a special legal status to the French language. The experience of Quebec served as a model for many other national groupings that wished to assert their identity within states that had failed to give them special status.

Identity politics is also a means by which each individual perceives his or her identity. The American liberal philosopher Francis Fukuyama (1952–) demonstrated the importance of identity politics thus:

Modern identity politics springs from a hole in the political theory underlying liberal democracy. That hole is liberalism's silence about the place and significance of groups.

From 'Identity and migration' in *Prospect Magazine*, February 2007

Key Term

Identity politics

A militant form of politics that places a group's identity at the centre of political action. It has been best known in terms of the radical politics of ethnicity, gender and sexual orientation. In the context of multiculturalism it can be seen as the politics of liberation and anti-oppression among specific ethnic and cultural groups or communities. It may also refer to the resistance of a dominant culture to such liberation movements.

Fukuyama thus places the blame for the rise of radical identity politics, especially religious terrorism, on liberalism itself. While tolerating minority groups and granting them equal status, liberal society in the West has nevertheless failed to recognise that they have their own, special identity needs. In other words, they need more recognition than is provided by mere tolerance and legal protection. Fukuyama's Canadian colleague, Charles Taylor (1935–), had already recognised the conflict between liberal pluralism and identity politics in Canada several decades earlier, but the challenge of Islamic terrorism brought the issue back to prominence after 2001.

In order to illustrate this we will use this example of Islamic identity. Islamic culture is, naturally, based upon religion. Devout Muslims can say that it is their religion that defines them as an individual most precisely. Islam is a special case, it has to be said, because it is a religion that provides a mode of behaviour for all aspects of a person's life – in marriage, parenthood, education, social life and even business and commerce. To say that a person is such a devout Muslim tells us all we need to know about that person's identity. While this would also be true for an orthodox Jew, it would not be true for a moderate or liberal Jew. They have multiple identities. They may see themselves as Jewish *and* British or American or French. Many Muslims in Britain hesitate to call themselves 'British', not necessarily because they are anti British but because they do not consider their British citizenship as a definition of their identity. It merely states where they live and what appears

on their passport. In the twenty-first century, fundamentalist Islamic identity has turned itself into a liberationist movement. Not only are some Islamic countries seen as victims of political and economic imperialism, but Islamic communities *within* non-Islamic states see themselves as oppressed and systematically discriminated against. In recent history many other groups have also adopted militant identity politics to counter their perceived oppression, including blacks in the USA, Aborigines in Australia and native Americans in the USA.

We also need to see this kind of deep cultural identity in terms of communities. Here we are asking what defines a community. In simple terms, a community may be nothing more than a group of people who live in a geographical location – a village or a district of a town or city. A 'cultural community', by contrast, does not concern itself with geography. It defines itself in terms of a common set of values, attitudes and beliefs that may be linked, typically, to religion (Jewish, Islamic), ethnicity (East African, Chinese) or historical experience (American blacks or native Indians).

Identity politics suggests that these differences in cultural identity have, or should have, political significance. The clearest example of such identity politics is when a cultural group considers itself to be systematically discriminated against. In such cases the cultural group may be seeking equality and legal protection. This was the basis of the black rights movement in the USA in the 1950s and 1960s and is a key element in modern Islamic movements. A further example is when the culture believes that its very identity is under threat. This is certainly true, as we have seen above, of those communities for whom language is critical, such as militant Welsh nationalism.

A less radical view of identity is represented by '**communitarianism**', largely associated with the Canadian philosopher Charles Taylor. Taylor, a critic of individualistic conceptions of liberalism, argues that the community within which the individual lives is crucial to his or her

perception of themselves. In other words, we see ourselves very much in terms of our ethnic, religious or cultural community, and not just as a unique individual. Furthermore, Taylor argues that modern liberal society is guilty of excessive 'block thinking' – that is, a tendency to see cultural groups as 'monolithic', giving them a single identity. In fact, he asserts that all groups are internally varied and have a great number of sub-groups within them. For example, the term 'Islam' is both misleading and dangerous. In reality there are many types of Muslim and many variations of Islam. This kind of communitarianism has important implications for multiculturalism.

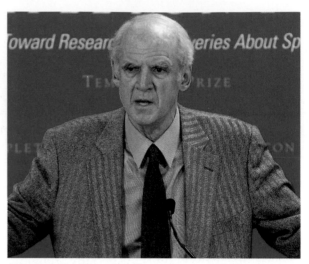

Charles Taylor, a leading advocate of identity politics

Key Term

Communitarianism

In general terms communitarianism is a challenge to social theories, especially liberalism, which sees society as made up of autonomous, unique individuals pursuing self-interest. The communitarian view challenges the liberal outlook, asserting that individuals do have a strong sense of community and recognise themselves in relation to the community. In multiculturalism, communitarianism implies that we see ourselves as members of particular communities that are distinctive in terms of religion, ethnicity or culture. It follows that communities should be recognised by the state and afforded respect, dignity and rights.

This so-called 'politics of recognition' argues that liberalism concentrates too much on individual identity and not enough on group identity. States do not recognise sufficiently the importance of community identity. This sense of group identity has not received enough respect and recognition. Politically, this has led to calls for greater recognition of group rights and identity in terms of anti-discrimination laws, positive discrimination and the legal protection of group rights. This concern with identity politics has become especially important in post-colonial states. Post-colonialism creates special problems for minority culture in new states.

Culture and pluralism

The liberal conception of pluralism is that modern societies inevitably contain many different groups and communities. The traditional circumstance of societies that are homogenous in terms of ethnicity and culture has now disappeared. Pluralism also recognises **particularism**. This is the phenomenon of individuals who see their own identity in terms of different layers of cultural distinctiveness. These layers may include ethnicity, race, religion and language. It becomes a rejection of the notion that individuals see themselves in terms of a single, overwhelming identity, usually nationality.

Key Term

Particularism

In general terms particularism simply means that individuals in a society see themselves in terms of a number of different identities, including race, ethnicity, religion, nationality, gender, sexual orientation, etc. In the context of culture, particularism refers specifically to one's social identity and is slightly more restricted towards nationality, ethnicity and religion.

Where a society contains such a plurality of identities it gives rise to the neutral, purely descriptive sense of the term 'multiculturalism'. A pluralist, multicultural society thus becomes no more than a society within which there are different cultures and different cultural identities that individuals use to define themselves. In the course of this chapter we will see multiculturalism as a contested term and a disputed goal, but here we are referring to the term purely as a description of a pluralistic collection of cultures co-existing in one national community. The implication of pluralism is that each group has equal status within a society, an idea that conflicts with both conservatives, who believe in natural inequality, and those who support identity politics (see above) and who demand special status for minority groups.

Although cultural pluralism is neutral, it leads directly to the most disputed aspect of multiculturalism, which is liberal in nature. This is known as 'cultural relativism'.

Cultural relativism

The concept of **cultural relativism** is a critical feature of multiculturalism and also forms the basis of its principal criticism. Cultural relativism is a belief that individuals see the world in terms of their own *culture*. In other words, our culture gives us a relatively different view of society and the world from other cultures. Thus, for example, according to cultural relativism, a Muslim sees the world differently to a Jew or a Christian, *because* he or she is a Muslim (or a Jew or a Christian). A simple example would be that a Muslim considers it immoral for one person to charge interest when lending another some money. This is in the teachings of the Koran. Jews and Christians, however, would find this kind of commercial behaviour quite acceptable and normal. More fundamentally, some cultures take a simple view of justice as 'an eye for an eye', etc., whereas others see justice as more complex, requiring a variety of remedies. Cultural relativism, therefore, asserts that neither concept of justice is *right*, but that both are equally valid according to the culture that adopts them.

This can become extremely controversial in some cases. Should, for example, such practices as female circumcision, child marriage, incestuous relationships or 'discrimination' against women be tolerated even though, in modern 'liberal' societies, they are considered to be unacceptable? Cultural relativists may argue that they can be tolerated because they are 'normal' within the cultures that operate them. In a global context, can it be acceptable for an American such as former Defence Secretary Donald Rumsfeld to describe parts of the Arab world as an 'Evil Empire' because it takes a different world view to his own?

As we shall see later, cultural relativism is the basis of much of the modern criticism of multiculturalism. These critics argue that cultural relativism paralyses governments, making them fearful of passing laws or prohibiting practices which may 'offend' a minority culture within the state (often known as 'political correctness'). Furthermore, it can tolerate practices and beliefs that many feel to be repugnant. Anne Phillips, a leading contemporary social theorist of culture and gender, has put this objection thus:

According to the critics, multiculturalism has promoted a cultural relativism that can no longer distinguish between right and wrong. Culture is operating as a reason for public inaction and an excuse for immoral behaviour.

From *Multiculturalism Without Culture*, 2007

We will see below that there are two answers to cultural relativism in the context of multiculturalism. One is to reject it totally in favour of 'positivism'. A positivist view would say that morality and ethics are absolute, notions of 'right' and 'wrong' are universal and eternal and so should not be subject to cultural interpretation. This was certainly a view taken at the Nuremburg Trials after World War Two to combat the Nazi claim that morality was a matter for the state. The other is to adopt the approach of Bhikhu Parekh, described in the next section. Parekh argues that multicultural society should accept that cultural relativism exists, but that it must be seen in the context of the dominant values of the society within which a minority culture exists. Thus, minority cultures should be tolerated as long as their practices do not contradict the fundamental values of the 'state culture'.

Key Term

Cultural relativism
A belief that the values, attitudes and morality of a culture should be seen in the context of that culture and not in the light of any abstract, positive sense of morality and values. In other words, individuals view the world in terms of their own culture.

Liberalism and multiculturalism

In order to set the scene for a discussion of liberal attitudes to multiculturalism we can use the words of Bhikhu Parekh (1935–), one of the leading liberal theorists on the subject. This is how he describes the challenge of multicultural societies:

Almost all contemporary societies are multicultural in the sense that their members entertain different conceptions of the good life and assign different meanings and significance to human activities and relations. This cultural diversity is a product of several interrelated factors, such as ethnic and religious diversity, moral individualism, decline in the traditional moral consensus, globalisation and immigration. Since none of these is likely to disappear in the foreseeable future, cultural diversity is a more or less permanent feature of modern life. Every society needs to acknowledge this fundamental fact and find ways of accommodating its demands without losing its cohesiveness and unity.

From *Prospect Magazine*, September 2005

Parekh here describes the essential dilemma for any society that is based on liberal ideals but which also wishes to maintain national unity. Historically, liberals have been more concerned by the threat to society posed by individuals and by the need for individual liberty. Modern multicultural theory, however, is interested in the impact of cultural groups, especially minorities, upon society.

Before examining the specific liberal case for multiculturalism, we need to remind ourselves of the liberal principles that underpin the debate and create problems:

- Clearly **liberals support individual liberty**. This creates a problem when the individuals within a minority culture believe that their own liberty is being threatened by the state's laws. Thus, for example, a member of a minority religion may see it as his undeniable and God-given right to force his daughter to marry a man of his rather than her choice. The father's freedom may not be upheld by a modern state; the state instead would seek to uphold the daughter's freedom to marry a man of her choice.

- The issue described above presents a second problem for liberals. In liberal tradition there is a strong sense of a **distinction between public and private spheres of life**. The state has no right to interfere with what is 'private' – i.e. has no negative impact on the rest of society – and what is public – a matter of public concern that *does* affect the rest of society. The case of forced marriage described above appears to be a private matter, an issue of that particular culture and/or religion. Thus liberals are constantly faced with the problem of where the public–private boundary lies, especially when minority groups place that boundary in different places.

- To complicate the matter further, **liberalism supports tolerance**. Here again, difficult questions arise as to how far a liberal society should tolerate minority activities and beliefs. This is especially difficult when a minority culture is *itself* intolerant. The liberal can argue that tolerance of 'self-regarding' actions, (activities and beliefs that do not affect others) can be easily sustained. If, however, a belief is 'other-regarding' and will adversely affect society, tolerance is severely tested. If such beliefs or actions are suppressed, liberals are open to the charge that they are oppressing a minority culture. This issue arose in the UK in the 1970s when Rastafarians, largely originating from the Caribbean, claimed that cannabis use was part of their religious belief and so should be tolerated even though, for most citizens, its use was illegal. Similarly Sikhs, for whom the carrying of a ceremonial dagger is obligatory for men, claim they should be exempt from laws relating to carrying such weapons.

- **Liberals support equal rights**, both for individuals and for groups. This is notable for its implications for minority rights. This may appear, at first sight, to present few problems as rights are simply enshrined in law. But, as we have seen above, the question remains whether society should allow minorities the right to engage in activities that, outside their own community, would be illegal. An example of this issue concerns the wearing of religious objects. If Christians in a predominantly Christian society may wear religious symbols, such as a crucifix, religious minorities should, according to the principle of equal rights, be allowed their own symbols. But some societies have sought to prevent women wearing a *hijab* (which covers much of the head and face) in certain circumstances, especially in schools. The French answer has been to ban *all* religious symbols by all groups and so preserve the principle of equal rights, but the problem remains in Britain, for example.

- **Liberals are pluralists**. This implies that they accept that society is made up of different groups and cultures and that they have a right to co-exist. It also goes further by claiming that the very diversity of society is a positive force. It enriches society and makes it more dynamic. This principle sits well with multiculturalism, but is also its greatest challenge as excessive pluralism may begin to threaten the stability and unity of the state and the nation.

The emergence of liberal multiculturalism

As we saw in the introduction to this chapter, multiculturalism was, to some extent, the product of necessity. This necessity arose from the need to accommodate the increasing movement of peoples with diverse cultures, ethnicities and religions into different societies, especially after the Second World War. This is not to say that multicultural societies had not existed before – the Roman and Greek Empires, for example, were in many ways multicultural in nature; indeed, many great empires have flourished *because* they understood it was better to tolerate and absorb the conquered cultures than to obliterate them. The USA, from its very birth in the eighteenth century, had been forced to deal with successive inflows of immigrants from all parts of the world. But the postwar era has seen the most extensive of all such challenges to the 'monoculturalism' (the acceptance that states have a right to impose one set of cultural norms upon its people) of the modern nation-state.

The problems coincided with the apparent 'victory' of liberalism and democracy over the forces of communism and totalitarianism in the modern age. Thus it was inevitably liberalism that sought to provide the answers to the issue of multiculturalism. A number of important principles of what we should call **liberal multiculturalism** thus came to the fore.

> ### ✔ Key Term
>
> **Liberal multiculturalism**
> The dominant form of multiculturalism, which became prominent from the 1970s onwards. Liberal multiculturalism accepts the reality of cultural diversity in modern societies and seeks to find principles and ways of reconciling such diversity with the other liberal ideals of tolerance, equal rights, the rule of law and the primacy of the nation-state, while also preserving the need to promote national unity and identity.

The neutral state

The celebrated American liberal philosopher John Rawls (1921–2002) was concerned with establishing the nature of a 'just' state. How, he asked, was a state to treat different cultures, religions and beliefs in a way that would prevent any of them unjustly imposing their beliefs and practices on others? He took, as his inspiration, the lessons of the Protestant Reformation and the liberal philosophers who had flourished within it. Such figures as John Locke, Jean-Jacques Rousseau and Voltaire had all argued for religious emancipation. For Locke it was arrogant for the followers of one belief to argue that their belief was superior to others. Voltaire had insisted that all had a right to express views, however repugnant they might be to others. Thus, those states that had attempted to enforce a 'state religion' on their people ultimately had to give way to religious diversity and tolerance.

Rawls argued that the modern liberal democratic state should remain 'neutral' in its treatment of different cultures and beliefs. There was, however, a proviso, which was that the freedom of one culture to express its views and carry on its practices had to be compatible with the freedom of all groups. The nature of Rawls' conception of the neutral state was that there should be no monopoly of belief about what constituted 'the good life'. Different groups' ideas of what constitutes 'the good life' must therefore be respected and protected. For Rawls there should be no orthodox state view of the good life. China and the Soviet Union have been clear examples of states that sought to do this and, in so doing, completely suppressed ethnic and cultural minorities within their borders. China continues to do so to this day (note its treatment of Tibet).

Pluralism

Rawls' conception of the neutral state did not go far enough for the supporters of multiculturalism. For them, pluralism meant that the cultural diversity of modern societies should be nurtured by the state. It was not sufficient for the state simply to remain unengaged with the issues. Thus states would have to engage actively in protecting minority cultures.

To a large extent this was achieved through legislation outlawing discrimination in such fields as law, politics, employment and education. In some cases law went further, offering 'positive discrimination' (known in the USA as 'affirmative action'), whereby members of religious, racial or ethnic minorities (as well as women in some cases) were offered an advantage in order to counteract the discriminatory effects of social discrimination. The main example of positive discrimination has been found in the employment field, where some employers in the USA and Europe have been forced to impose 'minority quotas' for some posts.

The principle behind such legal initiatives is that cultural diversity in all fields not only creates equality of opportunity but also ensures that all groups in society can play an active, positive role, can believe they have a stake in society and will thus be better integrated. As we shall see below, however, it is this conception of pluralism that also forms the basis of some of the most important criticisms of multiculturalism.

Perhaps the most controversial aspect of liberal pluralism in this context lies in the assertion that pluralism actually *strengthens* the unity of a society, rather than weakening it as some critics have claimed.

 Key Term

Toleration and Diversity
Implicit in liberal multiculturalism is the belief that all minority cultures have a right to toleration. The concept of diversity also implies that a culturally diverse society should be both tolerated and celebrated.

Liberal citizenship

The liberal conception of citizenship asserts that the rights of individual citizens are matched by obligations. Thus if individuals are to enjoy the rights bestowed on them by the state – for example, to take part in political activity, to be treated equally under the law and to be entitled to the benefits of the welfare state – they must also accept their civic duties – for example, to obey the laws, pay taxes and respect political institutions. This conception of citizenship is critical to multiculturalism.

Multiculturalism implies a contract with various groups in society. If their rights are to be respected and their cultural identity recognised and protected, they must also fulfil their obligations as citizens. The sociologist Amitai Etzioni (1929–) summed up the nature of this kind of multicultural citizenship in his so-called 'Golden Rule':

> Respect and uphold society's moral order as you would have society respect and uphold your autonomy.

However, the liberal conception of citizenship rights and equal rights created a problem for the multicultural movement. This related to the fact that different cultural and religious groups either claimed special rights that would enable them to preserve their own cultural identity or claimed some exemptions from obligations to obey laws that might offend their cultural identity. For example, Welsh nationalists have secured certain protections for the use of their language. These include the right to give evidence in court in Welsh and the right of school pupils to learn Welsh. Those who have travelled in Wales will have seen that road signs are written in both Welsh and English. Similarly, Sikhs have sought relief from the legal obligation in the UK to wear crash helmets when riding motorcycles on the grounds that it is a religious rule for them to wear a turban. Equally, Jewish school pupils are granted exemptions to attendance for religious holidays or to arrive home before dusk on Friday, the beginning of their sabbath.

These problems and exceptions have created challenges for liberal multiculturalists who seek to treat all groups equally and to reconcile different identities with an overarching national identity. This problem has led to the conception of 'multicultural citizenship'.

Multicultural citizenship

The liberal view of citizenship, as we have seen above, was largely concerned with individual rights and obligations. It took little account of group rights. The contemporary Canadian theorist Will Kymlicka has sought to develop multiculturalism is such a way as to accommodate group rights.

Kymlicka argues that multicultural, multi-ethnic societies are a fact of life. The challenge for liberal multiculturalism is not to ignore this reality or to seek to suppress it, but to recognise it and accommodate it within a liberal, pluralist society. The way to do this is to grant special group rights to minority communities. He describes this goal thus:

> So if ethnic politics are an enduring part of democratic life, it can nonetheless become a normal part of day-to-day democratic politics, not a uniquely explosive or destabilising issue. The long term goal, therefore, shouldn't be to extinguish or to solve ethnic politics once and for all, but rather to 'normalise' it.

From interview in *Eurozine*, 2008

The argument here is that ethnic and other cultural differences must be recognised by the modern liberal-democratic state, so much so that specific rights should be accorded to them. These can include the following:

- Special recognition for language and its use in public contexts, as in Canada (French) or in Wales.
- Positive discrimination for minority groups in the fields of politics, employment, education, etc.
- Exemptions from some legal obligations – for example, in dress regulations, holiday entitlement, employment regulation.
- Special rights in education to set up single-faith schools with distinctive curriculums.
- In some limited cases the right to use the state's legal system to enforce specific religious (as opposed to civic) laws. A more extreme version of this is to allow a religious minority to enforce its own laws within its own community. This debate has been most prominent in terms of the possible enforcement of elements of Islamic Sharia law.

Kymlicka and his followers therefore suggest that it is possible to accommodate such a recognition of separate group rights within a unified, cohesive society. This is often described in this context as communitarianism.

Following Kymlicka's ideas, Bhikhu Parekh has recognised the dangers of excessive communitarianism. His view is that modern multicultural societies should give equal importance to national and to group identity. He expresses it thus:

> Unity and diversity are equally important and neither should be secured at the expense of the other. If a multicultural society privileged unity and treated it as all-important, it would provoke resistance, violate an important human right, and forfeit the benefits of diversity. If it did the opposite, it would degenerate into a collection of mutely coexisting cultural ghettoes obsessed with their differences.

From *A Commitment to Cultural Pluralism*, 1997

Challenges to multiculturalism

The conservative/nationalist critique

This criticism of multiculturalism is relatively straightforward and predictable. It can best be understood in terms of a number of traditional conservative principles. These include the following:

- **Conservatives see society as organic**. This means that it should be seen as a single entity and that all its various parts are interrelated. The organic society is seen as natural and vital if good order and security are to be maintained. Multiculturalism challenges this organic view of society, stressing instead the fractured nature of the culture where many minorities are coexisting in the same state.

- **Conservatives are nationalists**. They see the nation as the natural community. Nations are, for them, based on common circumstances of birth. Cultural minorities do not share the common experiences of the dominant nation and so remain a threat to its unity. As a result,

more extreme conservatives seek to avoid a multicultural society by reducing or eliminating immigration. More moderate conservatives accept the reality of a multicultural society and seek to stress the need for minority groups to integrate and absorb the dominant culture.

- **Conservatives support traditional values**. The question arises, whose values? For a conservative the answer is simple, they are the values of the dominant nation. Clearly competing cultural values should therefore be discouraged or suppressed. As we have seen above, cultural relativism is unacceptable to a typical conservative.

- **Conservatives support traditional institutions**. Minority groups might not share an attachment to such institutions and so present challenges to their authority. The threat to established religion is the clearest example.

- **Conservatives promote law and order**. Multiculturalism is seen as a threat to both. Respect for law may be undermined by minority cultural attachments to competing conceptions of law (for example, Sharia law among Muslims). Order may be threatened from two directions. First, members of the dominant national culture may feel threatened by the rising status of other cultures and resort to conflict. Second, members of minority cultures may themselves feel discriminated against or oppressed and so promote their own conflict. Examples of both these effects have certainly been seen frequently in modern states over the past 50 years.

- **Conservatives believe that societies should evolve naturally**. Multiculturalism appears to them to be unnatural, being instead the artificial creation of societies with different cultures mixing together in ways they might not do naturally.

- **Conservatives are empiricists** and naturally sceptical. They can point to many historical examples of how multicultural societies have all, in the end, failed. Thus the multicultural

Roman Empire ultimately collapsed, as did the Ottoman Empire in which the dominant Turks had introduced a remarkable degree of religious and cultural tolerance.

It is perhaps all too easy to see the conservative critique as either simply 'racist' or xenophobic, but this would be to ignore the fundamental part played by the more reasoned conservative principles.

The liberal critique

Liberal criticisms of multiculturalism are more complex, largely because the multicultural movement itself was inspired by liberalism. So how is it possible for the philosophy that promoted multiculturalism to have become its greatest critic? One answer is that such critics are not actually seeking to abandon multiculturalism, but rather hope to modify it in the light of recent events and beliefs. The other is that some liberals now fear that multiculturalism has indeed gone too far and now threatens national unity and identity. Liberal criticisms have included the following:

- Perhaps the most strident critic has been Trevor Phillips, head of the former Commission for Racial Equality in the UK. His critique is all the more significant as Phillips was a former supporter of multiculturalism. Phillips' main argument is that multiculturalism is now causing inter-cultural conflict rather than reducing it. He famously suggested that, by giving minority cultures, especially ethnic groups, a special status, society is forcing them into 'ghettoes', which effectively separates such groups from mainstream society, rather than integrating them. In other words, multiculturalism has been achieving the very opposite of its main goal.

- Liberals have begun to argue that multiculturalism has been too 'essentialist' in nature. Essentialism in this context refers to the belief that each culture is a single, identifiable entity and that all members of a particular culture share the same *essential* characteristics. This, say liberal critics, is reducing cultural

analysis to simplistic terms. In fact each individual, they say, adopts his or her own version of their culture. Put simply, cultures are more complex and varied than many multiculturalists them give credit for. The danger is, therefore, that multiculturalism becomes a threat to people's individualism and individual needs. It can be especially dangerous when a cultural minority attracts negative reactions to itself. Thus it is extremely counterproductive to see all Muslims as fundamentalists who are engaged in a *jihad* against modern liberal culture. In fact there are many Muslims who are very moderate in their views and who wish to adopt a predominantly British identity. A similar analysis could be made of African-Caribbean or Jewish communities.

- The classical liberal tradition stresses the importance of individual liberty. It sees us all as free individuals with our own, sovereign will. Multiculturalism can be criticised by such classical liberals for denying individuality and, instead, assuming minorities adopt the will of their cultural community rather than their own individual will. In this sense, multiculturalism actually threatens liberty.

- Finally, it can be said that multiculturalism has created its own enemies. In this sense the 9/11 attack on New York and subsequent atrocities committed by Islamic jihadists in Madrid, Bali, London, Mumbai, etc. were traumatic blows to the multicultural movement. Some liberals suggested that attempts to impose liberal multicultural values upon the Arab (and other) parts of the world were, in themselves, intolerant of alternative cultural values. Thus, what was seen as a tolerant philosophy by its own adherents was seen as intolerant and imperialistic in other parts of the world. Some liberals have come to recognise this fault in their own philosophy.

Cosmopolitanism

The cosmopolitan approach is perhaps best seen as a new perspective rather than a critique. Cosmopolitanism sees people as 'global citizens' who have a consciousness that draws from many different cultures and not merely from one. Naturally cosmopolitanism has drawn strength from the growing phenomenon of globalisation. In particular, it recognises that there is an increasing mobility among many communities, which freely move from one part of the globe to another.

Cosmopolitanism also accepts that the individual may carry a number of different cultural identities simultaneously. Thus the characteristics 'black', 'Muslim', 'Arab', 'African', tribal allegiance and domicile (where the individual currently lives) may all exist in the same individual and may be seen as overlapping cultural identities, all of which influence the practices and values of that individual. Multiculturalism, especially when it is essentialist in nature, fails to recognise such overlapping identities.

It is also true that multiculturalism is concerned with maintaining national unity. By recognising cultural differences and the claims of minorities to their own rights, status and dignity, it is hoped to maintain national allegiance. Cosmopolitan thinking challenges national identity as a desirable goal. We have multiple identities in the modern, global context so multiculturalism becomes superfluous.

Issues in multiculturalism

Is multiculturalism dead?

The answer to this is almost certainly no. It is also undeniably true that multiculturalism has been transformed from its original 1970s' conception. We can simplify the discussion in the following way.

The weaknesses of modern multiculturalism
- Conservatives have now largely rejected multiculturalism on the basis that intercommunal tensions in many parts of the world – notably Paris, Northern English towns and cities, India and Holland – prove that encouraging cultural diversity simply creates

rather than suppresses conflict. The view of critic Trevor Phillips (see earlier on p. 251) is that multiculturalism has increasingly emphasised the 'differentness' of cultures to such an extent that it has come to threaten a dominant national identity and culture.

- Nationalists now see multiculturalism as a threat to the future of the modern nation-state. By weakening patriotism and national culture, multiculturalism threatens the authority of the national government within its own territory.

- Cosmopolitan thinkers argue that multiculturalism is outdated and takes little account of globalisation. The old model of seeing individuals as having a *dual* identity must be rejected as too simple. Instead, individuals have multiple cultural identities.

- Many liberals now believe that multiculturalism is threatening individual liberty. It places too much emphasis on national identity and cultural identity and not enough on individual identity (i.e. particularism). They argue we must return to the situation where the state respects the rights and freedoms of individuals rather than of whole communities.

- Terrorism has placed a huge stress on multicultural thinking. When minority groups are willing to attack the communities in which they have settled, it becomes increasingly difficult for other members of the community to tolerate their presence and their cultural 'deviance'. This may be an irrational reaction to the activities of a small, unrepresentative minority, but it is a reaction that severely undermines multiculturalism. As Francis Fukuyama has also famously commented, the reason why Islamic terrorism has shocked the Western liberal world (apart, of course, from the deaths and injuries it has caused) is that it had been assumed that the values of liberal democracy and capitalism were universally supported. Thus multiculturalism had been based on the belief that individuals could maintain a dual cultural identity, their own *plus* that of Western liberalism. The fundamentalists reject this notion as they do not accept liberal democracy as a desirable culture in itself. In other words, as Fukuyama continued, multiculturalism has been an 'ornament' for liberal democracy, but it cannot be sustained if the basis of liberalism is itself challenged.

The enduring strengths of multiculturalism

Despite a broad-based attack on multiculturalism, especially since 2001, the fundamental values of the movement have survived and retain important supporters. Though it has been extensively modified, multiculturalism is defended on the following grounds:

- The crisis in multiculturalism created by Islamic 'extremism' may be a temporary condition. If there is a settlement in the Middle East, resolutions to the conflict in Iraq, Afghanistan and Pakistan as well as in Israel/Palestine, it may be that Muslim groups in Western society will be able to return to integration.

- Some have argued that there are always tensions and difficulties when 'alien' groups are being absorbed into indigenous populations. The current problems are, therefore, nothing new and may be resolved in the long term.

- Critics, such as Trevor Phillips, have suggested that the weakness of multiculturalism has been the result of a failure by national cultures to assert themselves and their identity. Thus, it has not been the strength of minority cultures that has threatened multiculturalism but rather the *weakness* of national culture. The recent 'counter-attack' by those who wish to re-assert national identity, notably in Britain, Holland and France, may have the effect of restoring multiculturalism rather than damaging it further. Two factors lie behind this. One is the weakening of cultural relativism and the other is the recent attack on essentialism.

  - Cultural relativism weakened national identity because it suggested that minority groups should be tolerated even if they challenged Western liberal values. By reasserting the universal strength of those values and rejecting such a relative approach, multiculturalism can fight back.

  - Essentialism failed to recognise the different elements and variations within minority cultures. With increasingly sensitive understanding of the nature of cultural identity and its complexities, multiculturalism can save itself. Tariq Modood, a contemporary supporter of multiculturalism, has pointed out that cultural identity is not a simple concept and that it is common for individuals to adopt multiple identities. Policy on multiculturalism must and can, therefore, recognise this 'differentness' feature of most cultures.

- Tariq Modood summarises how multiculturalism can survive. In essence this requires two developments. One is to recognise that members of minority cultures have complex attitudes to their identity and this should be taken account of. Specifically attention must be paid to creating greater social mobility for members of ethnic and religious minorities. Second, there must be a re-assertion of national identity and a strong sense of citizenship to which all can subscribe.

The Report of the Commission for Multi-Ethnic Britain (CMEB, also known as 'The Parekh Report') summed up the hope that there is a way forward for multiculturalism on the basis of a synthesis between national aims and the future of each individual and each group. In the words of the report writers:

If people are to have a sense of belonging to society as a whole, to have a sense of sharing a common fate with fellow citizens and nationals they must be able to feel that their own flourishing as individuals and as communities is intimately linked with the flourishing of public institutions and public services.

From *Report of the Commission on Multi Ethnic Britain*, 2000

Why has multiculturalism been challenged by identity politics?

Identity politics, as we have seen above, can be seen as a response to the belief among certain minority groups that they have been the subject of oppression and discrimination by a dominant culture. This has sometimes been described as 'cultural imperialism'.

An important illustration of the clash between identity politics was provided during the civil rights movement in the USA in the 1960s. Martin Luther King represented the liberal (effectively multicultural, in modern terms) approach. While accepting the past oppression of the black population of America, King campaigned for liberal values such as equality of opportunity, equal rights, tolerance and the end of discriminatory policies and practices. A famous passage from his 1963 Lincoln Memorial speech ilustrates the King view:

> I have a dream that my four little children will one day live in a nation where they will not be judged by the color of their skin but by the content of their character.

The radical opponents of King's movement argued that, by advocating a 'colour-blind' approach to the liberation of his people, he was denying their very 'identity'. The militant black power movement, by contrast, hoped to assert black identity, not suppress it.

The modern equivalent of the schism in the black liberation movement of the 1960s is the position taken by fundamentalist Islamists in Europe, mainly in the UK. Here again, fundamentalists have resisted integration and assimilation on the grounds that it threatens the Muslim identity of its members, an identity that is fundamentally in conflict with liberal democratic values. Muslims in Europe see no distinction between the oppression of Muslim and Arab peoples in the Middle East and the 'suppression' of Islamic culture in Birmingham or Leeds.

Those who advocate identity politics reject the liberal claim that policies to provide equal rights, and equal opportunities and which outlaw discrimination do not address the real problem for minorities. The real problem is the failure of Western liberal society to recognise the identity of minority groups and to recognise its essential 'differentness'. Instead of the multicultural initiatives described above, identity militants wish to promote more positive, challenging developments. These include:

- Positive discrimination in favour of minorities (blacks in the USA).

- Recognition for national minorities in terms of political autonomy (Quebec nationalists in Canada, Basques in Spain).

- Special status for cultural institutions such as language, laws and and cultural 'social norms' (Welsh language militants, Sharia law among Muslims, tolerance of special culturally based marriage practices).

Identity politics of this kind claims that multiculturalism is seeking to suppress these distinctions in a number of ways, for example:

- By imposing equality upon cultures there is an attempt to reduce cultural differences by suggesting that all cultures have equal status.

- By encouraging minority groups to integrate with national culture, the dominant culture is actually attempting to 'assimilate' them and so destroy their identity.

- By insisting on the adoption of a dual identity – a national culture alongside minority cultures – by individuals there is an assumption that the national cultural identity is equal or superior to the group's. Certainly radical Scottish nationalists have presented this argument in support of full political independence.

- Religious minorities have claimed that the imposition of legal constraints upon their religious leaders in the guise of 'tolerance' is, in fact, an attempt to suppress religious belief and practices.

- Minority ethnic groups have argued that multiculturalism seeks to eliminate ethnic 'awareness', in the guise of the outlawing of 'colour prejudice'. Groups with a strong ethnic identity seek to protect that identity rather than de-emphasise it.

How do feminists view multiculturalism?

First, there is one clear feminist critique of multiculturalism and this rests with the attitude towards cultural relativism. As we have seen above, cultural relativism places no moral or ethical judgements upon cultural practices but accepts them as embedded in the culture. However, the problem for many feminists is that a wide range of cultural practices seems to involve the unequal (at best) or oppressive and cruel (at worst) treatment of women.

On the milder scale we see the reduced status of women in some (but certainly not all) Muslim communities. At the extreme level the Afghan Taliban have sought to deny women access to education and will not allow them paid employment. Until recently women in Saudi Arabia were forbidden from driving cars. Similarly many Islamic societies demand the wearing of clothes that obscure most of the female form and face. In many cultures forced marriage is practised and in some cases child brides are tolerated. At the more extreme end of the spectrum we see female circumcision, the stoning to death of women caught in adultery and 'honour killings' by family members when a woman takes an 'unsuitable' partner. Most feminists will not accept the relativist view that such practices might be tolerated because they are culturally embedded. So feminists criticise advocates of multiculturalism who give support for such cultural practices.

On a more general level, feminists have noted that many so-called 'traditional' societies tend to be intensely patriarchal in nature. Here again opposition to multiculturalism has a clear agenda – that if feminism is opposed to patriarchy, it must, by definition, be most opposed to the most patriarchal cultures. This was very much the view of leading liberal feminist Susan Okin (1946–2004). She argued that the subjugation of women was immoral and therefore any culture that allowed it should be suppressed or at least it should be subjected to demands to reform itself if it is to take its place in modern society. Okin adds that, because the institution of the family is, in itself, oppressive to women, traditional cultures that have especially strong family values oppress women more than cultures with weaker family structures. Here again she is denying John Rawls' original position – that all cultures are fundamentally equal.

However, the feminist opposition to multiculturalism is not universal. There are some who argue that women are equally subjugated in the West and in traditional societies. Indeed they argue that traditional societies, by controlling the status of women and by laying down strict rules of conduct for women and for men in their relations with women, are actually protecting women from exploitation. The dignity and identity of women is better protected in traditional culture, say many post-colonial feminists. Colonialism, they argue, sought to impose upon subject peoples a Western, therefore patriarchal, view of women. Those countries that have liberated themselves from colonial rule can, therefore, also claim to be liberating women from a subordinate status in society. When post-colonial cultures come into contact with Western society, it follows, respect should be shown for their cultural practices.

In summary, it would probably be accurate to say that most modern feminists remain anti-multicultural on the grounds that cultures that do not respect women should not be tolerated. However, there is a liberal, compromise position, which states that multiculturalism is appropriate, but that any practice that is clearly against the interests of women, oppressing and exploiting them, should be held as illegal, while other cultural practices can be tolerated. Women's rights are regarded by such feminists as an absolute, and multiculturalism must never endanger them in societies where such rights have been hard won.

How have socialists and Marxists viewed multiculturalism?

As background to this question it can be clearly stated that Marx himself, and his close followers such as Lenin and Karl Kautsky, saw interest in cultural identity as a diversion from an understanding of the true nature of class and capitalist exploitation of workers. They were, therefore, unsympathetic to movements that sought to raise the issues of culture and the liberation of minorities as dangerous threats to the cause of true socialism. In the communist states of the twentieth century it was common that cultural minorities were suppressed. The reason for this was the fear that well-developed cultural identity would inhibit the development of true socialist consciousness. It could therefore be said, with a great deal of evidence from the Soviet Union and China, that Marxist-inspired communism is mutually exclusive to multiculturalism.

Modern, post-Marxist socialists have tended to see multiculturalism as a classic liberal attempt to create an illusion of equality (by treating all cultures as having equal value) and thus disguising the inherent inequality of capitalism. But a more thorough critique suggests that multiculturalism can be seen as an element of post-colonial exploitation. A socialist perspective is that in the colonial era, the poor of the Third World were exploited in the interests of international capitalism. No surprise in that. In the post-colonial era, however, the matter is less simple. Many modern socialists have seen the mass immigration from Third World countries to Western capitalist states as an extension of colonialism. By this analysis, the immigrant groups are no longer exploited in their own country but are exploited in modern, developed states instead. Multiculturalism is seen by such socialists as an element in this exploitation.

The liberal policy of encouraging different cultures to flourish and be tolerated in modern capitalist states may not seem to involve exploitation. Socialists, however, have suggested that the integration of minority cultures has been used as a means by which the groups *can* indeed be economically exploited. If ethnic and religious minorities from poorer countries were not encouraged to integrate and were subjected to cultural suppression (as they had been in communist states), the nature of their exploitation would be brought into focus and conflict would undoubtedly result. By embracing such groups, liberals are disguising the fact that they remain subjects of exploitation – providing cheap labour, working in poor conditions and often suffering unemployment when there is an economic downturn. Even the liberal claim that there is now equality of opportunity for all groups can be combated by evidence suggesting that social mobility is largely absent from many ethnic and cultural minorities. Both socialists and supporters of identity politics agree that, if liberals were serious about multiculturalism, they would introduce *positive* ways of offering economic opportunity for the minorities.

If we consider moderate social democrats, however, we find a more sympathetic view of the multicultural agenda. Indeed multiculturalism has been seen as the product of a liberal–social democrat alliance. Inspired by the views of John Rawls, social democrats (including New Labour) have stressed the principle that all groups in society should be treated equally. In a just society, Rawls stated, freedom, rights and opportunities must be evenly distributed. This equal distribution applies both to individuals and to specific cultural, ethnic or religious groups. The view that all human beings are of equal value is thus extended to all groups having equal value.

The social democrat agenda of granting equal rights, extending equality of opportunity, providing welfare when capitalism fails to serve the interests of the worst off in society and promoting social mobility sat well with multiculturalism. The communitarian aspects of social democracy, influenced by Amitai Etzioni (1929–), insisted that minority cultures should adopt the dominant values of their 'parent state', while, in return, the state would respect their own freedom, values, customs and practices. This creates a balance between the state and its component groups, an equality with which such moderate social democrats can readily agree.

As we have seen, therefore, there is no single answer to the question of how socialists view multiculturalism. It totally depends upon what kind of socialism is being considered. In general we can say that, as socialism has moved further away from its fundamentalism roots it has become increasingly sympathetic to multiculturalism.

Key multicultural thinkers

Charles Taylor (Canada, 1931–)

Taylor is a philosopher who became best known for his championing of the cause of recognition for French Canadians in Quebec as a separate cultural group from the rest of Canada. His philosophy of identity became known as the 'politics of recognition'. This idea asserts that multiculturalism of a liberal kind has tended to ignore the claims of minority cultures to full recognition as *different* and *separate*.

It is not sufficient, as liberals have suggested, to tolerate minority cultures and to give them legal rights and protection. More must be done to ensure that these cultures survive. The reason for his assertion that minority cultures are too important to ignore lies in his claims concerning the nature of individual identity. Liberals see us as individuals and therefore create social and political systems that guarantee the assertion of one's individualism. Taylor says that we see our identities in terms of the cultural communities in which we grow up and in which we live. Therefore political systems must recognise the importance of such groups. A clear example is Taylor's belief that it is not sufficient simply to tolerate the use of the French language in Quebec. It is also necessary, argues Taylor, to protect the language positively and even to require all

French-origin inhabitants of Quebec to learn the language and to use it in specific circumstances.

Taylor also criticises liberals for concentrating on individual rights and ignoring group rights. He therefore proposes that modern societies should add statements of group rights as well as individual rights to their constitutional arrangements. Further to this, he argues that all minority communities should flourish on the same basis and status as the national state as a whole. In practice this may well mean political autonomy for national minorities and legal protection for their language and cultural practices.

Thus, Taylor is a critic of multiculturalism, but also proposes his own version of the doctrine, usually known as communitarianism. Integration and assimilation, possibly the long-term goals of multiculturalism, are thus to be opposed because they are a fundamental denial of cultural identity and will lead to alienation, the very negation of integration.

Bhikhu Parekh (British-Indian, 1935–)

Parekh rose to prominence when he chaired a British-based Commission on Multi-Ethnic Britain in 2000 in response to inter-communal strife in some industrial towns and cities in Northern England. He is a strong supporter of multiculturalism, but pleads for its modernisation and adaption to an increasingly global and diverse world. He makes three key assertions about culture:

1 Every individual understands the world in terms of both his or her own cultural identity and membership and the view of other cultures. He describes the cultural experience of each individual as 'cultural embeddedness'. This phenomenon suggests that people largely view the world in terms of their cultural upbringing, though not exclusively.

2 No single culture has a monopoly of understanding of what constitutes the best sort

of life, though many claim to do so. In fact all cultures can make a contribution to our understanding of the ideal 'good life'. Furthermore, not all cultures are of equal value, though all minority cultures do have *some* value.

3 Cultures are not single entities with only one single identity. They are themselves internally pluralistic and have different strands of thought and belief. Cultures are also constantly changing and responding to pressures placed on them from the outside world.

Parekh has criticised multiculturalists for not recognising sufficiently these three features of minority cultures. But he has also suggested that multiculturalism became weakened because it ignored the importance of developing a shared sense of national identity. This is how he expressed his support for national culture:

A multicultural society cannot be stable and last long without developing a common sense of belonging among its citizens. The sense of belonging cannot be ethnic and based on shared cultural, ethnic and other characteristics, for a multicultural society is too diverse for that, but must be political and based on a shared commitment to the political community. Its members do not directly belong to each other as in an ethnic group but through their mediating membership of a shared community, and they are committed to each other because they are all in their own different ways committed to a common historical community.

From *What is Multiculturalism?* India Seminar, Delhi, 1999

Parekh also criticised multiculturalism on the grounds that, while expecting greater commitment by minority cultures to national identity, too little had been done to ensure that the national society recognised the separate identity of minorities. In this sense he is a follower of Charles Taylor, albeit a moderate one. Parekh has advocated the need for differential rights, where necessary, giving special recognition to the need to pay attention to the different cultural perspectives of groups. This is not to say that 'evil' or even 'bad' practices by minority groups should be tolerated, but it does mean that different norms of behaviour should be recognised. Furthermore, Parekh is a supporter of positive discrimination for minorities and special legal protections against discrimination and prejudice.

In his analysis of alienation, Parekh believes that it is possible to enjoy all the rights of citizenship, to have one's rights protected, to be treated equally and with tolerance and yet still feel a stranger in one's own country. This is because **cultural embeddedness** is a reality and needs to be recognised, not suppressed, by the state.

 Key Term

Cultural embeddedness
This is the belief that the individual's personal identity is determined largely by the culture within which they have grown up. In other words, one's identity is embedded in one's own particular *culture* rather than in one's nationality or citizenship. Some critics of multiculturalism have suggested that such cultural embeddedness has not been sufficiently recognised.

Exam focus

Using this chapter and other resources available to you, answer the following questions.

Short questions

Your answers should be about 400 words long.
1 Why have conservatives criticised multiculturalism?
2 Why have some liberals criticised multiculturalism?
3 Distinguish between identity politics and multiculturalism.
4 Why has cosmopolitanism challenged multiculturalism?

Long questions

Your answers should be about 1200 words long.
1 How and to what extent do liberal and conservative criticisms of multiculturalism differ?
2 On what grounds do nationalists criticise multiculturalism?
3 How does multiculturalism justify the flourishing of separate cultural identities within the modern nation-state?
4 To what extent has multiculturalism been discredited?

Further reading

Gutmann, A. (ed.) (1992) *Multiculturalism and the Politics of Recognition*, Princeton University Press.
Kymlicka, W. (1995) *Multicultural Citizenship*, Oxford University Press.
McGhee, D. (2008) *The End of Multiculturalism?*, Open University Press.
Modood, T. (2005) *Multicultural Politics*, Edinburgh University Press.
Modood, T. (2007) *Multiculturalism*, Polity.
Parekh, B. (2005) *Rethinking Multiculturalism*, Palgrave.
Phillips, A. (2007) *Multiculturalism Without Culture*, Princeton University Press.
West, P. (2005) *The Poverty of Multiculturalism*, Civitas.

Chapter 9

Conclusion: Critically assessing ideologies

This concluding chapter suggests various approaches that can be taken when seeking to evaluate the ideologies that are described and analysed in this book. We have seen that all ideologies contain internal divisions, and this gives rise to internal criticisms. For example, fundamentalist socialists take issue with revisionists as the latter fail to understand the true exploitive nature of capitalism. Similarly, radical feminists have criticised liberal feminists for failing to understand the 'political' nature of patriarchy. Here we propose more general, external approaches that can be taken to criticism.

The Conservative Critique

As we have seen in the chapter on conservatism, the movement partly defines itself by its opposition to ideology and to political dogma in general. Here we can examine a more comprehensive criticism based on a conservative outlook, rather than on the conservative movement specifically. In other words we can here consider the argument that ideologies are flawed for three fundamental reasons. One is that they make assumptions about the nature of mankind that cannot be sustained. The second is that ideologies hope to transform society in artificial ways and so are a denial of natural evolution. Finally, conservatives fear that ideological thought and action tends to be oppressive in nature. In other words, sooner or later, ideological regimes will oppress their subjects in the name of the ideology.

Human nature

Anarchism is particularly susceptible to the first criticism, especially collectivist anarchism. It makes extremely optimistic views of mankind's nature, seeing us as naturally sociable and co-operative. Like all communists, collectivist anarchists assert that we are capable of living and working for the good of the social whole and not merely in our own, self-interested interests. Thus the charge of 'utopianism' is a powerful one. It is intensely utopian, say conservatives, to believe that communism can operate permanently. It will ultimately fail because it does not conform to human nature. Liberalism is another optimistic philosophy as it believes that mankind can use personal freedom largely for good ends. Here again conservatives are sceptical. Too much freedom, they argue, will lead to disorder because excessive liberty will lead to conflict between individuals. Ironically there is some common ground between individualist anarchists and New Right (neo-liberal) conservatives. Both these traditions see mankind as essentially competitive and individualistic. Thus, a world free of almost any interference by laws and governments can conform to human nature.

Feminism also makes assumptions about the nature of men, about women and about relations between them. Though there are many variations on this theme among feminists, they have one feature in common: that is, that women are, or have the potential to be, *at least* equal to men. Conservatives have argued strongly that the reason for patriarchy is natural – society has evolved in such a way that it is inevitable that men should play dominant roles. This does not necessarily mean that patriarchy is a desirable state of affairs, merely that it is *natural.*

Conservative and fascist views of human nature have some common features. Both philosophies see mankind as having two characteristics. One is a drive to power ('will to power' as Nietzsche famously described it), the other is frailty and 'herd instinct'. This implies clearly that men (specifically men in the case of fascism) will seek to exercise power over their fellow men, but that they are also easily led. Edmund Burke, in his 1790 commentary on the French Revolution, noted the effect of both these tendencies. Clearly conservatives reject fascism because of its complete denial of individualism, but their criticism of fascism's view of human nature is relatively muted.

Conservatives take issue with many ecologists on one clear level. This is the controversy over whether mankind has been granted – by God or nature – dominion over the natural world. If conservatives are right and humans are separate from and superior to the natural world, much radical environmental thought becomes invalid. This is not to say that a conservative cannot be an environmentalist, rather that he or she is likely to take the 'shallow' rather than the 'deep' green perspective. The conservative view would be that environmental protection is part of our duty as 'guardians' of the natural world. Radical, deep, ecologists are calling for more fundamental change in the relationship between humans and nature – to one of equality – which conservatives would reject.

Social progress

Conservatives oppose artificial 'blueprints' for society. They argue strongly that society should be allowed to evolve naturally. There is no sense of 'progress' in traditional conservative thought and this is the opposite perspective to most ideological thought. As the great conservative philosopher, Michael Oakeshott, suggested, societies are like ships adrift in an open sea with no port of origin and no destination. Ideologies such as Marxism and anarcho-syndicalism do propose specific forms of society, which are either desirable or, as Marxists argue, the inevitable conclusion of the process of history. Supporters of liberal multiculturalism can be similarly criticised. Some conservatives accuse multiculturalism of proposing a kind of social structure that simply does not exist. The idea that different cultural groups should be able to respect each other and that they have equal value, may simply be impractical because societies do not evolve naturally in such a way. In other words, there is a natural tendency for different groups to seek exclusivity and to consider themselves somehow superior, certainly to others.

Ecologism can, perhaps, avoid the conservative criticism on practical grounds. If, they would argue, human society is allowed to evolve naturally, it will simply destroy its own natural environment and, ultimately, itself. If mankind is to survive, therefore, perhaps intervention is essential. If human progress is headed towards a cliff, therefore, conservatives have to accept that a change of course may have to be imposed. Even so, many American neo-conservatives (such as George W. Bush) have even suggested that no intervention is needed to 'save the planet'. They suggest that, ultimately, free market forces will provide their own solutions. These are likely to be technological in nature. Neo-conservatives are certainly not ecologists.

The fascist view – that there is also no specific destination for history – accords with conservative thought. However, fascists also believe that societies should aggressively pursue certain goals, and this cannot be supported by conservatives. For fascists it is the role of the dominant leader to determine the destiny of a people. For conservatives there is no such thing as destiny. Society changes according to the forces of natural evolution and in accordance with the traditions and inclinations of the people, they insist. The idea that a single individual should lead a whole people towards their own vision of the future cannot be supported by conservatives. This is not to be confused with the conservative liking for strong, paternalist political leadership. The typical strong conservative leader is one who rules in accordance with the traditions of the people and takes note of their needs and goals. The fascist leader is not at all inclined to listen to his people, and pursues his own vision relentlessly.

But is it fundamentalist socialists, especially Marxists, who come in for the severest criticism by conservatives. The Marxist analysis of history follows a German (after the philosopher Hegel) tradition that history is moving through a series of stages towards its own, inevitable conclusion. This is a world where there is no alienation, and no contradiction between the goals of individuals and the goals of society as a whole. This world is one where there is perfect freedom because those contradictions have been removed. For Marxists this was known as the final, communist, stage. Conservatives completely reject such a view of history. This is on two fundamental grounds. First, there are no such thing as 'historical forces' and, second, because there can never be a world where individualism is made compatible with socialism. As we have seen above, it is based on a false view of human nature.

Radical feminists have not adopted a single, common view of the future, but they are nevertheless criticised by conservatives on the grounds that all feminists are denying the natural order of society whatever change they are proposing. A world where men and women are truly 'equal' is perfectly acceptable to conservatives. The issue concerns how we reach such a situation. If it occurs naturally conservatives can accept it. If it is achieved through radical political action, on the other hand, it should be resisted. A similar criticism can be levelled by conservatives against liberal multiculturalism. If it occurs naturally, so be it.

But multiculturalism should not be treated as though it were a fixed ideology.

Oppression

We can turn to the experience of the French Revolution to guide us towards the most important conservative fear of ideological oppression. It was Robespierre's Jacobin Party that was largely responsible for the 'reign of terror' which followed the revolution. From this experience the term 'jacobinism' is derived. Jacobinism can be described as the 'tyranny of ideas'. It involves the ruthless imposition of ideas upon a people.

In the case of the French Revolution there was a considerable irony involved. The high ideals of the revolutionaries famously included liberty, equality and fraternity, yet the way in which they were imposed became a denial of the very values on which they were based. The idea that 'freedom' could be imposed is a contradiction in terms. This experience informed conservatism for the next two hundred years.

The experiences of the Soviet Union and its communist allies, of Nazi Germany, Mao Zedung's China, and, in more recent times, of some religious fundamentalist regimes such as the rule of the Taliban in Afghanistan, confirm the conservative fear of ideology. The problem is that ideologies will never be supported actively by all the people. Yet the supporters of ideologies do seek complete compliance. Therefore oppression becomes necessary.

The ideologies that come in for most criticism by conservatives are those that require complete subservience by the people and which break down the barriers between what is 'public' and what is 'private'. When all aspects of human life and behaviour become relevant to a ruling ideology, totalitarianism takes over. In any religious fundamentalist regime (we may describe religious fundamentalism as an ideology here) every aspect of a person's life is subject to ideological limitations and guidance. Almost the same was true in Hitler's Germany and Mao Zedung's China.

Of course, not all ideologies necessarily involve such oppression. Feminists, ecologists and individual anarchists all would deny that their ideas should lead to such oppression – and indeed there is certainly no prospect that any of them could spawn a society approaching Nazi Germany or the USSR. Nevertheless, conservatives do assert that all supporters of an ideology have a tendency to try to impose their views on others. Even liberal supporters of multiculturalism have been accused of this.

Conservatism and nationalism

There is little contradiction between conservatism and nationalism on the whole. Indeed conservatives are, on the whole, nationalists by nature. It therefore follows that conservatives do not normally criticise or oppose nationalism. That said, there is one sense in which conservatives are concerned. This relates to more radical forms of nationalism that may become a threat to peace and security and which may become overly ideological in nature.

Fascism as a form of radical nationalism is the best example of this. Conservatives can support the fascist goal of uniting a people around a common sense of national identity. But when radical nationalism becomes too expansionist, xenophobic and even racialist in nature, it carries a threat that conservatives cannot tolerate. When nationalism becomes a *divisive* rather than a unifying force, it is to be opposed. Thus, militant British nationalism, represented by the British National Party (BNP), is criticised partly on the grounds of its racist elements, but also because it threatens the unity of British society.

When we consider nationalism that becomes imperialism, the picture is less clear. Traditionally conservatives have supported imperialism, mainly on paternalistic grounds – that it is a way of spreading civilisation throughout the world. Contemporary conservatives, however, have pragmatically accepted that the age of imperialism is now past. They have therefore, joined the generally accepted world view, that imperialism is no longer acceptable.

The Liberal Critique

There are some liberal traditions that can themselves be described as ideologies. Classical liberalism of the nineteenth century, together with its offspring, social Darwinism, has sometimes been described as ideological. Its dogmatic attachment to free markets and minimal government certainly has an ideological element. This is also true of modern neo-liberalism, which became part of a wider political movement known as the New Right in the 1970s–1990s. Opposition to government intervention and a belief that free markets have a solution to all social and economic issues have been rigidly supported by neo-liberals. Certainly conservatives, as we have seen above, were almost as opposed to these doctrines as they were to socialism and fascism. But mainstream liberalism, as we generally understand it today, is not usually described as an ideology.

Much of the liberal concern with ideologies is held in common with conservatism. Above all there is the danger of oppression and the loss of liberty that would automatically result from that. To some extent, liberals have criticised radical feminism on these grounds. Conservatives see the militant approach of the radicals as a danger to the liberty and individualism of both men and women. Some liberals have even begun to challenge multiculturalism on the grounds that it is too dogmatic in its approach to culture and society.

Liberals also see ideology as a threat to tolerance. Supporters of ideology, they point out, are intolerant of both their opponents and of other, rival ideologies. The more ideological a political movement is, the more intolerant it becomes, say liberals. Indeed, John Locke, one of the 'fathers' of liberalism, saw such dogmatism (in his case, religious dogma) as an exercise in arrogance, a belief that one's own beliefs are superior to another's. Tolerant liberals accept that all beliefs have their merits as long as they do not propose harm to others. They all have a right to co-exist. But ideologies tend to be exclusive, they do not tolerate rivals and so oppress those who hold other beliefs.

Flowing from their belief in tolerance, modern liberals also support pluralism. Social and political systems can and should encompass a wide spectrum of interests and beliefs. This is not only desirable in the interests of freedom and tolerance, it also makes society more dynamic. The free interplay of values and ideas can stimulate progress on all fronts – economic, technological, intellectual, social and aesthetic. By contrast, ideologies threaten pluralism. It is remarkable that ideological regimes, such as fascism, soviet communism and religious fundamentalism, all tend to make the destruction or subversion of civil society a priority. Indeed, it could be said that ideology is the direct enemy of pluralism.

Liberal critics of ideology have a problem. This is the question of the extent to which they should tolerate ideologies. A liberal's instincts for tolerance tell him or her that ideological beliefs are all valid. On the other hand, liberals recognise the threats to liberty, tolerance and pluralism presented by ideology. As a general rule they tolerate beliefs that share their beliefs in freedom and tolerance, but making judgements on this basis are often difficult.

The 'End of Ideology' Critique

Two contemporary thinkers have led the way in this movement: Daniel Bell (1919–) and Francis Fukuyama. Both proposed that the age of ideology is dead and that the world has entered a new era in which ideologies have disappeared or have become unimportant. Their criticism is, therefore, based on a belief, not that ideologies are undesirable or simply wrong, but on the theory that they have become irrelevant.

Bell's best-known work, *The End of Ideology* (1960), foresaw the end of the Cold War. He argued that class warfare was becoming an outdated idea, that capitalism, democracy and liberalism had triumphed and that left-wing ideologies, especially Marxism, were no longer

relevant. As ideology was largely the product of class conflict, Bell argued, it would wither away. In place of conflict society, he described a modern 'post industrial society' or 'information society', where mass production no longer dominates, replaced by service industries and information technology. Ideology thrives on the existence of large masses of alienated people, but contemporary economic and social structures are eliminating such alienation. Everybody can take part in the new information society (this was astonishingly predictive as it pre-dated the development of the internet). However, Bell himself can be criticised as he under-estimated the development of new conflicts to replace those involving economic class. Thus, the politics of gender, ethnicity and religion have come to replace the socialist perspective, which is very restricted.

Francis Fukuyama also announced the end of ideology, but he, like Bell, has been greatly criticised and has, indeed, accepted the flaws in his own theory. In his great work, *The End of History and the Last Man* (1992), Fukayama proclaimed the triumph of Western liberalism thus:

> *The most remarkable development of the last quarter of the twentieth century has been the revelation of enormous weaknesses at the core of the world's seemingly strong dictatorships, whether they be of the military-authoritarian Right, or the communist-totalitarian Left. … liberal democracy remains the only coherent political aspiration that spans different regions and cultures around the globe.*

Fukuyama, until recently a neo-conservative, was not so much opposed to ideology as such, but argued that one ideology – a combination of neo-liberalism and neo-conservatism – would come to dominate the world. The shock of the 9/11 attack on New York and the 'War on Terror' that has followed have gone some way to dispel his theory and he has indeed largely recanted. He now accepts that the aggressiveness and intolerance of neo-conservative ideology is actually promoting rival ideologies, notably

Islamic fundamentalism. This provides us with a further critique of ideology – that attempts to impose ideology upon different cultures will simply result in the creation of new ideologies to oppose it. This becomes a kind of 'dialect' approach to the development of ideology, following Marxist analysis of economic and social history. However, Fukuyama's perspective is largely traditionally conservative in nature.

The Postmodernist Critique

Postmodernist philosophy embraces a wide variety of human thought and activity, including the arts, media, science and religion. At its centre, however, lies some fundamental beliefs that provide a profound criticism of political ideology. Postmodernism is an extremely complex movement with many facets. We must concentrate on a few basic ideas.

Science and history

Postmodernists such as Jean-Francois Lyotard (1924–98) and Michel Foucault (1926–84) have challenged the supremacy of science and history in human thought. It had been assumed that the physical sciences (and social science to some extent) and the established histories of civilisations were examples of universal truths. They were based on the proposition that there is one 'true' version of the world and its history and their truth can be judged on the basis of how well they conform to the observable world.

Postmodernists, however, do not accept the idea of one version of truth. Scientific explanations of the world, together with its histories, are only *one version* of truth. There may be other explanations of truth that are equally valid. Indeed, Lyotard argued, every culture develops its own versions of science and history. Thus, for example, Shakespeare's history plays – widely criticised as flawed by conventional historians – are seen as valid versions of events even though they were written to entertain and to carry the playwright's reflections on the human condition. On a wider basis, all major cultures have developed their own versions of their own history. Such beliefs have also given rise to 'feminist history' or 'black history'.

The implication of this for ideology becomes clear when we consider that Marxism, for example, is based upon an analysis of history that Marx claimed to be scientific in nature. Similarly, some radical feminists have proposed their own histories, which again can be criticised by postmodernists. They are not opposed on the grounds that they are 'false', but on the basis that they claim to be the only true version of history.

Similarly with science, which is criticised by postmodernists. Here again, Marxism comes under attack. Environmentalists who base their beliefs on scientific research have thus been questioned. Their interpretations of research into the deterioration of the natural world should not be accepted as 'truth'. Indeed some postmodernists have suggested that such science is ultimately futile because changes in the natural world must be the result of such complex influences that no single explanations can be trusted. In other words, there is no discoverable 'truth'

It follows from this brief review of post-modernist perspectives that those ideologies that are most criticised by portmodernism are those that are based on a fixed interpretation of history and/or a claim to understand scientific truths. Interestingly, anarchism, which has been rejected on the grounds of its lack of scientific basis, can be most easily embraced by postmodernists.

Discourse

Postmodernists are particularly concerned by the importance of language. For them, language is crucial in transmitting cultural attitudes from one generation to the next and in relationships between different cultures. Ideologies are characterised, they argue, by very specific 'discourses', which determine the consciousness of those who support those ideologies. Put another way, ideology is understood in terms of its own specific language.

This is very clear when we consider socialism and its emphasis on ideas such as class war, alienation and exploitation. Feminism, too, has its own discourses such as patriarchy, 'the personal is the political', sex and gender, etc., while ecologists have developed ideas such as 'Gaia' and anthropocentrism.

The problem with such discourses is that they have the effect of 'locking' the followers of ideology into a kind of straitjacket of discourse from which they cannot escape. Language becomes, in other words, a form of totalitarianism in itself. In reality, the experience of each individual is unique to that individual and so they should express it using their own voice, their own discourse. If an individual describes their experience merely in terms of the language of an ideology – such as feminism, Marxism or anarchism – the true nature of their position will be hidden. Putting this more simply, ideologies are flawed because they do not take into account the individual circumstances of people, all of which vary slightly. In order to be able to use a universal discourse, ideologies have to make assumptions that groups of people all have the same experience.

Summary

We have now established a number of approaches that one can take when assessing ideologies. We will always tend to favour some ideologies over others because we are individuals with our own values and attitudes. In academic studies, however, it is important to see ideologies *as others have seen them*. In that way we can reach more objective conclusions and find more universal ways of judging them.

Chapter 10

Answering examination questions

This section is a guide to answering typical examination questions on political ideologies. It explains how to tackle each type of question, gives worked examples, lists generic essay questions and explains the command words used by examiners.

Short questions

The demands of short questions on ideologies generally fall into the following categories:

- Defining political principles as used by the followers of an ideology, e.g. the meaning of freedom, equality, order, the state.

- Explaining distinctions between the ways in which different ideologies have used principles, e.g. comparing how liberals and anarchists view freedom, or how liberals and anarchists view the state.

- Explaining typical ideological attitudes towards certain phenomena, e.g. the conservative attitude to human nature or Marx's attitude to social class.

- Giving short descriptions of how ideologies demonstrate internal distinctions, e.g. liberal and radical feminism or collectivist and individualist anarchism.

It is vital to focus clearly upon the question, to avoid unnecessary analysis where none is required and to ensure that as many relevant facts and illustrations as possible are included within the limited time available.

Examples

Three examples of short questions are given below, together with suggestions on how to structure a response.

Question 1
What do feminists mean by the term 'patriarchy'?

This is an example of a requirement to explain an important concept used within an ideology.

Short introduction

This should give a generalised description of patriarchy as a system of rule by men. You should give information such as the notion that it arises from the model of the family in which fathers are traditionally dominant.

Main answer

It is important when describing a concept or principle that you explain how different branches of an ideology have used the term. In this case, you should explain that liberals see patriarchy as the general domination of society by men. Make sure you give examples, such as the position of men in employment and politics, and refer to discrimination. Mention that radicals, however, see partriarchy as a more complete, all-embracing system. Explain that 'the personal is the political'. Illustrate ways in which radicals have insisted that patriarchy exists in public and private life, including personal relationships. Note that socialist feminists see patriarchy as economic in nature and explain why; add that other radical feminists have emphasised the sexual nature of patriarchy (e.g. Greer). Your answer should contain some references to leading authorities.

Conclusion

Write a sentence or two summarising what you have said, emphasising the fact that there are different usages, but that there is also a common meaning.

Question 2

What is a typical conservative attitude towards human nature?

Note that 'typical' invites some degree of critical analysis. As the answer shows, there may not be a typical attitude.

Short introduction

This should explain that there really is no 'typical' attitude. Instead, there is a traditionalist attitude and perhaps two modern versions. You should state how influential this concept is on the whole philosophy of conservatism, since it affects issues such as the role of the state, authority and morality. In particular, explain that conservatism was originally a reaction against Enlightenment thinking; it opposed the view that humans are rational beings, seeing them as being driven more by appetites than by reason.

Main answer

Explain the traditional view – for example, as exemplified by Burke. This includes pessimism about human nature, humankind's imperfectability, original sin and related ideas. Then give the modern view, which accepts that individuals can be improved through education and the creation of a more moral society – the

'traditional values' argument. Contrast this with the neo-conservatives, who have reverted to the pessimistic view, citing decadence, family breakdown, crime and so on as proof that humanity needs firm moral guidance and perhaps even religious observance. You could quote authorities such as Strauss. Perhaps you could note that conservatism thus appears to have come full circle.

Conclusion

Return to your two main themes. First, state that there is a basic traditional, fundamental view, and, second, explain that there have been adaptations of this view by modern conservatives, although some basic principles remain.

Question 3

Distinguish between an anarchist and a liberal view of freedom.

'Distinguish' questions are common and can be tricky. It is important to make sure you draw distinctions and don't just assume them. Avoid the temptation to describe one view and then the other, thereby leaving the reader to identify the differences. Distinctions must be clearly identified and stressed.

Short introduction

Make general comments about the importance of the concept to both ideological traditions. State that it might initially appear that there are no significant distinctions, but that you will show this is not the case.

Main answer

The liberal, at least classical liberal, view was that freedom is 'negative'. Explain negative liberty and emphasise that it means an absence of external restraint. Contrast this with the anarchist view that people should exercise private judgement. We do not need external restraint to indicate good actions as opposed to bad ones. Quote Godwin, for example, on how moral individuals use private judgement well.

Then go on to discuss positive liberty. Liberals see it as a widening of opportunity and choice. The anarchist view is similar, but concerns self-realisation. Explain this term. Show that, for liberals, the state can promote liberty, whereas anarchists insist that liberty can be genuine only within voluntary societies.

Third, explain that anarchists propose that the social existence we choose must be voluntary and a matter of free choice. For liberals, by contrast, political society arises from collective consent. We are free because we have consented. Anarchists do not accept that consent represents free choice.

Conclusion

Write one or two sentences explaining that both philosophies see freedom as fundamental and place it at the centre of their belief system, but note that it arises from different premises in each case. Stress again that the whole basis of a free political society – liberal consent versus anarchist voluntarism – is disputed.

Essay questions

Generic questions

Whichever politics course you are taking, certain generic questions will arise. The actual wording of these common types of question may vary, but the essential elements of a good response are the same. By learning the material for these answers and practising them, you can give yourself the basis for a good examination answer. Of course, it is imperative that you address the specific demands of the actual question too.

Below is a list of generic questions that commonly arise in ideologies examinations. It is not exhaustive, but it is based on the questions that have appeared in recent years.

Anarchism

- Distinguish between individualist and collectivist anarchism.

- Do you agree that anarchists are united on principles but divided on ends?

- Is anarchism nothing more than utopianism?

Conservatism

- Distinguish between traditional and New Right conservatism.

- Distinguish between neo-liberalism and neo-conservatism.

- How has the conservative attitude to the state and society evolved?

- To what extent has the modern Conservative Party abandoned traditional principles?

Ecologism

- Distinguish between deep and shallow ecology.

- To what extent is ecologism an ethical movement?

- What is the significance of the distinctions between anthropocentrism and ecocentrism?

Feminism

- Distinguish between liberal and radical feminism.

- Why have feminists argued that the personal is the political?

- In what ways have feminists disagreed about the nature of patriarchy?

- Has feminism finally succeeded?

Liberalism

- Distinguish between classical and modern liberalism.

- Why have liberals traditionally been suspicious of the state?

- Why do liberals stress limited government and constitutionalism?

- How have liberals sought to control the power of the state?

Marxism

- Examine Marx's claim to be a scientific thinker.
- Why did Marx believe that revolution was inevitable?
- How much were Leninism and Stalinism distortions of Marxist theory?
- What were the main distinctions between Leninism, Trotskyism and Stalinism?

Nationalism

- Distinguish between liberal and right-wing nationalism.
- Is nationalism necessarily racist in character?
- Is nationalism necessarily expansionist in nature?
- Are all nationalists right wing in nature?
- Why has fascism been closely linked with nationalism?

Socialism

- Distinguish between revolutionary and evolutionary socialism.
- Do you agree that socialism has disagreed more about means than ends?
- To what extent has modern social democracy abandoned traditional socialist principles?
- What have been the most typical socialist attitudes towards capitalism?
- Is Marxism still relevant today?

Command words

Most essay-based questions include important command words or phrases. Here are the most common ones and suggested approaches.

To what extent?

Make sure you give an evaluation. Put it in the introduction and the conclusion, and assemble evidence to back it up. The answer to this kind of question would usually be 'a great deal', or 'the arguments are balanced', or 'not very much'. Note that none of these answers is a simple 'yes' or 'no'.

Discuss

This usually follows a quotation. You are being asked to explain its meaning. Explain why the quotation has been said and then evaluate it. It is acceptable to challenge a statement or to support it fully, but it is generally best to give a balanced assessment. Ensure that you assemble enough evidence to support your conclusion.

Distinguish

As was shown in the third short question example, it is vital to bring out the points of distinction and not just expect the reader to work them out. Go through each of the key points in turn. This a better technique than simply describing each point of view and then attempting a few distinctions at the end.

Why?

The answer to 'why?' is 'because', and your answer should be a full version of 'because'. Make sure you answer the question and use relevant evidence.

Essay structure

Quality of writing and essay structure have always been important, but this is even more true as, at Advanced level, a separate mark will be awarded for the quality of communication. The following principles apply to writing good examinations essays.

1 You should use 'appropriate vocabulary'. This means in practice that you should try to use as many key words and phrases as you can. Here are a few examples.

   If answering questions on liberalism, phrases such as *negative and positive liberty, tolerance, constitutionalism, welfarism, equality of opportunity* are likely to be useful, and examiners will be looking for them. With ecologism the key words and phrases might include *anthropocentrism, deep ecology, shallow ecology, ecocentrism, ecological ethics.* For multiculturalism it is likely you should be referring to *cultural relativism, assimilation, integration, identity politics, particularism.* The same can be applied to all the ideologies. In each chapter we have explained 'key terms' and these should be used as much as possible where it is appropriate.

2 Essays should have an introduction. The question is, what should this contain? There are a number of alternatives. The most obvious and safest is to explain how you intend to answer the question. The second is to explain (or 'deconstruct') the question. What you should avoid is a rambling historical introduction that does not address the question. Here are three ways of introducing an answer. Two are valid, one is to be avoided.

Question: Why is anthropocentrism significant in ecologism?

Introduction (a) shows how you intend to tackle the question: Most ecological theories fall into one of two categories. One of these categories is anthropocentric in nature. Such theories place humankind at the centre of nature and see issues in terms of man's place in it. Other theories reject anthropocentrism and instead see humans as having an equal status and position in nature to other living (sometimes inanimate) parts of nature. I shall examine these two types of theory, examine the significance of anthropocentrism for them and, in so doing, analyse the importance of the concept. **This is a useful beginning.**

Introduction (b) analyses the question: Anthropocentrism – the belief that humans have a central, possibly superior, place in nature – plays a key role in environmental thought. Its significance rests with the fact that it has a profound influence on the nature of ecological thought. The anthropocentric thinkers reach very different conclusions to those who reject anthropocentrism. In other words,

anthropocentrism is the key influence on environmental thought. **This approach also works.**

Introduction (c) is an historical narrative: Environmentalism is a movement that arose in the 1960s when the first major concerns about the environment were being considered. Before then, environmentalism had been confined to romantic visions of the relationship between man and nature. In more recent years environmentalism has become increasingly ideological in nature. It is now divided into deep ecology and shallow ecology. **There is nothing drastically wrong with this, but it does not address the question and therefore is unlikely to attract any credit. The effort is, thus, wasted.**

3 Half the marks in essays are for analysis and evaluation. Therefore the main content must address the key command words, as described below. This does not mean that half the wordage needs to be analytical, but it does mean that special attention needs to be paid to it.

4 Try, whenever possible, to give evidence to support your assertions. This may be the beliefs of leading thinkers or authorities and may be examples of specific events and movements. Thus, when suggesting that right-wing nationalism is largely expansionist in nature, you need to mention some specific nationalist movements that have behaved in that way – Nazism or Russian nationalism might be used. If describing the classical liberal opposition to the large, powerful state, you might use John Stuart Mill or perhaps Herbert Spencer.

5 All ideologies have different branches. If the question specifies one of the branches, you should obviously concentrate on that. If it does not – for example, *'To what extent has socialism embraced collectivism and rejected individualism?'* – make sure you consider as many branches of the ideology as you can. In this case look at Marxism, other fundamentalists, gradualists, revisionists, democratic socialism, social democracy.

6 Essays should be balanced. Where there is an evaluation, make sure that all sides of the conflicts and all opinions about ideological belief are included. So, for example, when discussing patriarchy in feminism, you should include radical, liberal and perhaps socialist views on this key idea. However, balance does not mean failing to give firm conclusions. However balanced your content may be, it is important to offer a firm answer. It does not matter what conclusion you reach, as long as you have justified it with your evidence.

7 Conclusions are less important than you might think. However, where the question requires an evaluative response, this should be the subject of a conclusion. If such an evaluative conclusion does not seem to be required, the ideal conclusion simply brings out what you consider to be the most important points. So, for example, if you have answered a question about traditional conservatism, you might conclude that, ultimately, it is the traditional conservative view of human nature and human motivation that lies at the centre of the philosophy, influencing all its other beliefs and values. This approach – identifying a key feature – may also get you a few marks for additional evaluation.

And finally...some dos, don'ts and misconceptions

- Do write a plan.
- Don't cross out your plan.
- Do write an introduction.
- Do explain how you intend to answer the question.
- Don't start your essay with a long historical background that is not directly related to the question.
- Do address the question directly.
- Don't ignore what the question asks.
- Do plan your time.
- Don't run out of time.
- Do use bullets if you are running out of time.
- Don't use bullets in any other circumstances.
- Do refer to leading authorities.
- Don't attempt to quote them at length.
- Do use as many real-world examples as you can.
- Do write a conclusion that states concisely what your conclusions are.

Bibliography

General reading

Adams, I. (1998) *Ideology and Politics in Britain Today*, Manchester University Press.
Adams, I. and Dyson, R. W. (2003) *Fifty Major Political Thinkers*, Routledge.
Crick, B. (1994) *In Defence of Politics*, Penguin.
Eccleshall, R. *et al.* (2003) *Political Ideologies: An Introduction*, Routledge.
Goodwin, B. (2007) *Using Political Ideas*, Wiley.
Heywood, A. (2007) *Political Ideologies: An Introduction*, Palgrave Macmillan.
Heywood, A. (2002) *Politics*, Palgrave Macmillan.
McLellan, D. (1995) *Ideology*, Open University Press.
Rosen, M. and Wolff, J. (eds.) (1999) *Political Thought*, Oxford University Press.
Vincent, A. (1995) *Modern Political Ideologies*, Blackwell.

Websites

The internet is not the most useful medium for finding additional information about political ideologies, but by using leading search engines, and keying in the names of major thinkers, you can find interesting biographies, critiques, summaries and quotations.

The best general site is probably Wikipedia, which can be accessed at http://en.wikipedia.org. It has an excellent search engine, which is particularly useful for finding information about major authorities and works on each ideology. It is interesting to view the current policies of the main UK and US political parties in relation to the ideologies that originally underpinned them. The three key UK party websites are:
www.conservatives.com
www.labour.org.uk
www.libdems.org.uk

For information on political parties in the USA, see the following:
www.democrats.org
www.rnc.org
www.politics1.com

Classic works

The following list includes many of the great works that have been written within each ideological tradition. They are available in virtually all large academic libraries.

Liberalism

Hobhouse, L. *Liberalism*
Locke, J. *Two Treatises of Government*
Mill, J. S. *On Liberty*
Rawls, J. *A Theory of Justice*
Rousseau, J. *The Social Contract*
Smiles, S. *Self Help*

Socialism

Benn, T. *Arguments for Socialism*
Giddens, A. *The Third Way*
Laski, H. *Democracy in Crisis*
Lenin, V. I. *What is to be Done?*
Shaw, G. B. (ed) *Fabian Essays in Socialism*
Tawney, R. H. *Equality*
Winstanley, G. *The Law of Freedom*
Marx, K. *The German Ideology*

Conservatism

Burke, E. *Reflections on the Revolution in France*
Disraeli, B. *Sybil*
Friedman, M. *Capitalism and Freedom*
Hayek, F. *The Road to Serfdom*
Hobbes, T. *Leviathan*

Nationalism

Carr, E. H. *Nationalism and After*
Kedourie, E. *Nationalism*

Anarchism

Kropotkin, P. *Anarchism*
Nozick, R. *Anarchy, State and Society*
Thoreau, H. *Walden*
Wolff, R. *In Defence of Anarchism*

Feminism

de Beauvoir, S. *The Second Sex*
Friedan, B. *The Feminine Mystique*
Greer, G. *The Female Eunuch*
Millett, K. *Sexual Politics*

Ecologism

Bookchin, M. *The Ecology of Freedom*
Capra, F. *The Web of Life*
Lovelock, J. *Gaia: A New Look at Life on Earth*
Thomas, K. *Man and the Natural World*

Multiculturalism

Taylor. C. *Multiculturalism*
Kymlicka. W. *Multicultural Citizenship*

Index

Note: Page numbers in **bold** refer to keyword definitions.

Acton, Lord 138, 148, 155
Adam, Robert 36
Adorno, Theodore 119
Afghanistan 162
air pollution 219, 220
alienation 106–7, **113**, 114, 258, 264
Althusser, Louis 147
'American Cause' 59–60
American Christianity 53, 60, 62
American Constitution 11, 28, 139
American Declaration of Independence 2–3
'American Dream' 10
American Revolution 4, 133
anarchism ix, x, 132–58
    and capitalism 134–5, 137, 140–4, 148
    and collectivism 152–3, 155–6, 260
    see also anarcho-communism
    and common ownership 140, 151–2
    and community 132–3, 135–6, 138, 140–3, 145, 149
    and consent theory 138–9
    contemporary 146–7
    core values 132–3, 135–41, 153
    critique of modern society 133
    definition 132
    early development 133–4
    eco-anarchists 140
    and equality 143, 156–7
    exam questions on 268–9
    and exchange of goods 132
    and free society 155
    and freedom 268–9
    and human nature 133–4, 137, 142, 148, 151, 153, 156–7, 260
    and inequality 140
    issues in 151–3
    key thinkers 147–51
    lack of a living example of 133
    and law 136, 137, 141, 144, 154
    and liberalism 154–5
    and liberty 136–7, 138–9, 143, 152–3, 154, 156–7
    and Marxism 155–7
    and mutualism 144–5
    and nationalism 141
    and natural law 136, 137
    nihilist 132, 135, 146, 153
    and property 132, 139–41, 144–5, 151, 156
    and religion 141
    revolutionary 134–5, 145–6, 149–50, 153–4, 156
    as single ideology 153–4
    and social justice 143
    and socialism 155–7
    and the state 132, 134–5, 137–41, 143–6, 148–50, 153–7
    types of 141–7
    as unscientific socialism 157
    and utopianism 137, 141, 144, 151–3, 157, 260
anarcho-anarchists 132
anarcho-capitalists (libertarians) 18, 51, 132, 139, 144, 147, 150–1, 153, 155
    see also anarcho-individualism
anarcho-communism 129, 133, 135, 140, 141–2, 147, 151–3, 155–6
anarcho-environmentalism 222, 225–6, 227–8
anarcho-individualism 135, 142–4, 147, 152–3, 153–4, 155
    see also anarcho-capitalists (libertarians)
anarcho-syndicalists 132, 140, 145–6, 149–50, 153
Ancient Greece 107
androgyny 203, 210, **211**, 212, 214
animal rights movement 225, 229
anthropocentrism 221–2, **221**, 229, 234–5, 237, 239, 271–2
anti-feminism 215, **215**
anti-globalisation 227–8, 237
anti-industrialisation 222
apartheid 184
appetite 40
Arab peoples 161, 179, 245, 251, 254
Aristotle 107, 229
Arvidsson, Adolf 176
Asquith, Herbert 19
assimilation xii, 254, 257
Atkinson, Ti-Grace 212
Austen, Jane 193
'Austrian School' of economics 144, 150
Austro-Hungarian Empire 162, 163
authoritarianism 42, 55
authority 41–2
autonomy **137**

Babeuf, Gracchus 71
Baker, James 53
Bakunin, Mikhail 117, 134–8, 140–2, 146–9, 151–2, 155, 157
Basque peoples 242
Baumgardner, Jennifer 216
Bell, Daniel 264
belonging 258
Benn, Tony 92, 97, 104
Bentham, Jeremy 6, 7, 8, 13, 14, 23
Berlin, Isaiah 7, 18
Bernstein, Eduard 86, 88, 95, 98, 129–30
Beveridge, William 9, 12, 19–20, 25–6, 29, 104

Bhopal disaster 228, 238
Bible 217
biodiversity 220, **220**, 224
biological sex difference 197, 202–3, 209–15
biosphere 232
Bismarck, Otto von 49, 170
black rights movement 254
Blair, Tony 27, 31, 36, 60, 89, 91, 96, 102
Blanqui, Auguste 85, 94, 97, 99, 129
'block thinking' 244
BNP *see* British National Party
Bolsheviks 86, 98, 105, 117–18, 121, 123, 149
Bookchin, Murray 147, 225–6, 228–9, 235, 238
Booth, Charles 9
bourgeoisie
    definition **109**
    and Marxism 109–10, 116
    and socialism 74
Bright, John 15, 16
British National Party (BNP) 33, 188–9, 231, 241, 263
Brown, Gordon 92
Buchanan, Pat 59–60
Buddhism 222, 234, 236
Bunch, Charlotte 206–7, 212
Burke, Edmund 38, 40–2, 46, 52, 55–6, 62, 134, 261, 268
Bush, George, Senior 53
Bush, George W. 16, 60, 231
Butler, R. A. 49

Cambodia 125
Cameron, David x, 31, 44, 54, 67, 68
Canada 242, 257
capital 111–12
capitalism x–xi, 107
    and anarchism 134–5, 137, 140–4, 148
    benevolent 83
    and class 73–4
    collapse of 114
    and conservatism 39, 48–9, 61–2
    cooperative 143
    cultural hegemony of 119, 125, 128
    definition **3**
    development 112–14
    and ecologism 222, 230, 231–2
    and exploitation 73–4, 106, 109, 112, 117–18, 137, 143, 148–9, 222, 230–2
    and feminism 195, 199, 204
    and inequality 140
    and liberalism 3–4
    and Marxism 101, 106, 108–14, 117–21, 125–6, 127, 128–30
    and multiculturalism 256
    nature of 111–12
    and social class 73–4
    and socialism 70–4, 76–9, 83–8, 93–8, 100–2, 106,

108–14, 117–21, 125–30
    see also anarcho-capitalists (libertarians); post-capitalism
Capra, Fritjof 220, 234, 235, 238
Castro, Fidel 85, 92, 126, 178
Centre for Policy Studies 59
Chamberlain, Houston 173, 178, 181
Chamberlain, Joseph 100
Chartist movement 74, 106
chauvinism 170, **170**
Chavez, Hugo 120
chemical industry 228, 238
Cheney, Dick 16, 52
Chesterton, G. K. 42, 47
Chicago School 50–1, 61–2
China 92, 118–19, 124–5, 128, 161, 248, 262
Chipko movement 207
chlorofluorocarbons (CFCs) 220
Chomsky, Noam 147
Christian democracy 60, **60**
Christiania 133, 142
Christianity 245, 247
    American 53, 60, 62
    and the Enlightenment 36–7
    fundamentalist 60
    Nonconformist 87
    and socialism 97, 106
Church 48
Churchill, Winston 39
citizenship
    active 91
    global 251–2
    liberal 248–9
    multicultural 249–50
civil society 10, **10**
Clarke, Kenneth 49, 57
class
    and capitalism 73–4
    and conservatism 37–9
    definition **74**
    exploitation 110
    and ideology xi
    and the Industrial Revolution 3
    polarisation 109, 110
    and socialism 73–4, 76–7, 79, 88, 91, 96, 102
    underclasses 68
    women as subordinate sex class 202, 212–13
        see also bourgeoisie; hierarchy; middle-classes; ruling class; working classes
class conflict 74, 76–7, 95, 113–14, 170
class consciousness 76, 110, 114, 127
class solidarity 110
classless society 110, 111, 116
Clause IV 89, **89**, 101, 102
Clean Air Act 1956 219

Clinton, Bill 27
Cobden, Richard 15, 16
Cold War, end of the 128
collective consciousness 24, 106–7, 109, 206–7
collectivism
    and anarchism 152–3, 155–6, 260
    and individualism 80
    and socialism 79–80, 102
colonialism 113
colour-blindness 254
Commission for Multi-Ethnic Britain (CMEB) 253, 257
    Report of the 253
common good 7, 27
common ownership
    and anarchism 140, 151–2
    and socialism 71–2, 80–2
communications 185
communism x, 84, **84**, 109, 116–17, 152–3
    and anarchism 132
    definition 105
    failure 105, 128
    final transition to 117
    free 152
    and freedom 152–3
    and Marxism 116–17
    and the state 116
    see also anarcho-communism
Communist Manifesto 106, 108, 110, 114
Communist Party 121–3
communitarianism 91, 243–4, **244**, 250
communities
    and anarchism 132–3, 135–6, 138, 140–3, 145, 149
    cultural 243–4
    and socialism 93
    women-only 203–4, 206–7, 210, 211–12, 214
competition 15, 128
consciousness 119
    class 76, 110, 114, 127
    collective 24, 106–7, 109, 206–7
    and ecologism 221–2, 226, 232–3, 235–7, 239
    false 107, 178, 221–2
    and female oppression 202–4, 209–10, 213–15
'consensus' politics 20, 27
consent theory 138–9
conservatism xii, 16, 35–69
    and authoritarianism 42, 55
    and authority 41–2
    Cameronian 54–5
    and capitalism 39, 48–9, 61–2
    chameleon-like nature 39–40, 61
    and class 37–9
    contemporary US 52–3, 59–60, 62–3
    continental European 53–4
    core values 40–55
    and crime 67

crisis of 63–4
critique of ideology 46–7, 260–3
early 47–9
empiricism 47, 250–1
exam questions on 269
and fascism 261–2, 263
and feminism 215
and hierarchy 43–4
and human nature 37, 40–1, 46–7, 58, 260–1, 268
and ideology 39–40, 60–1
and individualism 35, 39, 44–5, 58, 65–7
and inequality 43
issues in 60–2
key thinkers 55–60
and the law 62, 250
liberal 54–5
and liberalism 1, 4, 31–2, 51, 53–5, 61, 65–8
and liberty 41–2, 44, 45, 51, 65–7
and multiculturalism 55, 60, 250–1, 252
and nation-states 62, 164
and nationalism 49–50, 52–5, 160, 169–70, 179, 183–4, 190, 250, 263
nationalist-authoritarian right 49–50
New Right 16, 17, 31, 50–2, 55, 58–62, 65, 67–8, 260, 263
'one-nationism' 28–9, 39, 54–5, 57
and oppression 262–3
and order 41–2, 56–7, 58, 62, 68, 183, 250
and organic society 43–4, 54, 56, 61, 65, 68, 250
origins of 36–7
pragmatism 44, 48
and preservation 42–3
and property 45–6, 67
reactionary nature 35, 48, 63
and reform 46, 55
and rights 67
and scepticism 47
social conservatives 49, 54–5
and social progress 261–2
and socialism 43, 51, 61
and the state 44–5, 51, 54–5, 58–9, 61–2, 65–7
and tradition 35, 42–3, 56, 65
types of 47–55
in the United Kingdom 63–5
    see also neo-conservatism
Conservative government 44
Conservative Party 36
    and liberalism 31–2
    and nationalism 190
    power loss 68
    weaknesses 63, 64
Constant, Benjamin 5–6
constitutionalism 28, 29
    definition **28**
    and liberalism 11, 32

constitutions 11–12, 31
  see also American Constitution
consumerism 222, 232
consumption 14, 194–5, 222
contract theory 139
cooperatives 81, 93–4
cosmopolitanism 251–2
Countryside Alliance 54
Crick, Bernard 159
crime
  and conservatism 67
  and liberalism 21
critical theory 119–20
Cromwell, Oliver 71, 82
Crosland, Anthony 96, 97
Cuba 85, 92, 126, 128, 178
cultural assimilation xii, 254, 257
cultural communities 243–4
cultural embeddedness 257, 258, **258**
cultural hegemony
  capitalist 119, 125, 128
  male 199
cultural identity 167, 241, 256, 257
  dual 251–3, 254
cultural imperialism 254
cultural institutions 254
cultural integration 257
cultural nationalism 176–7, 179, 180, 185–6, 190
cultural relativism 245–6, **246**, 253, 255
Cultural Revolution 119, **124**, 125
culture 163, **163**
  of dependency 17, 24, 29, 59, 65
  and identity politics 242–4
  mass 194–5
  national 161, 163–4, 175–7, 179–80, 253–4, 258
  nature of 241–2
  neutral conception of 242
  and pluralism 244–5, 248
  and race 241–2
  right-wing conceptions of 241–2
  state 246

Darwin, Charles 16, 173, 236
date-rape drugs 212
de Beauvoir, Simone 197, 198, 212, 214
de Gaulle, Charles 54, 170, 181–2, 183
de Gobineau, Arthur 173
de Saint-Simon, Henri 99, 101, 106
de Tracy, Antoine x
d'Eaubonne, Françoise 207, 230
Debray, Regis 126
decentralisation 21, 29
democracy
  Christian 60, **60**
  direct 133, 141, 145

and fascism 174
and liberalism 15, 27–9, 32–3, 174
and nationalism 175
representative 15
see also social democracy
'democracy of the dead' 42, 47
democratic centralism 122, **122**
dependency culture 17, 24, 29, 59, 65
deprivation
  cycle of 9, 59
  and equality of opportunity 79
  and liberalism 18–20, 25–6
Descartes, René 36, 236
determinism 114, **114**
  economic 108–9
dialectical materialism 108–9
dialectical process 106–7, 108–9, 110, 129, 265
diaspora 165, 183
'dictatorship of the proletariat' 99, 115–16, 118, 148
'difference principle' 27
discourse
  feminist 217
  postmodern 265–6
discrimination
  class-based 79
  culturalist 243, 248, 254
  liberal views on 9
  positive 79, **79**, 201, 248, 249, 254, 258
  sex 196, 201
  see also racism; sexism
Disraeli, Benjamin 37–9, 41, 47–9, 56–7, 63, 65, 68, 170, 183, 190
distributive justice 78, **78**, 104
diversity **248**
divorce 208
doctrine 1, **2**
dogma 263
domestic violence 201
dominant ideology x–xi, 1, 110
Dworkin, Andrea 204, 212

Earth 232–4
Eastern Europe 118
eco-anarchists 140
ecocentrism 234
ecofeminism 207, 230
ecologism 219–40
  and air quality 219, 220
  and anthropocentrism 221–2, 229, 234–5, 237, 239
  and anti-industrialisation 222
  and biodiversity 220, **220**, 224
  and capitalism 222, 230, 231–2
  and consciousness 221–2, 226, 232–3, 235–7, 239
  core values 221–2
  dark green 219, **225**

deep ecology 223–7, 229, 232–3, 235–9, 261
definition 219
Earth first 226–7
ecofeminism 230
eight-point platform 226–7
ethical ecology 229–30
exam questions on 269, 271–2
and globalisation 227–8, 232, 237–8
and habitat destruction 220–1
holism 220, 224–5, 228–9, 233–4
and human nature 261
issues in 235–9
key thinkers 232–4
left-wing 231–2
light green 219, **225**, 229
and Marxism 231–2
and natural quality of life 222
as politics 238–9
and resource depletion 221, 222, 224
right-wing ecology 230–1
as science 238–9
shallow ecology 223–5, 227, 229, 235–6, 238–9, 261
social ecology 228–9
and social progress 261
and sustainability 221
types of 222–32
utopian 236–7
and water quality 220
see also anarcho-environmentalism
economic determinism 108–9
economic development 237–8
economic imperialism 182, **182**
economic patriotism 60
economic planning 123–4
ecosophy 232, **233**
education
    elementary 19, 25
    universal 9, 19, 25
egoism 142, 155
elections 11, 111
empiricism 47, 250–1
'end of ideology' 264–5
endangered species 221
energy production 234
Engels, Friedrich 83–4, 85, 93, 94, 99, 108, 114, 204
English Civil War 71
Enlightenment x, 36–7, 56
    and anarchism 133
    and feminism 193
    ideology 36
    and liberalism 2–3
    philosophies of 2, 36, 56
    and rationalism 2, 36, 37, 56, 173, 193
    reactions to 37, 48
entrepreneurs 37, 45, 54, 66, 145

environmental degradation 230–2
environmentalism
    core values 221–2
    definition 219
    ethical 229–30
    instrumental 230
    issues in 235–9
    key thinkers 232–4
    liberal 222–4, 227, 229, 235–6, 238–9
    post-modern critiques of 265
    types of 222–32
    see also anarcho-environmentalism
equal rights 8–9, 13, 247
    women's 207–9, 255–6
equality
    absolute 75, 76
    and anarchism 143, 156–7
    and feminism 192, 193–6, 198–204, 206–10, 214–16
    and socialism 71–2, 74–9, 88, 90, 97, 100, 102–4, 156
    of welfare 75, 76, 83
equality of opportunity
    definition **9**
    and feminism 199, 206, 208
    and liberalism 1, 2, 9–10, 19, 21, 25–7, 29, 31
    and socialism 75, 76, 79, 90, 100, 103, 104
equality of outcome 76
essay questions 269–72
    analysis and evaluation 271, 272
    balance 272
    example 269–70, 271–2
    generic questions 269–70
    introductions 271
    structure 270–2
    supporting evidence 271
essentialism **205**, 206, 217, 251, 253
Etzioni, Amitai 249, 256–7
Eurocommunism 98
European integration 62, 64, 164–5
European People's Party 54
European Social Chapter 101
European Union (EU) 164
Euroscepticism 64
exams 267–72
    command words 270
    dos and don'ts 272
    essay questions 269–72
    short questions 267–9
    supporting evidence 271
exchange of goods 132
existentialism 146
expansionism 171, 176, 186
exploitation
    capitalism and 73–4, 106, 109, 112, 117–18, 137, 143, 148–9, 222, 230–2
    class and 110

of immigrants 256
post-colonial 256
of women 197, 199–200, 203, 204–6, 211–14, 216, 255

Fabian Society 85–6, 87, 95, 98, 99–100, 115
Fabianism 85–6
'Fair Trade' 145
falsification 58
family unit, as source of female oppression 202–3, 204–5, 210, 211, 215
Fanon, Franz 115, 125–6, 128
farmers 37, 45, 54
fascism ix, xi, 39
    and anarchism 146, 150
    and conservatism 261–2, 263
    and democracy 174
    Frankfurt School critique of 119–20
    and nationalism 171–6, 180, 181, 263
    and nihilism 146
    and organic society 167
    and racialism 172–3
    and rationalism 173–5
    and romanticism 173–5
    and social progress 261–2
    and syndicalism 87
female circumcision 196, 200–1
feminism 192–218
    and capitalism 195, 199, 204
    and conservatism 215
    core values of 196–200
    definition 192
    ecofeminism 207, 230
    and equality 192, 193–6, 198–204, 206–10, 214–16
    and equality of opportunity 199, 206, 208
    exam questions on 267–8, 269
    and female careers 196, 198–201, 206, 208–9, 214, 216
    first-wave 192, 193–4, 200
    and gender 198–9, 203, 214, 215
    and human nature 260–1
    and inequality 193, 198–200, 207–10, 213
    issues in 213–17
    key thinkers 207–13
    lesbian 206–7
    liberal 192, 195, 199–201, 205–9, 213–14, 216
    and liberation 199–200, 203, 211, 213–14, 217
    Marxist 195, 202, 204–5, 211–12
    matriarchal 196
    militant 192, 201–4, 212
    and multiculturalism 255–6
    and otherness 197–8
    and patriarchy 192, 194–7, 199, 202–4, 210, 213–16, 255, 261, 267–8
    and property 192, 194, 204, 208

radical 192, 195–200, 201–6, 211–17, 262
    and revolution 202
    second-wave 192, 194–5, 205, 209, 216
    and social progress 262
    socialist 199–200, 204–5
    and the state 192
    third-wave 196, 205–6, 215, 216
    types of 200–7
    see also anti-feminism; postfeminism; postmodern feminism
feudalism 108–9, 111, 126
    see also neo-feudalism
Feuerbach, Ludwig 107
Fichte, Johann 163, 170, 175, 177
Finland 176
Firestone, Shulamith 195, 202, 203–4, 211–12, 216
Five Year Plans 123–4
Forster Education Act 1870 25
Foucault, Michel 205–6, 265
Fourier, Charles 71–2, 83, 93, 99, 101, 204
France 53–4, 94, 173–4
franchise 57
Frankfurt School 115, 119–20, 126
fraternity **74**
free market
    and anarchism 132, 144
    and conservatism 39, 41, 48–9, 50, 55, 61–2
    and ecologism 231, 261
    and liberalism 15–16, 17, 29, 33
    and socialism 92–3
free society 155
free trade 13
free will 2, 4
freedom see liberty (freedom)
French nationalism 159
French Revolution 4, 42, 55–6, 71, 82, 126–7, 238
    and anarchism 133
    and feminism 193
    and the nation-state 162
    and oppression 262
Freud, Sigmund 119
Freudian theory 202, **203**, 209
Friedan, Betty 194–5, 197–202, 206, 209–10, 213–14
Friedman, David 144
Friedman, Milton 16, 50–1, 61–2
Friends of the Earth 237, 238–9
Fukuyama, Francis 93, 242–3, 252, 253, 264–5
fundamentalism **105**, 262
    Christian 60
    Islamic 53, 253, 254, 265
Furies 207

Gaia **227**, 229–30, 232–4, 236–7
Galloway, George 92
Garibaldi, Giuseppe 170

Gaullism 54
gemeinschaft 167, **167**
gender issues 198–9, 203, 214, 215
gender roles 198, 209
gender stereotypes 198–9
genderless/sexless society 203–4, 207, 210–11
genocide 164
ghettoisation 251
Gilmour, Ian 47, 49
Gladstone, William 9, 19, 24–5, 29, 56
global citizens 251–2
global warming 220, 221, 237
globalisation
    and the decline of the nation-state 185
    and ecologism 227–8, 232, 237–8
    and liberalism 164
    and nation-states 164–5
    see also anti-globalisation
Glorious Revolution 1688 21
Gobineau, Count 178
Godwin, William 6, 133–4, 136, 137, 147–8, 152, 207
'Golden Rule' 249
good, desire to do 7
government
    and anarchism 143, 148
    by consent 10–11
    conservative notion of 41, 45
    limited 11–14, 15, 21, 23
    local 88, 99
    over-powerful 6, 11
    paternalistic 6
    rational 174
    representative 37
    and social contract 22
    see also self-government
Gramsci, Antonio 115, 125
Great Depression 25
'great myth' 150
Green, Thomas Hill 7, 18–19, 24, 29, 31, 167
Green Party 223–4, 237
green politics 219, 236
greenhouse effect 221
greenhouse gases 220
Greenpeace 237, 238–9
Greer, Germaine 195, 199, 202, 203, 211
group identity 244, 250
guerrilla movements 120, 126, 128, 180–1
guild socialism 87, 146

Habermas, Jürgen 147
habitat destruction 220–1
Hailsham, Lord 47
Hamilton, Alexander 10
Hanisch, Carol 206, 211, 217
happiness, pursuit of 2–3

Hayek, Friedrich von 16, 50–1, 61–2
Heath, Edward 51
Hegel, Friedrich 94, 106–7, 108, 109, 167
Hegelians
    left 107
    right 107
hegemony **177**
herd instinct 261
Heseltine, Michael 49, 57
'hidden hand' 4
hierarchy 43–4
Hindu nationalism 170
Hinduism 222
historical materialism 115
history
    Hegelian/Marxist theory of 106–10, 114–15, 117, 121, 126, 128–9
    postmodern conceptions of 265
Hitler, Adolf 171–2, 174, 175, 176, 178, 181, 189
Hitler Youth 231
Ho Chi Minh 178
Hobbes, Thomas 3, 10–11, 41–2, 136, 169
Hobhouse, L. T. 19
Hobson, J. A. 19
holism 220, 224–5, 228–9, 233–4
home ownership 46
Horkheimer, Max 119
human nature
    and anarchism 133–4, 137, 142, 148, 151, 153, 156–7, 260
    and conservatism 37, 40–1, 46–7, 58, 260–1, 268
    definition **153**
    and ecologism 261
    and feminism 260–1
    and liberalism 260
    and socialism 156
Hussein, Saddam 162
Hyndman, H. M. 85, 98, 129

idealism, purposeful xii
identity
    group 244, 250
    racial 163, 254
    see also cultural identity; national identity
identity politics 242–4, **243**, 254–5
ideologies viii–xii
    blurring of the distinctions between x
    historical development x–xi
    nature of xi–xii
    variations ix–x
    see also specific ideologies
ILP *see* Independent Labour Party
IMF *see* International Monetary Fund
immigration
    and conservatism 60, 62

and multiculturalism 241, 247, 250, 256
and nationalism 188, 189, 190
imperialism
cultural 254
economic 182, **182**
and nationalism 165, 170–1
and self-determination 165
inclusiveness 57, **57**
income, redistribution 104
Independent Labour Party (ILP) 87–8
individual, sovereignty of the 132, 135–6
individualism
and collectivism 80
conservative 35, 39, 44–5, 58, 65–7
see also anarcho-individualism
industrial accidents 228, 238
Industrial Revolution 3
industrialisation 93
see also anti-industrialisation
inequality
and anarchism 140
and capitalism 140
and conservatism 43
and feminism 193, 198–200, 207–10, 213
and liberalism 103
and Marxism 75, 113
and socialism 74–5, 77–8, 91, 101, 103
see also equality
information society 264
interconnectedness 227
interests of the people 174
see also self-interest
international culture 185
International Monetary Fund (IMF) 92, 140, 164, 168, 228
international organisations 165, **165**, 185–6
and environmentalism 228, 237–8
international trade 164
interventionism 53
Iraq 162
Irish nationalism 168, 169, 187–8
Irish republicanism 188
Islam 242, 243, 244, 255
see also Muslims
Islamic fundamentalism 53, 253, 254, 265
Islamic Jihadists 251
Islamic law 249
Islamic terrorism 252–3
isolationism 53, 60
Italy 161, 171

Jacobin Party 262
jacobinism 262
Jainism 222
James II, King of England 21
Jefferson, Thomas 2, 10, 12, 67

Jesus Christ 97
Jews 177, 242, 243, 245, 251
Joseph, Keith 59, 61, 64
Jura Federation 142
justice
distributive 78, **78**, 104
and liberalism 12
social 12, 25, 29, 33, 77–8, 143

Kant, Immanuel 36
Kautsky, Karl 86, 256
Keynes, John Maynard 20, 29
Keynesian economics 64
Khmer Rouge 125
King, Martin Luther 254
Kinnock, Neil 89
Kohn, Hans 166
Kovel, Joel 232
Kropotkin, Peter 117, 134–6, 138–42, 147–9, 152, 155, 157, 228
Kymlicka, Will 249–50

labour
and capitalism 104, 109, 111–13
division of 117
exploitation 112
'surplus value' 112–13
unskilled 72–3
Labour Government 20
Labour Party 19
and class 74
and equality of opportunity 9
and European integration 64
and the Fabian Society 85–6
influences on 87
and liberalism 31
policies of and Conservative government 44
and revisionism 96
and socialism 87–8
values 88
see also New Labour
Labourism 87–8
laissez-faire **4**, 16, 64, **65**, 67, 68
land, ties to the 177, 181, 186, 230–1, 239
language
and culture 242, 249, 257
and feminism 200, 217
as form of totalitarianism 266
and nationalism 176, 180
and the transmission of ideology 265–6
law
and anarchism 136, 137, 141, 144, 154
and conservatism 62, 250
and multiculturalism 249, 250
natural 136, 137

religious 249
rule of 29
Le Pen, Jean-Marie 49
leadership
  conservative 262
  fascist 174, 262
Lebensraum (living space) 177, 181, 230–1
Lenin, Vladimir Ilyich 86, 116, 117–18, 120–3, 125, 127, 135, 149, 231–2, 256
Leninism 127
  see also Marxist-Leninism
Leopold, Aldo 229, 239
'*les philosophes*' 173–4
lesbians 196, 204, 206–7, 212, 216
Levellers (Diggers) 71, 80, 82
liberal citizenship 248–9
Liberal Democrat Party 21, 31, 32
liberal feminism 192, 195, 199–201, 205–9, 213–14, 216
liberal nationalism 160, 168–9, 174–5, 179
Liberal Party 19, 20, 31, 64
liberalism x–xi, 1–34, 39
  and anarchism 154–5
  and capitalism 3–4
  classical 4, 14–18, 22, 31, 51, 61–2, 263
    contemporary neo-liberalism x, 16, 29, 55, 61–4, 231, 263, 264
    libertarianism 17–18, 22
    Manchester School 15
    Millite 15
    social Darwinism 16–17, 24, 29, 31
  and conservatism 1, 4, 31–2, 51, 53–5, 61, 65–8
  and the constitution 11–12
  and constitutionalism 11, 29, 32
  core values 5–12, 20–1
  critique of ideology 263–4
  and democracy 15, 27–9, 32–3, 174
  as doctrine 1, **2**
  as dominant Western ideology 1
  and the Enlightenment 2–3
  and equal rights 8–9, 13, 247
  and equality of opportunity 1, 2, 9–10, 19, 21, 25–7, 29, 31, 103
  exam questions on 268–9, 270
  and the free market 15–16, 17, 29, 33
  and globalisation 164
  and government by consent 10–11
  and human nature 260
  and inequality 103
  issues in 27–31
  and justice 12, 25, 29, 33
  key thinkers 21–7
  and the Labour Party 87
  and liberty/freedom 2–8, 11, 13–15, 23, 25–7, 30–1, 66–7, 104, 136–9, 151, 154, 169, 183, 246, 251–2, 263–4, 268–9
  and limited government 11–14, 15, 21, 23
  modern 18–21
    contemporary liberalism 20–1, 22
    new liberalism 18–19, 22, 24
    policies 21
    principles 21
    welfare (social) liberalism 19–20, 22
  and multiculturalism 21, 30, 243–50, **247**, 251, 252–3, 256, 257, 261
  and nation-states 164
  and pluralism 10, 33, 247, 248, 264
  progressive 39, 53
  and property 67
  revolutionary 4
  and rights 3, 8–9, 12–13, 21, 32, 67, 103, 247
  and social democracy 1, 20
  and social responsibility 1, 5, 7, 18, 24
  and socialism 1, 39, 103–4
  and the state 1, 14, 16, 19–20, 23, 29–30, 66–7, 154–5, 184, 246
  and tolerance 7–8, 14, 15, 22, 27–8, 30–1, 32, 33, 246–7, 263–4
  and totalitarianism 119–20
  types of 12–21
  in the UK 31–3
  utilitarian 6, 13–14, 23
libertarians *see* anarcho-capitalists
liberty (freedom) 2–8, 11, 13–15, 23, 25–7, 30–1
  and anarchism 136–9, 143, 152–4, 156–7, 268–9
  collective 107
  and conservatism 41–2, 44, 45, 51, 65–7
  and constraint 6
  and deprivation 25–6
  enemies of 6, 11
  individual 5–7, 18, 44, 45
  and liberalism 2–8, 11, 13–15, 23, 25–7, 30–1, 66–7, 104, 136–9, 151, 154, 169, 183, 246, 251–2, 263–4, 268–9
  Mill on 6, 7, 14
  and multiculturalism 251
  negative 5, 7, 18, 136, 154, 268
  political 5
  positive 5, 7, 18, 19, 154, 269
  revolutionary 5
  right to 13
  and self-determination 5
  and socialism 71, 102, 104, 156
  'true' 6–7
Lincoln, Abraham 174
Lloyd George, David 19, 25, 29
local government 88, 99
Locke, John 2–3, 8, 10–12, 21–3, 30, 36, 67, 138–9, 165, 248, 263
Lotard, Jean-Francois 265
Louis XIV 169

Lovelock, James 221, 226–7, 230, 232, 233–4

Macmillan, Harold 65
Madison, James 10, 56
majority rule 15, 27–8
Malatesta, Enrico 137, 141, 142, 149, 151
male dominance 194, 195, 196–7, 199, 202–4, 207,
    209–14
male superiority 208
Mao Tse-tung (Mao Zedong) 118–19, 124–5, 262
Marcuse, Herbert 115, 119–20, 126, 147
marriages
    arranged 196, 200–1
    forced 246, 255
Married Women's Property Act 1869 194, 208
Marshall, Alfred 51
Marx, Karl x–xi, 23, 71–3, 76–7, 83–5, 93–5, 97–8,
    103–21, 126–30, 134–5, 148–9, 152–3, 157, 195, 202,
    204, 256, 265
Marxism x–xi, 83–4, 102, 105–30, 265
    and anarchism 155–7
    and capitalism 101, 106, 108–14, 117–21, 125–6, 127,
        128–30
    and class conflict 113–14
    and collectivism 79
    and communism 116–17
    contemporary 120, 128–30
    core ideas 108–17
    and dialectical process 108–9
    and 'dictatorship of the proletariat' 99, 115–16
    and ecology 231–2
    and equality 156
    exam questions on 270
    Frankfurt School 115, 119–20, 126
    and Hegelian philosophy 106–7
    and inequality 75, 113
    issues in 126–8
    key figures 120–6
    and Leninism 127
    and multiculturalism 256
    and nationalism 177–8
    in practice 117–20
    and revisionism 95, **95**
    and revolution 105–6, 108, 110–11, 114–19, 121–2,
        124–30, 156
    and the Russian Revolution 1917 115, 117–18
    scientific 126–7
    and social class 73–4, 76, 109–11, 113–14
    and social justice 77
    and social progress 261, 262
    and socialism 129–30
    and Stalinism 127–8
    and the state 98, 99, 111, 116, 119, 122, 123, 127,
        152, 156

    theory of history 106–10, 114–15, 117, 121, 126,
        128–9
    utopian 126–7
Marxist feminism 195, 202, 204–5, 211–12
Marxist-Leninism 121, 122, 123, 124
mass culture 194–5
maternity rights 201
Mazzini, Giuseppe 169, 180–1, 183
Mead, Margaret 198
means of production 73, 109
Mensheviks 118
meritocracy 9
middle-classes
    and conservatism 37, 38–9, 45–6, 48
    and feminism 194
Mill, James 23
Mill, John Stuart 6–9, 14–16, 18, 23–4, 27, 29–30, 33,
    104, 111, 179, 193–4, 208–9
Millett, Kate 195, 197, 199–200, 202–3, 210, 211, 216
minority cultures 245–7, 249–55, 258
    and anarchism 141
    discrimination against 27–8
    oppression of 247
mission statements 189
Mitchell, Juliet 204, 216
Modood, Tariq 253
monarchy 43
    absolute 37
monetarism 51–2, 61
Monnet, Jean 164
monoculturalism 247
monopolies 15
Montesquieu, Charles 174
Moral Majority 53
morality
    and anarchism 137, 151–2
    and conservatism 62, 68
    and environmentalism 229–30
More, Thomas 82
Morris, William 72, 83, 93, 150, 231
Mosley, Oswald 163, 172
Mozart, Wolfgang Amadeus 36, 173
Mugabe, Robert 177, 178
multiculturalism ix–x, xii, 241–59
    and capitalism 256
    challenges to 250–2
    and citizenship 249–50
    and conservatism 55, 60, 250–1, 252
    and cosmopolitanism 251–2
    and cultural relativism 245–6
    death of 252–3
    definition 241
    and equal rights 247
    and equality of opportunity 248, 254
    exam questions on 271

and feminism 255–6
and identity politics 242–4, 254–5
issues in 252–7
key thinkers 257–8
and liberalism 21, 30, 243–50, **247**, 251, 252–3, 256,
   257, 261
and liberty 251
and Marxism 256
and nationalism 250–1, 252
and the nature of culture 241–2
and pluralism 244–5, 247, 248
and social democrats 256–7
and social progress 261
and socialism 256–7
strengths of 253
and tolerance 241, 246–7
multinational corporations 227–8, 232, 237
multiracial nations 184
Muslims 200–1, 242, 243, 244, 245, 247, 251, 254, 255
   see also Islam
Mussolini, Benito 87, 125, 167, 172, 186
mutual aid 149
mutualism 144–5
mysticism 234, 236

Nader, Ralph 237
Naess, Arne 225, 232–3, 235, 236, 238
Napoleon Bonaparte 159, 162, 179
Nasser, Gamal Abdel 161
nation
   definition 160–2, **184**
   fascist concepts 175
   liberal notions of 174
   multiracial 184
   and race 163–4, 184
   and self-determination 165
nation-state 162, 164–5, 168–9, 175
   and conservatism 62, 164
   decline of the 185–6
   definition **185**
national culture 161, 163–4, 175–7, 179–80, 253–4, 258
national identity 48–9, 159–61, 163, 165, 170, 175, 183,
   184, 253, 258
National Organisation of Women (NOW) 209
national sovereignty 60
national superiority 160, 164, 170
national unity 246, 247, 248, 250, 252
nationalisation 96, **96**
nationalism ix, 159–91
   and anarchism 141
   British 188–9
   and conservatism 49–50, 52–5, 160, 169–70, 179,
      183–4, 190, 250, 263
   core values 165–8
   cultural 176–7, 179, 180, 185–6, 190

Czech 169
and decline of the nation-state 185–6
defensive 186, 190
definition 159
development 159–60
exam questions on 270
and expansionism 171, 176, 186
and fascism 171–6, 180, 181, 263
and independence 167–8
Irish 168, 169, 187–8
issues in 183–6
key thinkers 179–83
left-wing 160
liberal 160, 168–9, 174–5, 179, 183–4, 184, 186, 190
and multiculturalism 250–1, 252
myths of 167, 175
and organic society 166–7
post-colonial 177, 179, 186
racialist 178–9, 181, 184–5
radical 171–6
right-wing 52, 160, 170–1, 179, 184, 188–9, 190
romantic 179, 180, 186
Scottish 32, 169, 183, 187
and self-determination 162, **163**, 165–6
socialist 177–8, 179, 182–3, 190
and sovereignty 183
types of 168–79
and unity 183
in the United Kingdom 186–90
Welsh 32, 167–8, 176–7, 187, 249
natural law 136, 137
natural order 43–4
natural rights 3, **3**, 8, 12–13, 150, 168–9
nature 207, 220–2, 229–33, 235–6, 238, 261
Nazism (National Socialism) 163–4, 171–3, 175–8, 181,
   184, 186, 189, 230–1, 241, 245, 262
Nechaev, Sergei 135, 146
neo-classical economics 51–2
neo-conservatism 52, 61–3, 264–5
neo-feudalism 37
neo-liberalism x, 16, 29, 55, 61–4, 263
   dominance 264
   and ecology 231
New Harmony 93–4, 143
New Labour 88–91, 96
   Clause IV 89, **89**, 101, 102
   and liberalism 31
   policies 101–3
   and socialism 101–3
   and the state 100
New Left, feminism of 194–5, 201
'New Right' 16, 17, 31, 50–2, 55, 58–62, 65, 67–8, 260,
   263
   paradox of 61–2
New World Order 53

Newton, Isaac 36, 173, 236, 238
nihilism 132, 135, 146, 153
Nixon, Richard 53
noblesse oblige 38, 44, 57, 68
North Korea 120
NOW *see* National Organisation of Women
Nozick, Robert 18, 51, 103, 133, 139
nuclear fission 234
nurturance 209–10
Nyerere, Julius 176, 177, 182–3

Oakeshott, Michael 44, 45, 46, 47, 58, 61, 63, 261
Obama, Barack x, 53, 67
Okin, Susan 255
'one-nationism' 28–9, 39, 54–5, 57
oppression
    and conservatism 262–3
    and the French Revolution 262
    of minority cultures 247
    and self-determination 165
    and the state 137
    women's 202–3, 206, 210, 211, 213, 217
order
    and conservatism 41–2, 56–7, 58, 62, 68, 183, 250
    natural 43–4
    New World Order 53
Organisation for African Unity (OAU) 179
'original position' 26–7
original sin 37, 40
Orwell, George 93, 138
other 197, **198**
other-regarding actions 6
otherness 197–8
    internalisation 197
Ottoman Empire 162, 163
over-population 207
Owen, Robert 72, 83, 93–4, 99, 101, 106, 142–3

Paine, Thomas 3, 8, 12, 67
Palestine 162
Palin, Sarah 52
Pan-Arabism 161, 179
Parekh, Bhikhu 245–6, 250, 257–8
Paris Commune 1871 94, 108
particularism 244, **244**
paternalism 38, 40, **41**, 48, 52, 65
patriarchy
    and environmental degradation 230
    and feminism 192, 194–7, 199, 202–4, 210, 213–16,
        255, 261, 267–8
patriotism 189, **189**
pay, equal 201
peasantry 109, 118–20, 123–4, 126
    and anarchism 134, 140, 145
Peel, Sir Robert 48, 56

Peelites 48
penis envy 203, 209
'personal is the political, the' 211, **211**
personality cults 127
'petite bourgeoisie' xi, 109
Phillips, Anne 245
Phillips, Trevor 251, 252, 253
philosophy xii, 2, 36, 56
Plaid Cymru 176
Plato 107
pleasure, pursuit of 13–14
pluralism **33**, 264
    and culture 244–5, 247, 248
    and liberalism 10, 33, 247, 248, 264
Poland 166
political correctness 217
political parties, Marxist views on 111
'politics of grandeur' 182
'politics of recognition' 257
pollution 219, 220, 228
Popper, Karl 40, 47, 58–9, 115
populism 52, 54
pornography 196, 204, 212
Porritt, Jonathon 225
Portillo, Michael 47
positive discrimination 79, **79**, 201, 248, 249, 254, 258
positivism 245
post industrial society 264
post-capitalism 107
post-colonial exploitation 256
post-colonial nationalism 177, 179, 186
postfeminism 192, 195–6, 205, 206, 215–16
postmodern feminism 196, 205–6, 215, 217
postmodernism 205–6, 265–6
poverty 90
Powell, Enoch 50
power
    in gender relationships 210, 217
    of liberal governments 11, 12, 13
    Marxist views on 111
'power of things' 104
pragmatism 44, 48
'private judgement' 137, 152, 154
private property **81**
    see also property
private sphere 44–5, 200, 213–14, 246
privatisation 65, 100, 144
producer cooperatives 81
proletariat 109–11, **109**, 113–14, 117–18, 123, 127, 130
    dictatorship of the 99, 115–16, 118, 148
'propaganda by deed' 145, **145**
property **81**
    and anarchism 132, 139–41, 144–5, 151, 156
    and conservatism 45–6, 67
    and feminism 192, 194, 204, 208

and socialism 71, 80–2, 156
prostitution 212
Protestantism 37
Proudhon, Pierre-Joseph 138, 139, 144–5
Prussia 107
public sphere 200, 213–14, 246
Pym, Francis 47, 49

quality of life 222
Quebec 242, 257

race 184, **184**
    and culture 241–2
    and identity 163, 254
    and nation 163–4
    and notions of superiority 164, 175–6, 177, 181
racialism 172–3, 178–9, **179**, 181, 184–5
racism 172, 179, **179**
rainforests, destruction of the 220–1, 229, 238
rape 212
Rastafarians 247
rational society x
rationalism 36, 37, 55–6
    definition **2**
    and fascism 173–5
    and feminism 193
Rawls, John 12, 20, 26–7, 29, 30, 78, 103, 104, 247–8, 255, 256
Read, Herbert 150
Reagan, Ronald 16, 39, 50, 51
recession 59, 64, 68, 113
Reclus, Elisée 141, 142, 147, 149
referendums 21, 41, 64
Reformation 248
religion
    Abrahamic 221–2, 229
    American 53, 60, 62
    and anarchism 141
    dogma 263
    and the Enlightenment 36–7
    state 248
    and tolerance 8
    see also specific religions
representation 37, 41, 56
Republicanism 52, 53, 59
resources
    depletion 221, 222, 224
    scarcity of 77–8, 113, 128
Revisionism **86**, 95, **95**, 96
revolution
    and anarchism 134–5, 145–6, 149–50, 153–4, 156
    definition **84**
    and feminism 202
    and liberalism 4

and Marxism 105–6, 108, 110–11, 114–19, 121–2, 124–30, 156
    permanent 125
    see also socialism, revolutionary; specific revolutions
rewards, rational distribution of 77–8, 116
Ricardo, David 4, 94
Rich, Adrienne 206
Richards, Amy 216
rights
    animal 225, 229
    black 254
    and conservatism 67
    and constitutions 12
    equal 8–9, 13, 207–9, 247
    and liberalism 3, **3**, 8–9, 12–13, 21, 32, 67, 103, 247
    maternity 201
    natural 3, **3**, 8, 12–13, 150, 168–9
    women's 207–9, 255–6
    see also equal rights
Robespierre, Maximilien 262
Rocardo, David 111
Roman Catholicism 36–7, 40, 109, 188
romanticism
    and fascism 173–5
    and nationalism 179, 180, 186
Rosenberg, Alfred 175, 181
Rothbard, Murray 144, 150–1
Rousseau, Jean-Jacques 3, 12, 27, 36, 70–1, 133, 136, 137, 139, 174, 179, 248
rule of law 29
ruling class
    and anarchism 137
    and conservatism 37–8
    and ideology x–xi
    and Marxism 110, 111
Rumsfeld, Donald 245
Russian Revolution 1917 115, 117–18, 120–1

Santayana, George 57–8
Sarkozy, Nicolas 54
scarcity of resources 77–8, 113, 128
scepticism 47, 64
Schumacher, Ernst 147, 222
scientific method 58
scientific truths 265
scientism xii, 73, **73**, 126–7, 171, 173
Scottish nationalism 32, 169, 183, 187
Scottish Nationalist Party 32
SDLP see Social and Democratic Labour Party
self-actualisation/self-realisation 18, **18**, 24, 196
    and ecologism 226, 232–3, 235, 236
    see also self-fulfilment
self-determination 5, 162, **163**, 165–6
self-fulfilment 7, 9
    see also self-actualisation/self-realisation

self-government 133–6, 138, 141–2, 145, 147–50, 152
self-interest 27–8, 111
    anarchism and 136, 144, 151, 155
    enlightened pursuit of 6, 7, 13–14
    national 182
self-regarding actions 6
Sessions, George 226
sex (biological) difference 197, 198, 202, 202–3, 209–15
sex class, subordinate 202, 212–13
sex discrimination 196, 201
sexism 196–7, 209, **209**
sexual liberation 203
sexual reproduction, without men 203–4, 211–12
sexuality, female 202, 211
Sharia law 249
Shaw, George Bernard 85
Shiva, Vandana 207, 230
Sikhs 247, 249
Sinn Fein 183, 188
Smiles, Samuel 17, 29
Smith, Adam 3–4, 111
Smith, John 31, 89
social conditioning, of femininity 209, 212, 213, 214
social conflict 170, 264
social contract 22
social Darwinism 16–17, 24, 29, 31, 164, 173, 176, 178, 263
social democracy x, 73, 76–7, 87–91, 97, 101
    and class conflict 77, 95
    definition **89**
    and equality of opportunity 79
    and inequality 75
    key thinkers 95
    and liberalism 1, 20
    and multiculturalism 256–7
    principles 102
    and social justice 78
    and the state 100
Social Democratic Foundation 85
Social and Democratic Labour Party (SDLP) 188
social ecology 228–9
social exclusion 91, **91**
social justice 12, 25, 29, 33
    and anarchism 143
    and socialism 77–8
social mobility 9, 55, 92
social progress 261–2
social responsibility 1, 5, 7, 18, 24, 48–9
social solidarity 136
socialism x, 70–31, 143
    and absolute equality 75, 76
    and anarchism 155–7
    and capitalism 70–4, 76–9, 83–8, 93–8, 100–2, 106, 108–14, 117–21, 125–30
    and class conflict 76–7, 95

and collectivism 79–80, 102
and common ownership 71–2, 80–2
and conservatism 43, 51, 61
contemporary 92–3
cooperative 73
core values 75–93
death of 93
definition 70
democratic 73, 76–7, 78, 79, 87–91, 97, 100, 101–2
early ideas 71–2
and economic equality 71–2, 74–5, 97
and equality 71–2, 74–6, 77–9, 88, 90, 97, 100, 102–4, 156
and equality of opportunity 75, 76, 79, 90, 100, 103, 104
and equality of outcome 76
evolutionary 85–6, 98
exam questions on 270
guild 87, 146
and human nature 156
and inequality 74–5, 77–8, 91, 101, 103
issues in 97–103
key thinkers 93–7
and liberalism 1, 39, 103–4
and liberty 71, 102, 104, 156
Marxist 83–4, 102, 105–30
militant 74–5
and multiculturalism 256–7
municipal 100
and natural order 75
and New Labour 88–91, 101–3
post New Labour 92
primitive 82, 83
and property 71, 80–2, 156
revolutionary 76–7, 84–6, 95, 97–8, 102, 105–6, 108, 110–11, 114–19, 121–2, 124–30
and rights 75, 103
rise of 106
scientific 73, 126–7
and social class 73–4, 76–7, 79, 88, 91, 96, 102
and social justice 77–8
and social progress 262
and the state 79, 81, 85, 88, 97, 98–100, 99, 102, 156
syndicalist 86–7
types of 82–93
utopian 72, 82–3, 87, 93, 99, 126–7
socialist 'experiments' 81
socialist feminism 199–200, 204–5
socialist nationalism 177–8, 179, 182–3, 190
society
    civil 10, **10**
    collective consciousness of 24
    destination of 107
    free 13, 155
    natural 148

open 59
organic 7, 24, 43–4, 54, 56, 61, 65, 68, 167, 250
rational x
Socrates 107
solidarity 110, 136
Sorel, Georges 87, 140, 145, 149–50, 151
South African apartheid 184
sovereignty
    of the individual 132, 135–6
    and the liberal constitution 12
    national 60, 162
    and nationalism 183
    of Parliament 21, 32
    and self-determination 165
    state 162, 183
Soviet Union 105, 118, 121–4, 127–8, 262
spaceship Earth 221, **221**
Spain 171
Spanish Civil War 135
Spencer, Herbert 16–17, 18, 23–4, 29, 155
Stakhanov 124, **124**
Stalin, Josef 116, 118, 123–4, 125, 127–8, 149
Stalinism 36, 127–8
Stanton, Elizabeth Cady 217
state
    and anarchism 132, 134–5, 137–41, 143–6, 148–50,
        153–7
    centralised 79, 81, 97, 98, 99
    and communism 116
    and conservatism 44–5, 51, 54–5, 58–9, 61–2, 65–7
    corrupting nature 138
    culture 246
    definition 160, 161–2
    failed 162
    fascist 171
    and feminism 192
    and freedom 138
    functions of the 185
    and liberalism 1, 14, 16, 19–20, 23, 29–30, 66–7,
        154–5, 184, 246
    and Marxism 98, 99, 111, 116, 119, 122, 123, 127,
        152, 156
    minimal 17
    multi-national 186
    nanny 61
    neutral 247–8
    oppressive 137
    regulatory 100
    and socialism 79, 81, 85, 88, 97, 98–100, 99, 102, 156
    sovereign 162, 183
    as unnatural 138
    withering away of the 116, 152, 156
    see also nation-state
state religions 248
status quo xi, 35, 38

stereotypes, gender 198–9
Stirner, Max 135, 136, 142, 144, 146, 147, 151, 155
Strauss, Leo 59
strikes 145
subjugation, of women 195, 197, 212, 255
suffrage 15, 194, 208
supranationalisation 165, **165**, 185–6
'surplus value' 112–13, **112**
'survival of the fittest' 16, 17, 173
sustainability 221
syndicalism 86–7
    see also anarcho-syndicalists

Taliban 255, 262
Tamworth Manifesto 1834 48
Tanzania 92, 182–3
Taoism 236
taxation 26, 55
Taylor, Charles 243–4, 257, 258
Taylor, Harriet 23, 193–4, 208–9, 214
Taylor, Helen 23
teleocratic society 45
terror 146, **146**, 262
terrorism 251, 252–3, 264
Thatcher, Margaret 16, 29, 35, 39, 40–3, 46, 48–52, 59,
    61, 63–5, 68, 89, 170, 190
Thatcherism 59
Thatcherite era 67–8
Third Reich 171, 172, 176
Third Way 88–91, **90**
Third World 230, 232, 237–8, 256
Thoreau, Henry 135, 136, 139, 143, 144, 150, 154
threats, external 165–6
Tocqueville, Alexis de 10, 15
tolerance
    definition **248**
    and liberalism 7–8, 14, 15, 22, 27–8, 30–1, 32, 33,
        246–7, 263–4
    and multiculturalism 241, 246–7, 252, 254
    political 14, **15**
Tolstoy, Leo 147, 153–4, 157
Tory **38**, 57
Toryism **38**, 48
totalitarianism 46, 51, 119–20, 262
    language as form of 266
    Stalin's 123
trade
    fair 14
    free 13
    international 164
trade unions 114
    and New Labour 103
    and socialism 86–7, 88, 94
    and Thatcher 65
tradition 35, 42–3, 56, 65, 250

traditional societies 200–1, 255–6
transnational corporations 227–8, 232, 237
Trotsky, Leon 98, 123, 125
truth 265
Tucker, Benjamin 135, 143, 144, 145
tyranny
    of ideas 215, 262
    and ideology 46
    of the majority 15, 27–8

UK Independence Party (UKIP) 50, 170, 190
Ulster Unionists (Northern Ireland) 168, 187–8
underclasses 68
Union Carbide Company 228
United States
    Constitution 11, 28, 139
    contemporary conservatism 52–3, 59–60, 62–3
    and equality of opportunity 10
    see also American...
universal will 167
utilitarianism 6, 13–14, 23
utilities 96
utility 13, 14
utopianism xii, 72, **72**
    and anarchism 137, 141, 144, 151–3, 157, 260
    and ecologism 236–7
    Marxist 126–7
    socialist 72, 82–3, 87, 93, 99, 126–7

vanguard 116
'veil of ignorance' 26–7
velvet revolution 84
Venezuela 120
volk 163, 175, 177, 188, 230
volkism 177, 189
Volksgemeinschaft 24, 48–9, 172–3, **172**, 230
Voltaire 8, 174, 248
voluntarism 114, **114**
von Herder, Johann Gottfried 167, 175, 179–80
voting
    liberal attitudes to 15, 23, 28
    see also elections; suffrage

wages 112–13
Wallace, William 5
war 166, 176
Warren, Josiah 142–3, 144, 145
water pollution 220
wealth
    rational distribution of 77–8, 116
    redistribution of 104
Wealth of Nations, The (Smith) 3–4
Webb, Beatrice 85, 99
Webb, Sidney 85, 99

Weber, Max 162
welfare 20, **20**
    equality of 75, 76, 83
welfare state
    and conservatism 55, 59, 65, 68
    and liberalism 17, 18–20, 24, 26, 29
    and socialism 88, 90, 92
Wells, H. G. 85
Welsh nationalism 32, 167–8, 176–7, 187, 249
Welsh Nationalist Party 32
Weltanschauung xi, **xi**
Whig Party 45, 55
White Russians 121
will
    free 2, 4
    general 27
    of the people 27
    to power 261
    universal 167
William III, King of England 21
Wilson, Woodrow 163
Winstanley, Gerrard 71, 82
Wittig, Monique 207, 212–13
Wolfowitz, Paul 16
Wollstonecraft, Mary 193, 207–8, 213, 214
women
    enslavement 199, 211
    'inferiority' of 197–9, 202–4, 206, 208–9, 212–13, 217
    oppression 202–3, 206, 210, 211, 213, 217
    and the social conditioning of gender 209, 212, 213, 214
    subjugation 195, 197, 212, 255
    'superiority' 199
    as victims 213
    and work 196, 198–201, 206, 208–9, 214, 216
women's liberation 199–200, 203, 211, 213–14, 217
women's rights 207–9, 255–6
working classes
    and capitalism 72–4, 112–14
    and conservatism 38, 48
    and Marxism 109, 112–14, 121–2
    and socialism 72–4, 76, 84, 85–7, 93, 95, 96
World Bank 92, 168, 228
World Trade Organisation (WTO) 140, 164, 168, 228
world views xi

xenophobia 171, 190

'Young Italy' movement 169, 180

Zeitung, Reinische 112
Zimbabwe 92, 177
Zionism 177